THE INFORMATION PROCESSING THEORY OF ORGANIZATION

To my wife, Jo

The Information Processing Theory of Organization

Managing technology accession in complex systems

JOHN L. KMETZ
University of Delaware

Ashgate

Aldershot • Brookfield USA • Singapore • Sydney

Published by
Ashgate Publishing Ltd
Gower House
Croft Road
Aldershot
Hants GU11 3HR
England

Ashgate Publishing Company
Old Post Road
Brookfield
Vermont 05036
USA

British Library Cataloguing in Publication Data
Kmetz, John L.
  The information processing theory of organization :
  managing technology accession in complex systems
  1.Information resources management 2.Organizational
  sociology
  I.Title
  654.4'038

Library of Congress Cataloging-in-Publication Data
Kmetz, John L.
  The information processing theory of organization : managing
technology accession in complex systems / John L. Kmetz.
    p. cm.
  Includes bibliographical references and index.
  ISBN 1-84014-427-0 (hb)
  1. Communication in organizations. 2. Organization.
3. Technology--Management. 4. Airplanes. Military--Testing.
I. Title.
HD30.3.K59 1998   98-22478
658.5'14--dc21   CIP

ISBN 1 84014 427 0

Printed in Great Britain by The Ipswich Book Company, Suffolk

Contents

List of Figures

vii

List of Tables

ix

Acknowledgments

In the roughly twenty years of field research work represented in this book, there have been more people who have taught me and helped me than I could ever hope to thank. This is a very short list of some of those people. First, my former colleagues at the University of Southern California Systems Management Center, where all of this work began in 1976, gave me my first opportunity to learn how complex electronic-test technologies work, and to look at the organizations that enabled them to do it. Bill Schuler saw the need for the kind of services and study we did in the early days of this work, and gave me that "first shot" when he formed the Systems Research Corporation and assembled the initial study team. Later, Kurt Wasserman at Harris Corporation gave me an opportunity to expand the scope of what I did as the study moved into later phases; that work progressed along with many of Kurt's colleagues at Harris, and I particularly want to thank Dick Monis and Bob Frye for their help and flexibility. Through Kurt, I met Wolf Gaston and many of his colleagues in the Canadian Forces, who gave me a chance to look at automatic test equipment in an environment totally different from where I had begun.

During this same era, and through some of these early studies, I had the privilege to work with John Griffin and his team at Joint Research Group. Grif, Jim Langanke, and many friends and colleagues at JRG spent a lot of time trying to figure out how the repair system worked and how to use what we had learned to make the next ones better. Every time I worked with them I came out a lot smarter than when I started.

Along the way, and threaded through these other activities, I was fortunate enough to meet John Gray at the Aircraft Intermediate Maintenance Support Office. By this time I had joined the faculty at the University of Delaware, but just to remind us that the world is very small, John was a graduate of the Southern California program I had taught in, and we were immediately *simpatico*. It was a great privilege for me to work with John and his team on the information system he was developing, and I learned an enormous amount from him.

Partly as an outgrowth of my work with John Gray, I met Chuck Diesel and the team at Dynamic Science, Inc. Chuck and I spent quite a lot of time working on advanced study of the system, and over the course of numerous sessions at our respective homes and offices, we went through a lot of erasers doing endless flowcharts and diagrams.

The work involved to extract research data from the Navy's maintenance-data system was a long, grueling process that required concentration, persistence, and a willingness to pore through huge amounts of data many times until we were sure we had it right. My graduate assistant, Ernie Talbert (now Lt. Col., USAF, and commander of the Delaware Air National Guard detachment), was the literal "right-hand man" who got that work done for me. I never would have had the time to complete these analyses without his help and his unwavering concern for quality.

Finally, there are many, many personnel in the Navy who had the patience to teach us what we had to know to do our jobs in these studies. There are too many dedicated men and women out there to ever properly acknowledge by name, but I think they know who they are, and how much they contributed to this work. I certainly do, and am forever in their debt.

List of Abbreviations

AIMD	Aircraft Intermediate Maintenance Department
AIMSO	Aircraft Intermediate Maintenance Support Office
AIRLANT	Naval Air Force, Atlantic Fleet
AIRPAC	Naval Air Force, Pacific Fleet
AMSU	Aeronautical Material Screening Unit
AMT	Advanced Manufacturing Technology
APMM	Automated Production Management Module
ASO	Aviation Supply Office
ATE	Automatic Test Equipment
ATI	Automated Technical Information
ATLAS	Abbreviated Test Language for All Systems
ATS	Automatic Test Systems (Department of Defense program)
ATS V1	Automatic Test Set Version 1
AWACS	Airborne Warning and Control System
AWM	AWaiting Maintenance
AWP	AWaiting Parts
BB	Building Block
BCM	Beyond Capability of Maintenance
BIT	Built-In Test
BPR	Business Process Reengineering
BU/TD	Build-Up/Tear Down
CAINS	Carry-Aboard Inertial Navigation System
CASS	Consolidated Automated Support System
CATE/ILSMT	Common Automatic Test Equipment Integrated Logistics Support Management Team
CAT-IIID	Common Automatic Tester, Version IIID; F-14A, E-2C SRAs
CCI	Comfort/Capability Index
CDI	Collateral Duty Inspectors
CIP	Cognitive Information Processing
CLAMP	Closed-Loop Avionics Maintenance Program
CM	Configuration Management
CNI	Communication, Navigation, Instrumentation
CNM	Chief of Naval Material
CNO	Chief of Naval Operations
CSE	Common Support Equipment
CSS	Consolidated Support System
CTE	Commercial Test Equipment
CV(N)	Aircraft carrier (Nuclear)

DIMOTE	A-7E SRA tester
DSA	Defense Supply Agency
DSI	Dynamic Science, Inc.
D-level	Depot level maintenance
EC	Engineering Change
ECM	Electronic CounterMeasures
ECP	Engineering Change Proposal
EI	Engineering Investigation
EMT	Elapsed Maintenance Time
EV	Expected Value
EW	Electronic Warfare
EXREP	EXpedite REPair—no replacement item available for squadron
FAMMS	Fixed Allowance Management and Monitoring System
FIFO	First In, First Out
FMS	Flexible Manufacturing Systems
FRAMP	Fleet Replacement Aviation Maintenance Program
GAO	General Accounting Office
HATS	Hybrid Automatic Test Set (for S-3A SRAs)
HID	Hybrid Information-Decision matrix
HTS	Hybrid Test Set, F/A-18 SRAs
ICRL	Individual Component Repair List
ID	Interconnecting Device
IFF	Identification Friend or Foe
ILSMT	Integrated Logistics Support Management Team
IMA	Intermediate Maintenance Activity
IP	Information Processing
IPPR	Information Processing Procedures and Rules
IPT	Information Processing Theory of organization
IT	Information Technology
IW	In Work
I-level	Intermediate level maintenance
JIT	Just In Time
LSR	Logistic Support Representatives
MAD	Magnetic Anomaly Detector
MAF	Maintenance Action Form
MAM	Maintenance Assist Module
MAU	Multi-Attribute Utility decision model
MESM	Mission Essential Subsystem Matrix
MIRP	Minnesota Innovation Research Project
MCCs	Material Control Coordinators
MRMS	Maintenance Resources Management System
MRP II	Manufacturing Resource Planning version II
MTBF	Mean Time Between Failure

MTBUMA	Mean Time Between Unscheduled Maintenance Actions
MTTR	Mean Time To Repair
NAEC	Naval Air Engineering Center, Lakehurst, N.J.
NALCOMIS	Naval Aviation Logistics Command Management Information System
NAMP	NAVAIRINST 4790.2, The Naval Aviation Maintenance Program
NAVAIR	U.S. Naval Air Systems Command
NAVAIRINST	U.S. Naval Air Systems Command Instruction
NAVMASSO	(1) Navy Management Systems Support Office, (2) Navy Maintenance and Supply Systems Office
NAVSUP	U.S. Naval Supply Command
NTCSS	Navy Tactical Command Support System
OA	Operational Availability
OMS	Operational Management System
OPEVAL	Operational Evaluation
OR	Operational Readiness
ORGEVAL	Organizational Evaluation
O-level	Organization level (squadron) maintenance
PC	Production Control
PCO	Production Control Office/Officer
PEB	Pre-Expended Bins, or bit-and-piece parts
PGSE	Peculiar Ground Support Equipment
POOL CRITICAL	Only one item remaining in stock
PRD	PRD Electronics, the VAST manufacturer (later Harris/PRD, then Harris Government Support Systems Division)
Q.E.D.	Q.E.D. Systems
RFI	Ready For Issue
SIDMS	Status Inventory, Data Management System
SMS	Stimulus and Measurement Section
SNAP	Shipboard Non-tactical Automated data Processing
SPAWAR	Space and Naval Warfare Systems Command
SPORT	Specialized Program for Oceana Repairables Tracking
SRA	Shop Replaceable Assembly
SRASTAT	Database on SRA tester status
SRC	Systems Research Corporation
SRS	Supply Response Section
SSC	Supply Support Center
SSM	System Synthesis Model
TAT	TurnAround Time
TECHEVAL	Technical Evaluation
TPS	Test Program Set
TR	Trouble Report

UUT	Unit Under Test
VAMP	VAST Automated Management Program
VAST	Versatile Avionics Shop Test system
VIDS	Visual Information Display System
VITAL	VAST Interface Test Application Language
VLSI	Very Large Scale Integrated circuit
WAFL	Waveforms Analysis Language
WC	Work Center
WFA	Workflow Analysis
WRA	Weapon Replaceable Assembly
WYSIWYG	What You See Is What You Get

Foreword

Objectives of This Book

The Information Processing Theory of Organization

This is a book about many things. At the core of the book is the Information Processing Theory of organization (IPT), and the first purpose of this book is to advance that theory. IPT is a theory of organizations which has been in development for years, and one of the major objectives of this book is to advance IPT as a way of understanding and improving organizations. IPT posits that everything an organization does can be represented by information. Further, IPT posits that the functioning and control of an organization is achieved through information processing, ranging from processes as simple as the exchange of information for coordination, to the complex transformation of information for purposes ranging from software development to strategy formation. Information is therefore the "common currency" of organizations, and can be used to describe them, model them, diagnose them, and design them. Like Egelhoff (1991), I regard IPT as the "physics" of organizations—the rules and processes which govern how parts of the organization are related to each other and how the whole behaves.

IPT incorporates the concepts of General Systems Theory (von Bertalanffy, 1948) and cybernetics theory (Weiner, 1948) to describe how organizations function. Like Ashmos and Huber (1987), I believe that systems theory concepts have enormous potential as theoretical tools for the study of organizations, but that potential has never been fully exploited. IPT conceptualizes all organizations as dynamic systems. The words *dynamic* and *system* connote many things and are somewhat overused in our literature, but they are accurate. Organizations are in a state of balanced, constant internal motion; Katz and Kahn (1978) refer to this property as *dynamic homeostasis*. For that reason alone, static models of organizations are generally incomplete representations of them, and static studies do not capture important data on them.

Managing Technology Accessions

A second purpose of this book is to advance our understanding of technology management using IPT as the conceptual basis. The field of technology management is relatively new, both as an academic discipline and an applied field. "Technology" itself is a broad term, and used in many ways. Part of the problem of the academic legitimacy of technology management seems to be related to this conceptual diffuseness. In common usage, "technology" connotes bodies of knowledge, information technology (both hardware and software), machines, products, and processes. In the academic world, it is not yet entirely resolved that technology management is a distinct discipline or, if it is, how it is related to technical fields of study (Kanz and Waterhouse, 1995). There are journals specializing in technology management, which establishes a sort of scholarly legitimacy, but the scope of inquiry is still more a matter of editorial policy than strong paradigms. In the applied world, technology management is often an afterthought—the technical issues of work are the primary concern, and the management of their development or application is someone else's problem.

I use the word "technology" in the sense of its dictionary definition—a body of knowledge, and I will expand this definition in Chapter 2. Elements of a body of knowledge may be tangible, but this is not necessary to a technology. The major technology management focus of this book is on the accession of new technologies in organizations. *Technology accession* refers to the replacement of old technologies by newer generations, and the processes by which organizations do this. It is not necessarily the transfer of technologies, or the wholesale, abrupt replacement of one form of technology by another, although these are both mechanisms by which some accessions occur. Most organizations, however, have to cope with problems of the gradual turnover of old technologies for new. This is a process which is increasingly visible at every turn: in the adoption of new manufacturing and service technologies; the automation of offices and office work; and the transition of the former centrally-planned economies into market economies.

It may be helpful to clarify exactly what characterizes technology accession in contrast to other forms of technology change. In my view, technology accession does not refer to the process of "innovation," which usually refers to the creation or major development of a novel idea. Neither is technology accession "technology transfer," the application of existing technologies in new environments. Rather, technology accession refers to the process by which organizations apply technologies to serve established objectives or clients, and which must continue to serve those clients as the technologies change and evolve. For example, suppose we have decided that 220-volt electricity is a better choice for residential applications than the 110-volt service now used in North America. An accession to this "new" technology requires resolution of two problems simultaneously—how to change the wiring and electrical devices that consume power, and how to serve the "installed base" of 110-volt users while the new system is phased in, without interrupting service to the users of either voltage or incurring unacceptable costs. The first problem is actually trivial: changing a few connections in the circuit breaker or fuse box is all that is needed to supply 220-volt electricity; the wiring devices (mostly outlets) are more involved, but still a simple problem. The second problem of serving the "installed base" is the larger problem by far. Any power company choosing to make such a conversion must figure out how to solve both problems. This is the nature of accessions: they are linked to multiple clients (who may have quite different objectives); they are achieved over a span of time (which may be quite long); and they must provide continuity. To the final client, the end user of the organization's output, the accession should be totally "transparent," in the current lexicon—things get done, programs run, life goes on, and needs are satisfied, hopefully with fewer hassles than before.

For an organization, the total problem of using technologies encompasses a multiple set of problems and challenges, each of which can be resolved in a variety of ways. Depending on its situation, an organization may simply choose to offer clients a new service and abandon those who do not accept the new technology; it may force the change and impose the costs on its clientele; it may offer both old and new technologies; it may leave the field entirely; and so on. The path any organization selects involves the resolution of a set of tradeoffs, and is never simple. Technological obsolescence, externally-driven service requirements, and other variables may have an impact on the decision, depending on the organization. But in any case, difficult choices must be made between paths that are never entirely definable before the fact.

Technology accession, therefore, is woven into the fundamental processes of many organizations. It cannot be understood through superficial analysis, and in my experience, it cannot be understood or managed by looking at either the technology or the organization in isolation from each other.

A *Longitudinal Study of Technology Accession*

A third purpose of this book is to report a longitudinal study of a technology accession while looking into a key premise of IPT. I have a coffee cup which conveys a message familiar to anyone who has ever worked in an organization dependent on technology. The cup shows a logo for a machine very few people have ever heard of—the Versatile Avionics Shop Test (VAST) system. VAST is an automatic tester, and was designed to solve a number of technical problems the U.S. Navy faced in the maintenance of its carrier-launched aircraft since the mid-1970s. This was a major new maintenance technology when it was introduced, and unlike its sometimes error-prone manual predecessors, this one would get the job done the right way and do it quickly—as the logo claims, "Everytime (*sic*), baby." While it is unlikely that most of us have ever heard of VAST, we all know the promise of a new technology to do things better, faster, and cheaper. VAST, and its accession, are the focus of much of the research reported in this volume.

VAST is an automated electronic tester used to maintain the aviation electronics ("avionics") for the U.S. Navy's principal carrier-launched aircraft. Avionics consists of everything from navigation and communication gear to ultra-secret electronic warfare equipment. Most of the studies reported in this book occurred during the height of the Cold War, when there was serious concern that conflict between the U.S. and the former Soviet Union could break into the open—a hot war. VAST was developed during the late 1960s and early 1970s to provide avionics maintenance ("support") for a new generation of carrier aircraft. In preparation for these aircraft, VAST was deployed into the Fleet throughout the 1970s and 1980s, with initial carrier deployment and "real" at-sea operations beginning with outfitting of the USS *Enterprise* in 1973. The final outfitting was the USS *Forrestal* in 1985, although many VAST testers were "recycled" to newer carriers, as we will see.

VAST is a type of technology which is now relatively commonplace: automatic test equipment (ATE). Anyone who has ever taken a car into a service facility and had a machine attached to it to "read out the codes" has had an encounter with ATE. Like many technologies, consumer ATE evolved from hardware developed for military applications. ATE may seem a mundane and unlikely thing on which to base a large study, but the importance of these testers was enormous, and still remains so. VAST is the grandparent of today's commonplace ATE, and has continued to be an important U.S. Navy tester almost through the end of this century. Newer generations of ATE will be discussed later, but VAST was the first major accession into truly automatic test technology, and it will be the focus of much of this book. Although not the intention of this study when it was begun over 20 years ago, events have made it possible to study the management of this technology through what is effectively its entire life cycle.

Three new aircraft were being brought into the Fleet when VAST was deployed, and by design they depend on VAST for avionics support. These are the F-14A, the Navy's long-range standoff fighter, and one of the world's most complex weapon systems; the S-3A, the carrier's primary antisubmarine warfare aircraft; and the E-2C, the Navy's carrier-borne radar-surveillance and communications aircraft (its "AWACS").[1] These three aircraft are absolute necessities to Fleet performance in the event of a shooting war, and are critical to the mission and survival of a carrier battle group.

My involvement with VAST began in 1976, when I was invited to join a team of consultants who had been contracted by the U.S. Naval Air Systems Command ("NAVAIR") to look into reasons why the newly-acquired VAST system did not seem to be meeting its performance requirements. VAST was (and is) a critical element of a long chain of interdependence on a modern aircraft carrier. It seemed that this new tester was unable to do the job for which it was designed, and as a result the Navy was often faced with situations where a carrier at sea was unable to use a large fraction (sometimes up to 50 percent) of its aircraft. Fifty percent was the extreme case, but it was common during the late 1970s and 1980s to find that Operational Readiness (OR) rates for VAST-equipped carriers were between 60 and 80 percent—a major carrier with 85 aircraft aboard might be able to fly 60 of them in fighting shape, if needed. Individual aircraft types often had worse OR rates, and the S-3A was sometimes completely unavailable. Since VAST supported the three new aircraft, and was the major change in the Navy's avionics maintenance technology, the finger of blame for this poor readiness was pointed at VAST. There were no substitute testers to do the job that VAST was designed to do, so somehow VAST had to be made to work. The study team's job was to try to understand the problem and to make recommendations to help get VAST working.

Following this initial study, I became increasingly interested in the complex technological problems of aircraft maintenance and support, and thus became involved in a number of additional studies, served as a consultant to several military organizations and defense contractors, and contributed to proposals to develop the next generation of automatic test equipment, now in deployment. Much of this book is focused on the research done in the VAST studies, but it also examines a number of broader implications of the entire body of work. These include issues of interest to managers of technologies and technology-intensive processes, as well as the more theoretical focus on IPT.

Some of the work in this book has been published previously in *Administrative Science Quarterly* or presented to various professional meetings, both academic and practitioner. Preliminary analyses of some of the performance data discussed in Chapter 6 were published in the *Proceedings of the U.S. Naval Institute*. But this book is the first complete accounting of much of what has been learned from these studies and activities over nearly 20 years, and is the first publication of much of the data from the workflow analyses done in the 1970s and early 1980s and related work done in the late 1980s and early 1990s.[2]

The organizational science literature tells us very little about how organizations manage technology accessions; indeed, two schools of thought suggest that many organizations do not. Population ecology, on the one hand, asserts that different forms of organizations evolve to exploit opportunities and resources at different times, and basically are not able to adapt to changed environments (Hannan and Freeman, 1977; Freeman and Hannan, 1983). Quantum ("configuration") theories of organization assert that organizations tend to assume one configuration from a limited number of alternatives, and that movement from one configuration to another comes in sudden, discontinuous jumps (Bensaou and Venkatraman, 1995; Miller and Friesen, 1984). In either case, the underlying implication is that organizations do not manage accessions or gradual change as a normal means of adaptation, and many simply do not survive the circumstances that make change necessary. While it is clear that many organizations do not manage accessions very well, I think it is equally clear that many do. In part, my motivation is to expand our knowledge of how such accessions succeed.

A Field Quasi-Experiment

A fourth purpose of this book is to report a field "quasi-experiment" which studies several key implications of the VAST technology accession from the perspective of IPT. The quasi-experiment examines the fundamental theoretical proposition of IPT, that organizational performance is a function of organizational information processing capacity. The design of the experiment permits us to examine the role of organization "slack" in this relationship, and how slack is related to organizational performance more generally; in addition, it includes the effects of information technology mediation as a component of IPT and as a contributor to performance. This study therefore evaluates a key question regarding the payoff of information technology, and provides some implications for how people and information technology can interact effectively to manage complex organizations.

This experiment enabled me to do several things I believe in very strongly as a researcher. I think that taking the time to do a detailed investigation of a real operating organization is a worthwhile and rewarding experience, no matter what the outcome. I strongly believe in field research, based on deep involvement with real organizations. My primary reason for that belief is simply that if we are to advance the science of organization, then the first thing we must do is understand and observe operating organizations, in depth. I do not believe understanding of the complexities of organization can result from short-term or superficial study. The advance of the "hard" sciences clearly shows the need for persistent, long-term observation of phenomena before comprehension is possible, and I think that is more true for contrived systems like organizations than it is for natural systems. What has come to be termed "normal science" by some, i.e., essentially the model of the "hard" sciences, is a model I regard as having enormous untapped potential for the study of organizations. I find this approach very useful not only for the study of technology management, but also for my increasing interests in assisting change in the economies and organizations of Central and Eastern Europe and the former Soviet Union.

Some Practical Implications

Following the discussion of this quasi-experiment, the book next discusses practical developments since VAST was first deployed by the Navy, including current work to update it and eventually replace it with a successor technology, the Consolidated Automated Support System (CASS). The VAST quasi-experiment occurred during the late 1970s and early 1980s; the CASS technology accession began during the 1980s, and will continue well into the next century. As we will see in Chapter 7, however, it has taken much longer to supplant VAST with CASS than was ever intended, and in part that may be because some of the lessons of the VAST accession were not fully learned or applied to CASS.

Thus, a final purpose for this book is to convey some of the lessons learned from our experience with VAST and newer generations of ATE to the management of technology in general. I believe these lessons can be useful not only to people who maintain weapon systems, but to scholars of organization and managers in other fields, both in manufacturing and service organizations. As we will see, many characteristics of the flow of work and the management of that flow in avionics repair are similar to those found in other organizations, and the problems of integrating new (and newer) technologies into those workflows are similar. Thus, much of what was learned in connection with the development of VAST and other ATE has value to a wide range of organizations.

Part of this final purpose is that for all of the attention paid to the cost of military preparedness and individual weapon systems in the continuing debate over defense spending, testers and support equipment like VAST are nearly invisible to the general public, despite being extremely important parts of the whole picture. For all of the coverage given to the aircraft VAST supports, or the challenges facing the Navy during the Cold War, VAST and other test equipment are seldom mentioned even in specialized publications like *Aviation Week and Space Technology*, and virtually never anywhere else. With this book I hope to make them, and the contribution they and logistics management make to the success of any organization, more visible. VAST is now a mature technology, and in the process of its own succession by CASS,[3] which will eventually replace not only VAST but a number of other testers. However, for the Fleet's deployed aircraft, VAST is still a critical asset.

Reading this book will take some willingness to wrestle with Navy acronyms and military jargon. The Navy began using acronyms during the days of wooden ships and semaphore signals, and never got over the habit. Nearly everyone who gets involved in this kind of work initially hates the acronyms, and then begins to use them as it becomes apparent that they are better than repeating the same words over and over. To make reading the book easier, I will minimize the use of acronyms and I define them in the List of Abbreviations, but there still exists an irreducible minimum of them. Unfortunately, they work—they are, in fact, a useful form of information processing in a technical environment.

Organization of the Book

Depending on the reader's interests, the chapters one wants to read may not follow the sequence I have chosen, which is largely chronological. Chapters 1, 2, 6, and 8 are the recommended minimum set for organizational researchers. The theoretical model for this book, the Information Processing Theory (IPT) of organization, is developed in Chapter 1. This chapter is likely to be of greatest interest to scholars and organizational researchers. The IPT model develops the concepts of "information" and "information processing" more completely than elsewhere in the literature. These basic concepts are not new to the literature of organization or management, but they have not received adequate theoretical development or articulation, and this chapter is a major effort to address these deficiencies. These concepts are fully integrated into IPT, which is the theoretical framework used to evaluate the data on VAST and ATE functioning and performance described in subsequent chapters. Appendix 1.2 explains some of the reasons why I have chosen some of the research and other material included in this book, and why some other was not included. I encourage my academic colleagues to read this appendix closely.

Chapter 2 defines "technology" and provides some necessary background information on the Navy, aircraft carriers, maintenance and electronic support, and the evolution of VAST. It describes how VAST was intended to work, and what some of the problems were from its early evaluations and studies during its development. Finally, it gives an overview of the research in this book, particularly the field experiment reported in Chapter 6. Chapter 6 will be of particular interest to researchers, as it is a longitudinal test of the fundamental theoretical argument of IPT, i.e., the relationship between organizational information processing capacity and organizational performance; this chapter also empirically evaluates the nature and role of organization slack. Chapter 8 extends the IPT model using the findings of the ATE technology studies reported in Chapters 2 through 7.

Chapters 3 and 4 go into considerable technical detail on the VAST technology and the organization encompassing it. While these chapters are primarily of technical importance, the information in them also provides the background for full interpretation of the field experiment and field work reported in Chapters 5 through 7, for those wanting to evaluate those details. Chapter 3 describes VAST and its operation, and some of the differences between ship and shore operations. It provides more detailed background on the organization of the Navy's aircraft maintenance organization, and shows the intended and unintended results of the first "experiment," which was the introduction of VAST itself. Four appendices to Chapter 3 give more technical details on VAST and the Navy's maintenance organization and IP system.

Chapter 4 includes a detailed review of the technology accession process the Navy used to bring VAST into the Fleet, and some of its successes and shortcomings. The chapter discusses findings from the early studies of the VAST shops themselves, and the logistics support of VAST. Organizational scholars may find Chapter 4 to be heavy going, but if they want to know more about variables in the avionics maintenance system which should be considered when examining the performance data discussed in Chapter 6, they may want to look into it fairly closely. Appendix 4.1 also provides more detail on the Navy's maintenance measures, which were used to capture the performance data discussed in this chapter.

Chapter 5 continues the investigation of the Naval avionics repair process, using the concepts of IPT developed in Chapter 1, and going beyond the original level of the first VAST-shop studies reported in Chapters 3 and 4. A system analysis incorporating both "hard" and "soft" system variables is provided. The background and origins of "Experiment 2," the field quasi-experiment, are also described.

Chapter 6 reports the results of "Experiment 2," which is a three-wave longitudinal study of the entire avionics repair cycle, using hard measures of performance to assess the impact of information processing changes on performance in the Naval avionics repair system. Again, "Experiment 2" is an empirical test of IPT. This field experiment was quite fortuitous, in that I was able to do a quantitative analysis of performance data from the VAST shops and the entire avionics repair process. These data are derived directly from the VAST shops as described in Chapter 3 and the avionics repair workflow as described in Chapter 4; both of these chapters provide the technical background to understand the nature of the information processing changes which occurred in the experiment. The descriptions in these chapters are important to explain and interpret the outcomes of the experiment.

Chapter 7 discusses the development of the next generation of testers, and the experience of the Canadian Forces in managing workflows with newer aircraft and next-generation testers derived from VAST, but operating in a land-based environment. Developments in the management of related technologies in the Naval maintenance community are also discussed, and as we will see, these define the next "frontier" for much of the technology accession begun with VAST. Chapter 7 also discusses the current results of "Experiment 3," the replacement of VAST with CASS and the accession toward a single automatic electronic tester for the entire Fleet.

Finally, Chapter 8 summarizes the lessons learned from this work, and uses those to extend IPT as well. Pragmatic implications for the management of technology and related issues are discussed, along with theoretical implications. These are interwoven, and draw on the theoretical models and concepts of Chapter 1 to integrate and assess the lessons learned from Chapters 5, 6, and 7.

Notes

1. AWACS is an acronym for Airborne Warning and Control System. Electronic equipment from the E-2C has already been transitioned to other testers, which will be discussed in more detail in Chapter 7. The F-14A and S-3A (not so much the S-3B model), however, still largely depend on VAST.

2. Much of this interest in technology follows back to the days of my dissertation (Kmetz, 1975), when I became interested in some of the pioneering work of Joan Woodward (1965) and the subsequent work of the "Aston group" on the impact of technology on organization structure. My primary argument then, as it has remained, is that technology is best conceived of as "knowledge," and that organization structure and processes must reflect changes in organizational knowledge (Kmetz, 1978).

3. For those interested in what CASS looks like, a home page on the World Wide Web is maintained by the CASS Technical Working Group. Many other items discussed in connection with automatic test equipment in this volume are also found on this site. The address is (http://spectra.crane.navy.mil/cass/).

References

Ashmos, Donde P., and Huber, George P. (1987), The systems paradigm in organization theory: Correcting the record and suggesting the future. *Academy of Management Review*, 12 (4): 607-621.

Bensaou, N., and Venkatraman, N. (1995), Configurations of international relationships: A comparison between U.S. and Japanese automakers. *Management Science*, 41 (9): 1471-1492.

Egelhoff, William G. (1991), Information-processing theory and the multinational enterprise. *Journal of International Business Studies*, 22 (3):341-368.

Freeman, John, and Hannan, Michael T. (1983), Niche width and the dynamics of organizational populations. *American Journal of Sociology*, 88 (6): 1116-1145.

Hannan, Michael T., and Freeman, John (1977), The population ecology of organizations. *American Journal of Sociology*, 82 (5): 929-964.

Kanz, John, and Waterhouse, Michael F. (1995), Technology management: An escalating challenge for business and academia. *Business & the Contemporary World*, VII (2): 79-93.

Katz, Daniel, and Kahn, Robert L. (1978), *The Social Psychology of Organizations, second edition*. New York: Wiley.

Kmetz, John L. (1975), Technology and Organization Structure: The Relationship between Contextual Variables and Structure Variables in Manufacturing and

Service Organizations. University of Maryland: unpublished doctoral dissertation.

Kmetz, John L. (1978), A critique of the Aston studies and results with a new measure of technology. *Organization and Administrative Sciences*, 8 (4): 123-144.

Miller, Danny, and Friesen, Peter H. (1984), *Organizations: A Quantum View*. Englewood Cliffs, N.J.: Prentice-Hall.

Von Bertalanffy, Ludwig (1968), *General Systems Theory*. New York: George Brazilier.

Wiener, Norbert (1948), *Cybernetics or Control and Communication in the Animal and the Machine*. New York: Wiley.

Woodward, Joan (1965), *Industrial Organization: Theory and Practice*. New York: Oxford.

1 Foundations of IPT: the Information Processing Theory of Organization

Introduction

This chapter develops an integrated theoretical model, the Information Processing Theory (IPT) of organization. The IPT model provides the orientation for the research reported in the remainder of this book. There are three major components of IPT: information, information processing (IP), and the dynamic and cybernetic properties of systems. The first two elements, information and IP, are closely related, and I will discuss them and the relationships between them first. The third element, cybernetic theory and general systems theory, will be integrated into IPT in the final part of the chapter.

The General IPT Model

The general model of IPT postulates that organizational performance is the dynamic interaction of information and information processing, within the context of a cybernetic system linked internally and to its external environment by information flows. The general form of the IPT model is:

$$G = f (I \times S \times C)$$

where G = Goal attainment (organizational performance),
        I = Information,
        S = Information Processing Structure, including Information Technology,
and C = Cybernetic System dynamics.

Conceptualizing organizations as streams of information and IP activities, linked dynamically as conceptualized by both cybernetics theory and systems

1

theory (hereinafter "cybernetic systems theory"), is a unified way to understand organizational processes and outcomes. In this model, *Information* interacts with the information processing *Structure* to form *organizational information*. Similarly, the information processing structure interacts with the *Cybernetic* Systems dynamics to form the *information processing capacity* of the organization. I use the term "cybernetic system" to mean the larger organization within which organizational information is created and used, and also to connote specific properties of systems, which will be explained later in this chapter. Similarly, I use the term "information processing structure" to differentiate it from organization structure. Therefore, organization performance is a function of organization information interacting with the capacity to process that information. This model can apply to a case of a single goal, which is unlikely to be the case in most organizations, but can easily be generalized to encompass multiple goals, even in situations where those goals conflict.

As I have already begun to do, I will frequently use the acronym "IP" in this book to refer to Information Processing. This acronym specifically refers to the interaction between information and the processing of it through the IP structure. The IP structure will be discussed in detail in the next two sections of this chapter.

At the outset, it should be noted that IPT is concerned with information processing rather than information content. This does not mean that content is immaterial to the theory or that it is ignored by the theory. On the contrary, there is one body of content which is requisite to IPT, as will be discussed later in this chapter. However, the model is intended to be general, where the content of information is largely specific to the organization being considered. Content is therefore treated implicitly in most of IPT, and in my view this property of the theory contributes to its robustness and applicability to many organizations.

In the foreword to this book I said that I have come to think of IP as the "physics" of organizations. I mean that in a very literal sense, and explain this as we proceed through this chapter. The essential point to recognize at this juncture is that information and IP are related to each other in ways analogous to the dynamic relationship between matter and space-time: matter tells space-time how to curve, and space-time tells matter how to move. One cannot fully comprehend either in isolation from the other.

Most of this chapter will be given to consideration of the basic concepts of information and IP. Interestingly, more work has been directed by earlier contributors to the organization structure and design implications of IP than to these underlying variables and processes. One major objective of this chapter is to balance this discussion and develop a fuller understanding of these fundamental variables. To do so requires consideration of each separately despite their inseparability, but it should always be borne in mind that any partition of them is artificial. Organization design implications are discussed later, but are of less immediate concern than these basic concepts.

Information and Information Processing: the Conceptual Groundwork

A number of authors have contributed to the development of the information processing model of organization, including both scholars and executives. The most comprehensive of these models from the perspective of organizations was Galbraith's; as he noted (1977: 24), major earlier contributors were Barnard (1938), Simon (1957), and Cyert and March (1963). Most of the ideas about information processing have emerged in parallel with the development of other concepts of organization during the past 40 years. As is usually the case, these early developments left many pieces incomplete and many concepts poorly defined. Indeed, even the definition of fundamental terms like "information" and "information processing" are not fully explained in these works. What is most surprising is to find that the concept of "information processing" has received more thought and conceptual attention than that of "information." Therefore, my first objective in this chapter is to develop more complete definitions of these terms.

Information

For those with either a practical or theoretical interest in information and IP, 1948 was "Year 1" in many ways, since one of the groundbreaking works in the field was published by Shannon (1948), who wrote a treatise on the theory of information transmission from the engineering perspective of the early telephone and telegraph industry, followed in book form by Shannon and Weaver (1949). The study of information and related feedback processes was also formalized as "cybernetics" theory by Wiener (1948). Cybernetics had considerable impact in both science and philosophy, being used in General Systems Theory as a way to study dynamic relationships between all manner of living and nonliving systems (von Bertalanffy, 1968). Cybernetics concepts have been incorporated into IPT, as will be seen.

Alluisi (1970) points out that Shannon and Weaver and most of the early contributors to information theory gave no consideration to the content of the communication, but were concerned only with the transmission of messages. In recognition of the engineering and telecommunications focus of this early work, I refer to these information theorists as the *telemetry* school. The telemetry school focused almost entirely on the bandwidth capacity and signal clarity of the transmission medium (i.e., "noise" in the transmissions, which is an engineering problem to be taken literally), so for mathematical or engineering analysis one needed have no concern over what it was that was transmitted, only that the method worked. "Signal loss" was the principal criterion to gauge how well the medium was working.

The telemetry school conceptualized "information gain" to be identical to "uncertainty reduction." The concept of uncertainty, which is so fundamental to much subsequent work in development of information processing concepts, follows directly from the telemetry theorists' work. By definition, if one gained information, uncertainty was reduced relative to an unspecified previous level of knowledge; in fact, Sayre (1976) referred to "information" as simply a difference between two levels of uncertainty. Interestingly, the telemetry school was concerned with effective communication, but their idea of communication was a primitive view based on closure of a connection—it was assumed that if there was a successful transmission, someone or something on the other end got the message, and thus communication had occurred. Whether there was comprehension of meaning, as the term "communication" is used in the social sciences, was not an issue they considered. The two major legacies derived from the telemetry school are the initial focus on information, and the concept of uncertainty, which is still pervasive in much of our thinking about IP.

The question of what was conveyed by information was the concern of the second school of information theorists, the *content* school. The content "school" is a loosely defined aggregation to which I have assigned many subgroups. Among them are information technologists, to whom we owe the conceptual distinction between *data* and information. Information is not raw data; the computer I am using to write this book manipulates electrical impulses (which we interpret as "1" and "0"), and this is simply meaningless data. By structuring these impulses in a number of ways, we convert them into meaningful symbols, such as an alphabet which I can recognize and use.

Another subgroup in the content school is concerned with how human beings extract meaning from the streams of data and information they receive. Many of these have contributed significantly to the study of how humans acquire and process information for decision-making, as well as for other general purposes. I refer to this latter subgroup as the cognitive information processing (CIP) group, of whom we will hear more later.

Also included in the content school are a large number of communication theorists from the social sciences.[1] One of the early contributions to the study of communication in organizations (and in my opinion, still one of the best) was the work of Farace, Monge, and Russell (1977). They defined information as "pattern recognition in matter/energy flows." A stream of symbols lacking any discernible pattern lacks information; therefore, uncertainty is lack of a pattern, or randomness in the stream of matter/energy. They also point out that information depends on the perceiver (1977: 23); there are no "objective" patterns which universally constitute information. I find this a particularly robust concept. Among other possibilities, it allows me to resolve a shortcoming found in other models: how does one accommodate codes and coded messages in information theory, when the principal objective of a code is to be highly effective at communicating on one hand, while being highly selective about your audience and those with whom you do not want to communicate, on the other?

A small but significant volume in the thinking about information and IP was the work of Knight and McDaniel (1978). Like Farace, Monge, and Russell, Knight and McDaniel implied the role of communication in information, in that their definition required a "flow from one point to another in an orderly fashion" (1978: 13). Their definition considered information in organizations from several perspectives, differentiating routine from nonroutine information, along with other characteristics, and remains one of the most analytical and thorough definitions of information to this day.

A final subgroup in the content school is the psychological or social process group, who argue that the meanings that we receive from information are socially or behaviorally mediated. In this subgroup, the content of information may be socially determined through reference groups, or through culture. Others in this group, including many communication social scientists, argue that much of information is not the content alone, but the interpretation mediated by the context; this group focuses on attributions made to nonverbal and other cues as well as the message itself. This group also brings with it a perspective that is often either ignored or unappreciated by many others, and that is the importance of political and interpersonal interactions in determining the content and meaning of information. Most of the theorists who have chosen a political perspective, in fact, are rather isolated from others. The different perspectives within the content school strongly suggest the reciprocal relationship between information and IP mentioned earlier. If information depends on internal CIP or social or other mediation to become information in the first place, then it is essentially meaningless to consider information in isolation from IP.

Information in organizations Our primary concern in this book is the processing of information in organizations, or organizational information processing (OIP). Given that interest, I want to briefly examine some of the concepts of information that have been used in the context of OIP. As Galbraith's (1977) work illustrated, most of what we conceptualized about information and OIP was measured in the negative—rather than information, we instead used the concept of uncertainty to organize our thinking about information and information processing. Again, this can be traced to the works by Shannon (1948) and Shannon and Weaver (1949), who used the term "entropy" to characterize the absence of information. The concept of uncertainty was developed somewhat farther by Edwards (1964), who added the distinction between "small-current" problems of control and "large-current" problems of energy, as conceptualized in German electrical engineering theory.

While Galbraith used the concept of uncertainty to refer to a lack of information, he defined uncertainty differently than the telemetry school, and was the first to consider it as a general problem of meaning within the context of organizations. He implied dissatisfaction with the concept; as he noted (p. 36), there was a "great deal of uncertainty about uncertainty." He considered uncertainty to be the *difference between the information required to perform a task and the amount of information already possessed by the organization* (1977: 36). The "information required" consisted of two parts: (1) the nature of the task, in terms of the diversity of goals, and the internal diversity of the organization (primarily a function of the division of labor); and (2) the level of performance required. With respect to the latter, higher organizational performance necessitates considering more alternatives, more variables, and more variables simultaneously (p. 37). Hence, greater uncertainty is associated not only with the stock of information on hand, but with the stock of methods and approaches the organization has available to use that information. His was the first model to explicitly consider organizational performance in relation to IP.

More recently, Daft and Lengel (1986) differentiated Galbraith's concept of uncertainty from Weick's (1979) concept of equivocality, which Weick defines as essentially synonymous with "ambiguity." Daft and Lengel argued that the principal underlying reason for OIP was the need to cope with these two informational problems. Like most earlier contributors to our concepts of information, their idea implied that information already existed, and the issue for the organization's users was more a matter of the lack of it, or insufficient understanding of what we had.

Together, these concepts suggest that information must be conceptualized in a way that takes into account not only the medium by which information is transmitted, or the success of those transmissions in purely telemetric terms, but must also account for the meaning conveyed. Further, since meaning is considerably dependent on the perceiver, the mediating role of the communication process cannot be excluded.

Information Processing

Having considered earlier concepts of "information" more fully, I would like to turn attention to information processing (IP). As I mentioned at the beginning of this chapter, IP has received more theoretical and applied attention than the more fundamental concept of information. However, that does not mean that the concept of IP is necessarily more completely developed or integrated into the literature than "information." In fact, IP has fared little better, even though more frequently discussed.

One of the earliest applications of the concept of IP in the context of organizations was the work of Aguilar (1967), who related the development of business strategy to environmental scanning practices. Several years later, Newell and Simon (1972) developed a model of cognitive IP (CIP) which has been a configural guideline for many subsequent scholars of both CIP and OIP. They conceptualized CIP as a cyclical relationship between information sensors, short-term memory, information which shifted between short-term, long-term, and working memory as needed for a specific task, and "effectors" which transmitted information back to the environment. Lawler and Rhode (1976) gave attention to the role of information in the control systems of organizations, although they did not define what they meant by either "information" or "control systems."

OIP was moved to the forefront by two contributions in 1978. The first was a widely-cited article by Tushman and Nadler (1978), who adopted the contingency-theory concept of "fit" between organizational components and processes, along with the idea of uncertainty as a product of three groups of variables, and argued that IP was a basic model for understanding organizations faced with uncertainty. At about the same time, Knight and McDaniel (1978) gave a very thorough treatment of the concept of information "processors," which they categorized as ranging from theories to people (groups and individuals), to machines, and to organizations.

The conceptual approach of IP theory has continued to be represented as a small but persistent voice in the literature of organization and international business. Its conceptual place in this literature has often been only loosely related to other theories, however. As a direct reflection of that, there have been a number of diverse theoretical orientations in the range and structure of IP models. I will not attempt to do more than summarize these here and provide some examples of each of the categories I have grouped them into; there are many overlaps between categories, and I do not intend my classification of these models to be definitive, since my purpose is to try to develop a model which integrates most of these, or is at least compatible with them.

A number of theorists regard "information" as a highly abstract but uniform and homogeneous entity in the context of OIP. I refer to them as the *uniformist* school; "uniformist" is a somewhat awkward term, but a number of people have spent significant effort developing theoretical arguments about the cost and value of information and IP, and have posited abstract or philosophical arguments about the implications of their analyses (Kennedy, 1994; Kijima, 1993; Malone, 1987; Refinetti, 1989). On the other hand, some have tried to encourage others in their field to abandon uniformist models which are seen as overly restrictive and artificial (Kose, Ronen, and Radner, 1990; Radner, 1996). Characteristic of both sides of this school, however, is a very high level of abstraction—typically, neither information nor IP are ever defined, and both are treated as uniform entities with properties which are entirely understood and completely interchangeable between organizations and contexts.

A second approach, and probably the largest group of contributors by far, is the *decision theory* school. This school consists of a large number of subgroups, many of which can be subdivided farther still. One subgroup is the *social process* group, which views IP primarily as a matter of how information is mediated by group and social influences. A number of people working in this group were stimulated to do so by the "social information processing" concept of Salancik and Pfeffer (1978). Another group focused mostly on the question of how human beings deal with problems requiring the exercise of judgment; examples are provided by Bazerman (1994) and Hammond *et al.* (1975). Others have used the decision process as the basis for organization design (Huber and McDaniel, 1986). Most of these models focus on CIP as done by individuals or groups. Lord and Maher (1990) grouped the models I place in this category into four types: rational, limited capacity, expert, and cybernetic.

In its most recent manifestation, IP has been represented in the concept of "organization learning" (Argyris and Schon, 1978; Cavaleri and Fearon, 1996; Senge, 1990). The *organization learning* school includes a number of very diverse contributors. Argyris and Schon come from a background in the applied behavioral sciences, and are widely associated with early work in sensitivity training and management development. Forrester (1970) is an early proponent of the use of computer-mediated simulation and modeling as a method for system analysis, although his early applications deal primarily with "hard" systems dynamics; more recently, Checkland (1988) has advanced the idea of "soft" system dynamics. Senge (1990) represents a synthesis of these approaches, and in many ways can be considered an example of the fusion of system dynamics and modeling with management and organization development.

A number of OIP models have been published over the years, most of them derived in large part from this body of work. In fact, with very few exceptions, most OIP models are derived from concepts reviewed above. The role of "uncertainty" as a motivator for IP is found frequently in the OIP models, and so Galbraith's (1977) and Tushman and Nadler's (1978) concepts are often used as a basis for creation of a particular model. Aguilar's (1967) model of environmental scanning is also widely cited.

Within this IP literature, descriptions of the functions comprising IP have tended to polarize into two broad sets. There is some conceptual agreement within these sets, but very little commonality between them. Each has been applied to various approaches to OIP and to a variety of organizations. One set conceptualizes IP in terms of the types of *sensory and intellectual subprocesses* performed to process information. These usually categorize IP as a set of steps, such as Aguilar's (1967) three: viewing, search, and interpretation. Newell and Simon (1972) modeled IP in terms of sensory input followed by various memory and processor activities, followed by output returned to the environment via effectors. While differing in the number of steps and subprocesses, these models generally agree on the overall nature of the steps used to process information.

Examples of applications of these OIP models include senior management use of environmental scanning (Auster and Choo, 1994); police organization enforcement strategies (Simms and Petersen, 1991); and top management teams in planning and strategy formation (Wang and Chan, 1995). A prescriptive approach using IP methods in planning for volatile environments was also proposed by Hartman, White, and Crino (1986).

The second set has taken a rather different approach, and discusses IP in terms of information pathways and subprocesses determined by *organization structures and integrating devices.* Galbraith's (1977) model is very widely cited, along with Daft and Lengel (1986), and Tushman and Nadler's (1978) model. Several other authors have categorized task characteristics and organizational relationships somewhat differently, and have focused on task analyzability and ambiguity and task interdependence after Perrow (1967). Many of these models presume that certain structural types are able to process information with different degrees of effectiveness, an assumption partially supported by Van de Ven *et al.* (1976) and empirically investigated by Egelhoff's (1988) study of a group of multinational firms. In this category, I include those studies focusing on the potential for information technology (IT) to mediate these processes and contribute to organizational performance. This potential was discussed as part of Galbraith's (1977) model; more recent illustrations are provided by Cash *et al.* (1993), or Jarvenpaa and Ives (1993) examination of the role of IT in multinational firms.

Examples of these models can also be found in Bensaou and Venkatraman's (1995) study of interorganizational relationships in the automobile industry; Ito and Peterson's (1987) study of boundary spanning as an OIP mechanism to compensate for information overload; and Leifer and Mill's (1996) propositions regarding control strategies in emerging organizations.

Obviously, these models tend to focus only on components of OIP. The first set examines the CIP between managers and organization members, and extends the scope of their CIP to include the goals and activities of the organization. The second set is more concerned with how the organization is structured to cope with its IP requirements. Most studies either ignore the other domain, or attempt to simply reduce them to subsets of the other. Rarely do we see studies which attempt to construct OIP models that combine the CIP of members and the organizational components of OIP. Two examples of these are Corner, Kinicki and Keats' (1994) construction of a "parallel process" model for decision-making, and Thomas and McDaniels' (1990) model of how top management teams interpret strategic issues.

One of the most thorough of the OIP models was Egelhoff's (1991), which he conceptualized specifically for firms operating in international business. I regard it as one of the best contributions in the field within this category, especially with respect to developing applicable theoretical constructs. Egelhoff does not differentiate between information and IP in the same manner as I do, and he combines a subset of the models I have put into the "content" information category, along with the "sensory and intellectual" and "organization learning" IP groups, which he refers to collectively as "cognitive" models of IP. Similarly, he groups some of the content subgroups with the organization structure subgroup and refers to these as "logistic" models.

His model develops a 2x2 matrix of the "structural" dimensions of OIP, consisting of the purpose and perspective of IP on one axis, and the content of IP on the other. Similarly, he uses a 2x2 classification for processing, where the two major variables are the routineness of information and the interdependence between the parties in the IP event. These can be used to describe IP capacity differences between major structural forms found in most multinational firms.

Egelhoff (1988) had previously tested the proposition that the location of knowledge and decision-making capability would correspond to his structure classifications, using a sample of 49 U.S. and European multinationals. The predictions were generally borne out, and Egelhoff's work is some of the best empirical support for the general OIP argument that different organization structures do, in fact, have different IP capacities. Although his major interest is specific to the multinational firm, I regard much of his work as relevant to organizations in other contexts, and recommend his work to others who share the objective of advancing information processing theory.

A critique of OIP models All of these models are beneficial in having helped clarify the processes by which organizations cope with enormous amounts of data and information. At the same time, almost all of these share one or more characteristics which limit their utility in understanding OIP. These limitations are:

1. The *assumption of linearity*. This property is common to many of the models of cognitive (or "rational") IP. In nearly all the models reviewed above, there is a progression through a number of specific levels, each of which is peculiar to a "stage" or "step" in the process. Each of these transitions is incremental, rational, explicit, and transparent, in the sense that one knows when the transition has been completed, and what was done within it. This conceptual approach persists despite significant evidence that it is a poor description of much OIP, whether for decision-making, strategy formation, or general internal processing. As significant conceptual and empirical contradictions to this approach, research from Hall (1976) has shown the inability of managers to effectively use information in the publishing industry; Lindblom's (1959) classic article emphasized the recurring problem of dealing with unknowns and conflicting

criteria; Mintzberg, Raisinghani, and Theoret (1976) have shown that while seemingly "unstructured" strategic problems have a deep, complex structure, these have many loops and repetitive cycles; and Nutt (1984) has shown the tendency to do nearly anything but go through the process of generating truly novel solutions to problems. Further, research into organizational communication consistently underscores the nonlinearity of these processes (Farace, Monge, and Russell, 1977).

2. *Implied explicitness.* This seeming oxymoron refers to the unspoken implication that all OIP is done in the formal system, as it was designed, using only the "right" information and within the boundaries of the formal system (see point (3) below). This is simply not true: companies routinely keep "three sets of books"—one for the shareholders, one for the tax authorities, and one for internal control; police organizations have quota systems for traffic enforcement, and universally deny their existence; academic departments engage in journal-article bean-counting, and ostensibly claim no interest in research production for any purpose other than the creation of new knowledge. The cleavage between actual and ostensible purposes for the collection and use of information is one of the earliest findings to emerge from the study of organizations. Informal channels of communication have long been recognized and are a fact well-known to practitioners, of course.

3. *Democratic functionality.* OIP in nearly all models is "democratic" in the sense that all components of information at all stages of OIP have equal weight, which is obviously naive; OIP is "functional" in that the models assume IP which is focused on an unequivocal goal. As Feldman and March (1981) have pointed out, much information gathered and consumed in organizations has no relationship to any outcome, and is purely symbolic. Nutt (1984) would agree, and add that the nature of the overall decision process seldom matches the ostensible description. Studies of organizations in the communication literature (Farace, Monge, and Russell, 1977) make it clear that one of the major problems in OIP is overload, and that information routinely drops through the cracks in the organization. Wildavsky (1983) presented a compelling argument that "data" at a point of entry into an organization is transformed into "information," but then becomes "data" again as further transformations move the information up the organization's hierarchy. Part of this devolution is the need to compress information into increasingly compact form

as it moves upward through the hierarchy and is added to other information, thereby creating overload.

4. *Unidimensionality.* This criticism of most OIP models is a composite of three major limitations. One of these is that while most of the models of OIP recognize flows of information between locations and subprocesses, they tend to assume that we deal with IP demands one dimension at a time. In fact, I believe that in complex systems the process changes over time, and both the breadth and depth of IP processes subsume a large number of variables. Second, most models assume a type of static processing which is unrealistic, in light of the amount of information in our literature showing that cybernetic processes are a much more accurate description of organizational functioning (these will be discussed shortly). While most of the more complex models recognize the existence of flows of information, they are better described as *quasi-dynamic* models. In complex cybernetic systems like organizations, it is much more likely that many different types of IP are being done concurrently, with different actors and participants over time. The classic "garbage can" model (Cohen, March, and Olsen, 1972) is probably a more accurate description of general OIP, in addition to organizational choice-making. Finally, most models assume some degree of closure, in the sense that an "end point" can be detected in the process. Closure may be an appropriate property to describe decision processes (although I would argue that in most cases it is not), but it clearly does not describe OIP in more general cases.

5. *Noiseless linkages.* Most OIP models fail to take into account one of the first and most fundamental concerns of both the telemetry and cybernetic theorists, the problems of noise in communication; further, most models fail to incorporate any of the literature on human communication processes. The "flows" in many of the quasi-dynamic models assume a level of automatic linkage quality and accuracy which is not supported by either the literature or by direct observation of the goings-on in most organizations. Connection quality, in short, comes in good and bad forms. The communication theorists are acutely aware of the effect of communication activities on IP, but only rarely does the communication process explicitly appear in these models (e.g., Bensaou and Venkatraman, 1995; Egelhoff, 1982). A better degree of incorporation of communication theory and processes is found in the organizational learning literature, but full appreciation of the impact of communication

processes is still not found in the majority of OIP work. Because of the incompleteness of models which do not account for communication processes, the internal politics of OIP are rarely recognized or taken into account (Bensaou and Venkatraman, 1995). Political processes, in my view, are an inevitable consequence of the properties of information, which will be discussed next.

Information and Information Processing: a More Complete Model

Information in the IPT Context

Taking the factors in the preceding discussion into account, I find it appropriate to define the term *information* to be largely synonymous with "knowledge." *Information* is *knowledge* which is *created*, in that it is the outcome of human thought processes; is *structured*, in that it is not random and that it is dependent on prior interpretations; and is *communicable*, in that it can be stored and transmitted, at least in part. I use the term "human thought processes" to retain generality in this definition, rather than terms such as "cognitive" or "affective" which usually connote rational or emotional processes. Through use of information, any of us can look into a night sky and differentiate stars from meteors; in the absence of that accumulated knowledge, the passing of a meteor could be interpreted in a multitude of ways (and usually was in antiquity), with both rational and emotional connotations. I take a somewhat phenomenological view in this definition, in that I argue that if information is not perceived, it is not there; this view is also implied by many early contributors to this stream of thought.

Information imperfections However, earlier theorists' work builds a strong case for the argument that not all information has the same kind or clarity of meaning. I use the term *imperfection* to capture the potential limitations and shortcomings that any item of information may be subject to. Imperfections can come in two major forms. The first is widely discussed in the literature reviewed above, and recognizes that a primary problem of information in organizations is its *incompleteness*, or the absence of it. However, not all states of incompleteness are the same—equivocality and uncertainty are not identical either in terms of the depth or breadth of what we do not know. As used by most researchers, a state of uncertainty implies that information is absent or missing to some degree, where equivocality means that we have information but cannot interpret it. This implies a structured relationship between types information incompleteness relative to some perhaps ideal or "perfect" state of information.

The second imperfection is almost completely unrecognized in our literature, and is an aggregate imperfection which I describe in terms of the *vector properties* of information. When we use the term "information" in most organizational contexts, we imply or assume that it is true, objective, factual, and consistent. In fact, it need not be any of these. Information can often be false, as with misinformation or disinformation; it can be subjective in many ways, based on incomplete or partial acquisition, perceptual filtering, and the like; it can be based on individual feelings, where those subjective feelings are regarded and used as objective facts; and it can be highly internally inconsistent, as people can easily harbor contradictory views on closely related issues without experiencing internal conflict.[2] The implication of rational purpose underlies almost every treatment of organizational information in the content school. Feldman and March (1981), however, make an eloquent argument for the use of information for a variety of purposes which have nothing whatever to do with the ostensible purposes of supporting better decisions. Factors such as an apparent commitment to rational decision- making are argued to account more for information-seeking behavior, rather than its use or application.

The concept of a vector property requires a bit of explanation. Information processing in organizations is usually discussed in terms of assumed validity and conditions of uncertainty. That is, we assume that the information we have (or will acquire) is all valid, and that most of the time the problem is that we do not have enough of it—the usual expression is, "If we had the right information...." While most people can be assumed to be truthful, or at least honest (but an assumption not shared professionally by intelligence specialists or auditors, among others), it is quite ordinary to find that such properties may not apply to much of the information we receive, and that it is difficult to sort out what is real. Permutations of information can result from many variables and include many types of "information" which satisfy the criteria of being created, structured, and communicable knowledge, and may still be completely invalid and counterproductive. Virtually everyone knows of cases where people became upset over situations where they had incomplete, incorrect, and subjective information. Awareness of such possibilities is embedded in many institutional dispute-resolution processes, which often quite appropriately begin with fact-finding. Thus, I am proposing that all information is best conceptualized as a "vector" representing positions along several continua. A summary of some of the more important properties is shown in Figure 1.1.

True _____ False
Objective _____ Subjective
Fact _____ Feeling
Consistent _____ Inconsistent/Contradictory
Specific _____ General
Particular _____ Aggregated
Explicit _____ Implicit/Experiential

"Information" is a vector representing the location of an information element on all of these properties, each of which is a continuum.

Figure 1.1 Properties of information

Each of the dimensions shown in Figure 1.1 shows one of the continua along which the properties of information may vary. Any item of information may contain elements of truth and falsehood; both objective and subjective data; both facts and feelings. It may be consistent with other items of data or information, or contradictory; it may refer to a very specific entity, or be a generalization; and it may be a very particular construct or an aggregation of other constructs. It may be explicit, in that it can be clearly articulated, or implicit, as the information gained through experience. In nearly any complex situation, then, it seems inevitable that multiple interpretations of the situation and available data and information will obtain. "Information," from this perspective, clearly establishes a domain of the type Bellman and Zadeh (1970) termed "fuzzy."

These information imperfections can take at least four major forms, depending on whether they are active or passive. This is illustrated in Table 1.1 below. Most incomplete information originates from passive sources, and is a function of uncertainty (i.e., lack of information) or general signal loss in communication. But active incompleteness can result from misinformation, disinformation, and noise in the system which overwhelms the receiver; if deliberate, this constitutes "jamming." Similarly, vector properties may have active or passive sources. Much of what is done to process information in organizations or other contexts is intended to discover underlying patterns or reliable facts; this may fail, and that failure may go undetected. In that sense, any active source of imperfection within vector properties might be categorized as "analytical error." However, the majority of vector-property imperfections have passive origins, and result from internal, pre-existing, and often unconscious sources, such as values, feelings and emotions, responses to information sources rather than content, or cultural predispositions.

Table 1.1   Forms of information imperfections

Form	Source of imperfection	
	Active	**Passive**
Incompleteness	1. Misinformation, disinformation, "jamming"	2. "Uncertainty," lack of information, signal loss or noise
Vector properties	3. Analytical error	4. Values, feelings and emotions, source-specific responses, culture

We should note that each of these components of information imperfection stimulate specific IP activities. Types 1 and 2 stimulate search responses, although the exact nature of the search is likely to be quite different when we believe we are being deceived as opposed to when we think we need to "do our homework."   Much of the literature of organizational information processing and decision theory is concerned with this kind of problem, and mostly Type 2 imperfections. Type 3 imperfection may not be detected, or may stimulate search to consider whether the cost of additional information to evaluate the possibility of error is warranted, relative to its value. Much of Type 4 imperfection is not overtly considered by IP theorists, nor by most decision theorists despite early recognition of its limiting effect on rationality (Simon, 1976). Those who study organization culture (e.g., Schein, 1985), international business culture (Ferraro, 1997), or communication processes (Farace, Monge, and Russell, 1977) focus much of their work on these imperfections and recognize their effects on organizational processes and outcomes.

Relative to most other treatments, the need to account for information imperfections creates a major difference in the perspective of information and information processing proposed here. For a theory of information and IP to be scientifically useful, in my view, it must be able to accommodate any and all of these imperfections. Further, the imperfect nature of information implies the duality between information and IP that I mentioned above—since information is knowledge, the content of it is partially a function of the processing used to create it. To fully understand the composition of information, both in terms of the content we know and do not know, and in terms of the properties of that content, we must first have a more complete understanding of what "information processing" means. I am therefore going to suspend the discussion of information and its properties until we have had an opportunity to examine a model of organizational IP in more detail. With a more complete conceptual basis for both information and OIP, I will return to the issue of the composition of information and its properties.

The Structure of Organizational Information Processing

Information processing elements Any model of OIP must be sufficiently flexible and robust to address the limitations of OIP discussed earlier, and accommodate the imperfections of information. In the IPT model, I am defining the term "information processing" to consist of a *structure* which is the interaction of two major elements: the *functions* of information processing and a *framework* for the functions. The framework may include the application of Information Technology (IT) as a mediator, but IT is not necessary to the definition of IP. The structure of IP is summarized in Table 1.2, and although my primary concern is with OIP, I propose that this structure is applicable to individuals and groups as well.

There are four IP functions. First, information must be acquired. We *acquire* information through a variety of processes, such as attending to selected phenomena in our environment, retrieving information from storage, choosing to search for it, or creating it from raw data. Second, we *store* information in many forms and locations, primarily to have it for future applications. Storage may require nothing more (or less) than human memory or may be mediated. Third, we *transform* information in many ways. Much activity is directed toward decomposing information into components through analysis; other activities are intended to build larger or different wholes through synthesis; we interpolate information to project future states; and we interpret information and find, create, or supply new meanings. Finally, we *disseminate* information to others.

The framework of IP also consists of four components. These components can be human or nonhuman, and frequently consist of both; they

Table 1.2 Information processing elements: functions and framework

Functions	Acquisition	• Search • Attention
	Storage	• Memory • Retrieval
	Transformation	• Analysis—decomposition • Synthesis—weighting, evaluation • Extrapolation • Interpretation
	Dissemination	• Voluntary output, response • Behavior
Framework	Sensors	• Senses, sensory devices • Sensory registers
	Memory	• Working memory • Short-term memory • Long-term memory
	Processors	• Supervisory processor • Functional processor
	Accessors	• Formal output media and transmissions • Structured access (contacts, databases)

correspond to the functions discussed above, but are not necessarily bound to the functions. First, information and data input occurs through *sensors* or diverse input channels, many of which are highly specific to the nature of information accepted. Second, storage requires *memory* devices. These include documents and storage through other media, and also include training and education. Third, a *processor* is required to perform all of the transformations which information may be subjected to, and to control the operation of other components of the system. Finally, *accessors* are output structures which enable the information generated or changed by the system to be accessible to others or which provide it on some predetermined basis. I am literally using this word to mean "that which gives or creates access." These are gateways for dissemination, for information to be accessible to others inside and outside the system. Unlike the CIP concept of "effectors" (Newell and Simon, 1972), I make no assumption that access to information requires an active framework element or role on the part of the processor or organization; indeed, much access is purely passive (and in cases of military or industrial espionage, actively resisted).

Finally, I want to point out that the choice of the term "framework" is not unrelated to the cognitive IP concept of decision "frame;" I consider the components of the IP framework described here to constitute a basis of support (or the "frame") for many IP activities, decision-making among them.

Information Processing (IP) The function and framework elements interact with each other in information processing. Figure 1.2 shows this interaction between framework elements on the horizontal axis and functions on the vertical axis. The primary IP activities are performed in the four cells along the main diagonal of the matrix, from upper left to lower right. In other words, acquisition is associated most strongly with sensors, storage with memory, etc. "Information Processing" literally means that at least one of these main-diagonal cells is engaged. Obviously this takes time, an issue which will be dealt with momentarily. However, there is no presumption or requirement that IP must necessarily move along the diagonal in a strict sequence; the movement from cell to cell can be iterative, or can jump from one cell to another in discontinuous fashion, although it would be most likely to proceed from one to another on the diagonal over time. This means that if a processing activity got "stuck" and constantly needed more or different information from memory devices, one would expect to see an iterative series of movements between the two middle cells on the diagonal before moving on to the next processing cell.

The remaining 12 cells are auxiliary to the main activities on the diagonal, but they are important contributors to IP. It is entirely possible that in the example of being "stuck" above, the final IP action could be to transform information into a result only placed in working memory for short-term storage; this form of storage, however, could serve as an "accessor" for those allowed to use it, and thus a route to disseminate information under controlled conditions. An example is to allow those who gain access to provide a password, which upon examination (by a processor) allows further access to memory and controlled dissemination of information.

Framework elements

Functions	Sensors	Memory	Processors	Accessors
Acquisition	x			
Storage		x		
Transformation			x	
Dissemination				x

Figure 1.2   Information processing as the interaction of functions and framework elements

It is important to note that OIP is not constrained to occupy only one cell at a time, and in many cases it does not. There is no reason why the "storage" referred to in the example above might not be another person or organization, and a processor in its own right. With multiple individuals involved in most OIP, it is likely that for most situations there will be multiple activities under way at any time, so that multiple cells in the matrix could be active at once.

Figure 1.3 shows a hypothetical transition through a subset of the 16 cells of OIP over time. The relationship is illustrated as a matter of movement through a series of the matrices shown in Figure 1.2 as an OIP task progresses. The "path" followed is the trace linking whatever cells are active at one time to those active at later times. Staying in one or more cells for a period of time constitutes a "stage" in the process. The "scope" of activity is the number of active cells during that stage. Movement through the successive matrices does not imply linearity, efficiency, determinism, or even purposefulness in OIP; in fact, it does not necessarily even require closure.

Information technology (IT) can obviously be used to perform many IP functions, and can serve as a major part of the IP framework for an organization, i.e., IT can *mediate* IP. However, IT alone is inadequate to meet the IP needs of the system unless it is designed to interact effectively with all elements of a system, and these usually include people. At the same time, as the processing in the system becomes more variable, managing the system effectively without the enhanced capabilities of IT mediation is likely to be more difficult than necessary, and perhaps dysfunctional. The role of IT, therefore, is one that I regard as auxiliary to the functions and frameworks used by human beings, and IT plays roles which are parallel and

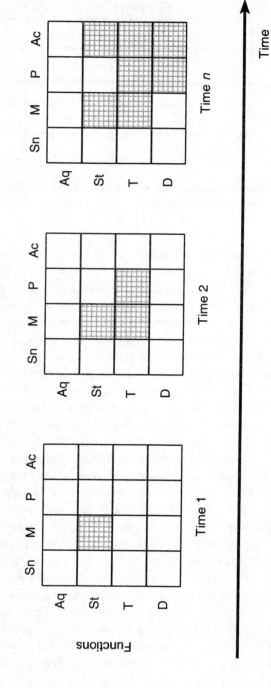

Figure 1.3 Organizational information processing

complementary to the people in the system and integrated into the dynamic matrix of Figure 1.3. There is no question that by now IT is embedded and integrated so completely into many organizational processes that it is impossible for most organizations to function in its absence.

For the remainder of this book, my use of the term "IP" will be taken to mean the processing of information as interaction between at least one function and one framework element of this model, i.e., within at least one cell of Figure 1.2. IT may or may not mediate this activity, but I do not regard IP as exclusively a human or an IT phenomenon. Where the role of IT is being considered explicitly, as will be the case in the discussion of performance and slack in Chapter 6, it will be made clear how IT is involved in the overall processing task.

A Hierarchical Model of Information in Organizations

Having now proposed definitions for both information and information processing, I want to return to the consideration of them as entities which are conjoint and interacting. These relationships are crucial to understanding information in the context of organizations. The hierarchy in Figure 1.4 illustrates the general properties of information in organizations, including information imperfections. I will first provide an overview of the hierarchical relationships between the levels of information in the model, and then use the model to define the levels and corresponding imperfections in more detail.

The model begins from the perspective of an ideal state of knowledge, which may be conceived of as *perfect information*. Perfect information is the state assumed by the telemetry school in their constructs of uncertainty or entropy, as the obverse of what we experience; it is represented by all areas outside the heavy line, which I define as the *imperfect information boundary*. At the level of perfect information, we know everything: whether there is an afterlife, whether time travel is possible, whether the "Immaculate Reception" of the 1978 American Football Conference playoff game really was a completed pass, and who wrote the "Book of Love."

Perfect information is unattainable to mere mortals, and so serves only as a point of reference for the rest of our analysis. Because we cannot have access to perfect information, we have to cope with whatever state of information (and data) we have at any time. IP is the enabling mechanism that provides enough closure to function in a world of imperfect information. In the information hierarchy shown in Figure 1.4, IP resolves different levels of imperfect information. This concept of "levels of imperfection" is

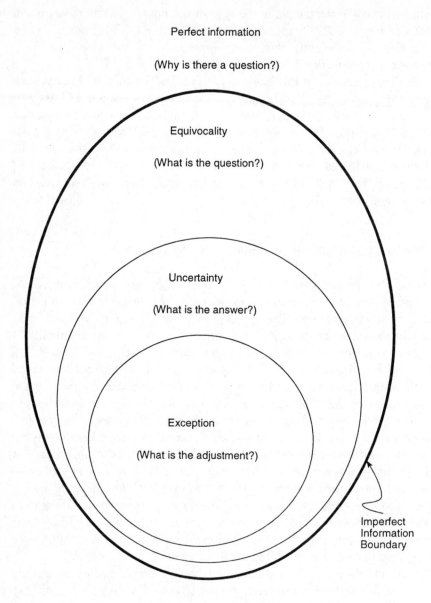

Figure 1.4 A hierarchical model of information

important, because not all IP activities are stimulated by the same type or scope of imperfection, as suggested above. Further, we should note that organizations *induce* information imperfections, both because they are artificial entities with fabricated goals and objectives, and because the structure of organizations causes information loss and creates noise in communication processes.

The simplest way to think about the relationships in Figure 1.4 is to view each of the four levels of information in the figure as representing a major issue or question to be resolved through IP, and from a point within any level there is always a different "horizon" to consider, in the sense that we can ask questions of larger or smaller scope. If we momentarily return to the imaginary world of perfect information, the IP issue at this level is very simple—"Why is there a question?"

Within our world, i.e., within the imperfect information boundary, the first IP imperfection we confront is that of *equivocality*. The fundamental IP issue of equivocality is, "What is the question?" Literally, deciding what to do, what to decide, and the real nature of the challenge confronting us at any time is the problem that must be resolved. This may not be realized by a decision-maker, of course, and I do not assume that rational awareness of this issue is a necessary condition for the model. By selection or default, however, passage through this level is a prerequisite for the next level; people have either chosen a question to pursue through active IP, or have begun to behave as if they have. Simple observation of human behavior, as well as much research on human judgment and decision processes, has long established the departure from rational IP in many instances (Simon, 1957; Cyert and March, 1963).

At the next level, we must deal with the issue of *uncertainty*. Uncertainty assumes we know the question, i.e., that equivocality has been resolved. The IP issue at this level is, "What is the answer?" Having selected or defaulted to a question, what outcomes to that question do we want? When that question has been answered, we can begin to enact it, and attempt to bring the desired answer into realization. This often does not work out as hoped, of course, and this brings us to the lowest level of imperfect information, the *exception*. I am using the term "exception" in the same way that March and Simon (1958) used it, to refer to those things that went wrong or were not intended outcomes, i.e., exceptions to what had been planned. The IP issue at this level is therefore, "What is the adjustment?"

Observation would suggest that in most organizations the largest volume of IP activity is concerned with the issues raised by exceptions, and the least with the resolution of equivocality. It may also be the case that the greatest importance is attached to the issues of equivocality, and the least to exceptions. This is a complex problem, and beyond the scope of the immediate discussion. What I want to point out for the moment is that there are fundamentally different IP requirements and informational properties associated with the different levels of imperfect information, and they should not be treated as equivalent (e.g., Schrader, Riggs, and Smith, 1993). These distinctions can be best understood from a clear definition of each of the levels.[3]

First, *equivocality* is defined as *an information imperfection where no single interpretation of a question can be made to dominate a different interpretation simply by the addition of more information*. Equivocality is not a matter of having enough information; it is a matter of having resolved the problem of what question to pursue. For example, if we have not decided what to decide, more information is not going to help us; in fact, it may simply add to our confusion. Organizations and managers lacking a clear set of goals to work toward cannot effectively process information to obtain outcomes—what outcomes are desired? This is one of the fundamental problems of decision theory, which often founders in attempts to help decide what problems are of sufficient value to warrant major investments of time and money. Whatever information is on hand can be processed to help make that determination. Since that determination is inherently made under conditions of imperfect information, there is no final resolution of whether it is the "right" question to pursue. We *choose* the question we want, or we *create* it. Issues under equivocality, in short, can be *resolved* through active IP, but they cannot be "reduced" or "eliminated."

At the next level, uncertainty is a quantitative issue—questions are resolved by getting more information, and in many cases the cost of that information can be considered as a factor in choosing whether to get it. *Uncertainty*, therefore, is *an information imperfection where the quantity of information is deficient for optimal processing*, i.e., we do not have enough information to get what we believe will be a good answer to a question. If we can get more information, or more knowledge about the cost of that information, we can make some relatively rational decisions regarding our next steps. It is in this range of questions where formal decision theory is best developed, and there are many procedures and algorithms to help us answer the questions that arise under uncertainty. (It should be noted that the term "risk," as it is used in formal decision theory and is discussed in Appendix 1.1, is a special case of this level of uncertainty. Any problem for which there is sufficient structure and information to permit an algorithmic or procedural resolution, in this model, is located at the level of uncertainty or lower.) Unlike equivocality, uncertainty can be *reduced* by acquisition of more information; the primary issue is the expected payoff of that information within the scope of the uncertainty.

Finally, exceptions are also a quantitative issue, but are constrained to the scope of the problem which defines the exception. That problem, in turn, is within the context of an earlier decision which created the "answer" that enables us to evaluate the outcome. An *exception,* therefore, is *an information imperfection where there is inadequate information to resolve an unanticipated outcome from a prior decision.* Unlike the problems of uncertainty and equivocality, it is much more likely that exceptions occur after resources and energies have been committed to an undertaking. I am restricting the term "exception" to situations where there is a "parental" relationship between a prior decision and the exception—the exception at issue can be traced back to a specific earlier decision. In that sense, the exceptions noted are usually negative outcomes relative to what was intended, and the somewhat tongue-in-cheek definition of a problem applies: a "problem" is a "deviation between expectation and observation." As Cyert and March (1963) noted, decision makers are most likely to start looking for an answer to a question in the "immediate vicinity of the problem," and that is very much the nature of exceptions.

Information processing over time   I said earlier that perfect information is unattainable to mere mortals. However, in the perception of most decision makers that is not quite true—over time, something resembling perfect information becomes available to us, in the form of history. After time has elapsed, information becomes far less malleable than in the future, and for many purposes, it is essentially "perfect," in that it is effectively fixed. Borrowing a term from grammarians, I refer to this state of information as *past perfect.* This apparent fixity of historical information provides us with linkages and anchors that are essential to human learning and decision-making.

The catch is that we may transpose events in time, and much CIP literature indicates that we often do. For example, it is well known that hindsight is related to decisions very poorly; rather than being able to use experience to form better judgments in the future, people are more likely to make attributions about what was known before the fact, and we are therefore unable to correctly reconstruct the situation before a decision was made. As a result, we change our perception of the information we had before the decision, in very familiar ways—the "Monday-morning quarterback" syndrome (Fischhoff, 1975), the "knew-it-all-along" syndrome (Wood, 1978), and the like. These and many other effects have been collectively described as *heuristics* and *biases* in decision-making. In his Nobel-prize winning work, Herbert Simon (1957) pointed out the difference between the rational evaluation of information that we like to think of as the way we make decisions, and the actual "bounded rationality" we really use. The latter approach is much more likely to be influenced by past knowledge we have acquired, which is one of the three "bounds" to our rationality.

This issue is related to the levels of information in Figure 1.5. What this figure suggests is a phenomenon we are all familiar with—degrees of freedom, as the potential to process information (i.e., decide what to do, decide how to do it, etc.) diminish as the point at which a decision must be made gets closer. If we designate a time for a decision ($t_{decision}$) relative to the present, we can see that as we move to the right, and that ($t_{decision}$) approaches the present, our ability to process these issues rapidly diminishes, and collapses to either a decision or a default. The area under the highest curve quickly decreases. Relevant information about that particular decision then becomes "past perfect" after ($t_{decision}$) passes. This model suggests some of the dynamics of IP behavior, an important property of IP for organizations and decision makers in them.

We can think about both the static and dynamic properties of IP as questions of which IP *horizon* we choose as appropriate to a problem. If we find that questions under uncertainty seem to be intractable, it may well be that the real problem is one of equivocality. The converse may also apply in those cases where no one pays adequate attention to the details of a problem. In any case, the decision maker has the option of evaluating an alternative horizon; obviously, freedom to evaluate any horizon is greatest when ($t_{decision}$) is remote.

Since perfect information is not possible, an unavoidable consequence is that any decision or attempt to resolve imperfections is itself imperfect. Organizations will always face the dilemma of simultaneously trying to avoid "paralysis by analysis" and "extinction by instinct." There are two consequences of this dilemma for the organization: tradeoffs necessitated by risk, and the adjustive role of organization slack, which may or may not be intended. Risk and tradeoffs are discussed in the next section; organization slack is discussed after examining the dynamic properties of organizations, the third major element of IPT.

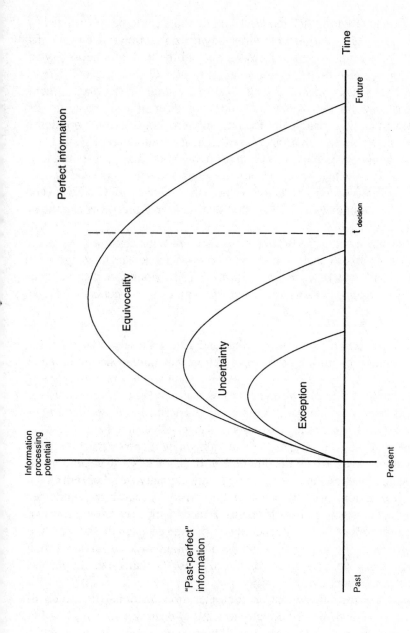

Figure 1.5 Information processing potential as a function of time

Expanding OIP: Risk and Tradeoffs

When I defined the basic IPT model, I said that this could be generalized to multiple goals. Most earlier IP theories pay little attention to the problems inherent in determination of multiple goals and the tradeoffs necessary to attain them. One of the most important attributes of this tradeoff is *risk*. Risk, of course, has received a great deal of attention in the management science literature, but this work usually does not differentiate the qualities of information, and then principally focuses only on "large-current" problems of choice of alternatives in a risky world. The determination of goals is an important act of equivocality resolution (or in my view, it at least should be). Once goals are selected, however, organizations and managers need to deal with several forms of risk; these involve both the "large-current" problems of threats to goal attainment as well as the "small-current" problems of control (Edwards, 1964).

This section extends the IPT model to encompass the concept of risk, and suggests some ways to broaden both the theoretical model and the pragmatics of dealing with the IP issues risk raises. The dynamic and cybernetic properties of organizations will be integrated with these concepts in the next section.

Risk and information processing Risk and IP are closely related. Risk describes a state of information imperfection, but unlike the hierarchical imperfections described in Figure 1.4, risk is a summary term for all types of imperfections as they apply to choices between alternatives. In general usage, "risk" is associated with negative outcomes; it is defined as the possibility of suffering loss or harm, or the possibility of danger. Decision theorists define risk somewhat more strictly, as the situation where a choice must be made between alternatives, where the outcome of the choice is also dependent on a future state of nature which is not known with certainty (see Appendix 1.1). Nearly all decision theorists consider this "risky" because the outcomes include possible negative ones. If one were faced with a set of only positive outcomes, the idea of "risk" as generally used in the decision theory literature would not really be applicable—while one might make a choice which precludes the best possible outcome, the only "risk" is that we might get less than the possible maximum.

Risk is a principal motivation for much organizational IP. Much of decision science is dedicated directly to ways of dealing with risk, whether through direct methods such as the payoff matrix and various decision tools, or indirectly through forecasting and predictive modeling. Companies and organizations spend a considerable amount of time and money in applying these methods to help them cope with risks, although in practice most of these methods are limited.[4]

As with any management issue, IP is necessary to cope with risk. This is hardly news. Kepner and Tregoe (1965: 39) pointed out that *"the raw material of management is information.* That is about all any manager has to work with...(emphasis added)." Simon (1957) recognized the limitations on individual IP capabilities; Downs (1966) recognized the limitations on organizational decision makers in six key areas, including lack of information (or affordable information), competition for attention, and individual limitations noted earlier. Altogether, these factors limit much organizational decision-making to what Lindblom (1959) called the "science of muddling through."

Most organizational decision makers are faced with a tradeoff between efficiency and effectiveness in their decisions—they can either make lower-quality decisions now, or better-quality decisions later. An unpredictable future is something we all face, but in some cases there are outcomes which are completely unacceptable, and must be avoided at any cost. In most situations (including many technology accessions), the risks are not so extreme, but reasonable effort needs to be made to avoid negative outcomes. Tradeoffs between the acquisition time and cost of information and potential negative outcomes constitute a first level IP problem, and the actual decision itself a second. Deciding these tradeoffs requires intensive IP activity and requires time, which itself may be an enemy. These multi-level problems are not generally dealt with in the decision theory literature. The value of information is reflected in Bayesian decision models, of course, but with respect to the primary outcomes under consideration, not with the issue of "deciding to decide" tradeoffs. That remains a problematic and more subjective issue.

For the primary choice problems in decision theory, the logic underlying the "payoff matrix" is still very appropriate. The calculation of an expected value (EV) for each alternative enables the decision-maker to use information in a systematic way, using probability theory in conjunction with information about alternatives and payoffs. While a useful process to go through, most decision-makers recognize the limitations of the EVs. The greatest of these, of course, is that the fundamental assumption underlying the use of probabilities, the idea of the "long run," is an inaccurate representation of reality. The majority of major organizational decisions are one-of-a-kind experiments, and will never be repeated; even if they were, the state of the universe would be so different in the future that circumstances would not be comparable to those in the present.

Further, the conceptual underpinning of the threat of loss is incomplete— risk is an expectation, and thus inherently a subjective phenomenon. It is equally a function of both the actual possibility of a loss, and of the interpretation of that loss by the individual. With respect to the latter question, risk is more a matter of how the decision maker (which can be an individual or a group) processes information about that possibility and its relationship to other subjectively relevant variables. The concept of *utility* best expresses this relationship, where a "utility" can be used to express the weighted value of one or more variables. Thus, a gambler who enjoys the game can look forward with relish to the entertainment associated with losing $200, while a person who does not enjoy gambling will choose not to participate because of the negative utility of the loss of money; both decision makers can be accommodated under utility theory. Further, utility can be expressed in the form of more than one attribute (multi-attribute utility, or MAU), making it very robust for many applications (Huber, 1980).

The concept of utility enables us to broaden the interpretation of outcomes, to include both multiple outcomes and different subjective values associated with them. However, utility itself is a subjective outcome, and the concept does not completely resolve the problem of risk assessment for practical decision-making. Information about utility does nothing to resolve the problem of imperfect information. Utilities add more variables (in the form of weights) to a process for which there already may be an excess of variables, i.e., information overload, and where the major issue is often the amount of time available to make decisions. In that connection, Simon (1973) observed that the problem faced by most managers is not a shortage of information, but of *attention*. Cyert and March (1963) argued that many decision makers cope with uncertainty by avoidance—they use short-term "feedback-react" decision rules and procedures, and thereby avoid problems with long-term outcomes. They negotiate conditions with key environmental actors, thereby reducing uncertainty. There is little reason to doubt that if an organization has resolved its major issue under equivocality, i.e., its goals and utilities, utility models can be effective, but at the cost of time and IP activity.

A composite model of risk IPT suggests that the conundrum in assessing risk is the basic problem of imperfect information, and there is no model which resolves that impossible problem. An alternative approach is to disaggregate risk in ways which focus on both the *inputs* to organizational goal attainment as well as the *outcomes*. A utilitarian approach to doing this is well-

established, in fact. Experience in technology-based industries, and the
military weapons-development process which will be discussed extensively
in much of this book, has led to the practice of differentiating between three
distinct categories of risk. As shown in Table 1.3, the three types of risk are
technical risk, *schedule* risk, and *cost* risk. I refer to this as a *composite
model* of risk.

Table 1.3   The composite model: three categories of risk

Category	Definition	Examples
Technical	• likelihood of a technical achievement or breakthrough	• ability to manufacture new component critical to avionics function • ability to instill Western management processes in former Soviet production facility
Schedule	• likelihood of accomplishing a task by a predicted time	• completing design phase for radically new avionics device within time limit for manufacturing tests • completing start-up and documentation requirements in Eastern Europe in feasible time
Cost	• likelihood of completing a task or set of tasks for a specified amount of money	• cost of radical new avionics design • cost of turnaround of Eastern European acquisition

From an IPT perspective, nearly any organization must be concerned with
these three categories of risk. In theoretical terms, these categories of risk
broaden attention from outputs alone to include inputs or resources. We can
characterize an end-point in a process in terms of having consumed a quantity
of resources, not solely as having attained some level of goal or outcome.

The framing of decisions is an important variable, as is well-supported in the decision literature (Bazerman, 1994; Taylor, 1984).[5] In practical terms, this composite model of risk helps us organize information without the presumption of information we do not have, such as probable states of nature or payoff values. Moreover, this approach allows us to evaluate the confidence we ascribe to each item of information, so that if our information is too far to the left on the scales in Figure 1.1, we do not treat all of it as having equal value or credibility. This is another area where communication theorists have more completely recognized the unequal weight assigned to information in contrast to many of the decision theories (Farace, Monge, and Russell, 1977). In addition, one of the "small-current" risks is that one may have information and not know it, whether this refers to potential future gains or losses.

Shifting theoretical attention to the composite of outputs of organizational processes and the inputs consumed by those processes offers the potential to study how decision makers relate risk to inputs. As Taylor (1984) notes, the problem of dealing with unmeasurable risk is very difficult to resolve; about the best we can do is improve on outcome-based methods by including more information and more variables. Unlike outcome-based models of risk, the composite model suggests that the decision maker think about risk in terms of commitment of resources without necessarily attaining the goals desired. In short, we can ask whether this project is worth its front-end cost; whether we can do this in the amount of time we have available; and so on. Closure is achieved through processing information about known costs rather than unknown futures.

This approach to assessing risk is conceptually similar to the Savage (1954) "regret criterion" (see Appendix 1.1), which argues that the way to choose between alternatives when faced with uncertainty is to think about them in terms of the regret you would experience if you had chosen an alternative, and the future turned out to be one where a different alternative would have been better, with hindsight. (A similar position is taken by Janis and Mann (1977), who argue that "anticipatory regret" is one of the preconditions for "vigilant" information processing.) The Savage method is also an outcome-based risk model, but one which focuses on anticipated knowledge of outcomes given full knowledge of the state of nature. It thus presumes "past perfect" information, but with the same limitations as other outcome-based models.

Using the three input risk categories allows the parsing of a more general level of risk. While these categories are distinct, they are not independent—schedule slips have cost implications, cost overruns typically threaten technical goal attainment, and technical risks increase the probability of overconsumption of the other two resources. Therefore, it is possible to consider implications of the interactions between risk categories, and to factor these interactions into our decision.

The composite approach to risk assessment is valuable in practical terms. We might find it improbable that a dry-goods retailer faces anything that could be characterized as "technical" risk, but the experiences of retailers attempting to open new stores in the former centrally-planned economies of Eastern Europe often suggest otherwise. The concept of "wholesaler" is still unclear to many in the region; indeed, the resale of goods at higher prices without modifying them was literally criminal "speculation" in the former Soviet Union, an offense for which one could be jailed. It is common experience that everything one wants to do in these economies takes much longer than projected, creating both schedule and cost risks. Retailers had much educating to do to get started in Eastern Europe, and some are still struggling with these problems. Thus, for any new venture, I argue that assessment of the three types of risk is a highly pragmatic step.

The robustness of these risk categories as a basis for risk assessment derives from the universality of them. Regardless of the clarity of any organization's goals, the undertaking of a new project or the recommitment of resources to an existing one raises these three types of risk. As organizations resolve equivocalities, these risks can be evaluated in terms of their utility for goal attainment, and weighted differentially if need be.

Project management methods, involving detailed schedules, task lists, resource allocations, and progress tracking, have become widely used in many organizations in recent years (Pinto and Kharbanda, 1995).[6] There are many reasons for this, including the tendency to do much more "custom" work for specialized customers, the very short response and delivery times now expected by customers (increasingly used as a competitive weapon by vendors), and the need to keep accurate records for electronic data interchange, quality tracking, and the like. The three risk categories integrate very effectively into the basic project variables which are the critical information for project management: cost, time, and individual task requirements. Project management is therefore conceptually related to composite risk assessment in its focus on the inputs for project goal attainment.

Finally, risk is associated with control processes, as I have noted several times. Control is fundamentally an IP activity, determining how an organization is monitored and measured, and what control actions are taken. While "small-current" problems, the processes used for control can dramatically affect the organization's balance between many opposing forces critical to its success. Control risks arise in part because organizations are *dynamic*—they do things over time, and are constantly in motion. Some of their activities are recurring and repetitive, while others are single events with consequences for the organization extending over varying lengths of time. The differentiation of an organization into dynamic components introduces a problem of integration and the nature of the linkages between the parts. Approaches taken to cope with risk require learning and feedback as part of OIP, since there are often considerable time lags between processing and outcomes. This raises consideration of the third element of IPT, which is the cybernetic and dynamic properties of organizations, and the implications of these properties for relationships between information and IP.

The Dynamics of Organizations

The third component of IPT is well-grounded in systems theory[7] and cybernetics theory—organizational dynamics. This expression means that things happen over time, and thus much of the future is a direct extension of past decisions and actions. In fact, it is usually best to think about the future in terms of what we create, rather than regarding the future as simply a state waiting to be discovered. How we perceive the future for an organization is partly a function of the relationships between properties of the organization, many of which are subtle and indistinct owing to their attenuation over time. In short, there is considerable lag between events and outcomes in organizations (Evan, 1966), so that even causally linked variables may appear to be unrelated.

This perspective is consistent with the definition of a "system" proposed by Schoderbek, Kefalas, and Schoderbek (1975:30):

a system is a set of *objects* together with *relationships* between the objects and their *attributes* connected or related to each other and to their *environment* in such a manner as to form an *entity* or *whole*.

Attributes are the properties by which system objects are known; i.e., attributes are information. While the number of attributes of any object are almost limitless, *defining* attributes are the primary ones of concern to IPT (Schoderbek *et al.*, 1975:38). Defining attributes can be properties of the objects themselves, or properties of the instrumentality of the objects in the functioning of the organization.

Basic Properties of Dynamic Systems

The dynamic properties and defining attributes of organizations can be expressed almost entirely in terms of information, primarily through *feedback* and *feedforward* processes. Both large current and small current issues are encompassed in organizational dynamics. *Feedback* is the consumption of some organizational outputs as inputs—a small quantity of production is sacrificed for measurement of quality, for example. *Feedforward* is also the consumption of some organizational outputs as inputs, but these are used to project the organization into a future state, and are consumed only gradually over a much longer period of time. Feedforward in the form of strategic planning, for example, is an important process in the resolution of equivocality; feedback is equally important for the reduction of uncertainty and to make adjustments for exceptions. Both processes are necessary to attain goals over time.

Figure 1.6 illustrates the typical input-process-output sequence commonly used to portray the generic functioning of a system. Inputs are acquired from the environment, and outputs returned to it. One set of such activities and relationships which results in a unit of output can be regarded as a *work cycle*. Such a cycle is the most elementary form of a system interacting with its environment. So long as the environment serves as a source of energy and a sink for outputs, the cycle can continue. Feedback, in this elementary system, is only achieved indirectly through the source-and-sink relationship with the environment.

Figure 1.7 shows the basic cycle of Figure 1.6, but with the addition of feedback and feedforward information loops within the organization. The addition of internal feedback enables the system to test its outputs for quality, in the sense of the suitability of the outputs relative to organizational goals. Some cost is incurred, but with the benefit of improved payoffs for the energies expended. The addition of feedforward enables the system to project future states as a control standard, so that better direction of efforts can yield more desirable future outcomes, avoid undesirable outcomes, and the like. Feedforward interacts with feedback—established goals enable more precise feedback to be collected and provide a baseline against which to evaluate the information acquired.

In many ways, it is appropriate to think of feedback as a small-current control requirement, and therefore a "cost" in the accounting sense, i.e., that once feedback is spent, it is consumed. In contrast, feedforward is concerned with organizational planning and direction, and is therefore better conceived of as an "investment," where present costs are incurred with the expectation

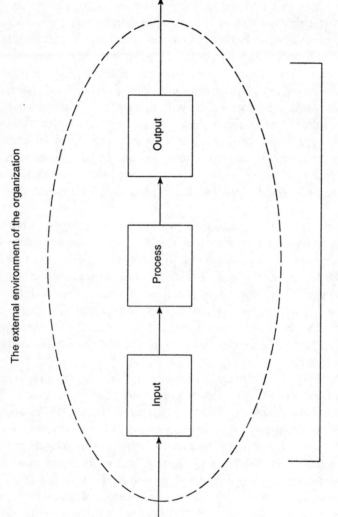

Figure 1.6 The basic system model

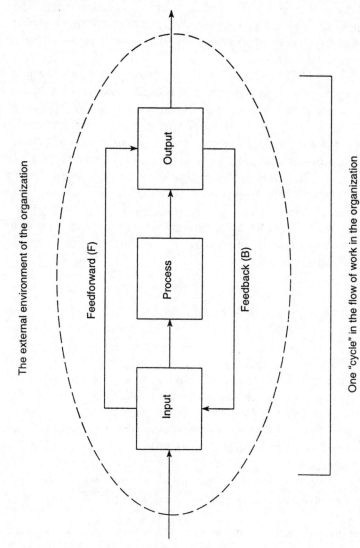

Figure 1.7   The basic system model with dynamic information flows

of future paybacks. Organizations acquire feedback information from their ongoing flows of activities and use that information for control. Larger-scale acquisition and transformation are used for feedforward, and most of the plans and projections from that process are widely distributed, which enables other members to process information locally in ways that contribute toward organizational goal attainment.

Figure 1.8 shows the relationship of feedback and feedforward to multiple work cycles over time. Feedback is returned to the system after a cycle has been completed; thus, feedback information is always historical. Also, feedback has a very short-term relationship to the system work cycle, in that it is collected and consumed very quickly. Feedforward, on the other hand, has longer-term value, although as Galbraith (1977) noted, plans decay over time and lose their utility, and therefore must be refreshed. This is reflected in the form of the utility curves above and below the timeline. The utility of a new or refreshed plan for goal attainment is considerable, and the relevance of that plan persists for a longer term, but it decays over time until refreshed. In contrast, the utility of feedback is less than that for a plan, and its value has a shorter lifespan.

Organizational Performance, Information Processing, and Organization Slack

Organization slack and information processing At the beginning of this chapter I pointed out that the primary focus of IPT is organizational performance. Decision makers must process information for virtually every organizational activity, ranging from setting broad goals and objectives, to the daily routine at the office, to the most mundane acts of data collection. Much of decision theory has incorporated IP, whether implicitly or explicitly, and has been concerned with improvement of the decision-making process, usually in the interest of corresponding improvements in organizational performance. *Performance*, again, is defined as the degree of attainment of organizational goals.

Goal attainment is not a foregone conclusion in a world of imperfect information, and this is one of the reasons that theorists discuss performance in terms of the *degree* of goal attainment. The linkage between what an organization plans and projects on the one hand, and what actually happens on the other, is nondeterministic and nonlinear (Mintzberg and McHugh, 1985). Accordingly any discussion of performance must take factors that create performance variation and necessitate IP into account. At the same

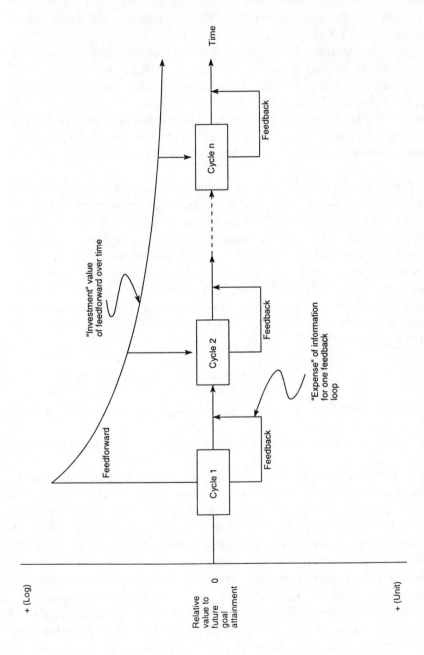

Figure 1.8   Feedback and feedforward over repeated work cycles

time, this variability makes it more difficult to rigorously link performance to IP. Within the past decade, the ability to demonstrate the payoff of investments in information technology has been a major challenge, for example. Strassmann (1985) argued that much of the early investment in information technology simply failed by automating obsolete methods of doing work. Since then, information technology has been argued by some to be a key to the rapidly increasing productivity of the U.S. economy (Farrell *et al.*, 1995; *The Economist*, September 16, 1995). But the time lags and lack of one-for-one correspondence between variables under observation in a complex system always make such relationships difficult to identify (Sichel, 1997).

The hierarchical model of information discussed earlier suggests a way to conceptualize this relationship within an organization. The desired or planned level of performance for the organization might be thought of as the outcome that would be attained under conditions of perfect information. Those exact outcomes cannot be obtained because we have only imperfect information. Imperfect information causes deviations from the outcomes that would obtain to perfect information, in the form of both costs and benefits, or as gains and losses. Considering both positive and negative outcomes, the performance of an organization in IPT may also be described in terms of the following relationship:

		outcomes as planned or		net payoff of [outcomes
Performance (G)	=	projected (assuming perfect information)	+	resulting from] imperfect information[8]

As shown in Table 1.4, the net payoff of imperfect information is the net value of all costs, benefits, gains, and losses resulting from both proactive and reactive organizational responses to imperfect information. Costs or losses may be incurred whether the organization attempts to deal with imperfect information either through proaction or feedforward, such as planning, market research, and forecasting; or they may be incurred through reaction or feedback, using adjustments and other means to correct or compensate for the costs of delay. In either case, the cost of coordinating organizational activities in the face of this imperfection must be borne, and there are always unforeseen costs and losses. Similarly, benefits obtain to both feedforward and feedback approaches to dealing with imperfect information, either through gains from anticipation and exploitation of new opportunities and competitive advantages, or through the avoidance of costs for unnecessary information and IP activities. An organization of any size usually does many of these things, and obtains many individual payoffs. The sum of all of these "payoffs" may be thought of as organization "slack." *Organization slack is therefore the net payoff of imperfect information.*

Table 1.4   Categories of slack: positive and negative outcomes as a function of imperfect information

Response mode	Payoff value	
	Cost or loss (–)	Benefit or gain (+)
Proaction/ feedforward	1. Planning and projection of future outcomes; coordination costs	2. Avoidance (errors), anticipation and exploitation (payoffs)
Reaction/ feedback	4. Opportunity costs of foregone outcomes and payoffs; coordination costs	3. Passive opportunism (a.k.a. IIABDFI— If It Ain't Broke, Don't Fix It)

Conceptualizing slack as the "net payoff of imperfect information" is conceptually clearer than earlier views of slack which treated it as "excess resources." Cyert and March (1953, 1963) used the concept of excess resources to describe the "cost of doing business" among organizational coalitions, in the form of "side payments" to induce cooperation among decision makers. As Galbraith (1977) used the concept, the scope of excess resources was broadened to include the costs organizations absorbed to achieve an objective; they were the costs of accelerating work on projects, of increasing IP capacity with information technology, and the like. These concepts imply the motivation for such use of resources in the first place—the promise of rewards for a front-end investment. However, these concepts fail to recognize that over time excess resources are a consequence of performance.

Specification of measurable excess resources also presents theoretical and practical difficulties. For example, is research and development a "slack resource" or not; if so, is all of it slack or is some a normal cost of remaining competitive? While simple to envision and describe, these tenuous linkages between "excess resource" slack and outcomes present great challenges to the researcher and to the practicing manager, and all beg the question of where the resources come from.

Galbraith's (1977) book stimulated a considerable amount of research into organization slack. However, as Marino and Lange (1983) noted, within a few years measurements of slack had diverged widely, and the concept was becoming muddled. This is not surprising in many respects, since from the excess-resource perspective one is considering resources that are consumed over long periods of time, often with no clear relationship to subsequent outcomes.

Resources can be consumed in the present for a future return, or they may be considered a feedback expense or a feedforward investment. In most cases, the reasons for such outlays are to deal with operational difficulties resulting from imperfect information. These costs may be to acquire information for decision-making, or may be the costs of tightly coordinating activities within and between organizations. An excellent example of the latter in recent years is the growth of Just-In-Time (JIT) vendor-customer relationships, where considerable initial cost is borne by both parties to tightly coordinate their production flows across organizational boundaries. The net payoff of the costs and benefits resulting from the expanded IP activity and changed relationships in JIT, however, is so great that for many firms any other approach to doing business is inconceivable.

Organization slack and organizational performance One of Galbraith's (1977) major theoretical contributions was that he was the first to explicitly link slack to performance. His argument is that slack can be created through *lowered* performance, i.e., that if an organization structure lacks adequate IP capacity to cope with its total information load, then an adjustive reaction is to reduce the level of output relative to what it might have been with adequate capacity. The theoretically and empirically difficult part of this concept is the question of "what might have been," either in terms of opportunity costs or foregone benefits. The other interesting possibility his concept implies is the obverse—if IP capacity is increased in a system, then at a later time there should be a measurable *increase* in performance, which has clearly been the argument of the information technology industry over the years. These effects might be moderated by the tightness of the coupling between components of the system, and the ability of the system to create buffers which might mask such effects, both of which will be considered presently.

But imperfect information often pays off in terms of many benefits. For those companies able to find a competitive advantage in their technology or market niche, returns far above those obtained by competitors may be earned. For those who adopt a wait-and-see approach to dealing with unknowns, problems often go away and the unnecessary costs of coordination and attempted mastery of new technologies and new markets are avoided—"if it ain't broke, don't fix it." Of course, many firms using either approach guess wrong, and fail—neither proacting or reacting are free of risk.

While risk is associated with organization slack, it is not the same. Slack is the net payoff of all outcomes derived from working under imperfect information; risk is the expectation (or perception) that a negative outcome might occur. Slack subsumes all payoffs, positive and negative, where risk is concerned primarily with costs or negative outcomes. In terms of the vector properties of information discussed in Figure 1.1, if a body of information was characterized as being at the extreme right of these scales, it would be assumed to be effectively "perfect," and no risk would be perceived from that information itself. On the other hand, information at the extreme left of the scales is "bad," and inherently risky and unreliable.

Organization performance, in short, is theoretically dependent on the ability of the organization to respond to market and environmental information imperfections, and to do this in ways that frequently cannot be predicted. This requirement creates risks, whether viewed from a proactive or reactive perspective—too much money can be "thrown at problems" to be acceptable, but at the same time the organization can suffer from excess constraints and the "want of a nail."

Conceptualizing slack as the net payoff of imperfect information helps to resolve problems with earlier concepts of it. Slack is derived from operations, and if these are successful, the positive net balance provides resources for future investment. The cycle then repeats. Resources consumed for anything from side payments to more IT are simply sunk costs—once gone, they may or may not result in future benefits, and if done poorly, or the fates are unkind, they may simply be waste. Through this "reinvestment" of prior payoffs, the organization chooses to invest in various kinds of buffering against anticipated problems, whether from internal or external sources.

Information Processing, Organization Design, and the Role of Slack

Galbraith's information processing model of organization design   As noted, Galbraith's (1977) book is a major contribution to the information processing theory of organization and particularly the role of IP in organization design. He argues that the need to process information, particularly that required to cope with task uncertainty, leads to a logical evolution of a basic "mechanistic" structure, the organizational pyramid with which we are all familiar. In his model, the development of the basic pyramidal structure progresses through five levels:

1. Specialize by subdividing jobs (differentiate). To use specialization alone, three conditions must be met: (1) the organization must be small; (2) interdependence must be low; and (3) low performance must be acceptable.
2. Introduce hierarchy. Specialists in processing information will be selected (or in natural groups, may gravitate) toward decision-making positions beneficial to attaining the group's goals.
3. Introduce rules, programs, and procedures. These are effectively "pre-made" decisions which can be widely applied.
4. Rely on planning or expertise ("professionalism"). In cases where judgment is needed, reliance on special expertise enables the organization to cope with task uncertainties (as Galbraith defined them).
5. Adjust the hierarchy. Additional levels of supervision can be added, different bases for aggregating tasks can be selected, and combinations of these along with the preceding steps can be used to modify the structure.

The progression through these stages is necessitated by information *overload*—as the IP capacity of any stage is exceeded, the next level must be used. Managers can mix, adjust, and tinker with the mechanistic structure, but the IP capacity of a basic hierarchy is limited. More elaborate structures can be designed, but at the tradeoff of higher cost. Galbraith describes two basic options for more elaborate organization structures, to cope with the limits to an overloaded hierarchy:

1. Reduce the need for information processing. This can be achieved by (1) managing the external environment, (2) creating slack resources, or (3) creating self-contained task units. Given my

definition of slack, I would reconceptualize his term of "creation of slack resources" as "buffering against potential exceptions."

2. Increase the capacity to process information. The two primary options here are to (1) invest in "vertical information systems," or (2) create lateral relations.

This model has considerable power to explain the evolution of organization structures, and in Galbraith's view organization slack plays an important role in the ability of the organization to achieve its goals under conditions of high IP demands. However, there are several limitations to this model. It does not define either "information" or "information processing." Furthermore, all determinants of IP requirements are treated homogeneously as uncertainty, when there is reason to differentiate between the need for types of information issues to be resolved, and for different IP functions to be applied to tasks. Finally, as discussed, the model treats slack in theoretically inconsistent ways. Still, Galbraith's concept provided an enormously useful tool to understand organizations. At the time the VAST studies in this book began, I had just completed reading Galbraith's book, and I found it helpful both to organize and extend my own thinking about "knowledge technology,"[9] and to serve as an analytical and explanatory tool to many people I worked with.

Organization slack and organization dynamics Feedback and feedforward are not free. In IPT terms, feedback and feedforward are costs of imperfect information; i.e., neither would be necessary under conditions of perfect information. Therefore, both are important components of organization slack. The net payoff of imperfect information is strongly affected by feedbacks that organizations acquire to prevent and correct error. At the cost of some output, larger losses are avoided. Similarly, feedforward enables the organization to avoid unproductive and uncoordinated activities, which improves performance on organizational goals and reduces losses through waste and lack of coordination. The dilemma for the organization designer is that the only component of these relationships that can be measured unambiguously are the initial costs. The benefits are always estimates, and often highly speculative estimates at that. This is one of the reasons why organization slack is often perceived largely in terms of cost and inefficiency, and seldom in terms of benefit; lowered performance remains completely hidden. In Chapter 6, we will attempt to unmask some of these hidden losses.

Monge (1993) points out that most of what we do in organization design (or reorganization) is a process of error reduction. We attempt to reduce the number of "misfits" between organizational variables and the outcomes those variables produce. This is an imprecise process at best, because the number of variables involved is so large. What is more, we really know very little about how organization design is related to outcomes—as Monge (1993: 325) points out, the research literature is limited by three major shortcomings: (1) most research is cross-sectional, static, and correlational; (2) most research is based on existing organizational forms, so that we know very little about the introduction of new forms; and (3) most research only examines pairs of variables, so we know very little about the interactions between the larger sets of relationships that make up complex systems and subsystems.

Monge proposes that dynamic relations between design variables and outcome misfits can be generally described in terms of six components or properties: (1) magnitude; (2) trend; (3) continuity; (4) rate of change; (5) cyclicity; and (6) duration. Duration should be examined particularly for discontinuous events. All of these properties of organizational variables can be examined over time, and through graphic displays and understanding of changes in them, Monge argues that we can do a great deal to improve our ability to reduce performance misfits through better design. The potential to use the dimensions he proposes is enormous because of their generality, and in my view could make important contributions to the theory of organization and to the pragmatics of organization design.

What is most evident in Monge's approach is the significance of feedback and feedforward in the process of error reduction. Monge's proposals, in some ways, can be considered as a generalized and institutionalized method of organization design based on practices which are fundamentally beneficial to any organization: careful planning and goal definition, systematic and continuous feedback for control and error correction, and analysis of information to learn about internal processes. All of these contribute to a positive net payoff of imperfect information.

Coupling, buffering, and interdependence The events that make up an organization's workflow are not independent. One of the key aspects of the dynamic relationship between organizational components is that events in one unit have direct or indirect effects on other units at a later time. How much time may elapse before these consequences become visible is often not predictable, nor is the nature of the resulting outcome itself. Much of the process-related IP in organizations is done specifically to cope with exceptions which arise from these linkages, and to make adjustments to them. These relationships and interactions are usually described in terms of three variables: coupling, buffering, and interdependence.

All three of these variables describe aspects of the interaction between system components, but they do it in different ways, and from different perspectives. *Interdependence* refers to the extent of jointly-determined outcomes in the system, i.e., interactions between subsystems. The ability of a subsystem to perform its role without interaction with other subsystems indicates little or no interdependence. *Coupling* refers to the nature of the linkages between subsystems; these linkages can be tight or loose, depending on the organization. Weick (1979) has argued that many of the seemingly irrational activities of organizations are a result of them being loosely-coupled entities, not the clockwork mechanisms implied by much of the organizational literature. *Buffering* describes the creation of stockpiles to reduce the strength of interdependent relationships between subsystems. The classic example is the work-in-process inventory on the factory floor, where workers and processes that move at different speeds can draw from pools of materials which are maintained along the workflow to decrease the interdependence of each on others.

Interdependence is the common denominator in all of these variables, and in organizations, interdependence is inherently an issue of information. To the extent that interdependence exists, elements of an organization require information about the state of outcomes and the processes of other elements, both to coordinate work with those elements and to maintain internal control. If one conceptualizes the information necessary for this purpose as a knowledge base, then interdependence is a matter of the degree of overlap of knowledge bases. Coupling, in this context, is "tight" or "loose" depending on the degree of overlap and rate of information exchange. Buffering, finally, consists of physical or informational mechanisms to compensate for the degree of interdependence. Buffering is not the same as loose coupling—buffering reduces the time-sensitivity of interdependence, but at the cost of stockpiling physical goods or information. Buffering compensates for interdependence, but does not reduce it. Buffering, from this perspective, is clearly a component of organization slack, where a known cost is incurred to mitigate against unknown costs that might occur if exceptions disrupt the achievement of interdependent organizational outcomes. It is done in the belief that the net payoff is positive.

Following Thompson's (1967) propositions, buffering is usually considered in terms of physical stockpiles which are used to reduce the tightness of linkages to the environment, on either the input or output sides of the "technical core." With buffering, a high degree of interdependence can exist between an organization's technical core and external elements, without fluctuations in those external forces disrupting the technical core. Despite the key role of uncertainty in Thompson's models of organization processes, he overlooks the fact that buffering can be done with information. Forecasts and histories, if acquired, can be as effective in "buffering" the technical core as physical inventories, and in my view, even more so. Reeves and Turner (1972) studied the British men's ready-to-wear clothing industry, and found that a key role in the factories was for people known as "progress chasers" to determine the status of large orders and speed their completion when the customer needed them quickly. By maintaining a "stockpile" of information about work in progress and customer needs, these individuals were able to coordinate schedule changes with plant managers, and actually disrupted the flow of materials in the technical core to benefit the overall performance of the company. Obviously, for some key customers, these firms believed the payoff of filling their orders quickly exceeded the costs of the schedule changes and holding inventories of other work in progress. In these cases, the organization was believed to be best served by opening the technical core to environmental influences, rather than protecting it.

Such complexities can all be different manifestations of functional adaptations to different environments. All of these can be subsumed under the general IPT model. The IPT model therefore provides a unifying framework to encompass these dynamic processes in organizations, and to understand these processes through their IP effects. Whether we consume resources to proactively deal with imperfect information or reactively to capitalize on gains or absorb losses, IPT is able to theoretically and practically accommodate such interdependencies.

Process vs. Content: the Rules of Organizational Information Processing

Since the primary focus of this book is on information processing, little has been said about the *content* of the information involved in the process. In the introduction to this chapter I noted that one body of content plays a pivotal role in IPT. The discussion of the vector properties of information earlier in this chapter suggests part of that role. The separation of IP into large-current and small-current processes also suggests part of the role of content in IPT. I have argued that information is knowledge, and that knowledge accumulates into specific bodies and subject areas, each of which is associated with a primary technical concern or issue. One of these bodies of knowledge is a "small-current" regulatory body which I characterize as the *Information Processing Procedures and Rules* (IPPR) of the organization.

IPPR is often expressed in terms of the "culture" of the organization (Schein, 1985), or as "getting to know the ropes," and so on, particularly in the context of the informal system. Understanding OIP in any organization requires not only a model of processing itself, but understanding of how data and information are admitted to the process. This requires knowing what processors, in terms of individuals, groups, and offices which do the organization's work, are actually involved in that processing. The designation of sensors, for example, specifies the gatekeeping roles which will be played by different persons and interests in the IP framework of an organization. For example, one of the dilemmas of technology management is the problem of finding managers with adequate technical background to comprehend the technology, while knowing how to make necessary business decisions involving it. Engineers and technical specialists tend to distrust "management types," and managers see engineers as laboratory technicians who will tinker until all the money is gone.

Similar IPPR issues surround the IP functions. The definition of "relevant" data to acquire, or populations to sample, in the resolution of equivocal imperfections is a great challenge for many organizations. The scope of equivocal questions themselves is often subject to enormous differences, and these may be the subject of power struggles which shape the future direction of the entire organization. Throughout this process, specific individuals may feel confidence in their choices and decisions, but uncertainty and equivocality are never very far from the scene.

For example, a key element of the IP structure is the supervisory processor. In many organizations, the term "supervisory" may take on literal meaning, in that who gets to do which analysis, make which presentation of the results, or even who is allowed to initiate requests and contacts with others may be very tightly controlled. Having had much experience in project-managed organizations, I have frequently observed that one of the greatest obstacles to effective use of project management is a function of such rules. When someone is appointed to the position of project manager, it becomes necessary for that person to take initiatives, make decisions, and exercise project-related authority on matters that would otherwise reside at a rank in the organization above that of the project manager. The mutual discomfort this can create may be terminal, and I have seen more than one project crash and burn for no other reason. Similar examples can be given for the other framework elements.

IPPR therefore shapes much of the actual IP done in any organization. While IPPR may be a body of knowledge which can be generalized, in the sense that all organizations have such a body of knowledge, the content of each set of IPPR is highly specific to the organization. This has long been recognized by those who study organizational cultures (e.g., Schein, 1985), and they devote considerable effort to specifying the kinds of procedures and rules which are found in the cultures of organizations. These organization microcultures exist within a larger-scale body of IPPR, which is the macroculture of the broader society. And as anyone who has observed nominally similar organizations in different cultures soon learns, the macroculture runs deep—there are many details within the IPPR that were operational long before the organization in question was ever imagined by its founders. The difficulty in changing organizational microcultures reflects this, in part.

For the remainder of this book, IPPR will not be overtly considered. However, its existence will become quite evident as soon as we begin a detailed description of the VAST system. One of the rules in Navy IPPR is that any commonly-used set of words will be reduced to an acronym on about the third usage, and I must warn some readers that they will know more about the U.S. Naval Air Force IPPR than they ever wanted to know. While consideration of IPPR may seldom be overt, however, the effect of this body of knowledge will be very evident, and it is never taken for granted.

Summary: the Information Processing Theory of Organization

At the beginning of this chapter, I defined the general model of IPT as

$$G = f (I \times S \times C)$$

    where G = Goal attainment (organizational performance),
                  I = Information,
                  S = Information Processing Structure, including Information Technology,
    and C = Cybernetic System dynamics.

In closing this chapter, I want to add a refinement to my description of the model, which reflects what I have argued about the nature of information and IP. In the first specification of this model, I said that Information interacts with the Information Processing Structure to form *organizational information*. I want to extend that description to point out that the interaction between I, S, and C defines *organizational knowledge*. What the organization knows about the world and how it might cope with the opportunities and challenges it finds there are enveloped within this body of organizational knowledge.

Despite the prominence of information technology in most of the general discussion of "information processing," little has been said of IT in this chapter. This does not mean that the role or significance of IT has been ignored or diminished. On the contrary, the role of IT in IP will become apparent in some of the early spontaneous IP changes to the system, as described in Chapter 5, and IT occupies a central position in much of the research in Chapter 6. However, within the framework of IPT, IT is primarily a tool or mediator, and not fundamental to the theory itself. Whether an organization uses IT as a central tool in its IP structure or as a minor contributor to achieving its objectives, IPT is argued to be an inclusive description of its information processing.

Further, I propose that one of the major strengths of IPT is its ability to describe an organization as a truly integrated system. Therefore, *the integration of a system can be expressed in terms of the time required for all relevant processing of information on all organizational activities on a workflow, to an equivalent level of knowledge about those activities on the part of all workflow members.* In one word, if all members in an interdependent chain of activities have the same quantity and quality of knowledge about processes on the chain, they have achieved information *closure* on the system. I define the term "closure" more conservatively to mean *having sufficient knowledge to be able to accurately and completely describe the state of the system at any time.*

From this perspective, organization slack can also be considered as the value of the time needed to achieve closure (i.e., integration) of its workflow activities. By definition, lack of closure creates a state of imperfect information, even where the best closure we can hope for is past-perfect information.

Finally, it follows that the principal function of organization structure is to be a macro-level information processor. Obviously, structure is influenced by factors such as the physical location of critical resources and clientele and by the content of its IPPR. But if we allow for such environmental imperatives, the test of a "good" or "effective" structure design is its ability to process information in ways that serve the organization in attaining its goals. The criterion for organization design is thus whether a structure meets the organization's needs in terms of the ratio of cost to IP capacity, relative to the value the structure enables. An "expensive" or "complex" structure like a matrix design is not desirable or undesirable in any absolute terms;

what matters is whether it is "cost effective" in helping an organization do what it wants to do.

IPT is a descriptive theory of organization, in the manner of the early models of decision behavior proposed by Cyert and March (1963). The fundamental model of an organization in IPT is that shown in Figure 1.7, and all organizations can be represented by elaboration of the relationships shown in that figure, to whatever level of detail is appropriate to the purposes of a system designer, a manager, or an organization researcher. Much of the remainder of this book will be an illustration of this basic model as applied to several analyses. The next three chapters give technical background on VAST, the focal technology of most of this study, and examine prior research on that technology. These provide the background for interpretation of IPT analyses in the remainder of the book. This includes the consideration of non-physical system attributes in Chapter 5, a study of organization IP capacity, performance, and slack in Chapter 6, and implications of IPT in several other technological contexts in Chapter 7. IPT is expanded and a model specific to technology accession is developed in Chapter 8.

Notes

1. Given the pervasiveness of communication and language among human cultures, I am often amazed that communication in this tradition has not long since emerged as the "mother lode" of all social sciences. For reasons I do not understand, it has not.

2. This can be true even for deeply-held values, such as safety or the sanctity of life. I always remember the incident where I was riding my bicycle on a clear day on a local country road. In a situation where oncoming traffic had to pass, where visibility was completely unrestricted but where there was no shoulder, I was nearly hit by a van whose driver refused to be delayed 5 seconds for an oncoming car to give him room to get around me. I noted with irony that as he passed, the van bore an anti-abortion bumper sticker saying, "It's a child, not a choice."

3. I have had a great deal of help with these definitions in earlier projects with colleagues, and owe a debt of gratitude to Diane Ferry here at Delaware, and to John Ogilvie at the University of Hartford. We put a lot of hours together into wrestling with these definitions; if we lost the struggle, that is my fault. I also want to point out that Diane Ferry and another Delaware colleague, John Sawyer, suggest that "ambiguity" is a level between equivocality and uncertainty. I do not show that level in my model, because I regard ambiguity as a subset of

equivocality. Nevertheless, I think their idea is a very good one, and it helps to incorporate the concept of ambiguity, as Weick envisioned it, within this framework.

4. For example, most large U.S. corporations no longer employ economists to predict future economic conditions, having found their predictions to be too unreliable; instead, they have chosen to use professional market research and data-acquisition services for some purposes, and to use different financial instruments and investment strategies to hedge against losses (Passell, 1996).

5. Unfortunately, we cannot generalize a great deal of this research to practice or to the general population with much confidence, because as noted by Tversky and Kahneman (1971), most experiments in the psychological and educational journals fail to give adequate attention to statistical power. They pointed out the irony that such research practices are consistent with a belief in a "law of small numbers," a misinterpretation of statistical principles exactly like that found in many of the heuristics and biases of the research subjects, and completely inconsistent with the statistical training social-science researchers are given. The problems of the social-science research model, particularly the inappropriate use of statistical significance testing, severely limits the ability to draw strong conclusions from this literature or to interpret it (cf. Meehl, 1990); these issues are discussed in Appendix 1.2. The lack of adequate power in most of the social sciences is a problem studied earlier by Cohen (1962) and replicated and updated by Sedlmeier and Gigerenzer (1988). Unfortunately, the latter study found that the inadequacies of statistical power Cohen had found in the research literature in 1962, had become considerably worse by 1988. Cohen also forcefully points out that there are other issues that limit the generalizability of this body of research; while some of the issues he raises have improved slightly in the last decade, the more fundamental problems associated with lack of power and statistical significance testing in Appendix 1.2 persist.

6. Although the use of project management methods has not been without its problems. One of the interesting points in this article is the observation that knowing the tools of project management does not necessarily mean knowing project management.

7. Most of the basis for systems theory can be traced to the 1954 meeting of the American Association for the Advancement of Science, where a biologist (Ludwig von Bertalanffy), an economist (Kenneth Boulding), a biomathematician (Anatol Rapoport), and a physiologist (Ralph Gerard) formed the Society for General Systems Theory, later renamed the Society for General Systems Research (von Bertalanffy, 1968). The focus of much of systems theory in the early days was modeled after the "hard" sciences, which we can

conceptualize as "hard" systems, but in recent years the concept of "soft" systems has been developed by Checkland (1988) to incorporate variables such as motives, cultural influences, and the like. I use the term "systems theory" to encompass both of these approaches.

8. In this discussion, I am using the term "payoff" in the sense of the payoff matrix as discussed in Appendix 1.1.

9. John L. Kmetz (1978), A critique of the Aston studies and results with a new measure of technology. *Organization and Administrative Sciences*, 8 (4): 123-144.

References

Aguilar, Francis J. (1967), *Scanning the Business Environment.* New York: Macmillan.

Alluisi, Earl A. (1970), Information and uncertainty: The metrics of communications. In DeGreene, Kenyon B. (Editor), *Systems Psychology.* New York: McGraw-Hill.

Argyris, Chris, and Schon, Donald (1978), Organizational Learning: A Theory of Action Perspective. Reading, Mass.: Addison-Wesley.

Auster, Ethel, and Choo, Chun Wei (1994), How senior managers acquire and use information in environmental scanning. *Information Processing and Management,* 30 (5): 607-618.

Barnard, Chester I. (1938), *The Functions of the Executive.* Cambridge, Mass.: Harvard University Press.

Bazerman, Max H. (1994), *Judgment in Managerial Decision Making, third edition.* New York: Wiley.

Bellman, R. E., and Zadeh, Lofti A. (1970), Decision-making in a fuzzy environment. *Management Science,* 17: B141-145.

Bensaou, M., and Venkatraman, N. (1995), Configurations of interorganizational relationships: A comparison between U.S. and Japanese automakers. *Management Science,* 41 (9):1471-1492.

Cash, James I., Jr., Eccles, Robert G., Nohria, Nitin, and Nolan, Richard L. (1993), *Building the Information-Age Organization: Structure, Control, and Information Technologies.* Homewood, Ill.: Irwin.

Cavaleri, Steven, and Fearon, David (1996), *Managing in Organizations that Learn.* Cambridge, Mass.: Blackwell.

Checkland, Peter (1988), Soft systems methodology: An overview. *Journal of Applied Systems Analysis,* 15: 27-40.

Cohen, Jacob (1962), The statistical power of abnormal-social psychological research: a review. *Journal of Abnormal and Social Psychology,* 65 3: 145-153.

Cohen, Michael D., March, James G., and Olsen, Johan P. (1972), A garbage can model of organizational choice. *Administrative Science Quarterly,* 17 (1): 1-25.

Corner, Patricia D., Kinicki, Angelo J., and Keats, Barbara W. (1994), Integrating organizational and individual information processing perspectives on choice. *Organization Science,* 5 (3): 294-308.

Cyert, Richard, and March, James G. (1953), Organizational factors in the theory of oligopoly. *Quarterly Journal of Economics,* 67 (1): 44-64.

Cyert, Richard, and March, James G. (1963), *The Behavioral Theory of the Firm.* Englewood Cliffs, N.J: Prentice-Hall.

Cyert, Richard, and March, James G. (1993), *The Behavioral Theory of the Firm, second edition.* New York: Blackwell.

Daft, Richard L. and Lengel, Robert H. (1986), Organizational information requirements, media richness, and structural design. *Management Science,* 32 (5): 554-571.

Downs, Anthony (1966), *Inside Bureaucracy.* Boston: Little, Brown.

The Economist, September 16, 1995. Back on top? 336 (7932): Survey 1-18.

Edwards, Elwyn (1964), *Information Transmission.* London: Chapman & Hall.

Egelhoff, William G. (1982), Strategy and structure in multinational corporations: An information processing approach. *Administrative Science Quarterly,* 27 (4): 435-458.

Egelhoff, William G. (1988), *Organizing the multinational enterprise: An information processing perspective.* Cambridge, Mass: Ballanger.

Egelhoff, William G. (1991), Information processing theory and the multinational enterprise. *Journal of International Business Studies,* 22 (3): 341-368.

Evan, William M. (1966), Organization lag. *Human Organization,* 25 (2): 51-53.

Farace, Richard V., Monge Peter R., and Russell, Hamish M. (1977), *Communicating and Organizing.* Reading, Mass.: Addison-Wesley.

Farrell, Christopher, Mandel, Michael J., and Weber, Joseph (1995), Riding high. *Business Week,* October 9, 1995.

Feldman, Martha S., and March, James G. (1981), Information in organizations as signal and symbol. *Administrative Science Quarterly,* 26 (2): 171-186.

Ferraro, Gary (1996), *The Cultural Dimension of International Business, second edition.* Englewood Cliffs, NJ: Prentice-Hall.

Fischhoff, B. (1975), Hindsight ≠ foresight: The effect of outcome knowledge on judgment under uncertainty. *Journal of Experimental Psychology: Human Perception and Performance,* 1: 288-299.

Forrester, Jay W. (1970), *Principles of Systems.* Cambridge, Mass.: Wright-Allen.

Freeman, John, and Hannan, Michael T. (1983), Niche width and the dynamics of organizational populations. *American Journal of Sociology,* 88 (6): 1116-1145.

Galbraith, Jay (1977), *Organization Design.* Reading, Mass.: Addison-Wesley.

Galbraith, Jay (1993), *Competing with Flexible Lateral Organizations.* Reading, Mass.: Addison-Wesley.

Galbraith, Jay (1995), *Designing Organizations: An Executive Briefing on Strategy, Structure, and Process.* San Francisco: Jossey-Bass.

Hall, Roger I. (1976), A System Pathology of an Organization: The Rise and Fall of the Old Saturday Evening Post. *Administrative Science Quarterly,* 21 (2): 185-211.

Hammond, Kenneth R., Stewart, Thomas R., Brehmer, Berndt, and Steinmann, Derick O. (1975), Social judgment theory. In Kaplan, M.F., and Schwartz, S. (Editors), *Human Judgment and Decision Processes.* New York: Academic Press.

Hannan, Michael T., and Freeman, John (1977), The population ecology of organizations. *American Journal of Sociology,* 82 (5): 929-964.

Hartman, Sandra J., White, Michael, C., and Crino, Michael D. (1986), Environmental volatility, system adaptation, planning requirements, and information-processing strategies: An integrative model. *Decision Sciences,* 17 (4): 454-474.

Huber, George P. (1980), *Managerial Decision Making.* Glenview, Ill.: Scott-Foresman.

Huber, George P., and McDaniel, Reuben R. (1986), The decision-making paradigm of organizational design. *Management Science,* 32 (5): 572-589.

Ito, Jack K., and Peterson, Richard B. (1986), Effects of task difficulty and interunit interdependence on information processing systems. *Academy of Management Journal,* 29 (1): 139-149.

Janis, Irving L., and Mann, Leon (1977), *Decision Making: A Psychological Analysis of Conflict, Choice, and Commitment.* New York: Free Press.

Jarvenpaa, Sirkka L., and Ives, Blake (1993), Organizing for global competition: The fit of information technology. *Decision Sciences,* 24 (3): 547-572.

Kennedy, Peter W. (1994), Information processing and organization design. *Journal of Economic Behavior and Organization,* 25 (1994): 37-51.

Kepner, Charles H., and Tregoe, Benjamin B. (1965), *The Rational Manager.* New York: McGraw-Hill.

Kijima, Kyoichi (1993), Characterization of desirable information processing and decision making systems in organizations. *European Journal of Operational Research,* 66 (1): 72-88.

Kmetz, John L. (1978), A critique of the Aston studies and results with a new measure of technology. *Organization and Administrative Sciences,* 8 (4): 123-144.

Kmetz, John L. (1984), An information-processing study of a complex workflow in aircraft electronics repair. *Administrative Science Quarterly,* 29 (2): 255-280.

Knight, Kenneth E., and McDaniel, Reuben R., Jr. (1979), *Organizations: An Information Systems Perspective.* Belmont, Ca.: Wadsworth.

Kose, John, Ronen, Joshua, and Radner, Roy (1990), Information structures, optimal contracts and the theory of the firm. Journal of Accounting, Auditing, and Finance 5 (1): 61-103.

Lawler, Edward E. III, and Rhode, John G. (1976), *Information and Control in Organizations.* Pacific Palisades, Ca.: Goodyear.

Leifer, Richard, and Mills, Peter K. (1996), An information processing approach for deciding upon control strategies and reducing control loss in emerging organizations. *Journal of Management,* 22 (1): 113-137.

Lindblom, Charles E. (1959), The science of "muddling through." *Public Administration Review,* 19: 79-99.

Lord, Robert G., and Maher, Karen J. (1990), Alternative information-processing models and their implications for theory research, and practice. *Academy of Management Review,* 15 (1): 9-28.

Malone, Thomas W. (1987), Modeling coordination in organizations and markets. Management Science 33 (10): 1317-1332.

March, James G., and Simon, Herbert A. (1958), *Organization.* New York: Wiley.

Marino, Kenneth E., and Lange, David R. (1983), Measuring organizational slack: A note on the convergence and divergence of alternative operational definitions. *Journal of Management,* 9 (1): 81-92.

Meehl, Paul E. (1990), Why summaries of research on psychological theories are often uninterpretable. *Psychological Reports,* 66: 195-244. Monograph Supplement 1-V66.

Miller, Danny, and Friesen, Peter H. (1984), *Organizations: A Quantum View.* Englewood Cliffs, N.J.: Prentice-Hall.

Mintzberg, Henry, and McHugh, Alexandra (1985), Strategy formation in an adhocracy. *Administrative Science Quarterly,* 30 (2): 160-197.

Mintzberg, Henry, Raisinghani, D., and Thèoret, Andre (1976), The structure of "unstructured" decision processes. *Administrative Science Quarterly,* 21 (3): 246-275.

Monge, Peter R. (1990), Theoretical and analytical issues in longitudinal research. *Organization Science,* 1: 406-431.

Monge, Peter R. (1993), (Re)Designing dynamic organizations. In Huber, George P., and Glick, William H. (Editors), *Organizational Change and Redesign.* New York: Oxford University Press.

Newell, Anthony, and Simon, Herbert A. (1972), *Human Problem Solving.* Englewood Cliffs, N.J.: Prentice-Hall.

Nutt, Paul C. (1984), Types of organizational decision processes. *Administrative Science Quarterly,* 29: 414-450.

Passell, Peter (1996), The model was too rough: Why economic forecasting became a sideshow. *The New York Times Business Day,* Thursday, February 1: D1, D10.

Perrow, Charles (1967), A framework for the comparative analysis of organizations. *American Sociological Review* 32 (2): 194-208.

Pinto, Jeffrey K., and Kharbanda, Om P. (1995), Lessons for an accidental profession, *Business Horizons,* 38: 41-50.

Radner, Roy (1996), Bounded rationality, indeterminacy, and the theory of the firm. *Economic Journal: The Journal of the Royal Economic Society,* 106 (438): 1360-1373.

Refinetti, Roberto (1989), Information processing as a central issue in philosophy of science. *Information Processing and Management,* 25 (5): 583-584.

Reeves, Tom Kynaston, and Turner, Barry A. (1972), A theory of organization and behavior in batch production factories. *Administrative Science Quarterly,* 17 (1): 81-97.

Salancik, Gerald R., and Pfeffer, Jeffrey (1978), A social information processing approach to job attitudes and job design. *Administrative Science Quarterly,* 23 (2): 224-253.

Savage, Leonard J. (1954), *The Foundations of Statistics.* New York: Wiley.

Sayre, Kenneth (1976), *Cybernetics and the Philosophy of Mind.* Atlantic Highlands, N.J.: Humanities Press.

Schein, Edgar H. (1985), *Organizational Culture and Leadership.* San Francisco: Jossey-Bass.

Schoderbek, Peter P., Kefalas, Asterios G., and Schoderbek, Charles G. (1975), *Management Systems: Conceptual Considerations.* Dallas, Texas: Business Publications, Inc.

Schrader, Stephan, Riggs, William M., and Smith, Robert P. (1993), Choice over uncertainty and ambiguity in technical problem solving. *Journal of Engineering and Technology Management,* 10(1,2): 73-99.

Sedlmeier, P., and Gigerenzer, G. (1989), Do studies of statistical power have an effect on the power of studies? *Psychological Bulletin,* 105 (2): 309-316.

Senge, Peter M. (1990), *The Fifth Discipline: The Art and Practice of the Learning Organization.* New York: Currency Doubleday.

Shannon, Claude E. (1948), A mathematical theory of communication. *Bell System Technology Journal,* 27: 379-423 and 623-656.

Shannon, Claude E., and Weaver, Warren (1949), *A Mathematical Theory of Communication.* Urbana, Ill.: University of Illinois Press.

Sichel, Daniel E. (1997), *The Computer Revolution.* Washington, D.C: Brookings Institution Press.

Simon, Herbert A. (1957), *Models of* Man. New York: Wiley.

Simon, Herbert A. (1973), Applying information technology to organization design. *Public Administration Review,* 35: 268-278.

Simon, Herbert A. (1976), *Administrative Behavior, third edition.* New York: Free Press.

Simms, B. W., and Petersen, E. R. (1991), An information processing model of a police organization. *Management Science,* 37 (2): 216-232.

Strassmann, Paul A. (1985), *Information Payoff: The Transformation of Work in the Electronic Age.* New York: Free Press.

Taylor, Ronald N. (1984), *Behavioral Decision Making.* Glenview, Ill: Scott, Foresman.

Thomas, James B., and McDaniel, Reuben B., Jr. (1990), Interpreting strategic issues: Effects of strategy and the information-processing structure of top management teams. *Academy of Management Journal*, 33 (2): 266-306.

Thompson, James D. (1967), *Organizations in Action*. Englewood Cliffs, N.J.: Prentice-Hall.

Tushman, Michael L., and Nadler, David A. (1978), Information processing as an integrating concept in organization design. *Academy of Management Review*, 3 (3): 613-624.

Tversky, Amos, and Kahneman, Daniel (1971), The belief in the "law of small numbers." *Psychological Bulletin*, 76: 105-110.

Van de Ven, Andrew H., Delbecq, Andre L., and Koenig, Richard (1976), Determinants of coordination modes within organizations. *American Sociological Review* 41 (2): 332-338.

Von Bertalanffy, Ludwig (1968), *General Systems Theory*. New York: George Brazilier.

Wang, Pien, and Chan, Peng S. (1995), Top management perception of strategic information processing in a turbulent environment. *Leadership and Organization Development Journal*, 16 (7):33-44.

Weick, Karl E. (1979), *The Social Psychology of Organizing*. Reading, Mass.: Addison-Wesley.

Wiener, Norbert (1948), *Cybernetics or Control and Communication in the Animal and the Machine*. New York: Wiley.

Wildavsky, Aaron (1983), Information as an organizational problem. *Journal of Management Studies*, 20(1): 29-40.

Wood, G. (1978), The knew-it-all-along effect. *Journal of Experimental Psychology: Human Perception and Performance*, 4: 345-353.

Appendix 1.1

A Brief Review of the Payoff Matrix

For those who have not recently reviewed the concept of a payoff matrix, or perhaps have never been exposed to one at all, this appendix provides a short summary of the idea and its application in decision theory.

A *payoff matrix* shows the unique outcomes jointly determined by each alternative a decision maker might choose, and each state of nature which may occur in the future, after the alternative is chosen. If a decision maker is considering three alternatives, and believes that one of two states of nature (or future states of the environment) might occur, there will be 6 (3 x 2) possible "payoffs" to consider in this decision problem. Only one of these will actually occur, of course, and the problem is to evaluate each of the *alternatives* fully in light of existing information, so that an acceptable choice can be made. The typical payoff matrix summarizing this information in general form is shown by Figure A1.1.1.

	State of nature	
	State 1	**State 2**
Alternatives	P (state 1)	P (state 2)
Alternative 1	payoff 11	payoff 12
Alternative 2	payoff 21	payoff 22
Alternative 3	payoff 31	payoff 32

Figure A1.1.1 A general payoff matrix

The first column of the matrix lists the alternatives the decision maker is considering. The remaining columns summarize the decision-maker's information about (1) the possible future states of nature which might apply, (2) the probability of each of those states of nature, *P(state n),* if any information is known, and (3) the most important information of all, the expected payoffs which occur as a joint product of having selected an alternative and then having one of the states of nature occur. The number notation of the payoffs refers to the row and column in which the payoff is located, respectively: payoff 11 is in row 1 and column 1 of the payoff area of the matrix; payoff 22 is in row 2 and column 2, and so on. Payoffs represent both positive and negative values—receiving a "payoff" in the general terms of a payoff matrix might represent losing your shirt.

It is important to understand the relationship between the alternatives and the states of nature, as they jointly determine the payoffs. The decision maker is considering one of the alternatives at the present time; however, at the present time, there is no way to tell which of the possible states of nature will actually occur. It is this unknown that is the source of the risk in the decision. After having selected one of the alternatives, the state of nature that will actually occur in the future will become known, and therefore the actual payoff which the decision maker will receive will become known. That payoff will be the one at the intersection of the alternative chosen and the column representing the state of nature which occurs. For example, if the decision maker chose Alternative 1, and the future state of nature was State 2, the payoff of the decision would be the value represented by payoff 12.

Here is an example of a payoff matrix with some actual data. A business owner is considering diversifying into a new line of business, different from the present one now owned. Three possibilities are under consideration: a travel-agency chain (since a "grayer" population will have more mature families with disposable income and more time to travel); a property modernization and upgrading firm (houses and new construction for small businesses are expensive, and economic growth will create opportunities to refurbish existing structures profitably); and a prepared-foods firm (since people always have to eat, and many families do not have the time to prepare meals). The two relevant states of nature are concerned with future economic growth rates, since these affect inflation, interest rates, and consumer optimism. Our decision maker believes that the most desirable state, sustained growth, has a probability of .70 (or 7 chances out of 10, or 7-to-3 odds); the other state of uneven, variable growth, has a probability of .30. The matrix relating this information, and the payoffs the decision maker must evaluate, is shown in Figure A1.1.2.

Alternatives	State of nature	
	Uneven growth	**Sustained growth**
	.30	*.70*
Travel-agency chain	– $10,000,000	+ $50,000,000
Property modernization and upgrading firm	+ $90,000,000	– $15,000,000
Prepared-foods firm	+ $30,000,000	+ $25,000,000

Figure A1.1.2   An investment-decision payoff matrix

This matrix tells the decision maker quite a lot. First, we should not overlook an obvious point—much thought and work has to go into assembling the information to create the matrix, and in practical terms that is often the greatest benefit of doing it. Important questions that force confrontation of equivocalities must be resolved to actually construct one of these: What objectives are you trying to attain? What states of nature do you believe will apply? How likely are these to occur? Why did you select the alternatives you did, and is there significant chance that others might be better for your purposes? How did you arrive at the estimated payoffs? How much confidence do you have in your knowledge? And so on. These questions alone are often the true "payoff" of the exercise, if it is done well.

Evaluating the matrix to select an alternative gets into procedures that are beyond the scope of this appendix. The primary means of evaluating a matrix such as this one is to use *expected values* for each alternative, which are the sum of the sum of the probability for each state multiplied by the payoff for the alternative under that state, for all payoffs in that row. For example, the EV for the travel-agency alternative is .3(-$10MM) + .7(+$50MM), or $32 MM. Thus, the expected values of this problems are $32MM for the travel chain, $ 22.5MM for the modernization firm, and $ 26.5MM for the food business. By this reasoning, the optimum decision is the travel-agency chain.

Risk, Uncertainty, and Regret

Of greater importance are two conceptual issues. A matrix such as the one portrayed here is technically referred to as a decision under *risk,* as most decision theorists define it. *Risk* means that we have reasonable estimates of the probabilities of the states of nature, and we are therefore engaged in somewhat of a "gambling" problem. Most real-world decisions have unclear or low-confidence estimates of these probabilities. In our example above, how can we be even reasonably sure that the probability of sustained growth is .70? Why not a 50-50 chance, or a .10 probability if the decision-maker feels pessimistic. These conditions, where we cannot estimate the probabilities of the states of nature, are termed decisions under *uncertainty* by formal decision theorists. Uncertainty is a more difficult problem to resolve than risk, primarily because it permits less direct application of mathematical methods.

There is one point which I do want to take from the decision-theory literature, which is Savage's (1954) idea of *regret.* In my discussion of risk in Chapter 1, I argue that risk is fundamentally an information-processing problem which is relative to the perspective of the decision maker. I also argue that both inputs and outcomes should be evaluated in the sense that sometimes known costs are a good investment toward reduction of later regret. In that discussion, I use the term *regret* in the same way as used by Savage to evaluate a decision when probabilities of states of nature are unknown. In his logic, Savage argues that one cannot estimate expected values or use other substitutes to calculate expected values without firm knowledge of the likelihood of the states of nature. Therefore, the real issue facing the decision maker is the regret he will experience after the state of nature becomes known in the future.

Consider the case of our investment decision maker above. Suppose he concludes that the future will be in the travel-agency business, as the expected value calculation suggests. Suppose he buys the firm, and unfortunately, while the economy grows it goes through several business cycles, is shocked by uncertainties in international events, and grows unevenly. Instead of receiving the payoff of $50MM, the ultimate outcome is a loss of $10MM on the investment.

The major point to realize from this scenario is that after the alternative is chosen, it is the actual state of nature which occurs that determines the payoff. Following this line of thought, Savage argued that the decision maker should evaluate the payoff matrix by looking at the amount of regret he would experience if one knew the state of nature for sure. *Regret* is defined as the difference between the best payoff for that state of nature (i.e., the column) and each payoff for other alternatives in that column. By definition, regret for the best payoff under each state of nature is zero. A *regret matrix* for this decision problem is shown in Figure A1.1.3 below.

	State of nature	
	Uneven growth	**Sustained growth**
Alternatives	*.30*	*.70*
Travel-agency chain	100,000,000	0
Property modernization and upgrading firm	0	65,000,000
Prepared-foods firm	60,000,000	25,000,000

Figure A1.1.3   A regret matrix for the investment decision

For the uneven growth state of nature, the regret for the modernization company is 0, since the outcome of $90MM is the best that could be obtained. For the travel company, however, regret is 100MM, which is the 90MM payoff you could have obtained from the modernization company, plus the 10MM you lose by selecting the travel company. Finally, for the prepared-foods firm, regret is 60MM, since you only made 30MM and might have earned 90MM.

With new information about the regret one would experience if we knew what the future state of nature would be, Savage advised that regret should be the basis for our decision. His best-known rule is called *minimax regret*, wherein he suggests that you should select the alternative associated with the *minimum of the maximum regrets*. In this case, that would change the investment decision to the modernization firm, since the minimax regret choice is 65MM for that company, under conditions of sustained growth.

Without necessarily following Savage's rule completely (consider the choice above if you feel that a loss of $15,000,000 is simply unacceptable under any conditions), I think that the concept of *risk* in information-processing terms is best conceptualized in this manner. It is this notion of "morning-after" regret that is most likely to influence the subjectively rational human decision maker. Even for those who appear to never consider the future consequences of their behavior, I would argue that the subjective construction of their payoff matrix differs from that of others, and that their time horizon is much more truncated. But I can see many cases of even nominally "dysfunctional" behavior fitting into Savage's framework.

Reference

Savage, Leonard J. (1954), *The Foundations of Statistics*. New York: Wiley.

Appendix 1.2

Social Science Methodology, Statistical Significance Testing, and the Use of Organizational Research in This Book

I decided to include this appendix to explain my selection and use of research from our scholarly literature in this book. Scholars and academic researchers have compiled a body of related work on many of the issues this book will investigate, loosely known as "organization science;" however, much of this literature will be noticeable by its absence. The reason for that absence, in some respects, may be regarded by some readers as troubling.

The problem that deters consideration of much research is that it has been developed under the current model of "organization science," which is essentially the general model of social science research applied to organizational matters. And the problem is that in far too many cases, "social science" is simply an oxymoron. That is a very strong word to use in this connection, but I find it to be appropriate when I carefully examine the model of science as it has been so well developed and applied in the physical and exact sciences against what we do in social science. Like Meehl (1967, 1978, 1990), I am greatly disappointed in the progress of the social sciences and the inability of the social sciences to learn from past problems and shortcomings.[1] This disappointment is especially keen in light of the length of time for which the problems with the social science model have been known.

An appendix, or even a small book, is too limited to address all the problems presently found in the social science model, so I will summarize the major difficulties, and provide more detail on two that cause me to either disregard or discount so much of our organizational literature. These are the incorrect interpretation of research results based on statistical significance, and the inability to cumulate research findings over time. The latter problem is really a cluster of related issues, but I will treat it as a single phenomenon. Hereafter, I will also restrict my concern to the pursuit of organizational questions, and hence will refer only to "organization science," but this in no way changes the substance of my arguments.

I want to be clear that in my discussion, I am concerned almost exclusively with the empirical process of theory testing and outcome interpretation as it is done in the social sciences. In the physical sciences, this is sometimes ironically referred to as the "normal science" model (Kuhn, 1962). (The term "normal" is used in our field to contrast to more innovative or unrelated approaches to the study of organizations, which may or may not actually use data to test ideas.) Unfortunately, the term "normal science" has come to be viewed in pejorative terms by many in the field, a state of affairs I find quite puzzling, since I am convinced normal science has never really been done in the social sciences.[2] Indeed, a large part of my argument here could be interpreted as an appeal to really try normal science, since it is a hugely unexploited asset in the study of organizations.

I have included an extensive bibliography with this appendix, in part because I know that for some my claims will be seen as controversial, and I want to expedite the process for colleagues to check the literature for themselves. Most of the materials in the references deal with statistical significance testing, which I will refer to hereinafter as "NHST," as used by Cohen (1994) to refer to Null-Hypothesis Significance Testing, since this is one of the two principal problems I discuss here. In summary, the literature on NHST shows several things: (1) most standard interpretation of NHST as we do it in the field now is unambiguously incorrect; (2) we have known that for decades; (3) leaders in the social sciences have been unable to change these incorrect practices (many prominent scholars are among the authors in this bibliography, for example); and (4) there is no counterargument—if one looks for literature supporting present practice with NHST, there is none. The only place there is support for NHST is in statistics texts that incorrectly create an amalgam of Fisherian and Neyman-Pearson methods, and get it wrong. Cohen (1994) alludes to that problem; a better reference is Carver (1978), who names names and gives examples of incorrect statistics texts. I have, incidentally, never found a rebuttal or refutation of the claims regarding those texts in his article.

When I use the expression "incorrect interpretation of NHST," I mean that in two ways. First, the primary problem is that we incorrectly use the p level of statistical significance as a substitute for having found an effect. That is, instead of judging our results in terms of the ability to explain a large percentage of variance in a dependent variable, or a relatively large difference between means (i.e., *effect sizes*), we claim to have found something meaningful because we have a low *p* value. For reasons I have never really been able to determine, we have attached a nearly-mythic importance to *p* levels of .05 or less. I really like Cohen's (1990) rejoinder, where he reminds us that the distribution of *p* is continuous, and "surely God must love the .06 level almost as much as the .05."

One of the myths surrounding NHST is that *p* levels are better measures of the importance of results than effect sizes, since they eliminate the possibility of effect sizes being misleading. However, as every one of the papers that looks at effect sizes points out (two of the best technical ones are Cohen (1962) and Sedlmeier and Gigerenzer (1989)), that belief is simply incorrect. The burden of making the call as to whether an effect size has some kind of importance falls entirely on the researcher, as it always has and always will—a *p* level of .05 or less does not confer importance or meaning on the effect. Significance levels are *not* a substitute for effect sizes, under any conditions, and the substitution of *p* for effects is one of the most pervasive errors associated with NHST.

The second problem with NHST is best expressed by Carver (1978) in his excellent summary of the problems with it. He describes three "fantasies" about statistical significance which permeate the research literature—

1.   The *"odds-against-chance"* fantasy. This is probably the most confusing of the misinterpretations of *p* levels. The *p* level is the probability of getting a research result when our method initially assumes that chance is why we got the result. Therefore, we cannot use the *p* value to be the probability that chance caused the difference between our groups, because (a) that probability was assumed to be 1.00 in the first place, and (b) we use the *p* value to decide whether to reject or accept the idea that probability is 1.00 that chance caused the difference! Carver uses an excellent example to clarify this point (1978: 384-385):

What is the probability of obtaining a dead person (label this part D) given that the person was hanged (label this part H); that is, in symbol form, what is $p(D|H)$? Obviously, it will be very high, perhaps .97 or higher. Now, let us reverse the question. What is the probability that a person has been hanged (H) given that the person is dead (D); that is, what is $p(H|D)$? This time the probability will undoubtedly be very low, perhaps .01 or lower. No one would be likely to make the mistake of substituting the first estimate (.97) for the second (.01); that is, to accept .97 as the probability that a person has been hanged given that the person is dead. Even though this seems an unlikely mistake, it is exactly the kind of mistake that is made with interpretations of statistical significance testing—by analogy, calculated estimates of $p(H|D)$ are interpreted as if they were estimates of $p(D|H)$, when they are clearly not the same.

The fundamental confusion in this fantasy is that the probability referred to by the p level is the *probability of getting the outcome data under the conditions of the null hypothesis,* or $p(D|H)$. It is *not* the probability of the hypothesis given the data. What the p level really tells us is the probability that we committed sampling error.

2. The *"replicability or reliability"* fantasy. This fantasy contends that the likelihood that the results of a study would be replicated if the study were repeated is $(1 - p)$. That is, if the p level of a difference is .05, the likelihood of a repeated result is .95. There is simply nothing in the estimation of sampling error under conditions of the null hypothesis to justify such a claim, but it is widely repeated, even in highly acclaimed statistics and research methods texts. Replicability depends on whether conditions can be controlled, variables can be controlled, measurements can be repeated, and so on, exactly as the word "replicate" is defined.

3. The *"valid [alternative] hypothesis"* fantasy. The last fantasy Carver discusses is the argument that if we can reject the null hypothesis, the alternative (or as he calls it, "research") hypothesis must be true. Further, it is argued that the more unlikely the incorrect rejection of the null hypothesis, the stronger the support for the alternative. For example, if we can reject a null hypothesis at $p < .001$, this fantasy implies that the probability the alternative is true is $> .999$. This is seldom stated explicitly, but it is the implicit argument underlying this fantasy. In fact, any such claims require use of Bayesian statistical methods to be valid, and these require investigation and procedures far beyond those found in the large majority of social science studies.

Carver is not alone in pointing out the weaknesses of standard practice in interpretation of NHST. Neyman and Pearson (1933) pointed out that one of the five factors determining whether a result was "significant" under NHST was the size of the sample. Thus, big samples will result in a significant p level every time for any "test." Many examples of the overwhelming impact of sample size have been reported in the literature. For example, in Meehl's (1967) discussion of an unpublished study of 57,000 students in Minnesota, he reported that his group collected 15 different measures, and ran off 105 chi-square tests. All of these were "significant," 96 percent of them at $p < .000001$! In a similar case, Bakan (1966) reported the results of a survey of over 60,000 school students. His group found that with a sample this large, they could subdivide the sample on any basis they chose (i.e., randomly), and obtain a "significant" difference between subgroup means on any variable they selected. This should not have been a surprise even 30 years ago—Berkson (1938) reported a problem interpreting chi-square tests with a sample of "only" 700, because all of the tests were statistically significant.

Many statistics texts (and I would suspect most), regardless of whether they teach NHST correctly, have always discussed the impact of sample size on significance levels. But very few caution that if a sample is big enough (and sample sizes very much smaller than the ones discussed above are sufficient), "statistical significance" is guaranteed regardless of effect size.

Thus, by incorrectly drawing conclusions from these NHST fantasies, we base our theories on incredibly weak findings—no one would write up a result claiming to have strong support for a theory on the basis of the *inability* to explain 96 percent of the variance of their dependent variable, but there is no need to look very far to find such claims based on "significant" r values of .20, and that correlation explains only four percent of the variance. I like Cohen's (1990) example of the "significant" relationship between height and IQ (and this is a real relationship): if you want to increase an average kid's IQ from 100 to 130, you have to give him enough growth hormone to make him 14 feet tall! (We'll temporarily ignore the fact that there is absolutely nothing causal in that correlation, by the way.)

The second major problem with present model of organizational science is the inability to cumulate findings over time, and to truly progress in the field as a result. A large part of this problem is a direct consequence of our misuse of NHST. Meehl (1986) argues forcefully that most of what we think we know from NHST is indistinguishable from background correlational noise, or what he terms the "crud factor." The crud factor refers to the fact that at some low level, virtually everything is correlated with everything else. Without baseline data to estimate the size of the crud factor in a population, we cannot really interpret research results at all. NHST *assumes* that there is absolutely no relationship between the variables under study, by definition; but assuming that to be the case for analytical convenience is in no way the same as knowing what the background noise factor is. To properly interpret our findings, we need to know it, and I have never seen a study to find out what happens when a set of variables is simply administered to the relevant research population at large to determine the level of the crud factor. We skirt the issue by sometimes examining variable scalability and reliability, but that is not sufficient. I see no good reason not to learn what the crud factor is for a study population, except that it would be almost impossible to publish it. With the number of graduate students we have trained around the world since the end of World War II, it would seem likely that by now detailed handbooks of such important data would be in wide circulation, as a key element to interpretation of data in our scientific enterprise. Like Meehl, I am forced to conclude that many of the significant "supportive" studies of many theories is nothing more or less than "discovery" of the size of the crud factor.

The cumulation problem is compounded by the nearly complete absence of replications in our research. I have done a study, only partially completed at present, wherein I had my graduate assistant survey 13,161 empirical articles from the ABI/Inform database, to search for those using the word "replication." The results of this search are shown in Table A1.2.1. Of these, only 68 used the word, or 0.51 percent. However, this figure is simply the result of a keyword search, since many of the articles use language to suggest that their results could be replicable (generally argued on the basis of the replication fantasy), but are not actual replications. It is common to find the expression "replication and extension" of research, but it is typically done in such a way that the "extension" destroys any close semblance of a "replication." We found 3,212 articles and 9 nominal replications on the subject of decision-making, for example; of those 9 articles, three that I have examined were not replications. Examining data from several subsamples in this way, I estimate the replication rate to be no higher than 0.32 percent.

As these data show, among the empirical articles in most organizational disciplines examined there were no nominal replications at all. It is worth noting that the fields sampled include both theoretical work and practical areas such as performance appraisal and training. Economics, considered a better-developed "science" by Pfeffer (1993), fares even worse than "organization science," with a 0.18 percent nominal replication rate.

We further compound the cumulation problem by using "voting" procedures to incorrectly accumulate evidence. A much more accurate procedure is meta-analysis (Hunter, Schmidt, and Jackson, 1982; Schmidt, 1992). Voting methods are actually likely to produce misleading results (Schmidt, 1992). Hunter, Schmidt, and Jackson (1982) provided a very clear argument on the need for meta-analysis rather than voting procedures, and one of the few rays of light to have penetrated the social science model in recent years is the publication of a number of studies using meta-analysis.

Table A1.2.1   Preliminary results of survey of replication in organization science and economics

Research category	N articles	Nominal replications
Communication (general)	2681	14
Compensation	1537	3
Contingency leadership	5	1
Contingency organization	30	0
Continuous improvement	14	0
Decision making	3212	9
ERG model	2	1
Expectancy theory	60	0
Goal setting	188	3
General motivation	942	5
Communication (organizational)	26	0
Planning (general)	810	19
Organization structure	67	0
Performance appraisal	311	4
Prospect theory	35	0
Quality circles	82	0
Quality management (general)	70	0
Strategic planning	814	0
Total quality management	23	0
Training (general)	2252	9
Total organization studies articles	13161	68
Economics articles (all subjects)	28571	51

However, given that the editorial and page-space requirements for universal reporting of data to support meta-analysis are so small (for example, correlational studies require only means, standard deviations, and item reliabilities), it is rather shocking to see the limited impact these requirements have made on journal editors. Hunter, Schmidt, and Jackson detailed the meta-analysis requirements for many common types of studies, and little was required of editors who wanted to change their practices to make such cumulations possible. Eminent statisticians like Cohen (1990, 1994) support the application of meta-analysis, but negligible change in editorial practices is evident over more than a decade. We continue to produce studies which use procedures rather like those intended to decide whether God exists by adding up all the supporting arguments on one hand, and all the contrary arguments on the other, and awarding the "decision" to the larger pile. This is very poor practice for either science or religion.

The combined interaction of NHST interpretation errors, unknown crud factors, nonreplication, and compilation through voting, is to make most of the research and reviews of our literature uninterpretable (Meehl, 1990); we literally do not know what we think we know. We cannot tell if a piece of research done in 1993 is an advance over work done in 1963, even if it is closely related. There are some exceptions to this, but they are rarities, and in the absence of cumulation, "new" "theories" constantly emerge instead. In her discussion of paradigms as a panelist at the 1995 Academy of Management meetings, Janice Beyer told a funny story about planning to submit a paper to a professional group. She was sent a form, and asked to check off which "theoretical group" best described her work; she had 66 categories to choose from, plus a category called "other!"

There are other problems with the social science model I might raise, as well. For example, the primary motivation for much research has been a largely economic motivation to gain tenure, with scientific progress taking a second seat (Anonymous, 1987; Campbell, 1967; Colander, 1991; Dunnette, 1966; Lorsch, 1979; Oviatt and Miller, 1989; Wachtel, 1980). Troubling questions have been raised about the "blindness" of the review process in organizational research (Anonymous, 1987; Ceci and Peters, 1984; Fiske and Fogg, 1990; Peters and Ceci, 1982), despite this practice being one of the claims to "objectivity" in organization science. Finally, the reliance on academic journals as both the primary outlets for our research and as primary sources for "relevant" work results in a dangerous and highly unrealistic form of academic inbreeding. One consequence of that is a loss of external validation of our research (Byrne, 1990; Colander, 1991; Lorsch, 1979; Oviatt and Miller, 1989; Price, 1985). Despite suggestion of approaches to resolve some of these problems (Cohen, 1962, 1990, 1994; Hunter, Schmidt, and Jackson, 1982; Kilmann *et al.*, 1994; Kmetz, 1992; Kupfersmid, 1988; Lorsch, 1979; Meehl, 1978; Price, 1985), there has been little observable impact on editorial practices or article content.

As I said at the beginning of this appendix, problems with the social science model are far greater than can be treated in a short discussion. The primary point I want to make is that I am very skeptical of much of the information I see in the professional research journals, and until there is clear evidence that the "science" being done is much more "scientific" as a whole, I will choose the option any scientist reserves: acceptance of any arguments will be suspended until there is convincing evidence that a body of work supports those arguments. I do not find that convincing quality in most of "organization science," as is the case with the overwhelming majority of my colleagues in the world outside of academic institutions.

I want to be clear that I do not consider these deficiencies to be a problem of carelessness, negligence, or deceit on the part of my academic colleagues. On the contrary, most of them take their research missions very seriously, and do the best research they can; their integrity as individual researchers is beyond question. What is more, many of them succeed in producing innovative, insightful, and valuable studies that truly advance our knowledge. As my own reference lists show, there is much that is good in our research.

This statement may seem inconsistent with most of what I have said about organizational research so far, but I think there is a rational explanation for this seeming anomaly. In my view, the problem is a function of two factors. The first has to do with the way that we process and disseminate information among ourselves, through our training and professional journals. In our training, we have learned research methods and statistics from texts written by authors who were faced with highly divergent points of view on appropriate methods and procedures. Much of this divergence resulted from a bitter dispute between Sir Ronald Fisher on one hand, and Neyman and Pearson on the other, in the early stages of development of modern statistics (Cohen, 1990; Meehl, 1978). The textbook authors, trying not to get caught between the camps, produced an artificial "hybrid" approach to statistical interpretation, but one which did not really resolve the differences (Carver, 1978).

Having produced this hybrid, generations of researchers were trained incorrectly, and it never occurred to them to use the journals to investigate statistical procedures when they would do their literature reviews—why question our methods when we already believe them to be right? Thus, even though the information necessary to interpret statistics correctly has been in our journals for a very long time, it goes unseen because no one looks for it. I never cease to be amazed at the extent to which the incorrect interpretation of statistical significance is rooted in the research we do. For that reason, I agree with Carver (1978) that use of NHST for any purpose beyond a minor initial check for sampling error should be completely banned. Many of the other problems I have discussed here are perpetuated by NHST, because we cannot make sense of what our research produces. That being the case, we should not be surprised that widely different views of the value or contribution of research are essentially reflections of our idiosyncracies as reviewers. If we were basing our evaluations of research on statistical power and the magnitude of effect sizes, it would be much easier to truly move ahead. Our weak procedures inhibit progress enormously.

Second, I agree with Colander (1991) that academic publishing makes obvious sense when it is considered as an economic undertaking. Anyone who has ever been involved in a promotion and tenure decision, whether as the subject or the experimenter, knows fully that one's academic future depends on the ability to produce an adequate quantity of journal articles which appear in journals that others agree are important. One cannot "make waves" in the system until one has paid the appropriate dues, and that is done by publishing under the rules of the established regime. If one examines the authors of many of the critical articles in the references to this appendix, it is clear that there are many luminaries in their respective fields. It is equally clear that nothing I have said in this appendix has not been stated by them. However, the feedforward of their criticisms and recommendations for change is countered by the need of many contributors to gain approval of their work under essentially subjective standards; the need to secure one's livelihood therefore creates a powerful feedback. When the operational objective of the enterprise is economic, the stabilizing power of such feedback more than offsets the destabilizing power of feedforward.

Many conscientious people thus make up a research enterprise which is as resistant to change as it could possibly be. Published replications, and particularly failures to replicate previous studies, are simply not to be found in our literature. Empirical studies of variables which might be useful to provide baseline data for the evaluation of theory-testing studies are never seen, typically because they are not themselves "theoretically grounded." I would love to be able to go into our literature and get some idea of the frequency of structural changes in real organizations, and the reasons cited for those changes, but such pedestrian research is not likely to be published if it were done; so it doesn't get done, and we have no good scientific data on how persistent organization structural forms are over time.

Given the technology-management focus of the research in this book, it would seem quite appropriate to review and include literature on the relationship of technology change to structure change. Such information would be very helpful, but I have no idea where I would get valid information on it. This is particularly ironic in light of the work that Joan Woodward (1965) and her colleagues began over 30 years ago, and was largely derailed by subsequent research with incorrect designs and incomplete tests, most of which relied on NHST. Woodward's argument was that different manufacturing technologies seemed best matched with different structures, in that firms of one technology type tended to cluster structurally, and those which deviated from the cluster tended to perform less well. In that connection, there were many studies which reported partial "tests" of her idea, but in fact, none of them did—they tested pairwise relationships which did not test the technology-structure-performance interaction, they added and deleted variables she discussed, and they never replicated what she did, even when the study was replicated elsewhere.[3] This replication of Woodward's design was done in the U.S., and it reported empirical data which strongly supported most of Woodward's major arguments (Zwerman, 1970). This study is largely overwhelmed by the noise of the major journals, however.

Perhaps Pfeffer (1993) is correct when he calls for an elite group to take control of the research enterprise, but given that the overall collective efforts of so many good people are so hard to redirect, I find it hard to believe that much would change. None of the problems I have addressed here are new, or have been for all of my career in academia; most persist in the same form as they were decades ago.

There are some rays of hope. As I mentioned, there are some journals where reporting of data necessary to support meta-analysis has at least been encouraged. Within the past several years, the American Psychological Association began to require publication of R^2 and adjusted R^2 in all studies, showing that the importance of effect sizes had begun to be appreciated. Shortly thereafter, the Academy of Management followed suit, and recent empirical articles in the *Academy of Management Journal* have prominently discussed effect sizes and even Type II error (Waller, Huber, and Glick, 1995). These are definite improvements over the majority of past practice, and are to be lauded.

Science is procedure, and in the framework of this book it is a body of information content, as a body of IPPR. The procedure is well-known, and the basic problem with the social and organizational sciences is that they do not follow that procedure. Organization science is far from being mature scientific discipline, for that reason.

In the meantime, I have to deal with whatever research I have, and most of that is simply uninterpretable. For that reason, many of my readers may find that seemingly important works have not been given their due consideration in this book. I can only argue that while they may have been seen, I have chosen not to cite them if they have not done the things necessary to avoid inclusion in that large mass of material which has been examined and rejected. That may not be very satisfactory, but he only thing I can offer right now is sympathy—this state of affairs is not satisfactory for anyone, and it will take more than a few people in the field to change it.

Notes

1. Most of my comments are directed toward the study of organization science in areas parallel to those that Meehl (1978) refers to as "soft psychology." There are no clear dividing lines as to what is "hard" and what is "soft" in any field, but I think his paper strongly reinforces the case for simply doing a better job of science in "social science." That would mean that studies linking constructs which have no objective referents, or cannot be directly traced to externally verifiable criteria, or have never been replicated, or depend entirely on the attainment of statistical significance for support, are not to be trusted. By this set of criteria, most of the empirical research in "organization science" is rejected. Like Meehl, I believe that the exact sciences provide a highly appropriate model for other sciences, and there is little excuse for not using better methods than we do.

2. As part of the audience at the August, 1995, meetings of the Academy of Management, I made a short version of these statements to a distinguished panel of scholars in a session entitled "Paradigm, paradigms, or Pfefferdigm" (the latter term refers to an article by Pfeffer (1993), in which he asserts the need for an elite to take more complete direction of the research establishment in the organizational sciences). No one rebutted or disagreed with my statements, but Henry Mintzberg did point out that when he suggested that a colleague in marketing actually did normal science, the colleague took huge offense, and never forgave Henry. The point I want to make with this comment is that many researchers in the field regard "normal science" as a commonplace activity that has pretty much run its course, and from which little more can be expected. I completely disagree, and my perspective is that normal science has yet to truly be done to any significant extent in the social sciences.

3. The absence of specific references here is deliberate. I am not trying to "beat up" any particular group or individuals, but illustrate a generic problem in a line of research which should be directly relevant to this book. A good summary of

the work in this field during the immediate post-Woodward era is given by Fry (1982). Unfortunately, his decision on whether studies support any arguments about these relationships is based on NHST, and his summary really tells readers less than we might hope.

References

Anonymous (1987), Beyond quality in the search for a lengthy vitae. *Journal of Social Behavior and Personality*, 2: 3-12.

Atkinson, Donal R., Furlong, Michael J. and Wampold, Bruce E. (1982), Statistical significance, reviewer evaluations, and the scientific process: Is there a (statistically) significant relationship? *Journal of Counseling Psychology*, 29 (2): 189-194.

Badia, Pietro, Haber, Audrey, and Runyon, Richard P. (1970), *Research Problems in Psychology*. Reading, Mass.: Addison-Wesley.

Bakan, David (1966), The test of significance in psychological research. *Psychological Bulletin*, 66: 423

Berkson, Joseph (1938), Some difficulties of interpretation encountered in the application of the chi-square test. *Journal of the American Statistical Association*, 33: 526-542.

Berkson, Joseph (1942), Tests of significance considered as evidence. *Journal of the American Statistical Association*, 37: 325-335.

Bolles, Robert and Messick, S. (1958), Statistical utility in experimental inference. *Psychological Reports*, 4:223-227.

Byrne, John A. (1990), Is research in the ivory tower, 'fuzzy, irrelevant, pretentious'? *Business Week*, October 29, 1990: 62-66.

Campbell, John (1967), Editorial: Some remarks from the outgoing editor. *Journal of Applied Psychology*, 66: 691-700.

* Carver, Ronald P. (1978), The case against statistical significance testing. *Harvard Educational Review*, 48: 378-399.

Ceci, Stephen and Peters, Douglas (1984), How blind is blind review? *American Psychologist*, 39: 1491-1494.

Cohen, Jacob (1962), The statistical power of abnormal-social psychological research: a review. *Journal of Abnormal and Social Psychology*, 65 3: 145-153.

* Cohen, Jacob (1990), Things I have learned so far. *American Psychologist*, 45 (12): 1304-1312.

* Cohen, Jacob (1994), The earth is round (p < .05). *American Psychologist*, 49 (12): 997-1003.

Colander, David C. (1991), *Why Aren't Economists as Important as Garbagemen? Essays on the State of Economics*. Armonk, N.Y.: M.E. Sharpe.

Cummings, Larry L., and Frost, Peter J. (1985), *Publishing in the organizational sciences*. Homewood, Ill.: R. D. Irwin.

Dunnette, Marvin D. (1966), Fads, fashions, and folderol in psychology. *American Psychologist*, 21: 343-352.

Fiske, Donald W., and Fogg, Louis (1990), But the reviewers are making different criticisms of my paper! *American Psychologist*, 45: 591-598.

Fry, Louis W. (1982), Technology-structure research: Three critical issues. *Academy of Management Journal*, 25 (4): 532-552.

Goodman, Steven M. and Royall, Richard (1988), Evidence and scientific research. *American Journal of Public Health*, 78 (12): 1568-1574.

Grant, David A. (1962), Testing the null hypothesis and the strategy and tactics of investigating theoretical models. *Psychological Review*, 69 (1): 54-61.

Greenwald, A. (1975), Consequences of prejudice against the null hypothesis. *Psychological Bulletin*, 82: 1-20.

Hays, William L. (1963), *Statistics*. New York: Holt, Rinehart and Winston.

Hunter, John E., Schmidt, Frank L. and Jackson, Gregg B. (1982), *Meta-analysis: Cumulating research findings across studies*. Beverly Hills, Ca.: Sage.

Kilmann, Ralph W., Thomas, Kenneth W., Slevin, Dennis P., Nath, Raghu, and Jerrell, S. Lee (Eds) (1994), *Producing useful knowledge for organizations*. San Francisco: Jossey-Bass.

Kmetz, John L. (1992), Proposals to improve the science of organization. Paper presented at the annual meeting of the Academy of Management, Las Vegas, NV.

Kuhn, Thomas S. (1962), The Structure of Scientific Revolutions. Chicago, Ill.: University of Chicago Press.

Kupfersmid, Joel (1988), Improving what is published: A model in search of an editor. *American Psychologist*, 43: 635-642.

Lorsch, Jay W. (1979), Making behavioral science more useful. *Harvard Business Review*, 57 (2): 171-181.

Lykken, David T. (1968), Meta-analysis: Cumulating research findings across studies. *Psychological Bulletin*, 70(3): 151-159.

Meehl, Paul E. (1967), Theory-testing in psychology and physics: a methodological paradox. *Philosophy of Science*, 34 (2): 26-37.

Meehl, Paul E. (1978), Theoretical risk and tabular asterisk: Sir Karl, Sir Ronald, and the slow progress of soft psychology. *Journal of Consulting and Clinical Psychology*, 46: 806-834.

Meehl, Paul E. (1986), What social scientists don't understand. In Fiske, Donald W. and Shweder, Richard A. (Eds): 315-338, *Metatheory in Social Science*. Chicago: University of Chicago Press.

* Meehl, Paul E. (1990), Why summaries of research on psychological theories are often uninterpretable. *Psychological Reports*, 66: 195-244. Monograph Supplement 1-V66.

Morrison, Denton E. and Henkel, R. E. (1970), *The Significance Test Controversy: A Reader*. Chicago: Aldine.

Neyman, J., and Pearson, E. S. (1933), On the problem of the most efficient test of statistical hypotheses. *Philosophical Transactions of the Royal Society (A)*, 231: 289-337.

Nunnally, Jum C. (1960), The place of statistics in psychology. *Educational and Psychological Measurement*, 20(4): 641-650.

Oviatt, Benjamin N. and Miller, Warren D. (1989), Irrelevance, intransigence, and business professors. *Academy of Management Executive*, 3: 304-312.

Peters, Douglas and Ceci, Stephen, (1982), Peer-review practices of psychological journals: The fate of published articles, submitted again. *The Behavioral and Brain Sciences*, 5: 187-195.

Pfeffer, Jeffrey (1993), Barriers to the advance of organizational science: Paradigm development as a dependent variable. *Academy of Management Review*, 18: 599-620.

Price, Raymond L. (1985), A customer's view of organizational literature. In Cummings, Larry L., and Frost, Peter J. (Eds), *Publishing in the Organizational Sciences*. Homewood, Ill: Irwin.

Rosenthal, Robert (1979), The "file drawer problem" and tolerance for null results. *Psychological Bulletin*, 85: 185-193.

Rosnow, Ralph L., and Rosenthal, Robert (1988), Focused tests of significance and effect size estimation in counseling psychology. *Journal of Counseling Psychology*, 38 (3): 203-208.

Rosnow, Ralph L., and Rosenthal, Robert (1989), Statistical procedures and the justification of knowledge in psychological science. *American Psychologist*, 44: 1276-1284.

Rozeboom, William (1960), The fallacy of the null-hypothesis significance test. *Psychological Bulletin*, 57: 416-428.

* Schmidt, Frank L. (1992), What do data really mean? Research findings, meta-analysis, and cumulative knowledge in psychology. *American Psychologist*, 47(10): 1173-1181.

Sedlmeier, Peter, and Gigerenzer, Gerd (1989), Do studies of statistical power have an effect on the power of studies? *Psychological Bulletin*, 105 (2): 309-316.

Tanur, Judith M. (1994), The trustworthiness of survey research. *Chronicle of Higher Education,* XL: B1-B3.

Tukey, John W. (1960), Conclusions vs. decisions. *Technometrics*, 26 (4): 416-422.

Tversky, Amos, and Kahneman, Daniel (1971), The belief in the "law of small numbers." *Psychological Bulletin,* 76: 105-110.

Wachtel, Paul L. (1980), Investigation and its discontents. *American Psychologist,* 35: 399-408.

Waller, Mary J., Huber, George P., and Glick, William H. (1995), Functional background as a determinant of executives' selective perception. *Academy of Management Journal,* 38 (4): 943-974.

Woodward, Joan (1965), *Industrial Organization: Theory and Practice.* New York: Oxford.

Zwerman, William L. (1970), *New Perspectives on Organization Theory.* Westport, Conn.: Greenwood.

* Highly recommended for understanding the fallacy of statistical significance testing.

2 Avionics Maintenance and Technology Accession

Introduction

This chapter serves two purposes. The first is to define the concept of "technology" in IPT terms. The second is to define the specific technology studied, and provide the reader with the necessary information to understand the role it plays in the U.S. Navy, and why its accession is an issue to the organization. We begin with a definition of technology which incorporates the IPT concepts developed in Chapter 1; then we examine the U.S. Naval Air Force and the role of the Versatile Avionics Shop Test (VAST) system in it; and we conclude with a review of the general problem of technology accession.

Defining Technology

"Technology," in the sense that the word is usually used, has not yet been fully defined in this volume. Having discussed IPPR and the broader context of IPT in Chapter 1, however, I propose the following definition: *technology is a goal-specific body of knowledge, comprising both a body of information and an interacting body of IPPR guiding the deployment of that information.*

The relationship between the two elements of a technology is important. The form of the elements is not. A computer, for example, consists of an enormous body of knowledge made tangible in the form of hardware, semi-tangible in the form of firmware and software, and operable with a minimum body of intangible IPPR to turn it on and use it. The latter is usually supplied by the interacting user. What computers can do well can also be done without them, although at the cost of much more time and energy than with IT mediation. The goal-specificity is embodied in the computer, in many ways—a computer cannot do brain surgery, but with the proper programming, and in the hands of the appropriate surgeon who also brings a considerable body of intangible, interacting, goal-specific knowledge to an operation, it can be a powerful mediating tool. If the knowledge of brain surgery can be specified to the level of industrial robotics, then the computer might actually do brain surgery. But in any of these cases, it is the simultaneous deployment of knowledge and rules for use of that knowledge that defines the technology.

Technology is therefore fundamentally information. But while a body of knowledge is a necessary component of technology, knowledge by itself is not necessary and sufficient. The application of knowledge to specific goals requires a "methodology," which is specific to a goal, and therefore requires IPPR. Computers are not much use for unclogging a stopped toilet.

In some cases the IPPR is more important than the body of information with which it interacts. Long before the advent of industrial civilization, the Japanese perfected the art of making the Samurai sword. This was a marvelous weapon, able to combine the resiliency and resistance to breaking of soft iron, with the hardness and ability to hold an edge of high-carbon steel; the latter is quite brittle, a property not desirable for swords. The technology consisted of a highly-formalized ritual of putting a pig-iron billet in a hot charcoal fire, and reheating, cutting, and folding it many times as the blade was hammered and drawn into its final shape. The effect of this ritual was to alternate layers of hard carbon steel with resilient iron, and marry the properties of both metals. No one knew or could explain the chemistry or metallurgy of the process, but it worked.[1] The technology was embodied in the ritual, i.e., the IPPR, long before steel-making was understood; in fact, not even fire was correctly understood.

The body of knowledge and the goal-specific IPPR interact to create a technology. This interaction creates two important properties of a technology: tangibility and specificity. I mean the term *tangibility* to mean both something which may be material or substantial and to mean something which is complete or can be fully comprehended. *Specificity* refers to the extent to which the technology may be applied to only one purpose or goal, or may be applicable to a range or group of related goals (I am tempted to use the term "domain" in this connection, but not in the mathematical sense).

Figure 2.1 illustrates these properties and provides a few examples of them. Tangibility may vary from none (intangible) to extremely high. In the case of intangibility, a body of knowledge can interact with associated IPPR to produce a technology which is entirely independent of any physical manifestation. At the other extreme, tangibility may be thought of as the existence of a "device." Specificity, unlike tangibility, must exist relative to some goal or purpose. The most specific technologies have only one purpose or goal; the least specific have multiple, related applications. A single-purpose intangible technology is represented in the figure as that of art appraisal, which requires several comprehensive bodies of knowledge, although the work is completely internal to the appraiser and entails no physical elements. At the other extreme of tangibility, a "smart weapon" represents a highly tangible, extremely specific technology.

Tangibility incorporates what the British frequently describe by the term "know-how." In many ways, know-how is an excellent description of the core of a technology. "Technology" has come to connote the tangible manifestation of a body of knowledge alone, which I find to be both constraining and incomplete. On the other hand, "know-how" alone does not include the growing and significant physical or manifest elements of what we know how to do, and so that term is also somewhat deficient. In my view, both of these properties must be accommodated by the concept of technology. I have illustrated this with the area labeled "medical technology" in Figure 2.1. This area shows a region where pure knowledge can interact with many devices conjointly. The region is the area of medical technology, but it accommodates a major hardware item in the form of a Magnetic Resonance Imager (MRI), which is an important piece of technology in its own right.

If one examines less specific technologies in Figure 2.1, an example of a tangible but broadly applicable technology is that of computers and some forms of information technology. At the other end of the continuum, management methods are an example of a multi-purpose intangible technology. Relative to different organizational goals, there are some management technologies which are effective and some which are not. This may also be observed across cultures, where the highly specific body of knowledge and "macro"-IPPR that characterize a national or ethnic culture lead to important differences in how to get things done. This can also be the source of many dysfunctional fads in management.

Finally, since the organizational knowledge discussed in Chapter 1 is a body of knowledge like any other, the addition of organizational IPPR creates an organizational technology in its own right. When one speaks of organizational or managerial "know-how," this is technology is implied. But I want to be clear that the organizational technology consists not only of the information the organization employs to conduct its daily business through its internal body of IPPR, but also includes a fundamental definition of the goals the organization pursues and knowledge of the dynamic relationships between the components of the organization, its IP system, and its environment. In resolving the basic equivocalities and uncertainties the organization confronts, the organization literally creates its definition of itself, in terms of what it is going to do in the future.

VAST, as we can also see in Figure 2.1, is a technology which is similar to a smart weapon or an MRI in terms of its specificity and tangibility. (This

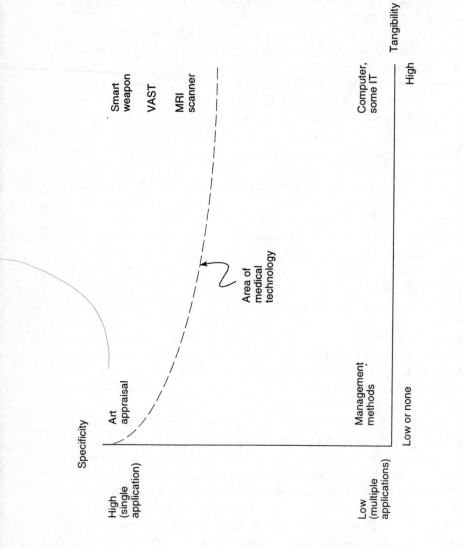

Figure 2.1 Specificity and tangibility as properties of technologies

point may not be clear at the moment, but will become so in this chapter and Chapter 3.) Like an MRI, VAST physically embodies a huge accumulation of knowledge and experience in a very specialized field. Also similar to an MRI, there is little that can be done with an avionics tester other than its primary job. Unlike an MRI, however, VAST is even more critical to a broader flow of work and to the performance of many interdependent, interacting units in the Naval Air Force. Understanding this role will be the next topic of attention in this chapter, and in Chapter 3 we will examine the avionics maintenance workflow in great detail. First, we must turn our attention to the specific context of Naval aviation, and we will thus leave the theoretical discussion of technology.

Background on the U.S. Naval Air Force

To understand why a relatively uninspiring item such as an electronic tester like VAST can command as much attention as it did, and be an important cog in a much larger machine, the reader has to have some feel for the environment in which this system works. My use of the term "system" is very deliberate and not only for the theoretical reasons discussed in Chapter 1—I found that in trying to understand anything in this huge, interconnected, interdependent set of activities, it was always necessary to have a complete model of the details of the organization. This experience helped me to develop my working definition of a system: a thing made up of other things and connected to all other things.[2]

Aircraft Carriers

A necessary place to start, or at least a pretty good place to start, is to understand an aircraft carrier. A carrier (or "CV" in Navy parlance; "CVN" if nuclear-powered) is not what most people think it is. Most are aware that during World War II the carrier became the primary Fleet weapon system, and it has been ever since (at least for conventional warfare). Whatever the image of a carrier most people have, few realize that it really is a floating maintenance facility. Of the roughly 5,500 personnel on a fully-complemented *Nimitz*-class carrier, about 2,300 do everything to operate the ship (the "ship's company"), about 300 are aircrew, and the remaining 2,200 tend and repair aircraft; the latter two groups comprise the carrier's "air wing." The ship's crew is a large group of "sailors," who are also "technicians." A large proportion of the sailors are trained in complex technical skills, some in more than one area, and all have "collateral duties" in addition to their main job. I use the terms "sailor" and "technician" interchangeably, for that reason.

To support this crew and accomplish their missions, aircraft carriers are huge, self-contained floating cities. In part they have no choice in the matter, but the Navy has always designed them to operate as independently of shore support as possible once a deployment has begun. The theory of operation is that the carrier can go into harm's way and do its job with no support from anyone other than the members of its battle group. That battle group consists of the carrier, and other specialized ships and submarines, all of which protect each other from various threats, whether from surface ships, submarines, aircraft, or missiles, and their resupply and support ships.

Aircraft carriers all have home ports, where major refitting, repairs, and reprovisioning are done. The air wing on the carrier is made up of a number of different aircraft squadrons, each of a different type (fighter, antisubmarine warfare, etc.), and each of these squadrons has a master base on shore where the squadrons return after deployment. A typical air wing on the USS *John F. Kennedy* in 1980 is shown in Table 2.1. The U.S. Navy has two major fleets, the Atlantic Fleet and the Pacific Fleet. Major port cities on both coasts support the ships and the aircraft, and other support functions are scattered throughout the United States. Major repairs, training for aircrew and support personnel, and other support functions are done at the master base. There are, of course, major ports and support functions in other nations around the world, but for the Naval Air Forces, deployments are from shore sites in the continental U.S., and deployed aircraft are supported by their carriers.

Sailors on deployment usually work 12-hour shifts for the length of the deployment, and that is ordinarily at least six months, interspersed with a few shore liberties. Since the carrier is self-supporting, everything needed to do its job and support itself has to be carried.[3] That means that beans, toilet paper, jet fuel, shoe polish, shirts, soap, tires for aircraft and deck gear, bomb loaders, movies for the crew, missiles, and things most people could never imagine have to be taken to sea with the ship. One of the principal limiting factors for everything the ship carries is therefore volume—how much storage space does it take?[4]

Table 2.1   Typical air wing for USS *John F. Kennedy*, 1980

Aircraft role	Squadrons	Aircraft type
Fighter	2	F-14A *"Tomcat"*
Light attack	2	A-7E *"Corsair II"*
Medium attack (including 4 tankers)	1	A-6E *"Intruder,"* KA-6B
Antisubmarine warfare	1	S-3A *"Viking"*
Helicopter antisubmarine warfare	1	SH-3 *"Sea King"*
Electronic warfare	1	EA-6B *"Prowler"*
Airborne early warning	1	E-2C *"Hawkeye"*
Reconnaissance	1	RF-5C *"Vigilante"*

Source: Harris Corporation, Consolidated Support System Preliminary Systems Engineering Study

Aircraft

From the perspective of the aircrew, the only reason for existence of the entire battle group is to get aircraft launched and on the way to perform their missions. While a somewhat aircrew-centered point of view, there is a great deal of truth in it—the entire battle group is unlikely to succeed as an offensive force, or protect itself as a defensive force, unless the carrier is able to get aircraft "off the pointy end of the ship." This is difficult enough when things are going well, and the Navy has had many years to practice it. But there are many factors working against flying aircraft from carriers, and one of them is the nature of the aircraft itself.

Modern military aircraft are enormously complicated machines. They are no longer referred to as "aircraft" so much as "weapon systems," which they really are. Increasingly, any modern weapon system is dependent on aviation electronics ("avionics") to accomplish anything, whether on the aircraft itself or as part of a larger group force. An F-14 relies on several on-board computers to fly and control its weapons. While flying defensive patrol an F-14 may use its own radar to seek targets, but since it will be in communication with an E-2C "Hawkeye," which uses a powerful radar to track both friendly and hostile aircraft within the "bubble" above the battle group, the F-14 may rely on the Hawkeye for target guidance during an encounter with hostile aircraft. The E-2C can guide the F-14 to its targets instead of having the F-14 betray its position by turning on its radar; once the fighter "lights up" its radar and electronic systems, it can be seen by others, and so it depends on a number of electronic systems to sense threats, and it relies on Electronic CounterMeasures (ECM) to protect it from some of them.[5] The F-14 may be on a long patrol, in which case it will be refueled by a KA-6B or S-3A tanker, also on patrol. They will be "vectored" into refueling position by others using shipboard electronics or by the E-2C; airborne refueling depends heavily on stable flight by both aircraft, impossible without the help of on-board computers. In the event of enemy electronic surveillance and sensing, all of these aircraft might be under the protection of an EA-6B "Prowler," actively jamming and engaging in other kinds of electronic warfare. The F-14 also jams and dispenses decoys, and all aircraft have some types of defensive ECM on board. All of these aircraft rely on an electronic Identification Friend or Foe (IFF) signal to tell who is whom. And so on. The sky gets very busy under these conditions, and so does the carrier. This kind of flying involves a lot of avionics and generates a huge load of maintenance work.

These complicated avionics all have some likelihood of failure over time. Failed avionics may render an aircraft completely unsafe or unable to fly, or prevent it from having the mission capabilities it must have to be an effective weapon. The inescapable result is that the carrier air wing has to do huge amounts of maintenance work at sea. For example, the F-14 requires about 100 hours of maintenance for every hour of flight, consisting of everything from cleaning the canopy to repair of the avionics.[6] When deployed, the maintenance load the carrier will have to manage will be (100 x total flight hours for all F-14s); and the F-14 is but one of the aircraft aboard.

When an avionics device has failed in flight, or does not pass a pre-flight check (using Built-In Test (BIT) devices on the aircraft), or external test equipment, the failed avionics device is replaced with a working one so the aircraft is made operational again. This replacement generates a cascade of maintenance actions, and this "downstream" flow of activity is where this study focuses most of its attention. This maintenance process will be examined in more detail shortly.

The avionics devices referred to above are electronic "boxes," most no larger than a desktop computer, and many quite a bit smaller. The desktop computer is a good analogy for most of them—the computer consists of a "system board" or "motherboard" into which other components or "cards" are inserted.   Most of that technology is derived from military electronics designs. Each of these "boxes" is mounted somewhere in the aircraft (a few are carried externally in "pods"), and because they are all replaceable assemblies mounted into a weapon system, the Navy refers to these "boxes" (along with engines and other components) as Weapon Replaceable Assemblies, or WRAs.

While not physically large for the most part, many of these WRAs are extremely complicated and perform multiple functions. They are typically expensive. Based on predicted usage and failure rates, a fixed allowance of spare parts for each of the many WRAs in the air wing is loaded aboard the carrier; the minimum number possible (i.e., the smallest volume) is taken to sea. These WRAs are only the beginning of the demand for space, however, and to understand why we need to look into the nature of aircraft maintenance in a little more detail.

Maintenance, Logistics, and the Support of Aircraft

The ratio of aircrew to aircraft maintenance personnel suggests why much more space is needed than just for storage of replacement parts. When we use the expression "an aircraft and spare parts," there is actually a much larger set of items accompanying the aircraft than replacement parts alone; this is the case for any aircraft but is especially true in military aviation. "Spare parts" refers to the aircraft requirement for a full "logistics support" program to ensure that it can be maintained and kept in operational condition. In modern military forces, that logistics program is the "belly" of the military Napoleon referred to in the 19th century, and consists of a number of standard elements, shown in Figure 2.2. An F-14 requires a number of people on the hangar deck with everything needed to fuel it, arm it, move it, and store it for normal operations. There are also on-deck testers, along with cables and tools to check it out when something goes wrong. When something does, that failure requires a spare WRA, and the spare WRA then requires a tester and workshop, trained personnel, publications and technical manuals, and specialized tools; when the failed component in the WRA is located, a spare component is needed, etc. The point, which I hope is obvious by now, is that each type of aircraft brings with it a huge logistical "tail" which must be dragged around with it, and much of this is aboard the carrier.

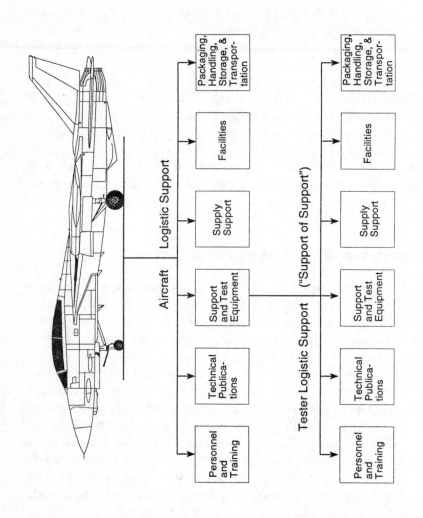

Figure 2.2 The logistics "tail" of aircraft maintenance

As Figure 2.2 shows, the logistical tail consists of six major parts or "elements:" personnel and training, technical publications, etc. These are considered to be relatively standard, and any discussion of "logistics elements" in the U.S. military or most of NATO refers to these six activities. There are two levels of support in the tail. The first, and largest, is the direct support for the aircraft. This is the area of greatest concern to the carrier. As one example of the logistics demands created by increased aircraft complexity, it is illuminating to consider the growth of technical documentation. The propeller-driven F-6F of World War II had 950 pages of manuals; the first carrier-launched jet, the 1950 F-9F, had 1,880 pages of manuals; the current F-14A has 300,000 pages of manuals.

The second level of logistics is "support of support." Each of the testers is an electronic device itself, and these can also fail. Failed testers must be repaired, and they often require recalibration and additional work to set them to very precise specifications, since they are the standard used to measure performance of the aircraft WRAs. Thus, manuals for the testers, and all the rest of the logistics elements, along with more highly skilled and trained technician-sailors are needed to do this work. Some higher-level maintenance cannot be done aboard ship, but more and more of logistic support is taken to sea each year, since that is how high Operational Readiness (OR) and independence from shore support are achieved.[7]

To make matters even more interesting, the level of maintenance and operability of aircraft during a cruise has to be as high as possible. In the event of war, the battle group has to be able to launch as many aircraft as possible for both offensive and defensive purposes, and this can be a significant fraction of the total number aboard at any one time. OR, the ability to respond quickly, is the name of the game, and this must be as high as it can be. For the support process, this means that Operational Availability (OA) of every element of the logistics "tail" must also be kept as high as possible throughout the deployment. Everything and everybody on the ship has to be able to absorb an extended surge in maintenance demands, and keep OA high for long periods, and therefore OR. Time is not on anyone's side.

The OR requirement, for all the armed forces, means continuous training. Very little about life on a ship or the operation or maintenance of complex weapons is intuitive, so constant practice is necessary. This involves not only practice for doing one's primary job, but drills in fire control, radiation decontamination procedures, crew evacuation, and so on. Everyone on the ship has multiple jobs, and all of these are interdependent with other people and units. This would be difficult for any organization to master, but in the military there is regular turnover among the personnel, so there is a constant loss of expertise. The only way to attain high OR is to train constantly. This applies to the aircrew as well, so flight operations become continuous as soon as the ship gets underway and "worked up." Every cruise brings a new learning curve for the ship to climb, and no two cruises are the same.

The learning curve is not easy—many operations on the carrier are extremely hazardous, especially on the flight deck and the hangar deck. At full operations, the noise level alone on some parts of the flight deck can kill; jets either want to suck people down an air intake or blast them over the side; propellers and rotor blades are always ready to decapitate the careless. Tow vehicles, safety equipment and aircraft with running engines are all over the deck, elevators move aircraft up and down from hangar storage, slippery spots result from fuel and fluid leaks (between deck scrubs), and all of this is happening on a deck with a 50-knot wind across it, because for air operations the carrier turns into the wind and then comes up to at least 30 knots itself. To make it really interesting, this is also done at night and in snow.

The process works. Despite all the operational challenges and physical hazards, serious accidents are remarkably rare. There have been serious fires at sea, and there are regular "industrial" injuries which are not usually life-threatening; but the overall capability of the ship is described by Weick and others (1987) as indicative of a "high-reliability organization." Even so, air operations are hazardous. The military usually projects that about 30 percent of all combat aircraft will be lost to training accidents over the service life of a design, assuming the type never goes to war. The Navy loses about six F-14s each year, at $38 million per copy.

Once a cruise is underway, this high level of activity begins to take its toll on aircraft, and maintenance becomes a critical factor to mission capability for the air wing, the ships, and the entire battle group. At full air operations with constant training activity, the number of WRAs to be maintained becomes significant. Table 2.2 summarizes a typical monthly avionics maintenance workload for the USS *John F. Kennedy* in 1980, and this is representative of most workloads at sea during the years when the studies reported in this book were in progress. This is a workload generated from operations of an air wing like that shown earlier in Table 2.1.

Maintenance of all of these WRAs, and the components in them, takes an enormous amount of tester capacity on the carrier. This brings us back to the issue of the volume of ship's space used by the test equipment. If each of these types of WRAs requires its own tester, then each of these will require physical shop space on board, and its own logistics tail.

Several factors have increased the demand for shipboard tester capacity over time. First, aircraft are increasingly reliant on avionics for nearly everything they do. Where a World War II aircraft had a radio, some limited navigation gear, and a few night fighters had airborne radars, the number of WRAs per aircraft was very small, and the boxes of that time were simple.

Table 2.2   Typical monthly WRA workload, USS *John F. Kennedy*, 1980

Category	WRAs per month	Percent
Magnetic Anomaly Detectors (MADs)	5	0.01
Recorders and cameras	17	1.01
Data handling	20	1.27
Altimeters	23	1.46
Communication/Navigation/Identification (CNI)	26	1.65
Infrared	38	2.4
Compasses and autopilots	74	4.8
Armament	80	5.1
Electronic CounterMeasures (ECM), Electronic Warfare (EW)	133	8.5
Flight systems	169	10.8
Communication and intercom	262	16.7
Navigation aids	328	20.8
All other	402	25.5
Total average monthly WRA workload	1577	100

Source: Harris Corporation, Consolidated Support System Preliminary Systems Engineering Study

By the 1960s, that number had exploded—an F-14 has 46 VAST-supported WRAs, and several others which are not tested on VAST. Second, each of the WRAs has become more complex for many reasons, including the increasing miniaturization of electronics, reliance on a larger variety of devices, increasing use of digital devices and "hybrids" of digital and analog components, and so on. Where a sailor using two probes to measure voltages and resistance at the end of World War II could repair a radio in a few hours, a single Very Large-Scale Integrated (VLSI) chip of the early 1980s would have required an estimated 10^{57} years to test by hand. Had a sailor begun such a job at the dawn of time, he would now have finished about one-third of the tests for the first chip!

Third, the larger number of roles each weapon system might play and the alternative ways to fill those roles put demands on aircraft that simply had not existed in the past. This meant much more complicated weapon systems—not only are there more avionics, but there are more ways for them to work, or to fail. For example, an E-2C might communicate directly with its carrier or aircraft on patrol, or indirectly by relay through a ship, a submarine, or a satellite; it might be sending different parts of a single message by different routes or the same message in different formats, etc. There are increased opportunities for things to go wrong, or to produce spurious indications of malfunction, all of which require tester time to check out.

However, the increasing capabilities of electronic systems also provided ways to use them to test other electronics. And while the devices being tested do much more than their predecessors, the basic technology of testing has changed very little: testing consists of applying stimuli to the unit under test and measuring the results, in a controlled sequence, until all circuits and functions have been tested. The stimulus is usually an electrical current, although sometimes physical stimuli are used to create those (a vacuum pump simulates high altitude to test an altimeter, for example), and the resulting measure is usually a voltage, a resistance, a change in these, or a waveform. Most of the stimulus-and-measurement cycle is very linear and straightforward, and thus relatively easy to automate; with the addition of a computer to follow a precise program of tests and compare each test result to a predetermined value, one has Automatic Test Equipment (ATE). VAST was the first true ATE device to be used by the military services.

Thus, the need for reduction of space, coupled with increased reliance on avionics and the capability of electronics to do avionics testing, logically led to the development of VAST and ATE. The decision to develop VAST was made in 1960. However, this decision did not resolve all of the issues facing VAST development—there were still issues of Navy policy, industry standards, and contractor integration to work through. These issues arose because the method of aircraft procurement prior to adoption of ATE meant that each weapon system prime contractor supplied the aircraft and its "spare parts." A manufacturer like Grumman Aerospace Corporation, who built both the F-14A and the E-2C, would provide the aircraft and its entire logistics tail—the test equipment, technician training and training courses, technical manuals, and all the rest. Making sure that all of this worked together was also the responsibility of the prime contractor.

With the adoption of VAST, the test equipment was manufactured by its own prime contractor, and the manufacturers of both the avionics and the aircraft prime contractor had to comply with design standards under which all of the WRAs and other designated components would be VAST-testable. NAVAIR had to formulate and enforce this policy, and do so over the long time required to get any aircraft from its conceptual phase to full-scale production.[8] In the case of the three VAST-supported aircraft, design started in the middle 1960s, and deployment did not begin until the early 1970s. Development of VAST had to completely parallel the development of the aircraft depending on it; when the aircraft started to be deployed in the early 1970s, VAST had to be there to support them. Table 2.3 shows a summary of the deployment schedule for VAST.

Avionics Maintenance—The Avionics Repair Cycle

A complete description of the avionics repair cycle will be given in the next chapter, but for immediate purposes it is helpful to understand the basic nature of the repair process as it is done for U.S. Naval aircraft (and most weapon systems in all U.S. services). Figure 2.3 shows a simplified version of the repair cycle. As the figure shows, the repair cycle is a series of remove-and-replace actions performed in different units ("work centers"), all linked by flows of materials specific to the job done in the individual units.

The repair cycle is actually rather straightforward, and quite effective: all WRAs and other removed items from an aircraft are replaced with working units obtained from the Supply Section. WRAs then go into a repair shop, where removed components are tested, and failed internal parts are removed and replaced with functioning ones if necessary (although not all removed components are actually defective, as we will see). The removed parts, in turn, are repaired in component repair shops. To the greatest extent possible, all repairs are done aboard ship, because of the importance of this capability to overall readiness.

Table 2.3   Schedule of VAST station deployments

Dates	Total stations	Recipients	
Dec 1970 - Nov 1973	41	• Grumman Aerospace (F-14, E-2C mfr.)	14
		• Lockheed Corp. (S-3A mfr.)	8
		• PRD Electronics (VAST mfr.)	4
		• VAST evaluation sites (3 shore, 1 carrier)	4
		• Training bases	3
		• Shore bases (F-14, E-2C squadrons, depots)	8
Dec 1973 - Dec 1974	24	• Carriers (*Enterprise, Saratoga, Kennedy*)	13
		• Shore sites (squadrons, depots, PRD)	10
		• Royal Iranian Air Force	1
Jan 1975 - Dec 1977	51	• Shore sites (squadrons, depots, training)	18
		• Carriers (*Saratoga, Enterprise, America, Constellation, Independence, Kitty Hawk, Eisenhower, Forrestal, Nimitz, Ranger*)	32
		• Ling-Temco-Vought (A-7E mfr.)	1
Feb 1978 - Jul 1985	19	• Shore sites (squadrons, depots, training)	11
		• Carriers (*Ranger, Vinson, Independence, Saratoga, Forrestal*)	8

Source: Operational Logistics Support Plan for AN/USM-247(V) VAST, 1980

What Figure 2.3 also shows is the high degree of interdependence between the flows and processes in the repair cycle. The development of bottlenecks, or the breakdown of processes, can prevent failed items from being repaired, and that results in lack of replacement items at other points in the chain; these disturbances culminate in failure of Supply to fulfill a requisition for a WRA when one is needed, and ultimately in the inoperability of an aircraft.

VAST is the primary tester in the Naval avionics maintenance system, but not the only one. There are numerous other work centers in the avionics repair organization, as will be seen in Chapter 3, although VAST receives about 50 percent of the total avionics workload on a carrier. VAST was

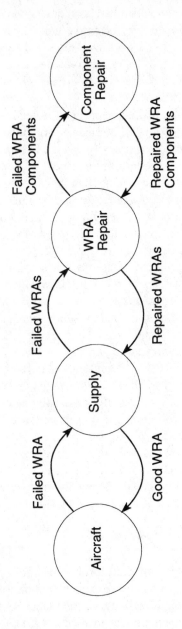

Figure 2.3 A simplified diagram of the avionics repair cycle

introduced into a repair workflow which had been developed over the course of many years and had developed very effective maintenance procedures. The flow of work from Supply after a working WRA had been issued to the squadron was to send each item to its respective "dedicated" repair shop, where they were repaired in the order received—what accountants refer to as a first-in, first-out (FIFO) workflow.

The logistics "tail" of aircraft maintenance, and the need to coordinate all of the logistics elements through a large number of organizational elements is one aspect of the organizational "complexity" which is fundamental to the issues studied in this book. A second major aspect of complexity is the nature of the organization itself, to be discussed in the next chapter. For now, logistics complexity can be regarded as a function of the need to coordinate every part of every logistics element with each other, and to coordinate these elements and procedures across physically and psychologically dispersed units. This is a task requiring significant IP capacity.

A third element of complexity is that the system is constantly changing. One change in a WRA necessitates changes in all documentation for that WRA, for the materials and equipment used to test it, and possibly in training, storage and handling, etc. Whatever the nature of any change, there will be effects on other logistics elements, and so all changes need to be checked and approved. If an upgrade in a failure-prone part in either VAST or a WRA is accomplished by substitution with a different part (a common occurrence), that modification will ripple through all of the logistics elements in the system.[9] A carrier deploying for a six-month cruise will need to be informed of all such changes, and the affect these may have on testing or repair procedures; if significant time is required to make such changes, it may be necessary to support both the old and new support procedures to the point of differentiating repair procedures by the serial number of the WRA—different boxes may go through different processes, depending on their upgrade status.

Measures of Performance and Effectiveness

An enormous amount of data is collected throughout the repair cycle, for many reasons. One of the most important reasons is to monitor performance of the system, and the operational readiness of the Fleet. As will be shown in Chapter 3, every maintenance action performed anywhere in the cycle is documented using a standard form and a set of standard codes. Navy training is effective, and despite the size and complexity of the system, the data obtained are quite accurate. This huge maintenance database is accumulated at the Naval Maintenance Support Office in Mechanicsburg, Pa., and from there large numbers of regular reports are sent to operating units worldwide. In addition, specialized reports can be requested, or raw data for special analyses, as was done for the analyses reported in Chapter 6.

For all of the complexity of the system and the number of transactions conducted at a site, there are only a few measures of performance which are truly critical. For the squadron, the time required to restore an aircraft to operable condition, whether for reasons of having just completed a mission, having a failure during a mission, or having failed a preflight check, is the key. For Supply, it is the ability to meet a demand for an avionics item when requisitioned. For the individual shops, it is the ability to repair an item inducted for repair, and return it to Supply. The shops can be evaluated on the time required for individual repairs to be performed within the shop, which the Navy calls Elapsed Maintenance Time (EMT). The full repair cycle can be evaluated on the length of time needed to repair a failed WRA and get it back to Supply in working order; this measure is TurnAround Time (TAT). TAT is the critical measure for the full repair cycle. In theory, TAT should be nothing more than EMT plus delays for transportation and physical movement, but that is often not the case, as we will see.

Given the technical nature of the work done in avionics repair and the central focus on technology, it is not surprising that the majority of people involved in avionics maintenance adopt an "engineering" concept of the organization. That is, they tend to see the organization as a machine, and if everything in it is designed and maintained properly, it will perform to specifications. That belief carries over into the working definition of effectiveness—individual unit performance is expressed as a proportion of maintenance successes to failures. Since there is a huge data-collection effort, it is easy to assess individual work-center performance, and this is watched closely by all managers at a site. For the work centers in the repair cycle, the question is, "What percent of WRAs inducted into the 'shop' were successfully repaired?" If each of the individual shops is working well, it is believed, then the entire site will work well, tester Operational Availability (OA) will be high, and aircraft readiness (OR) will be high.

As data to be reviewed in the next two chapters will show, this was often not the case; and that observation brings us to the point where this study begins. By 1976, it was widely believed that VAST performance was not meeting requirements either at shore sites or at sea, a situation that was unacceptable. VAST performance, it seemed, needed to be evaluated thoroughly to understand where the problems were, and to fix them.

As later chapters will show, the real problems were not what they appeared to be. The performance of VAST generally met, and soon exceeded, its design specifications. What was discovered was that problems in avionics repair performance were elsewhere in the repair cycle, not the VAST shops. The lessons learned from this work were not lost, although it was difficult to retain them at times. For example, in 1980 the Canadian Forces contracted to buy the F/A-18 Hornet (configured as the CF-18) to replace its aging fighters. Since that meant buying the support equipment for it, the Canadian Forces purchased the necessary automatic tester, a device which was known as "mini-VAST," although it is formally designated as the Automatic Test Set Version 1 (ATS V1). The "mini-VAST" label was applied because the ATS was manufactured by the same company that made VAST, used several of the same components, and used exactly the same testing approach; given advances in miniaturization of electronics, however, ATS is only a fraction of the size of VAST. By the end of the 1980s, when the CF-18 was fully operational, the Canadian Forces were having the same apparent "tester problems" the U.S. Navy had encountered earlier, i.e., ATS-supported WRA stockouts. As a result, I was contracted to evaluate their procedures and write a management course for their tester sites; in that process, I found the same problems with workflow management in the Canadian Forces repair cycle as in the U.S. Navy; the ATS tester was actually performing well beyond specifications. This work will be discussed in Chapter 7.

Some of these lessons were also carried into the design of the new Navy tester, the Consolidated Automated Support System (CASS). CASS is now being deployed, and while a modernized VAST is still working and still deployed with the same carriers and shore bases as before, the VAST WRA workload is slowly being transferred to CASS. Much of what was learned with VAST has benefitted CASS, i.e., the workflow management system has been automated to resolve the problems we found when VAST was a new technology. Those management lessons have also been extended into the maintenance of most other technologies in the Navy, and now into the civilian world, so that much more than avionics maintenance has benefitted from the experience with VAST and other ATE. These lessons will be discussed in Chapters 7 and 8.

Before turning to a more detailed description of the avionics repair organization and the early studies of it, it is useful to discuss some of the conceptual approaches used. Much of this study will be concerned with the first full decade of VAST deployment, from about 1976 to 1985. The primary reason for focusing on this part of the technology life cycle is that the

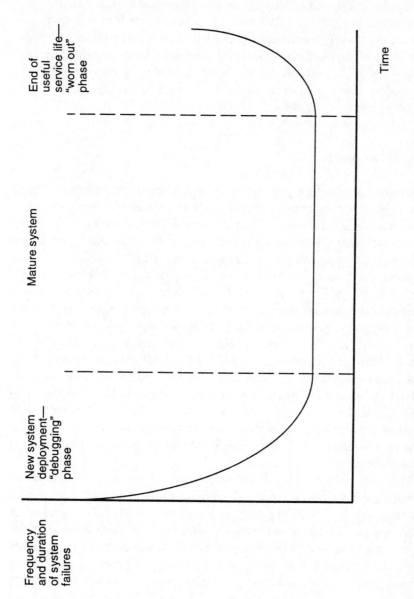

Figure 2.4   The "bathtub curve" of system failures over the system life cycle

great majority of adaptation and "debugging" in any new system occurs during these early years. This is a well-documented fact, as the life-cycle relationships in Figure 2.4 illustrate. As a result, much of this study will focus on events which considerably predate their actual publication, as did Hall's study of the old *Saturday Evening Post* or D'Aveni and Ravenscraft's (1994) study of the performance effects of vertical integration in the 1970s. It is seldom that we have a chance to see the beginning and end of a technology life cycle, and know how it comes out.

Three Experiments

In these studies, it became possible to observe the outcomes of three different "experiments:" the experiment of ATE itself, to observe what happened when a new technology was inserted into a stable system; a more traditional social-science experiment to evaluate the of impact of information processing capacity on an organization's performance, including the difficult question of organization "slack;" and a third experiment on the accession of the next generation of ATE, which is still unfolding. None of these three "experiments" could have been done in a different organization. The first and last of these are "experiments" in the broadest sense of the word, in that there was really no plan or intention to conduct an exercise in data collection and analysis. However, the intense study of VAST which was necessitated by its importance to the Navy meant that far more data were collected during these events, both in terms of quantity and duration, than would ever be likely to be the case in any other organization, and especially a cost-driven private sector organization. In that sense, we can evaluate the data within the context of its environment, and this permits the changes in technologies to approximate a field experiment.

The first of these experiments was the experiment of technology accession itself, i.e., the insertion of a new generation of technology into an operating system. The deployment of VAST permitted study of a complex technology from its inception to maturity, in terms of its specific performance and in terms of its impact on the organization. It was necessary to keep the rest of the organization working as the maturation problems of the new technology were resolved, and new management and information processing tools were developed to use it effectively. It is unlikely that a business could have afforded to pursue such a complex problem for this length of time at such high cost. Thus, the NAVAIR environment afforded much longer evaluation of the impact of technology change than would have been practical in other organizations. In many ways, however, the NAVAIR repair cycle is like many other production organizations, and its experience may be quite relevant to theirs.

The second experiment can be termed a "quasi-experiment" as described by Cook and Campbell (1979). Knowing the nature of the organization, the workflow, and its history in great detail, it was possible to evaluate the performance of the VAST shops and the entire repair cycle in objective terms, using objective Navy performance data (i.e., EMT and TAT). Circumstances even permitted a "control" group to be included in the design. The experiment was on the effects of changes in information processing capacity, including information technology, on organizational performance. For many of the same reasons discussed above, it is difficult for most organizations to even consider such "experimental" evaluations of changes in IP and IT. Despite the huge corporate and government investments made in IT in recent years, little objective evaluation of it has been done to show whether it has had the intended benefits on performance and productivity. The VAST experience afforded such an experiment, in terms of the impact of changes in IP capacity, both with and without IT mediation.

The third "experiment" is on the next technology accession, an experiment which is incomplete, and will not be finished for years to come. This is the accession of CASS and related tester and information-processing technologies into the organization. As will be seen in Chapter 7, much has changed since the initial design of VAST and its accession into the Fleet, and those changes extend far beyond logistics support alone, and include the total reconfiguration of global politics.

Technology Accession as an Organizational Problem

To close this chapter, I want to develop the concept of technology accession more fully and place it in perspective with other issues of technology management. The accession of technologies is a subset of the broader issue of technology management, and is somewhat distantly related to innovation. For clarity, I choose to consider accession a problem to be managed after the innovation process is complete and a technology has come into the marketplace. The question before us is therefore how to fit the technology into an ongoing organization, more typically as a consumer or user of that technology, and not so much as a creator of it. The organizational issue is a particular form of one of the most basic issues confronting any organization—how to simultaneously continue to do what we are doing, smoothly and without disruption of service to our clientele, while destabilizing the system as we introduce and integrate new technologies essential to the services we provide.

Innovation and Accession in the Technology Management Literature

Most of the existing literature is concerned with the processes of innovation *per se,* the management of innovation processes, or the adoption of new engineering and scientific technologies. Even with this large body of work, however, there are important unknowns in all facets of technology management. Different models and concepts of innovation are found— Benkenstein and Bloch (1993) classify these into four primary types: (1) the industrial development model, which focuses on the relationship between the innovation rate and product or process life cycle; (2) models with changing technological efficiency describing an S-shaped curve; (3) technology life-cycle models which link the S-curve model and life-cycle theory; and (4) systems models, which view most process and product innovations as large numbers of different variables operating together. Each type of model has significant implications for technology management.

Empirical assessment of the innovation process yields findings which are typically difficult to interpret or reconcile with the theoretical models. In evaluating the innovation process, Shenhar, Dvir, and Shulman (1995) discriminate between innovations as either incremental or radical; while Gopalakrishnan and Damanpour (1994) discuss the innovation process in terms of unitary and multiple sequence patterns. Schewe (1994) focuses on the question of whether it is the management of firm-related variables that is responsible for the success of a product innovation, or the management of project-related variables. From an empirical analysis of 88 innovation projects, he concluded that the firm-specific variables accounted for most of the variance in the successes.

Chidamber and Kon (1994) note that innovation researchers have frequently debated whether organizational innovation is driven by market demand or by technological shifts. The market demand school of thought suggests that organizations innovate based on market needs, whereas the technology proponents claim that change in technology is the primary driver of innovation. Collectively, empirical research studies on technological innovation are inconclusive regarding this "technology-push, demand-pull" debate. Chidamber and Kon examined eight key studies relevant to this issue for their methods, implications, and caveats, and suggest that much of the contention between the demand-pull and technology-push findings is due to different research objectives, definitions, and models, rather than market or technology forces.

These different concepts of innovation and factors that drive it, in sum, provide little help in understanding how innovation actually occurs. To make matters even more confusing, measures of innovation are hard to apply to different contexts or to apply over time. As Saviotti (1995) noted, the "heterogeneity-dispersion" of the technological population and the presence of qualitative change limit the accuracy and the meaning of measurements of technical change. This means that only in particular circumstances (e.g., long periods of observation and populations of unchanging shape, or developments along a particular trajectory) are measurements of innovation reasonably accurate or meaningful. Such circumstances are extremely rare.

Behavioral variables have also been studied in the process. Hurley (1995) studied "innovativeness," i.e., receptivity to new ideas and innovation, as an aspect of group culture. Innovativeness was hypothesized to be related to beliefs about four other dimensions of group culture: decision-making, power sharing, support and collaboration, and an emphasis on developing people and careers. Data from 8,969 individuals located in 38 groups in a large research and development agency of the U.S. government supported the positive relationship between innovativeness of the culture and innovative productivity as we might expect. But Gales and Mansour (1995) studied user involvement at the project level, and the relation between user involvement, organizational context, and performance. In 44 innovation projects, they found that the frequency of user involvement and number of users contacted increased as projects progressed from idea generation to commercialization. They also found that measures of uncertainty were related to user involvement. This finding suggests that as projects move from the "fuzzy front end" toward commercialization, the level of user involvement increases, rather that at the beginning where ideas are needed; further, the less certain the project, the more users get involved. Many innovation models posit a nearly opposite process.

In process innovations, Small and Chen (1995) looked into the usage of various justification activities in plants that adopted advanced manufacturing technology (AMT). They found that justification approaches and justification criteria preferences were important in explaining the adoption of the more integrated technologies. Further, the number of functional departments involved in AMT justification activities was more effective in explaining project performance than the other justification activities. This suggests that AMT is more likely to be adopted simply because more people get involved in evaluating it, and that this involvement had more to do with adoption than either the technical criteria or the evaluation method. Lowe and Sim (1993) studied factors influencing the adoption, timing of adoption, and implementation of manufacturing innovations—just in time manufacturing (JIT) and manufacturing resource planning (MRPII) in particular—in the context of Australian manufacturing industry. Their study indicated a slow rate of diffusion of such innovations which were already in the public domain, in spite of the demonstrated benefit of these innovations both in Australia and overseas. Generally, in spite of the major strategic payoffs from adoption of these technologies, few firms seemed to treat the innovations as major strategic decisions.

Such divergent findings tend to give little support to many of the models of innovation or technology adoption widely cited in the literature. Despite the rapid growth of the field of technology management education (Reisman, 1994), there is still much to learn about how these processes unfold. Further, few of these investigate what happens after an innovation occurs, to explain how the technology is deployed. A major research project in this body of work is the Minnesota Innovation Research Project (MIRP), which was launched in 1983 and has included the study of Navy systems development as one of its subject innovations (Van de Ven, Angle, and Poole, 1989). One of the major conclusions of the MIRP research is that innovation is a messy, nonlinear, and complex process—it follows few rules, and certainly is nothing like the stepwise models of innovation so often proposed in the literature.

There is a large body of research into the general process of technology management and innovation, and numerous professional outlets for scholarly works on different aspects of it.[10] Notable by its absence, however, are studies or models related to how new technologies get adopted into organizations and then go through "generational" changes as newer versions of those technologies are developed over time. What seems to be assumed by the literature is that organizations are entirely receptive and adaptable to such changes. This perception is difficult to reconcile with many of the empirical studies above, where it has been clear that new technologies and methods are not simply absorbed into the organization automatically and with few consequences. The primary research question of "Experiment 1," the case study of the introduction of VAST into an ongoing organization, is to evaluate this issue.

This study will propose a "messy" pattern for technology accession. However, accession is considerably farther along the technology life cycle than the innovation itself. A model of events beyond initial innovation was developed by Van de Ven (1993), and the incorporation of events he classifies as "process elements" comes closer to the nature of the accessions of interest in this book. Not only is the process of developing new technologies a nonlinear and somewhat unpredictable sequence of events, but I suggest that the same is true for the application of new technologies, even for organizations familiar with preceding generations of a technology. I am concerned with what happens when we have many interacting, interdependent technologies already integrated into an organizational workflow, and one of those is changed in some significant way. The particular change of interest is when a new generation of technology is replaced, supplanted, or upgraded by a successor. This is an ordinary occurrence, but one which is of no less importance to the organization which uses the new technology than the original innovation.[11] In fact, I would argue that it may be more important. Innovation can be deliberately stimulated, sought, and nurtured; but in many cases, it can also be contained within the R&D laboratory. When that new technology comes of age and is introduced into the everyday processes of the organization, the consequences may be very far-reaching, and not always quite what we had in mind.

The frequently contradictory findings on the innovation process predict similar complexity in the process of technology accession. The organizational change and learning needed to meld new processes and techniques into an existing stream of activity are not merely a sequence of adoption and scheduled replacement of the old with the new. Rather, I suggest that the complex relationships and interdependencies within an organization make the introduction of any "improvement" an organizational "problem." This problem exists in the sense that any change is disruptive and accession of any new technology disturbs the system where that technology change occurs. The old technology forms the mold in which we try to cast the new, and the materials of the new technology often cannot be shaped in those ways; moreover, in ways completely beyond the usual concept of "molding" something in these situations, the materials often reshape the mold.

VAST is a technology which changed the mold, as we will see. Chapter 3 will describe VAST in more detail to give the reader a clear understanding of what VAST is and what it does. In addition, Chapter 3 discusses the overall Navy organization structure that was in effect when VAST was introduced, and the aircraft maintenance organization in which VAST was the technology which succeeded earlier generations of testers.

Notes

1. The purchaser could specify the strength and sharpness of the sword by specifying the number of men it could cut through with a single stroke. Its ability to meet this test was demonstrated on prisoners, and a three-man sword was an envied blade. I understand this test is now done with packed straw.

2. It also supports my alternative, somewhat tongue-in-cheek definition: a system is an onion where each layer is a Mobius strip.

3. Within reason, of course. Oil-burning carriers must be refueled, mail to and from home must be delivered regularly, and so on. Food, jet fuel, ammunition, and any "consumables" have to be replenished regularly, with a normal schedule being weekly replenishment when at sea. The idea is to have a ship that is truly prepared to be at sea with minimal support, and to be ready to go on a nearly autonomous basis. The concept is that if shooting starts, the carrier can "button up" and do its job without ties to shore support for anything except the consumables.

4. The U.S. Navy still uses cubic feet to measure volume, unlike its NATO partners.

5. To illustrate one capability of this complex aircraft, once the F-14 radar is on it can monitor as many as 24 targets at a time at a range of over 100 miles. The fighter can select six of those targets and fire on them using the Phoenix missile which was specifically designed for the F-14, all the while continuing to monitor the remaining 18 targets. Most other contemporary fighters could select only one target at a time, and go "blind" to anything else in the sky when they select one for attack. This long-range, multiple-threat defensive ability is valuable to the Fleet, but comes at the cost of a heavy maintenance burden. In its early days, this particular radar was one of the high-failure WRAs that needed special attention to be made more reliable, if the F-14 was to achieve its readiness goals.

6. Hinkle (1993) categorizes "maintenance" into four types of activities: (1) cleaning, painting, lubrication and similar functions, which are done on an as-needed basis; (2) calibration and adjustment functions which are done on a periodic basis; (3) diagnostics and testing, which include both as-needed and periodic activities such as preventative diagnostics; and (4) repairing and replacing of faulty components. Avionics maintenance consists mostly of categories (3) and (4), but also involves the other two.

7. It is interesting to consider this logistics "tail" in the context of debates over defense spending. The cost of any weapon system can be divided into two parts: acquisition, the original price tag to buy the weapon, and operation and support, the cost of operating and maintaining the weapon over its life cycle. The operation and support costs are made up of consumables, such as fuel, lubricants, and ordnance; and maintenance costs, which is the logistics tail. What is almost never discussed in the media debate over defense costs is the fact that over the life cycle of the system, operation and support costs dwarf acquisition costs. A highly appropriate analogy is the life-cycle cost of a family: everything from the first date through the honeymoon is acquisition cost; the rest, including mortgages, car payments, vacations, food, orthodontia, Scouting, computer games, and alimony is operation and logistic support.

8. Most people do not realize how long the development cycle really is for a modern weapon system. Most considered the weapons used in the Persian Gulf war in 1991 to be the "newest" and "most advanced" in the arsenal. In fact, the large majority of those weapons were projects of the Carter administration, or earlier, and most were obsolete by the standards of technology at that time. VAST took 13 years from concept to carrier deployment.

9. Separate and rather complicated processes are followed to investigate and correct such problems after they are discovered in the field. A deployed system is seldom fully "mature" in its operational life, in the sense that it is finally "done." Changes, upgrades, and improvements are continuous.

10. See the Science and Technology Management Bibliography, *Research-Technology Management*, 36 (1): 54. Jan/Feb 1993. This bibliography, produced by Stargate Consultants, Ltd., contains over 7,500 titles to articles, books, and conference proceedings grouped in 34 specific categories.

11. I do not consider this process to be the same as the "diffusion" process often discussed in the literature. *Diffusion,* in my view, refers to how a specific technology becomes more widely distributed over time. Accession may accompany diffusion, and over long periods would be expected to; however, they are not the same process.

References

Anonymous (1993),   Science and Technology Management Bibliography. *Research-Technology Management,* 36 (1): 54.

Benkenstein, Martin, and Bloch, Brian (1993), Models of technological evolution: Their impact on technology management. *Marketing Intelligence and Planning,* 11(1): 20-27.

Berry, M. M. J., and Taggart, J. H. (1994), Managing technology and innovation: A review. *R and D Management,* 24 (4): 341-353.

Chandler, Alfred D. (1962), *Strategy and Structure: Chapters in the History of the American Industrial Enterprise.* Cambridge, Mass.: MIT Press.

Chandler, Alfred D. (1977), *The Visible Hand: The Managerial Revolution in American Business.* Cambridge, Mass.: Harvard University Press.

Chidamber, Shyam R., and Kon, Henry B. (1994), A research retrospective of innovation inception and success: The technology-push, demand-pull question. *International Journal of Technology Management,* 9 (1): 94-112.

Cook, Thomas D., and Campbell, Donald T. (1979), *Quasi-Experimentation: Design and Analysis Issues for Field Settings.* Chicago: Rand McNally College Publishing Co.

Consolidated Support System Preliminary Systems Engineering Study (1983). Syossett, New York: Harris Corporation, Government Support Systems Division.

D'Aveni, Richard A. and Ravenscraft, David J. (1994), Economies of integration versus bureaucracy costs: Does vertical integration improve performance? *Academy of Management Journal,* 37 (5), 1167-1206.

Gales, Lawrence, and Mansour, Cole Dina (1995), User involvement in innovation projects: Toward an information processing model. *Journal of Engineering and Technology Management,* 12 (1,2): 77-109.

Gopalakrishnan, Shanthi, and Damanpour, Fariborz (1994), Patterns of generation and adoption of innovation in organizations: Contingency models of innovation attributes. *Journal of Engineering and Technology Management,* 11 (2): 95-116.

Hall, Roger I. (1976), A system pathology of an organization: The rise and fall of the old *Saturday Evening Post. Administrative Science Quarterly,* 21 (2): 185-211.

Hall, Roger, I. (1980), Decision making in a complex organization. In England, George W., Neghandi, Anant R., and Wilpert, Bernard (Eds), *The Functioning of Complex Organizations.* New York: Oelgeschlager, Gunn and Hain, 1980.

Hall, Roger I. (1984), The natural logic of management policy making: its implications for the survival of an organization. *Management Science,* 30 (4): 905-927.

Hinkle, Gary L. (1993), Virtues of a broad based environment for test (ABBET), IEEE AUTOTESTCON Proceedings. IEEE, Piscataway, N.J. (93CH3149-2): 419-422.

Hurley, Robert F. (1995), Group culture and its effect on innovative productivity. *Journal of Engineering and Technology Management,* 12 (1,2): 57-75.

Kmetz, John L. (1975), *Technology and Organization Structure: The Relationship between Contextual Variables and Structure Variables in Manufacturing and*

Service Organizations. Unpublished doctoral dissertation, University of Maryland, 1975.

Lewin, Arie Y., and Minton, John W. (1986), Determining organizational effectiveness: Another look, and an agenda for research. *Management Science,* 32 (5): 514-538.

Lowe, Julian, and Sim, A. B. (1993), The diffusion of a manufacturing innovation: The case of JIT and MRPII. *International Journal of Technology Management,* 8 (3-5): 244-258.

Operational Logistics Support Plan for AN/USM-247(V) VAST (Versatile Avionics Shop Test) System (1980). Washington, D.C.: U.S. Naval Air Systems Command (AIR-417; OLSP-CGSE-0093; AA-RE). Revision E: October, 1980.

Reisman, Arnold (1994), Technology management: A brief review of the last 40 years and some thoughts on its future. *IEEE Transactions on Engineering Management,* 41 (4): 342-346.

Rubenstein, Albert H. (1994), Trends in technology management revisited. *IEEE Transactions on Engineering Management,* 41 (4): 335-341.

Saviotti, Pier Paolo (1995), Technology mapping and the evaluation of technical change. *International Journal of Technology Management,* 10 (4-6): 407-425.

Schewe, Gerhard (1994), Successful innovation management: An integrative perspective. *Journal of Engineering and Technology Management,* 11(1): 25-53.

Senge, Peter M., and Sterman, John D. (1992), Systems thinking and organizational learning: acting locally and thinking globally in the organization of the future. In Kochan, Thomas A. and Useem, Michael (1992), *Transforming Organizations.* New York: Oxford University Press.

Shenhar, Aaron J., Dvir, Dov, and Shulman, Yechiel (1995), A two-dimensional taxonomy of products and innovations. *Journal of Engineering and Technology Management,* 12 (3): 175-200.

Small, Michael H., and Chen, Injazz J. (1995), Investment justification of advanced manufacturing technology: An empirical analysis. *Journal of Engineering and Technology Management,* 12 (1,2): 27-55.

Van de Ven, Andrew H., Angle, Harold L., and Poole, Marshall S. (Eds) (1989), *Research on the Management of Innovation: The Minnesota Studies.* New York: Ballinger/Harper and Row.

Van de Ven, Andrew H. (1993), Managing the process of organizational innovation. In Huber, George P. And Glick, William H. (Eds), *Organizational Change and Redesign.* New York: Oxford University Press.

Von Bertalanffy, Ludwig (1968), *General Systems Theory.* New York: George Brazilier.

Weick, Karl E. (1987), Organizational culture as a source of high reliability. *California Management Review,* 29 (2): 112-126.

Appendix 2.1

VAST-Supported Aircraft

The five figures in this appendix show the aircraft VAST supports for avionics maintenance. The first three of these aircraft (the F-14A, S-3A, and E-2C) are the principal aircraft of concern to the studies reported here, as they were designed to be supported by VAST and no other tester could be substituted for it. The A-7E is an older aircraft and predated VAST. Seven of its updated WRAs were placed on VAST support, but the majority of A-7E WRAs used peculiar equipment.

The F/A-18 did not use VAST itself, but was supported by a newer tester popularly known as "mini-VAST." This tester was derived from the first version of VAST and used several VAST components; however, much of the technology was newer and digital, as were the avionics it supported. The importance of the F/A-18 to this research is that the Canadian Forces model (the CF-18) used mini-VAST for land-based support of the aircraft, and despite the newer and even more reliable hardware and software than used by VAST, stockouts of WRAs began to occur in exactly the same way as had happened in the U.S. Navy. As noted in Chapter 2, this part of the study is discussed in more detail in Chapter 7, and the significance of those stockouts will be explained there.

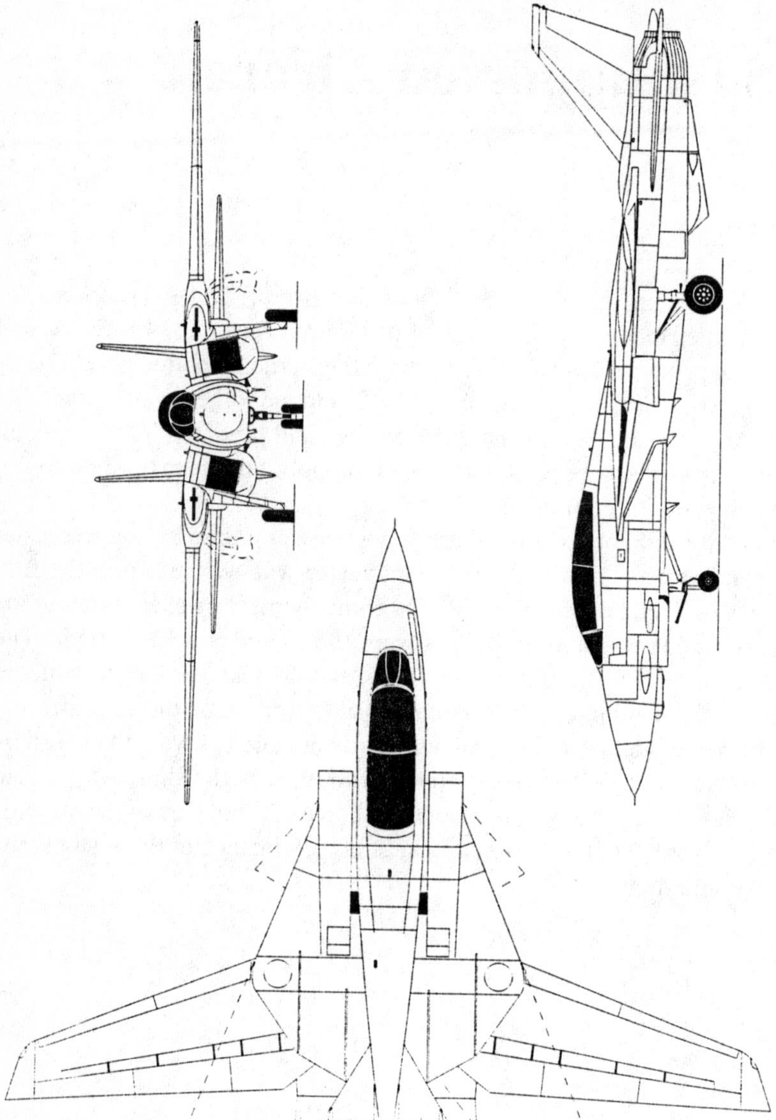

Figure A2.1.1 Grumman F-14A "Tomcat"

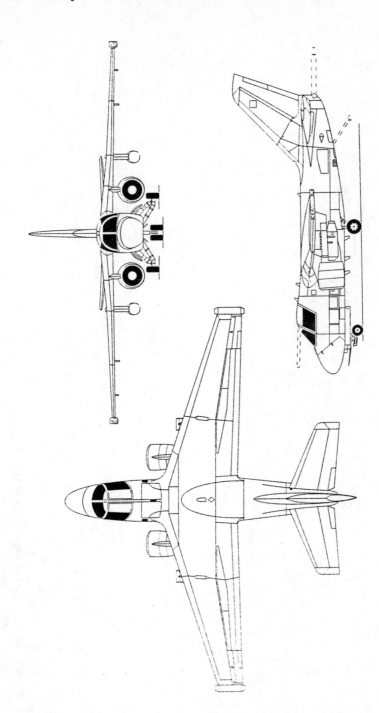

Figure A2.1.2   Lockheed S-3A "Viking"

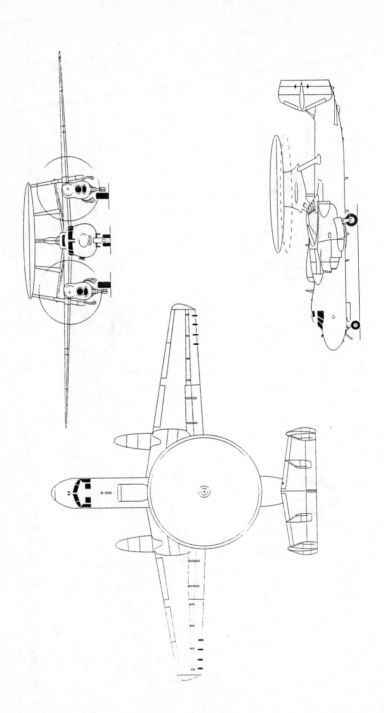

Figure A2.1.3 Grumman E-2C "Hawkeye"

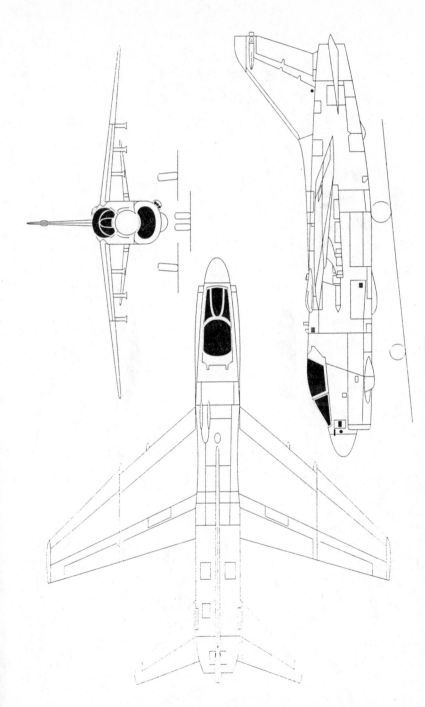

Figure A2.1.4   Ling-Temco-Vought A-7E "Corsair II"

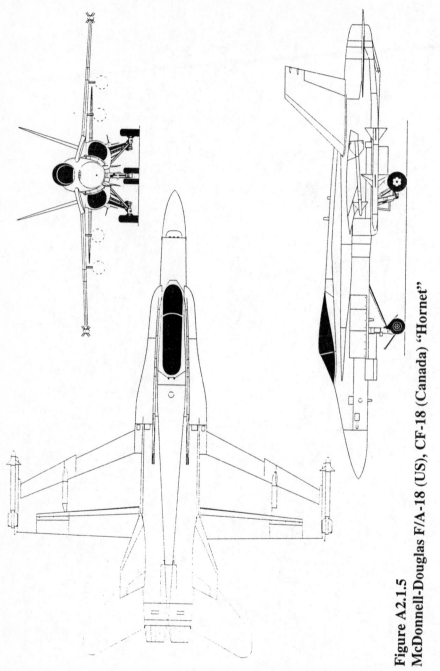

Figure A2.1.5
McDonnell-Douglas F/A-18 (US), CF-18 (Canada) "Hornet"

3   VAST and Avionics Maintenance

Introduction

This chapter has two purposes. First, it will give a more complete description of the VAST tester itself. Second, the U.S. Navy maintenance organization is described, progressing from the top of the Navy structure down to a detailed description of how VAST fits into the avionics repair cycle. Knowing the structure is necessary to understanding the nature of the maintenance workflow when VAST entered the system, and to understanding how VAST affected the workflow. Moreover, this background information provides the context for the analyses discussed in Chapters 4, 5, and 6.

Unfortunately, to understand VAST and the workflow in which it is embedded, we need to get through some fairly detailed technical descriptions and become familiar with a number of "alphabet soup" acronyms. This chapter will be the most difficult of the entire book in that regard. The payback is that knowing what VAST is, and how it fits into the overall Navy avionics repair cycle, will let readers see how the intended maintenance benefits from VAST were also accompanied by some unintended and undesirable consequences. To make this material easier to follow, I have provided a number of graphics to help visualize VAST itself, the maintenance organization, and the avionics repair workflow. Understanding the complexity of the system also makes it possible to see why the problems were not easy to discover.

The Versatile Avionics Shop Test (VAST) System

VAST and its function was introduced in Chapter 2—electronics "boxes" (like computers) are tested and diagnosed by other electronic "boxes," called "testers," one of which is VAST. The tester provides an input, (usually called a "stimulus") to the box (WRA), and the WRA responds with some kind of output, which is measured and compared to a known value, or standard. If a human being is required to measure the output and judge whether it is correct, this is a "manual" test; if an automated device does the work, it is called an "automatic" test. But the heart of the process is very simple, and anyone who has flipped a switch and observed that a light didn't go on, and then either changed the bulb or tried the bulb that didn't work in another outlet, has performed a basic "stimulus and measurement" electrical test. That is essentially all that electronic testers, including VAST, really do.

What makes electronic test more complicated is two things: (1) the WRAs have become very compact and highly complex, because they do an enormous number of things very quickly and in a very small space, and (2) consequently, there are many more tests and types of tests to do, and these have to be done quickly if the WRA is to be kept operational.

In the manual-test era, each WRA had its own "dedicated" tester, and each tester had its own workbench, technical manuals (for both the WRA and the tester), tool set, connectors, and whatever else was needed to repair the WRA. By the end of the manual-test era, there were large rooms on ships, and buildings at shore sites, all filled with testers that sat idle most of the time and were not turned on unless a WRA requiring them came in for repair.

VAST combined many different testers into one large physical device; it enabled the Navy to get rid of a large part of the avionics logistics tail, by requiring avionics manufacturers to build VAST-testable WRAs. Instead of having the entire set of testers and associated materials for each WRA, the WRA manufacturer provided a computer program which automatically tested the WRA, a set of cables and hardware to connect the WRA to VAST, standardized technical manuals and drawings, and everything needed to test the WRA on VAST. If the Navy required VAST testability, there was no choice for the manufacturer but to comply.

Figures 3.1 and 3.2 show line drawings of a VAST tester, known as a VAST "station.[1]" Figure 3.1 shows a station in perspective view. Figure 3.2 shows the physical layout of the station, and identifies the components by number and symbol; these will be discussed momentarily. As can be seen, a VAST station is composed of 14 separate cabinets called "racks," because that is literally what they are. Each rack holds one or more (usually more) tester components, each referred to as a Building Block (BB) because a VAST station is built up from these components. There is a computer rack; a switching unit to route internal data and signals to the correct BBs, which include an operator console with a monochrome CRT display and keyboard, and a small line printer (see Figure 3.1); a tape reader for the computer (since upgraded to disk drives); and 11 racks of stimulus and measurement BBs.

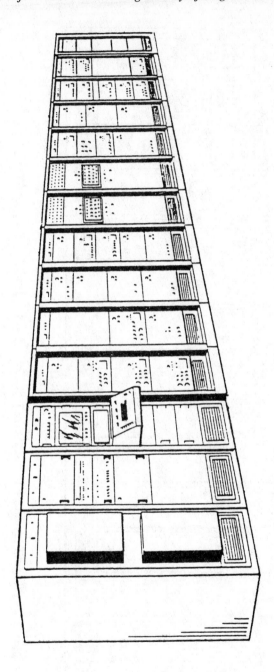

Figure 3.1   Perspective view of 14-rack VAST station

Source: Operational Logistics Support Plan for AN/USM-247(V) VAST, 1980

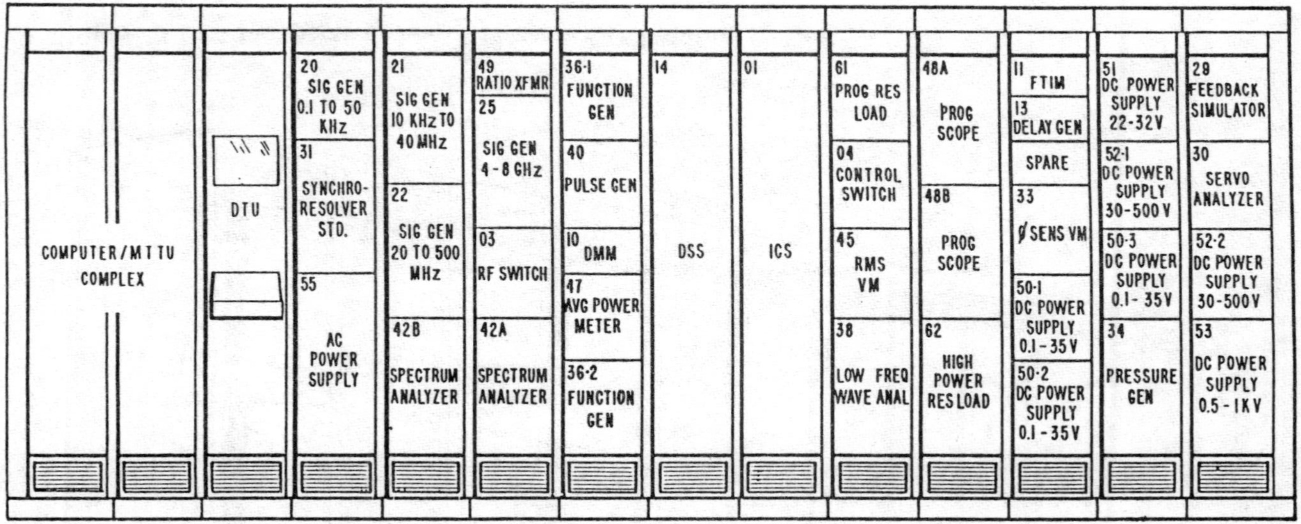

Figure 3.2 Physical layout of 14-rack VAST station, showing Building Blocks (BBs)

Source: Operational Logistics Support Plan for AN/USM-247(V) VAST, 1980

Each VAST BB performs a specialized function, and all of this activity is controlled by the computer program written specifically for the WRA being tested. Each BB is numbered, as shown in Figure 3.2, and is mounted in a particular rack. A typical Stimulus and Measurement System (SMS) rack is shown in Figure 3.3 (*Operational Logistics Support Plan,* 1980: p. I-17). The racks have large slide-out suspensions (like an office file cabinet), so that BBs can be moved in and out of the racks for individual maintenance. Racks are bolted and cabled together, so that the VAST station is a single device, both physically and operationally. A 14-rack station is a big machine. It is 78 inches tall, 34 inches deep, and 30 feet, 4 inches long. It weighs 18,620 pounds, and occupies a volume of 782 cubic feet. It has cables inside the racks and between the racks, and some externally mounted on the front to connect the BBs. Appendix 3.1 lists all the BBs in a VAST station, and provides a short description of their function.

In addition to the station itself, two other things are necessary to use VAST. One is actually a group of items, the Test Program Set (TPS). One TPS is specific to each WRA tested on VAST, and consists of (1) the computer program needed to test the WRA, on a tape (since replaced by disks); (2) the test program instruction manual; (3) an Interconnecting Device (ID), an interface box which mounts on the front of the VAST station and has the correct wiring and connectors for the WRA; (4) one or more cables to connect the WRA to VAST; and (5) supplemental data such as wiring diagrams and logic circuits, to assist the operator if something goes wrong with the test. Sometimes there is another "box" included in the TPS, for a few extremely complex WRAs which need intermediate signal processing or conversion. The other thing that makes up a VAST station is a rolling table (with locking wheels, of course) which holds the WRA being tested.

Because of its design, VAST is truly "versatile." VAST stations can be reconfigured to test WRAs from several different aircraft. They may be made up of as few as 11 racks for some purposes, but usually use 14 racks. Once a station is configured to test WRAs from a specific aircraft it is usually not modified unless exceptional circumstances arise, but stations can be reconfigured for other aircraft and WRAs. VAST was designed to test not only WRAs, but the "cards" that are taken from them when they are repaired. All that is needed to repair the cards is the correct TPS, and the availability of TPSs is one of the few factors limiting how versatile VAST is. The cards are electronic assemblies like the cards and adapters we buy for microcomputers; because they are assemblies replaced in the repair shop, the Navy refers to them as Shop Replaceable Assemblies, or SRAs. So long as

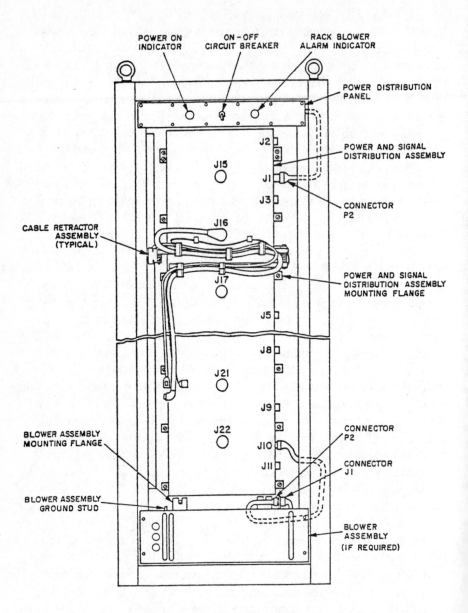

Figure 3.3 **Detail view of internal structure of empty stimulus and measurement system VAST rack**

Source: Operational Logistics Support Plan for AN/USM-247(V) VAST, 1980

the necessary BBs are in a station and one has the TPS, any WRA or SRA could be tested on VAST.

What is more, VAST can test many of its own BBs in addition to WRAs from aircraft. Since the BBs are electronic devices themselves, they need maintenance and calibration. VAST was designed to do as much of its own maintenance as possible, using automatic test. This design for versatility has meant that it can be upgraded and modernized, and its workload changed over time; and that is one of the reasons why an electronic tester designed in the 1960s is still a major item of support equipment in the late 1990s. VAST is still fully operational, and as of 1996 88 of the original 96 stations were still deployed in the U.S. and on carriers. These are not scheduled to be fully replaced until 2000.

Table 3.1 shows the original workload of WRAs and SRAs intended for VAST support. There are other testers required for some WRAs, notably radars, which pose radiation hazards, a number of electronic warfare and electronic countermeasures WRAs, and Forward Looking InfraRed (FLIR) test. The "versatility" of VAST is shown by its designed ability to test 409 different components, each of which requires its own Test Program Set.

The Three-Level Military Maintenance Organization Design

As with the other U.S. services, the Navy has organized its maintenance activities into three "levels." This model of organization is designed to maximize readiness rates for the squadrons by minimizing maintenance downtime for aircraft. The most basic level relies on both Built-In Test (BIT) on the aircraft and its major components, and on design of major components to be highly interchangeable (sometimes in very adverse conditions), so that a spare part can be quickly exchanged for a failed one by the squadron personnel. Having made such an exchange, the aircraft is back in service, and squadron needs are met. More complicated repairs, particularly those requiring special testers, training, and the rest of the logistics tail, can be done at the second level, which are the "shops" on a carrier. Only a few things are so complex or difficult to maintain that they have to go to the highest level, or back to the manufacturer. The idea is simple and effective—do major component swaps on the aircraft and get it back into service quickly; let the people with specialized knowledge and equipment worry about the innards of the removed part at a more leisurely pace and under better conditions. This model has worked quite well for a long time.

Table 3.1   WRA and SRA workload for VAST-supported aircraft

Aircraft or system	WRAs[1]	SRAs[2]
Grumman F-14A	46	35
Grumman E-2C	41	12
Lockheed S-3A	64	81
LTV A-7E	5	0
Carry-Aboard Inertial Navigation System (CAINS)	0	19
VAST	26	80
Totals	182	227
Combined total of repairable components		409

1   *Source:* U. S. Naval 3-M Maintenance Data System
2   *Source:* Automatic Test Equipment situation report (letter) 53424/MDM Ser 915, 1 October 1976

This three-level model is shown in Figure 3.4. The Navy refers to the squadron, where the first level of maintenance is done, as the "Organization" or "O" level; the deployed shops are the "Intermediate" or "I" level; and the third, most advanced maintenance level is the "Depot" or "D" level. The VAST work center is an I-level shop. This I-level organization is what makes up the majority of the people on the carrier. VAST and the rest of the I-level shops are physically contiguous to the O-level, and are operationally very closely linked to the squadrons since their purpose is to quickly replenish avionics needs for the O-level through Supply. D-level maintenance deals with repairs which are more complicated, and these facilities are neither operationally closely linked nor physically located near to O-level operations; they are also not as time-sensitive to O-level demands. Depot maintenance is provided by units called "depots" at major shore bases, or by manufacturers, but either source is referred to as "Depot" maintenance.

A long-term objective of all U.S. armed forces is to get the largest possible quantity of maintenance done by the "I" level. There are two excellent reasons for wanting to do this. First, for the O-level units, the support of intermediate maintenance reduces their maintenance downtime.

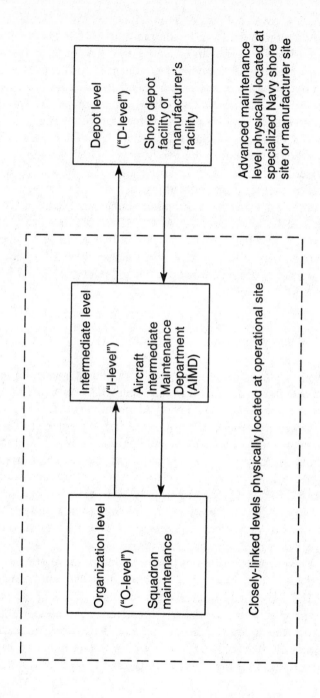

Figure 3.4   The three-level model of Naval aviation maintenance

The ability to quickly "swap out" major assemblies, i.e., WRAs, enables the squadron to repair aircraft quickly and with minimum technical complexity. Second, increased I-level capability means that few WRAs or other assets are removed from the operating site for depot maintenance; this keeps the assets moving through the local repair cycle, and puts them back into the Supply organization for reissue as needed. Supply, therefore, is the interface between the maintenance organizations at different levels. The squadrons exchange failed WRAs for working ones from Supply, and the I-level shops repair the removed ones and return them to Supply, in a closed loop.

Complete details of this organization design, the flow of physical materials and information, and operational instructions for all aspects of the repair cycle are provided by the Naval Aviation Maintenance Plan, or NAMP. The NAMP (technically knows as NAVAIRINST 4790.2) is an exhaustive three-volume document which covers everything that needs to be done to repair an aircraft and its WRAs. It was in releases B and C when this research was being done; it is regularly updated, and release 4790.2G is now posted on the World Wide Web.

The Navy Maintenance Organization

The Navy's matrix organization structure for aircraft maintenance during the time when this research was done is shown in Figure 3.5. The Chief of Naval Operations (CNO) is the highest-level Navy command officer. The Deputy Chief of Naval Operations for Air Warfare (OP-05), is in charge of the air operations, and commands the squadrons and operating units. Maintenance for operating units is under the command of OP-51, the Aviation Programs Division, and OP-514, in charge of Aviation Maintenance and Material programs. The Chief of Naval Material (CNM) is in charge of five organizations, two of which are particularly relevant to this study. One of those units is the Naval Air Systems Command (NAVAIR), and the other is the Naval Supply Systems Command (NAVSUP).

NAVAIR is responsible for initial research, design, development, test, acquisition, and logistic support of all aircraft, missiles, and associated materials in the U.S. Navy and Marine Corps inventory. Each of the offices in NAVAIR has program-specific relationships to the operating units, but the most important for this study is AIR-04, the NAVAIR office in charge of fleet logistics support. This office is concerned with on-going support and maintenance of aircraft after they have been acquired and deployed. Since

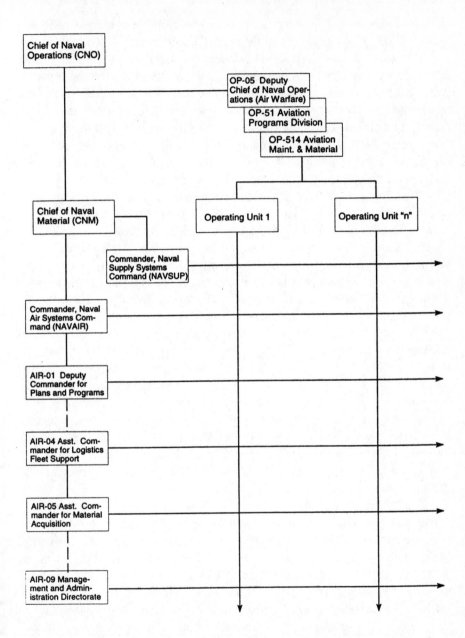

**Figure 3.5 The U.S. Navy matrix structure for maintenance and
logistic support**

electronic testers are one of the "associated materials" of concern to AIR-04, the NAVAIR office in charge of the VAST program was AIR-417.

In terms of the three-level model discussed above, Intermediate maintenance at any carrier or shore site is a responsibility of the operating air wing, to whom the maintenance personnel belong. While a VAST technician would never work on the aircraft itself under normal conditions, the VAST personnel nevertheless belong to the squadron whose WRAs they service. Maintainers at both the squadron and intermediate levels work with and through NAVSUP ("Supply") both to obtain materials needed for their maintenance work and to hold materials after repair.

This structure defines the second major aspect of the "complexity" referred to in this study. The Navy's matrix is in fact a three-way matrix, with different types of authority being exercised by functional managers, program (weapon system) managers, and by "cognizant" field managers and budgetary control. A Program Management office will be in charge of the development of a new system (like VAST, or the F-14), and will coordinate it with the different functional offices (including those in charge of the logistics elements), with each office having specific funding for different parts of the program. Systems in development will resolve issues within other units, with "hand-offs" of the system occurring as it moves through its development cycle toward deployment. As the new system moves into preliminary testing and field assessment, other units will become participants in their respective specialities, and so on until the new system becomes fully operational. At that time, control is passed to a "cognizant" field manager with different budgetary authority for operation and maintenance of the system. Coordination and control of all issues affecting operation, maintenance, and upgrading of the system will be passed to a specific base or field site.

The primary concern of this study is the operational sites, and the consequences of deploying a new generation of test equipment to them. The sites are all operating bases, whether on carriers or ashore. The principal focus of the study is the effectiveness of the maintenance departments at those sites in providing adequate levels of WRAs to the squadrons who need them to keep aircraft in operational readiness. However, the complexity of the Navy organization is a background factor which can never be overlooked or forgotten. If a problem in the operation of any deployed system is found, a potentially large number of organizational units may become involved in the investigation and correction of the problem, and for all deployed systems, the minimum number of participants will be the affected units of the logistics "tail," as described in Chapter 2.

The Aircraft Intermediate Maintenance Department

A generic intermediate-level maintenance organization in the Navy is called an Intermediate Maintenance Activity (IMA); the department within the IMA responsible for aircraft and avionics is the Aircraft Intermediate Maintenance Department (AIMD), and both carriers and larger shore sites have an AIMD. The AIMDs are responsible for maintaining everything that can be removed from an aircraft, i.e., WRAs. WRAs include tires, tailhooks, engines, hydraulics, guns, safety and survival equipment, and support equipment, as well as avionics. Figure 3.6 shows a summary of the divisions within the AIMD and the number of branches and Work Centers ("shops") within each division. VAST is only one shop in this total set—its Navy organizational code is Work Center 65P. A complete list of the organizational codes in effect at the time of the first wave of this study (from about 1976 through 1980) is provided in Appendix 3.2.

Each AIMD is under the command of a Maintenance Officer, and one or more assistants. An important office and function in the AIMD is the Maintenance and Production Control Office, which is notified of all "inductions" of repairable WRAs, schedules them for repair in the appropriate Work Center, and monitors and coordinates production with Supply and the air wing. The Production Control Officer (PCO) becomes very busy once air operations begin on a carrier. More than any other location in the repair cycle, Production Control (PC) is in a central informational location, being the hub of all inductions, scheduling, and feedback from the Work Centers. In addition to PC, each AIMD will contain a Technical Library, a Quality Assurance officer, various material screening and control officers, a safety officer, and as many as twelve training officers or functions, for all aspects of AIMD maintenance training.

Most Work Centers in an AIMD use the WRA-specific test equipment referred to in the general description in Chapter 2. This equipment is "dedicated" or "peculiar to" the WRAs it tests, and in Navy nomenclature it is known as Peculiar Ground Support Equipment (PGSE). Repairable items scheduled for repair with PGSE are sent to the appropriate shop on direction of the Production Control Office. It should be noted that prior to the introduction of VAST, all avionics WRAs were also repaired with PGSE.

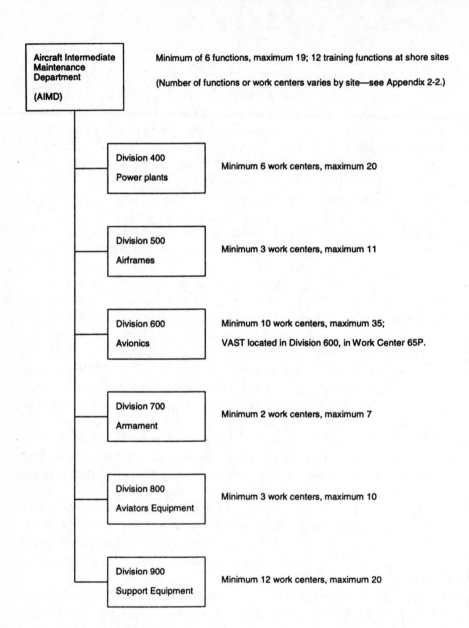

Figure 3.6   Aircraft Intermediate Maintenance Department organization and functions

Details of the Avionics Repair Cycle

This section provides a detailed description of the repair cycle, and shows the relationships between the O-level activities, Supply, and the various I-level shops involved in avionics maintenance. While other repair cycles follow a similar workflow, the avionics repair cycle is the most complex in the AIMD.

Figure 2.2 showed the concept of the remove-and-replace cycle of operations in the repair cycle. Figure 3.7 shows the actual repair cycle in terms of the three maintenance levels and their relationship through Supply and a related screening unit.

O-level maintainers remove the WRAs from aircraft. A removed WRA is taken to the Supply area and exchanged for a WRA which has been completely tested and is known to work correctly, which is termed Ready For Issue (RFI). Removed turn-in WRAs are then checked against a list of on-site repairables by a screening unit co-located with Supply; this screening unit determines if the WRA can be repaired on site, must go to D-level maintenance, or is disposable. The large majority of inductions are I-level repairables, and one of the Navy's objectives over time is always to maximize the number of WRAs that can be repaired on site at the intermediate level. Most D-level repairables are lost to the local site for a period of time, and this can create stockouts, especially on a carrier.

There will be some minor variations in arrangements at individual sites, but Figure 3.7 shows the overall workflow in any AIMD. Coordination of the workflow is managed by a Material Control office (not shown), which acts as liaison between Supply and the various shops on the site. Material Control establishes delivery and pickup points for materials in the repair cycle, routes materials to the proper repair shop, and advises individual departments on the stock status of materials stored there. In this connection, Material Control is an important source of information for determining repair priorities for components in the repair cycle. Each department at large sites has a Production Control Office, which sets the production priorities for the shops in the department, and provides information to Material Control to keep repair status current for each type of material. Depending on the site, the relationship between Material Control and Production Control will vary, but the functions described in this paragraph are performed at all sites.

The repairable WRA is sent to the appropriate shop in the AIMD. Testing identifies Shop Replaceable Assemblies (SRAs) which may be the cause of the fault; those SRAs removed in the I-level work centers are screened the same way as WRAs, and some must go to D-level maintenance.

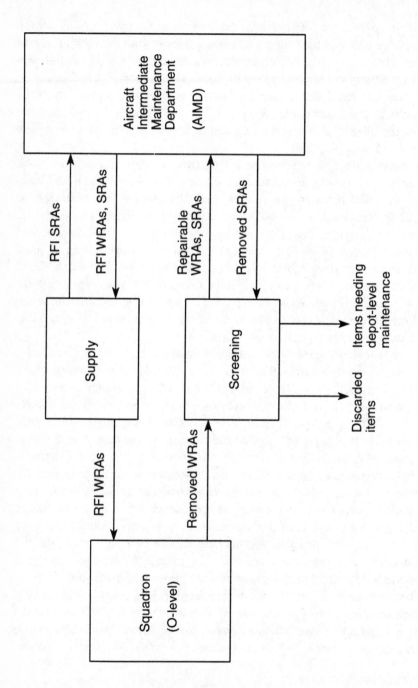

Figure 3.7   Expanded simplified model of avionics repair cycle

Working SRAs (i.e., RFI SRAs) are obtained by the I-level shop from Supply, used to replace the SRAs removed from the WRA under repair, and when the WRA completes the test cycle completely and correctly after SRA replacement, it is tagged as RFI and is returned to Supply. Note that while there are many details to be described in the workflow, the basic model operating throughout is a cycle of remove-and-replace activity, with I-level testers and Supply storage for each repairable item. The testers test and verify the functioning of the WRAs and SRAs repairable on the site. In Navy lexicon, a "repair" has not been accomplished until the unit which has had parts replaced has been tested and verified to be working as it should; thus, to "replace" parts is necessary for a repair, but a "repair" also requires a verification test.

The detailed avionics repair cycle is shown in Figure 3.8. This figure shows all of the major interactions between the three levels of repair, and expands the AIMD block in Figure 3.7 to show the VAST workflow within the AIMD. The flows between units in the repair cycle are numbered in order of a "chain of dependency" rather than a fixed sequence. The difference is that in the one-for-one exchange shown in Figure 3.7, the removed WRA from the squadron is immediately replaced with an RFI WRA. That may not happen if an RFI replacement is not available, and whether the RFI unit is available depends on what happens in this chain of dependency.

Each of the units in the repair cycle performs specialized functions; moreover, each is also a repository or "database" of one or more kinds of information needed to meet the repair cycle demands placed on that unit. I have designated these databases with italic acronyms. These databases will be described along with the flow of materials through the cycle. All actions taken in the repair cycle are recorded on a standard Maintenance Action Form (MAF), and the flows not only represent the physical movement of materials in the repair cycle, but the documentation of work performed by each unit before the component is released to the next work center. The MAF itself will be described in the next section. All description of the repair cycle will follow the flow of VAST-repairable avionics. The AIMD workflow in use at the time these data were collected is depicted as follows:

> **SQUADRON MAINTENANCE** (O-level) initiates the repair cycle when a WRA is removed from an aircraft. The WRA may not actually be malfunctioning, but has been identified as a potential source of trouble through in-flight failure, failure of pre-flight check, or by squadron maintenance testing. O-level maintainers remove one or more WRAs from an aircraft (depending on whether a problem or

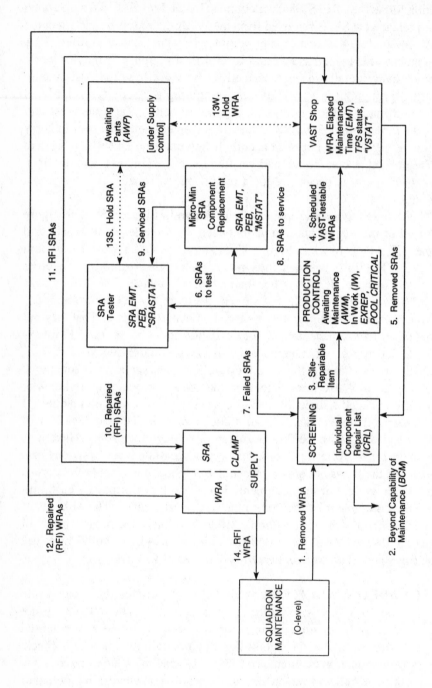

Figure 3.8   Workflow in the Aircraft Intermediate Maintenance Department (AIMD)

"gripe" can be identified with only one WRA) and complete an Aircraft Part Removal Form, the top part of which is placed in the cockpit and the bottom given to squadron maintenance control. A tag showing the part to be inoperable is attached to the WRA, and data are entered on a Maintenance Action Form (MAF) which is attached to the WRA also. *Databases:* (1) mission requirements for aircraft, dictating WRAs needed; (2) part removals and first information for demands on Supply and the AIMD repair cycle.

Flow 1. The removed WRA(s) are taken to the Supply Response Section (SRS) for turn-in and exchange; the removed unit is given to the Aeronautical Material Screening Unit (AMSU). The AMSU is actually part of Material Control, but is usually co-located with Supply.

SCREENING. The screening unit (AMSU) determines whether the removed WRA is on a list of on-site (I-level) repairables, and if so, it is forwarded to the AIMD for repair. *Database:* the Individual Component Repair List (ICRL), which identifies all site repairables. In coordination with Supply, this screening also identifies "EXREP" and "POOL CRITICAL" components, which are discussed in connection with Supply below. Material Control is notified of the induction of local repairables; any item which can be repaired on site is now classified as Awaiting Maintenance (AWM), and is moved to a designated AWM holding area if it cannot be repaired immediately.

Flow 2. Some removed components are not repairable and must be sent to D-level repair. These are nominally Beyond Capability of Maintenance (BCM); there are specific reasons why a component might be BCM, from lack of training to do the repair on site, to technical complexity requiring manufacturer servicing; BCM codes and explanations are shown in Appendix 3.3. These BCM items are temporarily lost to the local site, but are eventually returned when the repair has been completed. There are often substantial delays until these return, however.

Flow 3. Site-repairable items are forwarded to the AIMD, and almost always go through a preliminary cleaning and decontamination by Corrosion Control. Many WRAs, for example, come in covered in grease and exhaust soot from jet engines; they may be wet; they may be rusted or otherwise corroded, and so on. When cleaned and prepared, they are placed in the department's AWM holding area.

PRODUCTION CONTROL schedules the items received for the appropriate repair shop. (Note that this is an information-processing activity which actually precedes the physical movement of the WRA into the AIMD; it is placed in this location in Figure 3.8 because some WRAs will be BCM and not inducted into the repair cycle.) During the 1970s and until the latter 1980s, tracking of items in the AIMD was done using Visual Information Display System (VIDS) boards. Each VIDS board has rows of plastic pockets, each of which holds a number of MAFs. The pockets are lapped over each other like shingles on a roof. These are hung on the walls of the PC office, and each shop has its own display board. The MAF is folded in a fixed location so that a job control number on it can be seen, and the folded form is put onto the board when the item is received. Each VIDS board is divided into three columns: Awaiting Maintenance (AWM), In Work (IW), and Awaiting Parts (AWP). As the component moves through the repair cycle, its MAF is moved to the appropriate column on the VIDS board, and the MAF is removed from the board when the component is repaired.

For the large majority of repairable items received, the normal sequence of repairs is done on a First-In, First-Out (FIFO) basis, as described briefly in Chapter 2. A particular Production Control Officer (PCO) may often decide to do things differently, however, for many good reasons. For example, a PCO may notice that a group of one type of WRA is accumulating in Awaiting Maintenance, and decide to process the group as a "batch." Such "batch processing" allows the TPS to stay on the VAST station, and only connect and disconnect each WRA from the TPS in turn until the batch is done. Batching is typically done in consultation with the chief of the test shop, and sometimes in consultation with Supply and Material Control. *Databases:* all phases of production and production priorities—AWM, In Work (IW), EXREP, and POOL CRITICAL. AWP is monitored as well, although AWP components are controlled by Supply.

Flow 4. When a VAST station is available, the WRA is moved from the AWM holding area to the VAST shop.

VAST SHOP. A detailed description of the steps in the VAST test-and-repair process will be given in Chapter 4, in connection with data on a number of studies of the shop processes. At present, I want to summarize the steps an operator goes through with a WRA after it has been brought to the VAST shop, assuming everything goes as it should. The operator gets the WRA, usually bubble-wrapped, puts it on the rolling cart, and reads an identifying code from it.[2] This code is then referred to a master index card file located in the shop, which tells the operator which TPS to use, and where the tape or disk, cables, tools, technical manuals, etc., which make up the TPS are located. Everything is numbered, coded, and stored in specific locations.

When the TPS is gathered, the sailor goes to the VAST station, mounts the program tape or disk, and proceeds with a "Build-Up" of the WRA. The "Build-Up" means connection of the cables to the WRA; of the Interconnecting Device to the VAST station; and then the other end of the cable to the ID; locking down; grounding; and any other preparation activities needed to test the WRA. The test program is then begun, and the station computer takes over. The progress of the testing is shown on the station display, and instructions to the operator are given according to the results of the tests. These instructions could be to open the WRA when a "fault isolation" is indicated; or electrical safety precautions to take; or to remove one or more SRAs, all of which are identified by a letter-number code on the SRA, on the WRA frame or housing, and referenced on the display instruction; or to get replacement SRAs from Supply and insert them (Flow 11); and to repeat that part of the test which identified the SRA that was replaced.

To the greatest extent possible, WRAs are designed to be repaired while connected to the VAST station, and this is primarily a matter of removing and replacing SRAs once a fault isolation has been determined. The cluster of SRAs to which the fault is isolated is called the "ambiguity group" of SRAs, and the group can be as small as one SRA, or in some cases as many as five. Repair while the WRA is still connected to the VAST station is referred to as an "on-line" repair. In some cases an "off-line" repair is needed, and then the WRA must be detached and sent to another work center to have parts replaced. In a small number of cases, the VAST shop may be unable to repair the WRA, in which case it will be categorized as Beyond Capability of Maintenance (BCM), and sent back to the AMSU for disposition.

It is not necessarily true that a removed WRA has actually failed—other electronic interactions on the aircraft may have produced a spurious malfunction signal, a connector may have been loosened by a hard landing, or other factors may have necessitated removal of it. Once the WRA is removed, however, it must be tested and certified as Ready For Issue (RFI), and that cannot be done without a "clean" end-to-end test on VAST. All SRAs removed in the ambiguity group must also be tested and certified as RFI. Again, a "repair" has not been achieved until the WRA or SRA has been completely tested and no fault has been found. Simply replacing an indicated item is not a repair. The important point is that everything issued by Supply must be RFI, and nothing is returned to Supply for re-issue without proof of RFI status from a test.

When the WRA tests as RFI, the VAST station printer prepares an RFI tag to be attached to the WRA. The WRA is then bubble-wrapped, the RFI tag attached, and the WRA is returned to Supply to await the next time it is needed (Flow 12). The last step is the "Tear-Down," in which all of the TPS parts are removed from the WRA and VAST, and returned to their storage locations.

One final issue to be considered is the availability of the VAST station. Because it is a complex electronic device itself, VAST occasionally breaks down. However, many "breakdowns" involve only one of the Building Blocks (BBs), and the station may be able to repair WRAs which do not require that BB. What the station is able to test without that BB may not be the next item in the AWM queue, but at least some other WRA can be tested, and the queue continues to be reduced while the full station capability is restored. *Databases:* (1) Elapsed Maintenance Time (EMT) for complete WRA repair; (2) TPS status, and (3) station availability and capability (VSTAT).

I have designated this latter database on station availability as "VSTAT," to signify that it is the VAST station status; the Navy refers to this database as "test bench status." This database may be maintained in either the VAST shop or Production Control, and should be known to both. A station may be fully operational, partially operational (usually with one or more BBs degraded or not functioning, but still able to repair WRAs which do not require that BB), nonoperational, or operational but not in current calibration. This tester-status information is needed by Production Control to decide which WRAs to repair next.

Elapsed Maintenance Time. This database is especially important. Elapsed Maintenance Time (EMT) is the length of time (minutes, or hours and minutes) needed to complete the repair of a WRA in the VAST shop. It is measured and recorded for every repair. EMT comprises the setup time needed to gather the WRA and the TPS, the Build-Up/Tear-Down (BU/TD) time needed before and after testing, time needed for on-line repair, and the testing and retesting needed to ensure that the item is RFI. EMT is a significant measure of shop performance. Every shop in the AIMD repair cycle accumulates EMT specific to that shop.

Flow 5. Removed SRA(s) are treated in the same way as removed WRAs. They are screened for local repair capability, are then sent to Production Control for scheduling to the appropriate AIMD shop (Flow 3), and are held in AWM storage until the necessary SRA tester is available. SRAs which cannot be repaired on site are sent for D-level maintenance (Flow 2). Many more SRAs are likely to be BCM than WRAs; this can result in a serious reduction of spare SRAs for some items. Some of the BCM SRAs are disposable units which are not designed for repair when they fail.

Flow 6. When the appropriate SRA tester is available, Production Control releases the SRA from AWM storage and sends it to the shop.

SRA TESTER. These are also automatic testers like VAST, but usually specialized to test a particular category of SRAs, such as digital or analog SRAs. Three of these were most important to the repair of VAST-supported components.

In fact, VAST was equipped with TPSs which enable it to test SRAs as well as WRAs, and so both types of components should be tested and repaired in the same shop. But by the mid-1970s, VAST was so overloaded with work that specialized SRA testers were bought. SRA testers are also subject to failure, and most can operate with some degree of degradation. However, it is more likely that failure of an SRA tester will completely shut it down, and until it is repaired, SRAs requiring that tester will accumulate in an AWM backlog. Some SRAs contain "sub-SRAs," which are smaller replaceable boards which fit onto the SRA. Other components may be items such as relays, transistors, etc., and these are collectively known as "bit and piece" parts. All bit and piece parts which an SRA shop is authorized to replace are provided in batches, or "kits," and held in the SRA shop until needed.

The SRA Test shops also test SRAs on which parts have been replaced by the Micro-Min shop, discussed below. *Databases:* (1) Elapsed Maintenance Time for SRA repair; (2) station availability and capability ("SRASTAT," similar to "VSTAT);" and (3) inventory status for bit and piece parts (PEB), which will be explained in the description of Supply.

Flow 7. Failed SRAs are sent to the AMSU for screening for on-site repairability; as with other assets, some will be BCM, but many SRAs have replaceable components on them which are too small to replace in the SRA shop. These are sent to Production Control and held AWM until the Component Replacement Shop ("Micro-Min") is ready for them (Flow 3).

Flow 8. When the shop is ready, repairable SRAs and sub-SRAs are released for servicing.

MICRO-MIN, or actually the "Micro-Miniature" shop, can do repairs on very small, often nearly microscopic, parts on the SRA. A stereoscopic repair bench allows technicians to do a variety of mechanical and electrical repairs on the SRAs which cannot be done with the unaided eye. These shops have often become so proficient that they have been able to repair SRAs which were considered unrepairable, and were coded for disposal when they failed. *Databases:* (1) Elapsed Maintenance Time for SRA repair; (2) station availability and capability ("MSTAT"); and (3) inventory status for bit and piece parts (PEB).

Flow 9. Serviced SRAs are forwarded from Micro-Min directly to the SRA test shop for testing, to certify that the replacement of bit and piece parts actually have made the SRA operable.

Flow 10. When the SRA passes, it is tagged RFI and returned to Supply.

Flow 11. As discussed in connection with the VAST shop, RFI SRAs are drawn from Supply to repair WRAs in test.

Flow 12. When the WRA under test is certified as RFI, it is tagged, bubble-wrapped, and returned to Supply.

Flow 13. This flow has not been discussed until this point, because it only occurs when parts are not available for a repair. A stockout can occur in the repair of either a WRA (unavailability of an SRA—flow 13W) or an SRA (unavailability of a sub-SRA or a bit and piece part—flow 13S). In either case, the item in repair is removed from the tester, and put into an Awaiting Parts (AWP) holding area until the necessary replacement part arrives, which may take some time. The item in the repair flow is designated as AWP status in Production Control by moving the MAF for the item into the AWP column of the VIDS board. When the part arrives, the item needing it is removed from AWP storage, and the repair cycle resumes.

SUPPLY is the interface between all units on the repair cycle needing spare parts of any kind.[3] Supply is also the legal custodian of all materials in the repair cycle, even when they are physically removed and in the repair cycle. "Ownership" is actually technically given over to the on-site or off-site maintenance facility holding the item, but the final responsibility for government property rests with Supply. This is also true for bit and piece parts, which are technically known as "Pre-Expended Bins" (PEB), because they are pre-positioned in the work centers that consume them in bulk. For example, many bit-and-piece parts are used in Micro-Min to repair SRAs, so open bins of them are simply placed there by Supply.

In many ways, the repair cycle literally works for the Supply organization. So long as WRAs and SRAs are repaired and returned RFI, materials are available to any units needing them. Material Control, Supply, and the screening unit (AMSU) therefore provide information to the AIMD Production Control Office when stocks become too low. If a replacement item is not available for a removed one, the Maintenance Action Form for the removed item will be stamped "EXREP" for "EXpedite REPair." For a WRA, this means that there is an aircraft unavailable because of the stockout, and the item should be given top priority for repair. If a replacement is available for a removed item, but it is the last one from stock, the MAF for that item will be stamped "POOL CRITICAL," meaning that Supply is out of stock for that item, even though the most recent order was filled. Pool Critical items should be the first to be repaired after EXREPs. By communicating the status of critically low stocks to Production Control and being able to modify PC repair-priority decisions, Supply plays an important role in preventing stockouts and in keeping aircraft operational. One particular group of components is carefully monitored for that reason. This group is managed under a separate program known as the Closed-Loop Avionics Maintenance Program, or CLAMP. *Databases:* Status of inventories—WRA, SRA, CLAMP.

Flow 14. The final link in the chain of interdependence comprising the repair cycle is the ability of Supply to fulfill the request for an RFI WRA for a squadron. While this is ordinarily conceived of as a reciprocal to the removal of a WRA and its turn-in to the Screening unit, it is dependent on all other processes in the repair cycle.

Turnaround Time. A second particularly important database is Turnaround Time (TAT). TAT is the length of the AIMD repair cycle, from initial turn-in of a removed WRA until it is returned to Supply in RFI condition. TAT is measured in days and fractions of days. TAT is the most important overall measure of AIMD performance, since any component In Work in the repair cycle is unavailable to the operating squadrons. TAT may be thought of as a "system" measure of performance, where Elapsed Maintenance Time, the time required to do a repair in the VAST shop, is specific to only that one part of the overall repair cycle done in that shop. Unlike the other databases described here, TAT is not associated with individual shops or activities, but instead reflects the performance of the entire AIMD repair cycle.

Together, EMT and TAT are the most important performance measures to monitor for purposes of the research reported in this book. EMT is relevant to the VAST shops (or any other work center); it is the in-shop repair time for each WRA. TAT is the performance measure for the entire repair cycle, and it consists of four components: "processing time," the time needed to remove items by squadron personnel, exchange them for an RFI unit, screen them, and get them into the repair cycle;[4] "scheduling time," the time used to evaluate the AIMD workload and set a priority for the removed item of repair, plus Awaiting Maintenance, which is the delay until the WRA can be sent to the shop for repair; EMT, the time spent in the shop repair process; and AWP, the time spent Awaiting Parts after a repair process has begun, but for which a required part was unavailable (see Flow 13). Therefore:

$$TAT = processing + scheduling + EMT + AWP.$$

TAT for all repair cycles will include processing, scheduling, and EMT, whether the WRA was actually defective or not. Only those repairs delayed for unavailable parts will also include an AWP component.

As Figure 3.8 shows, there are 14 separate flows (each representing data entry on the MAF as well as physical movement of materials) and 19 databases contained within the AIMD repair cycle. This view is accurate and comprehensive, although still somewhat simplified. WRA TAT consists of all of the work necessary to take an inducted WRA through all necessary steps to put it back in the Supply storeroom, i.e., everything required to complete flow 12. That may vary from a simple test that indicates that the WRA was falsely identified as the source of an aircraft problem, in which case it is tagged RFI and returned to Supply, to having to complete every loop in the AIMD, and some loops more than once.

Documentation and Data Collection: The Maintenance Action Form

Throughout the U.S. Navy, all maintenance actions and materials movements are thoroughly documented.   The standard form for collecting this information is the Maintenance Action Form (MAF) introduced above. A MAF is designed to be used with the VIDS board in Production Control, and so the form is technically known as a VIDS MAF. A sample MAF is shown in Figure 3.9.

Volume III of the Naval Aviation Maintenance Program (NAMP) provides complete instructions for entering data on the MAF.   While technicians can enter some things in general language, the majority of the data collected on the MAF is entered using specific alpha-numeric codes, which are provided in the NAMP. Dates are always entered in Julian date format (year and day-sequence number, as 98069 for March 10, 1998; March 10 is the 69th day of the year). Specific codes for how a malfunction was discovered, the type of action taken, and other information, are used. The malfunction description codes used when these studies were conducted (and most remain current) are shown in Appendix 3.4. These codes are used to enter data into block A36 ("Mal Code") of the MAF. Codes which uniquely identify each WRA and SRA are provided in the NAMP, and these are used to enter the "Work Unit Code" in block A22; and similarly for part numbers, time cycles, and other data.   A large part of the training program for a maintenance technician is devoted to learning these codes and where to find them, to ensure correct data entry. MAFs are reviewed by shift supervisors in the work centers and periodically audited.   MAF data are therefore generally accurate and reliable.

In the repair cycle, a MAF is initiated by the squadron technician who first removes a WRA from an aircraft. That MAF will be attached to the WRA on turn-in to Supply and the screening unit when a new item is obtained. The same MAF will be annotated when the WRA is tested and repaired. If the WRA or its components need additional repair, new MAFs will be initiated for those items, and kept with the "mother MAF" until a full repair of the WRA is completed.

Copies of MAFs are sent to a site data-entry location, and cumulative data are sent to the Navy's central data depot in Mechanicsburg, Pa. Among other data collected on the MAF, dates and times for maintenance actions are recorded, so that MAF data are the basis for computation of EMT and TAT. Data used for analysis of the repair cycle in Chapter 6 were obtained from this depot.

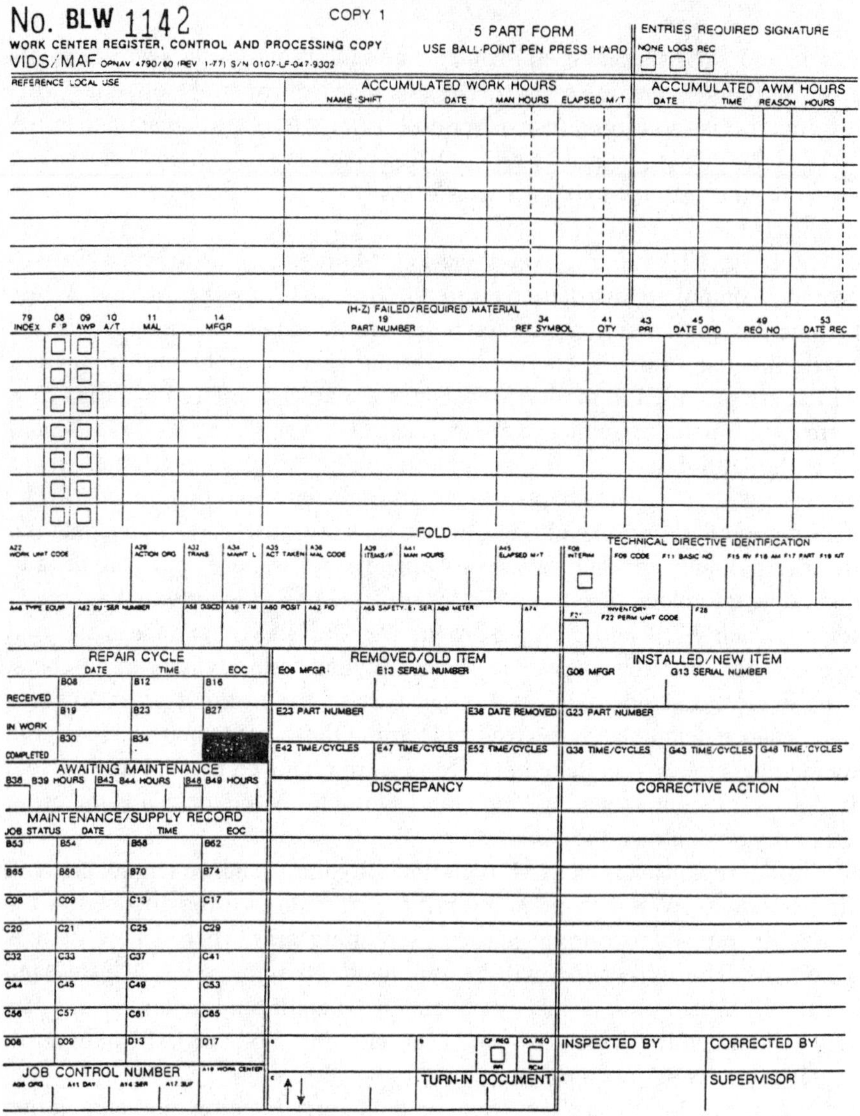

Figure 3.9   A standard Maintenance Action Form (MAF)
Source: NAVAIRINST 4790.2B, Naval Aviation Maintenance Plan

"Experiment 1:" The Deployment of VAST

To conclude this chapter, it is helpful to summarize some of the effects that the introduction of VAST had on the information processing done in the avionics repair workflow. We will begin by looking into the "experiment" that VAST imposed on an avionics workflow designed for dedicated PGSE shops. Following that, we will examine some of the IPT effects in a bit more detail, in preparation for a review of the first VAST shop studies covered in Chapter 4.

The AIMD workflow description in the previous section reflects the theory of operation of an AIMD, and for the VAST shop particularly. As is the case in any organization, there are some exceptions and local variations in actual operations in this workflow. What this description points out is that apparently simple reciprocal relationships depend on a great many things working well. Sometimes they do not work as intended, and small exceptions can amplify each other to become major system dysfunctions. The most important of these exceptions will discussed in Chapter 4, and their impact on the workflow will be examined there as well. For the present, I want to note that there were significant variations in the throughput of VAST shops. Some of these variations were specific to particular WRAs or their Test Program Sets, some were specific to VAST itself, and some were due to other variables such as technician skill levels. The main point is that the "automatic" in Automatic Test Equipment refers to the computer execution of the tests.

Actual VAST operations vary, as one would expect in such a complex workflow. One of the problems in understanding and analyzing VAST and AIMD workflow performance is this variability—it is very difficult to say what constitutes a "typical" repair process within the VAST shop alone. To provide some insight into how much variability there is, Table 3.2 summarizes the findings from a survey team which recorded data at a number of sites in 1979 and 1980. Each column of the table (after the left-most column of labels) shows the experience with one or more WRAs processed at each site on each survey. Note that different WRAs from different aircraft were observed, and in two observations multiple WRAs were processed. "Activities" in the table correspond to the description of VAST repair activities as described above, in summary terms; "idle time" refers to time when the station was connected to the WRA but not actually working, usually because operators were doing an "on-line" repair or were consulting technical publications or other personnel.

Table 3.2 Survey findings for VAST test and repair processing

Site	NAS Oceana	NAS Cecil Field	NAS Miramar	USS *Nimitz* (1)	USS *Nimitz* (2)	USS *Nimitz* (3)	USS *Nimitz* (4)
WRAs processed	F-14 fire control panel	2 S-3A ASCU computer power supplies; 2 S-3A armament control panels	F-14 electrical air temperature control unit	1 each F-14 yaw computer, RPM indicator; multi-channel auxiliary control	F-14 VDIG cockpit display converter	F-14 left glove vane switching assembly	S-3A switching logic unit
Activity	Minutes	Minutes	Minutes	Minutes	Minutes	Minutes	Minutes
WRA test	144	352	253	226	12	52	187
TPS Build-Up	30	56	42	68	7	29	29
TPS Tear-Down	6	47	13	38	1	7	0
VAST maintenance	153	228	178	0	31	0	131
WRA repair	85	62	81	44	15	0	140
Fetch materials	37	30	16	12	0	17	4
Paperwork	13	36	18	42	0	3	13
Idle time	0	153	156	102	40	4	127
Total minutes	468	964	757	532	106	112	631
Activity	Percent	Percent	Percent	Percent	Percent	Percent	Percent
WRA test	31	36	33	43	11	47	30
TPS Build-Up	6	6	5	13	7	26	4
TPS Tear-Down	1	5	2	7	1	6	0
VAST maintenance	33	24	24	0	29	0	21
WRA repair	18	6	11	8	14	0	22
Fetch materials	8	3	2	2	0	15	1
Paperwork	3	4	2	8	0	3	2
Idle time	0	16	21	19	38	3	20
Total percent	100	100	100	100	100	100	100

Source: ATE Operations Site Detail Report (undated). Syossett, N.Y.: Harris Corporation, Government Support Systems Division.

The upper block of rows shows the actual times in minutes as recorded by the survey team. Actual times correspond closely to the working times recorded by Navy guidelines on the MAF, i.e., they are the components of Elapsed Maintenance Time (EMT). The lower block of rows show those times in percentages. These rows are the most informative—for example, WRA test time varies from as little as 11 percent of the total to 47 percent; TPS Build-Up from 4 to 26 percent. Idle time varied from none to nearly 40 percent of total EMT.

Several sources of variability in EMT are apparent. The most important and obvious is that different WRAs take significantly different times to test, as noted above. The second is a function of whether the VAST station itself requires maintenance during the repair cycle—this varied from zero to 33 percent of total EMT. Third, complex TPS build-ups can require over 25 percent of total EMT, but usually take much less. TPS teardown, materials fetching (usually replacement SRAs), and MAF documentation generally take little time. Idle time, however, can vary significantly.

From its inception, the objective of VAST development was to reduce the number of discrete (PGSE) testers needed for aircraft maintenance, and VAST did that very well. But in doing that, VAST collapsed what would have been a large number of discrete workflows into a single workflow, and one which was still supposed to function as a discrete workflow on a FIFO basis. The nature of this change is shown in the comparison of Figure 3.10 to Figure 3.11, and its importance was not recognized for a long time.

What Figure 3.10 shows is that after screening and induction into the repair cycle, failed WRAs in the "dedicated tester" world each went to their respective PGSE repair shop. In queueing theory this is termed a "multiple-channel single-phase" model, where each WRA followed a specific channel, and was completely serviced in one phase, i.e., in one shop. Whether the WRA was simple or difficult to repair had no impact on the servicing of other types of WRAs in the overall AIMD flow. After the introduction of VAST (Figure 3.11), WRAs entered a queue and were repaired on a FIFO basis. If everything in the entire AIMD worked as designed, VAST would function as a "single-channel single-phase" model; but because of the need for off-line repairs, the inability to test SRAs on the station, and other factors that will be examined in Chapter 4, VAST actually functioned as an implicit multiple-phase shop, and each linkage between the phases was an opportunity for delay.

The importance of this change was that the priority assigned to "WRA-22," the last WRA to enter the queue, could change while the WRA was in the queue. That is, "WRA-22" may not have been EXREP or POOL

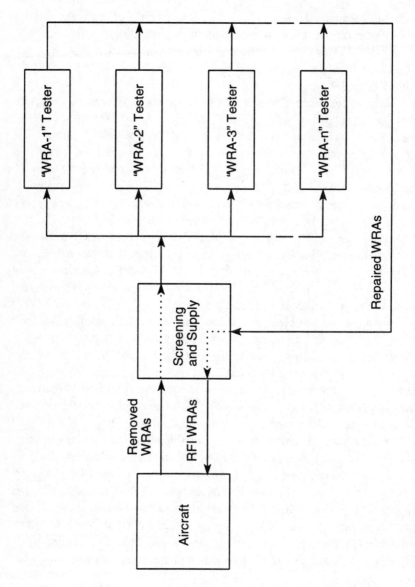

Figure 3.10 "Dedicated" (PGSE) avionics tester maintenance flow (before VAST)

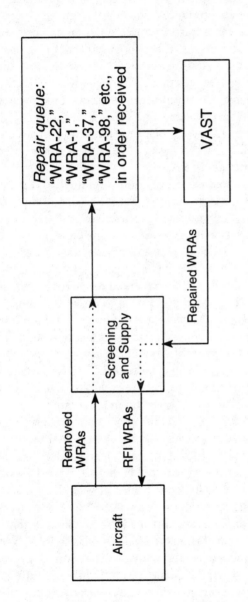

Figure 3.11   Avionics maintenance flow after introduction of VAST

CRITICAL when it entered the AWM queue, but several subsequent demands may have exhausted the RFI pool. If "WRA-22" was not moved to the top of the queue under these circumstances, an aircraft might be grounded. Many things could influence a repair priority for a WRA, as can be seen from the description of the workflow above. Since the AIMD organization design was considered to be valid for VAST, as for any PGSE tester, and since VAST was only one of a large number of other shops, there was no readily apparent need to change the management or information processing procedure. What is more, even if that had been realized when VAST was introduced, it would have made little difference, since at that time there was no effective way to monitor all the variables or to process all the information needed to make continuous repair priority decisions.

Further, given the intense focus on technological operations and maintenance in the Navy, it is no surprise that the design of the maintenance organization followed an "engineering" perspective.[5] What this means is that the design of the organization is very similar to the units which are repaired in them—everything can be taken apart, examined, "fixed," and evaluated as an independent entity. Each shop has a specific job to do, a logistics tail designed to enable it to do it, and documented measures of performance to tell how well it is working and suggest what to do when it fails. With the constant rotation of personnel inherent to military organizations, and the requirement to not endanger civilians in combat situations, which limits their use on carriers, there is probably no alternative to this model. The "engineering" perspective thus established a decision frame where workflow problems were specified in terms of concrete localized variables, not dispersed, non-specific issues like information processing.

The information-processing effect of VAST on repair priority decisions was to increase the amount of "variety" in the system (Ashby, 1964), in two important ways. First, the composition of the queue had to be continuously evaluated in ways that were never required in the PGSE world—with PGSE, once a WRA was released to its work center, it was "In Work" and of no further concern to Production Control. Even if the WRA was one which was difficult to repair, and might eventually lead to a stockout of that item, that repair process was independent from the repair of other WRAs. With VAST, an item might go into the queue, and while it was waiting, several more of other kinds would also go into the queue, resulting in a critically low supply of one WRA because of the accumulation in the queue. Getting stuck on one difficult WRA could now lead to shortages and stockouts of others, regardless of whether they were easy or hard to repair, and regardless of the stock level priority of the WRA when it entered the queue. Putting it another way, repair priorities for a WRA could change while the WRA was Awaiting Maintenance, as a consequence of repair-cycle processing rates rather than operational demands. The versatility of VAST created a new type of stockout which I refer to as an "interdependence stockout." This kind of variability did not occur in the PGSE AIMD.

The design of the AIMD for PGSE meant that each shop was a largely independent entity, with its own information database and repair procedures. While there is intensive control of the data collection and information processing procedures in the overall AIMD, each unit operates relatively autonomously and without central coordination. IP capacity in the AIMD was adequate for PGSE workflows, in other words. VAST created new ways for the system to vary because of the new interactions between individual WRA stock levels resulting from the creation of mixed-WRA repair queues within one shop. For the present, it should be noted that the Navy found arguments about IP capacity to be very counterintuitive, and hard to accept— VAST outwardly looked like PGSE in the flow of work, and there was no apparent reason to look into IP as an issue; it never had been before. Further, if one examines Figure 3.8, it applies to the PGSE workflow as a general model—there would be many "VAST" shops, not just one. The workflow, in any other sense, was exactly the same.

This led to a second counterintuitive effect on repair-cycle decision-making. If the difficult WRAs were the ones that created backlogs, or seemed to, it was appealing to try to clear them from the pipeline first and then repair the easy ones. If a technician got stuck on a difficult WRA, it was almost certain that a backlog would develop and create the interdependence stockouts described above. However, this effect could occur for other reasons; for example, it would seem more efficient to reduce time consumed for Build-Up/Tear-Down cycles by building up a batch of removed WRAs, and then test them all at once. While this practice did save BU/TD time (see Table 3.2), the probability of stockouts of that WRA became very high because the batch was being accumulated, defeating the intention of the increased repair-cycle "efficiency." Any variable which could create such backlogs implied a need to do batch processing to increase throughput, but this ultimately contributed to interdependence stockouts and reduced aircraft readiness.

Putting this point into IPT terms, any variation which led to backlogs also increased the likelihood of batch processing to reduce the backlog; however, the batch processing introduced a "hot" feedback into the system which had exactly the opposite effect of that intended and ultimately increased the probability of stockouts, rather than decrease it. A similar effect was discovered by Hall (1976) in his study of the old *Saturday Evening Post*. With the volume of test work to do, the number of testers, the constant flow of materials in the cycle, and the time lags involved between the time the queue began to change composition and its relationship to batch processing, there was no way for AIMD managers to detect this state of the system.

These points will be examined in more detail when the results of the VAST-specific studies are reviewed in the next chapter. What is most significant to note at the present time is that the accession of VAST over earlier generations of testers was indeed an experiment, a fact which was not recognized for many years following VAST's introduction into the Fleet. While early experience indicated that the experiment had unintended consequences associated with it, some of which were undesirable, it was not clear what caused the problems until the larger system, i.e., the entire AIMD repair cycle, was investigated. This does not mean that VAST was simply inserted into the repair cycle with no regard for the potential that it might not work out as planned—far from it. As we will see in the next chapter, VAST was evaluated carefully and given close scrutiny from its inception until its deployment. However, even with these precautions and preliminary evaluations, the accession of VAST into the AIMD workflow had effects far beyond simply those of replacing an earlier generation of testers with the new one.

Notes

1. A good color jpeg-format image of a VAST station may be found at http://www.concentric.com/~cjkilpat/vast.shtml. This photograph shows the exterior cables on the front of the machine very clearly. Several newer testers can be seen at the same site, as well.

2. In Navy and industry automatic-test lexicon, any component or item in a test process is referred to as a Unit Under Test, or UUT. For the sake of simplicity, I will use more generic terms like "WRA," "component," and the like.

3. Technically, the local Supply unit is a branch of the Aviation Supply Office (ASO) called the Supply Support Center (SSC), and it consists of the Supply Response Section (SRS), which provides the exchange units needed for turn-ins, a section which controls local pools of repairable WRAs and SRAs, and a section to store and control any items which are AWP because of a stockout. Nearly all sites refer to this group of activities collectively as "Supply," as I have been doing.

4. The definition of "processing time" was changed slightly during the early phase of our study, as will be discussed in Chapter 4. Until late 1978, processing time consisted only of the work done to get the WRA into the Supply area for exchange. If a WRA laid in a pile for two days until it could be screened for local repair, that time was not measured. The new definition, appropriately, considers the WRA to accumulate processing time until it is actually screened and inducted.

5. It is also noteworthy that early criticisms of the Navy's decision to develop VAST tended to focus attention on the testers. As early as 1971, the General Accounting Office had issued a draft report suggesting that VAST could not provide adequate avionics support for the new aircraft the Navy was procuring.

References

Ashby, W. Ross (1964), *Introduction to Cybernetics.* New York: Wiley.

ATE Operations Site Detail Report (undated), Syossett, N.Y.: Harris Corporation.

Consolidated Support System Preliminary Systems Engineering Study (1983). Syossett, New York: Harris Corporation, Government Support Systems Division.

General Accounting Office (1971), *Draft report on development, production, and planned utilization of the Versatile Avionics Shop Test (VAST) system.* (OSD Case No. 3314). Washington, D.C.: General Accounting Office, 26 July 1971.

Hall, Roger I. (1976), A system pathology of an organization: The rise and fall of the old *Saturday Evening Post. Administrative Science Quarterly,* 21: 185-211.

Ill, Charles L., Memorandum for the Assistant Secretary of Defense (Comptroller), 2 September 1971.

NAVAIRINST 4790.2 series, *Naval Aviation Maintenance Program* (3 volumes), Washington, D.C.: Department of the Navy.

Operational Logistics Support Plan for AN/USM-247(V) VAST (Versatile Avionics Shop Test) System (1980). Washington, D.C.: U.S. Naval Air Systems Command (AIR-417; OLSP-CGSE-0093; AA-RE). Revision E: October, 1980.

Appendix 3.1

VAST Building Blocks

Number	Function
01	Interface and configuration switch
04	Control switch
10	Digital multimeter
11	Frequency and time interval meter
13	Delay generator
14	Digital subsystem
20	Signal generator 0.1 Hz - 50 kHz (sinusoidal)
21	Signal generator 10 kHz - 40 MHZ (sinusoidal)
22	Signal generator 20 - 500 MHZ (sinusoidal)
25	Signal generator 0.4 - 18.0 GHz (sinusoidal)
30	Servo analyzer
31	Synchro/resolver standard
33	Phase sensitive voltmeter
34	Pressure generator
36(-.1,-.2)	Function generator (non-sinusoidal)
38	Low frequency wave analyzer
40	Pulse generator (non-sinusoidal)
42(-A,-B)	Spectrum analyzer
45	RMS voltmeter
47	Average power meter
48(-A,-B)	Programmable oscilloscope
49	Ratio transformer
50(-.1,-.2-.3)	Low voltage DC power supply
51	DC power supply 22 - 32 V
52(-.1,-.2)	DC power supply 30 - 500 V
53	DC power supply 0.5 - 1.0 kV
55	AC power supply 400 Hz
57	RF measurement augmenter
61	Precision resistive load

62	High power resistive load
63	Display stimulus generator
MTTU	Magnetic Tape Transport Unit (now disk drives)
DTU	Data Transfer Unit/Operator Console

Source: *Operational Logistics Support Plan for AN/USM-247(V) Versatile Avionics Shop Test.* AIR-417, OLSP-CGSE-0093; AA-RE, Revision E: October 1980

Appendix 3.2

Work Center Codes

Work Centers

Organization And Intermediate Level

Code	Functions
*010	Maintenance Officer
01A	Assistant Maintenance Officer
01B	Maintenance/Material Control Officer
*020	Maintenance/Production Control
02A	IM-General Maintenance Branch (Shipboard only)
02B	IM-Avionic/Armament Branch (Shipboard only)
02C	IM-Ground Support Equipment Branch (Shipboard only)
*030	Maintenance Administration
*040	Quality Assurance
04A	Technical Library
04B	Safety (Ground)
04C	Analysis
*050	Material Control
05A	Material Screening
05B	Material Procurement
05C	Accountable Material
05D	Aviation Tool Issue/Tool Control Center (Marines)
070	Naval Air Engineering Support Unit (NAESU) Technical Services
080	FRAMP Instructor
08A	Engine Mechanic Training (AD rating)
08B	Airframes Structural Mechanic Training (AMS rating)
08C	Airframes Hydraulic Mechanic Training (AMH rating)
08D	Safety Survival Equipment Mechanic Training (AME rating)
08E	Aviators Equipmentman Training (PR rating)

08F	Electronics Technician Training (AT rating)
08G	Electrical Technician Training (AE rating)
08H	Ordnance/Weapons Technician Training (AO rating)
08J	Fire Control Technician Training (AQ rating)
08K	ASW Electronics Technician Training (AX rating)
08L	Plane Captain Training
08M	Ground Support Equipment/AS Training

Intermediate Level Only

400	Power Plants Division
*410	Jet Shop
41A	Inspections
41B	Engine Repair
41C	Component Repair
41D	Complete Engine Repair (CER)
41E	Auxiliary Power Plants
*420	Reciprocating Shop
42A	Inspections
42B	Engine Repair
42C	Component Repair
*430	Propeller Shop
43A	Propeller Repair
43B	Component Repair
*440	Rotor Dynamics Shop
*450	Test Cell
*460	Auxiliary Fuel Stores
46A	Engine Mechanic (AD)
46B	Airframes Hydraulic Mechanic (AMH)
46C	Electrician (AE)
*470	Naval Oil Analysis Program (NOAP)
480-490	Unassigned
500	Airframes Division
*510	Structures Branch
51A	Structures Shop
51B	Paint Shop
51C	Welding Shop
51D	Machine Shop
51E	Tire Shop

*520	Hydraulics Branch
52A	Hydraulics Shop
52B	Brake Shop
52C	Strut Shop
*530	Non-Destructive Test (NDT)
540-590	Unassigned
600	Avionics Division
60A	Avionics Corrosion Control
*610	Communication/Navigation Branch
61A	Communication Shop
61B	Navigation Shop
61C	Computer Shop
*620	Electrical/Instrument Branch
62A	Electric Shop
62B	Instrument Shop
62C	Battery Shop, Lead Acid
62D	Battery Shop, Nickel Cadmium
62E	CSD Shop
*630	Fire Control Branch
*640	Radar/ECM Branch
64A	Radar Shop
64B	ECM Shop
64C	DECM Shop
64D	FLIR Shop
*650	SACE/Inertial Navigation Branch
65A	SACE Shop
65B	AFC/Inertial Navigation System (INS) Shop
65C	Weapons Systems Missile Component Shop
65P	VAST Shop
*660	ASW Branch
*670	PME Branch/Field Calibration Activity
67A	PME Receipt and Issue Shop
67B	PME Calibration Shop
67C	PME Repair Shop
67D	PME AWP Shop
*680	Reconnaissance/Photo Shop
68A	Sensor System Shop
68B	Camera/ADAS Repair Shop
68C	Film Processing Shop
*690	Module/Component Test/Repair Branch

69A	Module Test Shop
69B	Module Repair Shop
700	Armament Division
*710	Ordnance Shop
71A	Ordnance Pool
71B	Gun Shop
71C	Armament Equipment Repair Shop
*720	Special Weapons Branch
72A	Special Weapons Test/Repair Shop
72B	Special Weapons Magazine
730-790	Unassigned
800	Aviators Equipment Division
*810	Aviators Equipment Branch
81A	Parachute Loft
81B	Survival Equipment
81C	Regulator Shop
81D	Fabrication Shop
*820	AME (Safety/Survival) Branch
82A	Escape/Environmental Systems Shop
*830	Oxygen/Nitrogen Branch
83A	Oxygen/Nitrogen Shop
83B	Liquid Oxygen (LOX) Farm
840-890	Unassigned
900	Support Equipment Division
90A	Production Control
90B	GSE Pool
90C	GSE Training/License
*910	Support Equipment Engine Repair Branch
91A	Air Start Repair
91B	Tow Tractor Repair
91C	Servicing Power Engine Repair
*920	Support Equipment Structural/Hydraulic Branch
92A	Structural Repair
92B	Hydraulic Repair
*930	Support Equipment Electrical Repair Branch
93A	Electric Servicing Power
93B	Battery Shop
*940	Support Equipment Component Repair Branch
*950	GSE Inspection Branch
95A	Corrosion Control Shop

*960	Installed Air Start Branch (Shipboard Only)
*970	Air Conditioning Branch
*980	GSE Flight Deck Troubleshooter Branch
*990	Mobile Support Center Branch

Other Units And Functions

X00	Miscellaneous
X10	Supply MAG/Navy
X20	In-Flight Maintenance
X30	Away from Home
X3A	Engine Mechanic (AD)
X3B	Structural Mechanic (AMS)
X3C	Hydraulic Mechanic (AMH)
X3D	Safety Survival Equipmentman (AME)
X3E	Aviators Equipment(PR)
X3F	Electronic Technician (AT)
X3G	Electrician (AE)
X3H	Ordnance/Weapons
X3I	Technician (AO)
X3J	Fire Control Technician (AQ)
X3K	ASW Electronic Technician (AX)
X3L	Plane Captain
X3M	Tradesman (TD)
X40	Assistance Teams—All man-hours expended by special assistance teams, i.e., personnel from NARF facilities, factory personnel (excluding technical reps), etc., are documented to this work center. (Code X40 is not applicable to the man-hour accounting system.)
X50	Contractor Support
XX0	Aviation Maintenance Personnel—Aviation Maintenance personnel working outside maintenance should be assigned to this work center unless assigned below.
XXA	TAD AIMD/IMA
XXB	TAD Supply
XXC	TAD School
XXD	TAD Galley
XXE	TAD Compartment Cleaning
XXF	TAD Ship/Station

XXG	Aircrew Training
XXH	Nuclear Training
XXJ	IST LT/Command Master Chief
XXK	Operations
XXL	TAD CAG

* denotes minimum requirement

Appendix 3.3

Beyond Capability of Maintenance (BCM) Codes

Codes   **Definition**

BCM 1 Repair Not Authorized. Repair of the item is not specifically authorized by the ship/activity individual component repair listing.

BCM 2 Lack of Equipment. Repair of the item cannot be accomplished because of a lack of test stands, special tools, etc.

BCM 3 Lack of Technical Skills. Repair exceeds the skill capability of assigned personnel.

BCM 4 Lack of Parts. Parts needed to accomplish the repair are not available locally or will not be received by the activity within specified time limits.

BCM 5 Shop Backlog. Excessive shop backlog precludes repair within specified time limits.

BCM 6 Lack of Technical Data. Repair cannot be accomplished because of a lack of a maintenance manual, drawing, etc.

BCM 7 Excess to Ship/Activity Requirements. Item will not be scheduled for repair because it is in excess of ship/activity allowance.

BCM 8 Budgetary Limitations. Repair of item not scheduled because of insufficient funds or use of limited funds for repair of items with more urgent priority.

BCM 9 Condemned. Item cannot be economically repaired and will be processed for condemnation, reclamation, or salvage.

Appendix 3.4

Malfunction Description Codes

Note: The following tables list the Malfunction Description Codes prescribed for use in the U.S. Navy 3-M maintenance data system.

956 ABNORMAL FUNCTION OF COMPUTER MECHANICAL EQUIPMENT
314 ACCELERATION IMPROPER
931 ACCIDENTAL OR INADVERTENT OPERATION, RELEASE, OR ACTIVATION
030 ACCIDENT/INCIDENT (GROUND)
127 ADJUSTMENT OR ALIGNMENT IMPROPER
687 AFTERBURNER LIGHT, HARD OR LATE
651 AIR IN SYSTEM
007 ARCING/ARCED
694 AUDIO AND VIDEO FAULTY
693 AUDIO FAULTY
652 AUTOMATIC ALIGN TIME EXCESSIVE
458 BALANCE INCORRECT/OUT OF BALANCE
731 BATTLE DAMAGE
710 BEARING FAULTY/FAILING
780 BENT
135 BINDING
303 BIRD STRIKE DAMAGE
838 B-PLUS HIGH
839 B-PLUS LOW
050 BLISTERED
070 BROKEN
108 BROKEN, FAULTY, OR MISSING SAFETY WIRE/KEY
719 BROKEN OR FRAYED BONDING/GROUND WIRE
183 BROKEN MAGNETIC TAPE
160 BROKEN WIRE, OR DEFECTIVE CONTACT/CONNECTION
720 BRUSH FAILURE-EXCESSIVE WEAR
780 BUCKLED
900 BURNT OR OVERHEATED
080 BURNT OUT LIGHT BULBS OR FUSES
070 BURST
969 CANNOT RESONATE INPUT CAVITY
020 CHAFED
130 CHANGE OF VALUE
150 CHATTERING
425 CHIPPED

780 COLLAPSED
180 CLOGGED, OBSTRUCTED, PLUGGED
163 COMMUTATOR/SLIP RING FAILURE
181 COMPRESSION LOW
028 CONDUCTANCE INCORRECT
185 CONTAMINATION
989 COOLANT FLOW RATE LOW
970 COOLANT LEAK
170 CORRODED
606 COUNTER RUN-OFF: POSITION INDICATOR
190 CRACKED/CRAZED
029 CURRENT INCORRECT
070 CUT
105 DAMAGED HARDWARE
972 DAMAGED INPUT PROBE
973 DAMAGED OUTPUT PROBE
955 DATA LINK HIGH ERROR
318 DECELERATION IMPROPER
846 DELAMINATED
780 DENTED
117 DETERIORATED/ERODED
601 DETONATION
306 DIRTY
958 DISPLAY INCORRECT
780 DISTORTED
932 DOES NOT ENGAGE, LOCK, OR UNLOCK PROPERLY
974 DOES NOT TRACK TUNING CURVE
051 DRIFTS
923 ENGINE MONITORING SYSTEM INDICATES EARLY INSPECTION REQUIRED
921 ENGINE MONITORING SYSTEM INDICATES FURTHER INVESTIGATION REQUIRED
922 ENGINE MONITORING SYSTEM INDICATES OVERTEMP LIMITS EXCEEDED
142 ENGINE REMOVED-EXCESSIVE MAINTENANCE EXCESSIVE HUM
330 EXTENSION/TRAVEL INCORRECT
599 EXTERNAL POWER SOURCE
424 FAILED, DAMAGED, OR REPLACED DUE TO MALFUNCTION
602 FAILED DUE TO MALFUNCTION OF ASSOCIATED EQUIPMENT OR ITEM
242 FAILED TO OPERATE-SPECIFIC REASON UNKNOWN
292 FAILS ACCEPTANCE TEST
291 FAILS AUTO-CHECK
290 FAILS DIAGNOSTIC/AUTOMATIC TESTS
293 FAILS SELF-CHECK
294 FAILS SELF-TEST
959 FAILS TO TRANSFER TO REDUNDANT EQUIPMENT
051 FAILS TO TUNE/DRIFTS
069 FLAME OUT
037 FLUCTUATES, INTERMITTENT, OR FREQUENCY/RPM UNSTABLE
696 FLUID LOW
101 FOCUS POOR

304 FOREIGN OBJECT DAMAGE-SELF-INDUCED BY INGESTION OF AIRCRAFT
   PARTS (DZUS BUTTONS, RIVETS, FASTENERS, ETC.)
303 FOREIGN OBJECT DAMAGE-BIRD STRIKE
301 FOREIGN OBJECT DAMAGE (OTHER THAN 303 OR 304)
719 FRAYED BONDING/GROUND WIRE
020 FRAYED
982 FROZEN TUNING MECHANISM
177 FUEL FLOW INCORRECT
277 FUEL NOZZLE COKING
088 GAIN INCORRECT
001 GASSY
188 GLAZED
030 GROUND ACCIDENT/INCIDENT DAMAGE
653 GROUND SPEED ERROR EXCESSIVE
086 HANDLING IMPROPER
311 HARD LANDING
687 HARD OR LATE AFTERBURNER LIGHT
961 HIGH ANODE CURRENT
985 HIGH BODY CURRENT/BEAM INTERRUPTION
986 HIGH BODY MODULAR INVERSE
281 HIGH OUTPUT, READING, OR VALUE
065 HIGH VOLTAGE STANDING WAVE RATIO
317 HOT START
087 IDENTIFICATION IMPROPER
169 INCORRECT VOLTAGE
987 INPUT PULSE DISTORTION
350 INSULATION BREAKDOWN
037 INTERMITTENT OPERATION
374 INTERNAL FAILURE
819 IMPEDANCE HIGH
817 IMPEDANCE LOW
916 IMPENDING OR INCIPIENT FAILURE INDICATED BY SPECTROMETRIC OIL
   ANALYSIS
806 IMPROPER HANDLING
087 IMPROPER IDENTIFICATION
246 IMPROPER OR FAULTY MAINTENANCE
437 IMPROPER POSITION SELECTED, OR OTHER OPERATOR ERROR
135 JAMMED
481 KEYWAY OR SPLINE DAMAGED OR WORN
410 LACK OF (IMPROPER) LUBRICATION
687 LATE OR HARD AFTERBURNER LIGHT
158 LAUNCH DAMAGE
381 LEAKING-INTERNAL OR EXTERNAL
383 LOCK-ON MALFUNCTION
447 LOGIC WRONG-PROGRAM OR COMPUTER
730 LOOSE
105 LOOSE BOLTS, NUTS, SCREWS, CLAMPS, OR OTHER HARDWARE
988 LOSS OF VACUUM
989 LOW COOLANT FLOW RATE

004 LOW GM OR EMISSION
282 LOW OUTPUT, READING, OR VALUE
962 LOW POWER (ELECTRONIC)
537 LOW POWER OR THRUST
410 LUBRICATION—IMPROPER/LACK OF
183 MAGNETIC TAPE BROKEN
706 MAGNETIC TAPE ERROR
604 MANIFOLD PRESSURE BEYOND LIMITS
688 MANUAL TRANSFER IMPROPER
704 MEMORY PROTECT
372 METAL IN OIL STRAINER, FILTER, ETC.
009 MICROPHONIC
092 MISMATCHED (ELECTRONIC PARTS., ETC.)
106 MISSING BOLTS, NUTS, SCREWS
093 MISSING PARTS
064 MODULATION INCORRECT
425 NICKED OR CHIPPED
682 NO AZIMUTH OR DRIFT
799 NO DEFECT
800 NO DEFECT-COMPONENT REMOVED AND/OR REINSTALLED TO FACILITATE OTHER MAINTENANCE
807 NO DEFECT-REMOVAL DIRECTED BY HIGHER AUTHORITY
806 NO DEFECT-REMOVED AS PART OF A MATCHED SYSTEM
811 NO DEFECT-REMOVED DURING TROUBLESHOOTING
801 NO DEFECT-REMOVED FOR MODIFICATION
805 NO DEFECT-REMOVED FOR POOL STOCK
804 NO DEFECT-REMOVED FOR SCHEDULED MAINTENANCE
803 NO DEFECT-REMOVED FOR TIME CHANGE
957 NO DISPLAY
990 NO FOCUS CURRENT
607 NO-GO INDICATION-SPECIFIC REASON UNKNOWN
683 NO/IMPROPER IMC
255 NO OUTPUT
685 NO SHUTTER TRIP PULSE
823 NO START
008 NOISY
306 NON-METALLIC CONTAMINATION OR DIRTY
914 NON-REPEATABLE IDLE TRIM
913 NON-REPEATABLE MIL/INTERMEDIATE TRIM
758 OBSOLETE OR SURPLUS
257 OFF COLOR
916 OIL ANALYSIS LAB REPORT RECOMMENDATION
398 OIL CONSUMPTION EXCESSIVE
603 OIL IN INDUCTION SYSTEM
450 OPEN
003 OPEN FILAMENT OR TUBE CIRCUIT
437 OPERATOR ERROR
457 OSCILLATING
458 OUT OF BALANCE

991 OUT OF BAND FREQUENCY
416 OUT OF ROUND
766 OUT OF SPECIFICATION
191 OUTPUT INCORRECT
992 OUTPUT PULSE DISTORTION
440 OVERAGE
464 OVERSPEED
429 PEELED
520 PITTED
180 PLUGGED, OBSTRUCTED, CLOGGED
101 POOR FOCUS
964 POOR SPECTRUM
938 POWER OUTPUT DIP
525 PRESSURE INCORRECT
705 PROGRAM DETERIORATION
703 PROGRAM FAILURE
698 PROGRAM-FAULTY CARD
697 PROGRAM-FAULTY TAPE
447 PROGRAM LOGIC WRONG
070 PUNCTURED
567 RESISTANCE HIGH
568 RESISTANCE LOW
993 RF DRIVE IMPROPER
994 RF FEED-THROUGH ATTENUATED/DISTORTED
966 RF WINDOW SUCKED IN, BROKEN, OR CRACKED
686 RUNAWAY OPERATION
070 RUPTURED
108 SAFETY WIRE/KEY MISSING, BROKEN, OR FAULTY
583 SCOPE PRESENTATION INCORRECT/FAULTY
935 SCORED, SCRATCHED, BURRED, GOUGED
585 SHEARED
615 SHORTED
707 SHORTED, INTERNAL
689 SHUTDOWN IMPROPER
681 SHUTTER HUNG-DEFECTIVE
685 SHUTTER-NO TRIP PULSE
679 SIGNAL DISTORTED
163 SLIP RING/COMMUTATOR FAILURE
964 SPECTRUM POOR
481 SPLINE DAMAGED/WORN
279 SPRAY PATTERN DEFECTIVE
329 STARTING STALL-HUNG START
105 STRIPPED BOLTS, NUTS, AND OTHER COMMON HARDWARE
020 STRIPPED
135 STUCK
503 SUDDEN STOP
617 SULFIDATION
758 SURPLUS
649 SWEEP MALFUNCTION

695 SYNC ABSENT OR FAULTY
334 TEMPERATURE INCORRECT
664 TENSION LOW
784 TIRE BEAD AREA DAMAGED OR DEFECTIVE
786 TIRE BLOWOUT
785 TIRE INSIDE SURFACE DAMAGED OR DEFECTIVE
781 TIRE LEAKAGE EXCESSIVE
788 TIRE REMOVAL DUE TO OTHER PRIMARY CAUSE
787 TIRE REMOVAL-NORMAL WEAR
783 TIRE SIDEWALL DAMAGED OR DEFECTIVE
782 TIRE TREAD AREA DEFECTIVE (USE CUT, DELAMINATED, WORN, PUNCTURED, ETC., IF APPLICABLE)
070 TORN
167 TORQUE INCORRECT
877 TRANSPORTATION DAMAGE
599 TRAVEL OR EXTENSION INCORRECT
780 TWISTED
561 UNABLE TO ADJUST TO LIMITS
037 UNSTABLE RPM OR FREQUENCY
988 VACUUM LOSS
690 VIBRATION EXCESSIVE
694 VIDEO AND AUDIO FAULTY
692 VIDEO FAULTY
169 VOLTAGE INCORRECT
684 WEAK/NO STABILIZATION
878 WEATHER DAMAGE
622 WET
020 WORN
447 WRONG LOGIC-PROGRAM OR COMPUTER

4 The VAST Shop Effectiveness and Efficiency Studies

Introduction

By the middle 1970s, it had become evident that WRAs dependent on VAST for maintenance were not being repaired quickly enough or in adequate volume. It appeared that VAST was unable to do everything it had been designed or intended to do. This was unwelcome news to the Navy, for two major reasons. First, VAST had been extensively studied and modeled through computer simulations prior to committing to it, and early experience during test and evaluation had led to expectations that its performance would meet requirements. Second, VAST was the only WRA tester available for its newest and most mission-critical aircraft (the F-14A, S-3A, and E-2C), many of which were experiencing Operational Readiness (OR) rates far below what had been projected, or what was needed. This meant that Fleet vulnerability was much higher than acceptable in the event of a shooting war. The results of the VAST "experiment" were clearly not what had been expected, and the Navy was concerned.

The work reviewed in this chapter was primarily a major study of VAST shop operations begun in 1976 and published within NAVAIR in 1979. This study grew from a review[1] of earlier work on VAST development and operations, and developed into a completely new study, with a team of seven people and a much greater scope than any of its predecessors. The prime contractor for this study was Systems Research Corporation (SRC),[2] with whom I worked during the study.

One of the most important aspects of this study is that it was the first to evaluate all elements of the logistics support "tail" for VAST at one time. However, much of the work in this study went beyond evaluation of the logistics program alone, as will be seen. The overall scope of this work was thus the most comprehensive of any investigations of the VAST workflow.

Much of what will be discussed in this chapter draws on the Systems Research Corporation study. Some of my findings were published in 1984,[3]

177

and all of them have been presented or made public to a variety of audiences in both the Navy and the aerospace industry, in addition to some presentations to academic audiences. Since the best way to understand the evolution of the studies is to understand the evolution of VAST, I have organized the material in this chapter chronologically.

The Development of VAST

As noted in Chapter 2, the Navy committed to the concept of VAST support for its aircraft in the 1960s. As with any major weapon system, there is a protracted period of concept evaluation before any new technology is developed, and VAST was no exception. The Department of Defense has established an extensive program of competitions, reviews, and tests for development of any new weapon system technology. This process is intended to minimize both the cost of new systems and the risks of technical failure, since any new technology brings such risks with it.

All new weapon systems are evaluated rigorously before being deployed, and so was VAST. VAST was developed through a period of early technical evaluations (appropriately referred to as TECHEVAL by the Navy), both from the perspective of the technical feasibility of the system as well as its ability to meet operational requirements if deployed. The latter evaluation is known as an Operational Evaluation, or OPEVAL. While technical feasibility was being evaluated, a number of computer simulations were done, which modeled the flow of WRAs through an AIMD with simulated VAST properties.[4] Physical replicas of VAST were built and laid out according to the shop deck plan proposed for the new carrier USS *Enterprise*, and a physical flow of work based on the computer simulations was also evaluated.[5] From these studies, VAST was expected to have the capability to meet the avionics workload generated by the aircraft VAST was to support. But one of the problems with this type of development program is that it is usually impossible to evaluate the new technology in truly operational terms, since several new systems are being developed simultaneously. In this case, VAST was being developed in parallel with the three new Naval aircraft it would support, the F-14A, E-2C, and S-3A.

The physical design of VAST stations was also being evaluated and modified throughout this period, while the computer simulations of the workload and AIMD operations were underway. Test and evaluation reports were generated continuously, and by 1972 a development model of VAST was placed on the USS *Kitty Hawk* for at-sea trials under operating conditions.[6] This study concluded that VAST was able to meet actual maintenance demands for five WRAs from the A-7E aircraft (see Table 3.1), and could operate with an acceptable level of reliability.[7]

A significant point to be taken from this brief review of development activity is that VAST was not procured unadvisedly, or in the blind hope that it would work, with no data to support that expectation. On the contrary, VAST was extensively evaluated from its inception, as with any new system. It is also worth noting that in this development process Navy decision makers constantly hear of the benefits promised with new technologies, and it is probably difficult to find a more skeptical group of evaluators anywhere.

Some technical risks cannot be assessed, and that is part of what happened with VAST. By late 1973, there were the first opportunities to test VAST with workloads derived from all of its supported aircraft. The results suggested that VAST had several engineering deficiencies, and that its self-test capability was less able to identify faults in the station itself than was desirable. Even with these cautionary findings, however, it was concluded that VAST would probably be able to do its job once the problems were corrected.[8] By the end of 1973, as the program was coming into full-scale development and production, there appeared to be no reason to anticipate that VAST would not meet its design specifications.

Experience with Initial VAST Deployment

As was shown in Table 2.3, the first 41 VAST stations deployed through November, 1973, had gone to either evaluators or to aircraft manufacturers. The manufacturers of the three new aircraft were using their VAST stations to write the computer programs and document repair procedures for the Test Program Sets (TPSs) required for VAST to support their aircraft WRAs. Operational VAST stations did not reach either carriers or shore sites until December, 1973, by which time all preliminary test and evaluation had been completed. Fifty-one more stations were deployed between January, 1975, and December, 1977. It was during 1974 and 1975, with this set of deployments, that experience with VAST support of the full set of aircraft under operational conditions was gained.

During this period, Operational Readiness became a major problem for a number of complex aircraft.[9] The first deployment of F-14s was made in October, 1974; by March, 1975, OR was nearing 70 percent of the Navy's standard, and was progressing well for a new aircraft. But by the end of March, OR suddenly collapsed to about 50 percent of standard (on average,

47.1 percent of aircraft were classified as Not Mission Capable), and was becoming very difficult to improve. The Navy responded by launching a major readiness improvement program, beginning with identification of the "Top 20" troublesome systems to correct; of these, four were VAST-supported WRAs.[10]

Early Recognition of VAST Workflow Problems

Reports from the Fleet that VAST may have problems meeting operational demands, where all three new aircraft would simultaneously generate the repair workload, first appeared in 1976. The first report of problems with VAST was a letter from Lt. D. G. Craddock in February, 1976, suggesting that VAST manpower and training support was inadequate to cope with WRA diagnostic ambiguities from VAST.[11] The General Accounting Office (GAO) evaluated VAST, as it does with most new weapons programs, and also found that VAST had difficulties meeting its performance objectives.[12] Like the Craddock letter, the GAO report attributed VAST problems to TPS ambiguities and inadequate operator training, but also suggested that unreliable avionics WRAs, compounded by insufficient quantities of spare parts, created the impression that VAST had a negative effect on aircraft OR.

A more detailed study of VAST problems appeared at about the same time as the GAO report.[13] This study team reported problems in three areas. First, with respect to support for the three-aircraft "mix," they concluded that the VAST workflow would "saturate" under operational conditions and degrade aircraft OR, especially for the S-3A; that poor avionics reliability and inadequate VAST TPSs were the cause of this saturation; and that VAST could only support WRAs from these aircraft, rather than both WRAs and SRAs. Second, for the VAST station itself, they found that the stations were actually exceeding reliability and station-availability specifications, despite an apparent lack of adequate documentation and training for maintenance of the VAST Building Blocks. However, the team also concluded that operator training was inadequate. Finally, they found that the use of on-line TPS build-up and tear-down adversely affected VAST performance, since too much time was taken attaching and detaching cables and other parts while the station was idle. They recommended a management change to correct this practice and increase shop productivity.

These reports, along with observational data from several operating sites, suggested that procedures within the VAST shop themselves might be a major factor in the poor throughput of WRAs. Particularly, it seemed that

Elapsed Maintenance Time (EMT), the time to repair a WRA within the VAST shop, varied considerably for the same WRA at different sites. A study of this EMT variation was done by Q.E.D. Systems,[14] which investigated seven factors contributing to EMT in the shops: (1) time required on the station to diagnose a WRA failure; (2) station operator fault isolation techniques; (3) validity of TPS diagnostic recommendations for the WRA; (4) operator training and experience; (5) impact of local management policies and procedures on station utilization; (6) operator intervention to control station operation; and (7) failure of the VAST station and related equipment. Unlike previous studies, the Q.E.D. report recommended complete removal of some WRAs from VAST support (i.e., support through PGSE) because the ambiguity of the TPSs made repair of those WRAs on VAST very difficult. Q.E.D. Systems also recommended changes in maintenance policy and procedure, along with increased levels of VAST station maintenance; and development of interim "workarounds" for particularly difficult WRAs or TPSs. This group disagreed with earlier conclusions about the adequacy of operator training—while the Q.E.D. team agreed that operator training was a problem, their findings suggested that the deficiency was relative to unanticipated problems with the TPSs, and ambiguous fault isolations which could not readily be resolved, rather than with VAST itself. They also did not agree with the earlier studies suggesting that spare parts were insufficient. Overall, the strongest finding from this study was that while operator confidence in VAST was a significant problem, the underlying cause of that low confidence was TPS ambiguities, not VAST. The effect of low confidence was increased EMT, because operators would often repeat tests to verify them.

The Q.E.D. analysis of EMT also provided important new insights into shop operations. Overall, the report argued that EMTs for VAST-testable WRAs were "inflated," relative to the "actual" repair time. This inflation was accounted for by three factors. First, the complex VAST TPSs took considerable time to attach and detach, i.e., to go through the Build-Up/Tear-Down sequence necessary for every WRA. Ancillary activities also slowed production. For example, when a WRA is processed, whether having been repaired to return to Supply or shipped back to the manufacturer, it is wrapped with protective bubble-wrap and labeled. The operator also does this work as part of "repair," even though it is not. Second, operators often had to deal with problems in the TPS components themselves, such as pins on cables which had been bent or pushed up into the cable housing; Interconnecting Device (ID) components which were difficult to connect to the VAST station, or cables hard to connect to the ID; placing cables which were suspected of making poor connections in a precise position to keep a connection once made; and so on. Finally, low operator confidence in VAST fault-isolations caused many operators to repeat failed tests, to see whether the indicated fault would come up on the next pass.

As shown in Table 4.1, only 34 percent of the reported EMT was actually being taken to troubleshoot and repair WRAs. Of the five types of failures categorized in this study, 19 percent of them were "unclassified," which meant that operators would resolve a WRA problem through discovery of a loose SRA needing to be reseated, or by reconnecting a cable in the WRA, and the like. While these were often actual WRA failures, no parts or other repairs of the type normally recorded in the Navy maintenance data recording codes were required, although such actions are noted on a MAF. (One could argue that the EMT data in this study were not truly "inflated," since the time needed to repair a WRA on any tester is subject to any of the five types of failures. Further, most testers require some time for cable connection and set-up, and those cables are also prone to failure over time.)

Table 4.1   Summary of Q.E.D. Systems findings for components of VAST Elapsed Maintenance Time

Type of failure	Percent
WRA non-testable component failure	4
Interconnecting Device (ID) failure	17
Unclassified failure	19
VAST station failure	26
WRA failure only	34

At the same time, the Q.E.D. findings suggested that factors outside the VAST shop might also contribute to VAST difficulties in WRA maintenance. As part of their study, Q.E.D. measured actual EMT for a full year of activity at Naval Air Station (NAS) Cecil Field, Florida, and NAS North Island, San Diego, California. Data were examined at both sites for the period March 1, 1976, through February 28, 1977. During that year, Cecil Field processed 2,677 WRAs with an average EMT of 5.4 hours, and North Island processed

4,490 WRAs with an average EMT of 3.7 hours. The larger number of WRAs processed at North Island was due to a large percentage of the workload being false removals, which comprised nearly 21 percent of the year's total.[15] Over one-fifth of the workload in the VAST shop therefore consisted of tests which found no fault. While some of these false removals are inevitable, many can be prevented by more thorough troubleshooting on the aircraft. However, once WRAs are removed, they must be tested.

Another question that emerged while VAST was in early deployment was whether automatic test procedures were possibly less accurate than manual methods. One undated study by the Boeing Corporation shed some light on this issue—this study examined the frequency of false removals and ambiguous fault isolations of SRAs and "piece parts."[16] Boeing found that whether manual or VAST troubleshooting was used, about 30 percent of parts removed as a result of an initial fault isolation were actually defective, and that the other 70 percent retested as "good." All failed parts in this study were subjected to laboratory failure analysis, and real failures were usually due to mechanical or electrical abuse (the latter sometimes from improper testing). Use of VAST resulted in a somewhat higher percentage of non-failed SRAs being removed (the actual value was not reported), but when these were analyzed in the laboratory, the percentage of defective piece parts was found to be about the same. The study also found that in many cases the reason why a replaced part fixed a problem could not be identified! Overall, the study concluded that VAST and similar automatic test equipment did not necessarily make more incorrect fault isolations than manual equipment, but it suggested that more ambiguities in shop and test procedures might need to be overcome to improve WRA throughput.

Overall, this study and the first results with VAST suggest that the VAST TPSs, particularly the test program, simply automated the best collective wisdom of test and design engineers, and allowed the automatic system to do the "grunt work" of troubleshooting. The combination probably worked about as well as the best technicians could. On the other hand, the complexity of mechanical and electrical interactions on any SRA is so great that even in laboratory conditions, it is often hard to tell exactly what went wrong when an SRA fails, or why one piece part on that board fixes it and another does not. If these kinds of electronic ambiguities exist within a WRA, they can exist within the VAST station and components of some TPSs as well.

Problems with Support of the S-3A

Several of these reports found that VAST WRA production problems appeared to be more severe for the Lockheed S-3A than for the F-14A or E-2C. Part of the motivation for the Q.E.D. analysis of the EMT data at Cecil Field and North Island was that these are both S-3A shore sites, and both were experiencing severe WRA stockout problems. In particular, the S-3A was suffering from lengthy delays in WRA repair where SRAs were not available for them, and thus many WRAs spent more than a month Awaiting Parts (AWP).

NAVAIR wanted to determine why this backlog was so large (and growing); the situation was especially bad at NAS Cecil Field, and so a two-week sampling study was done there by Lockheed Corporation.[17] The study determined that nearly 77 percent of the total components on AWP status had been AWP for more than 30 days. The components had been caught in a loop between being In Work and AWP—when parts were received or repaired, they were inserted into a WRA, which was then retested. If that repair was successful, the WRA went back to Supply as Ready For Issue (RFI); if not, the WRA went back to AWP again. However, many AWP WRAs were being cannibalized to keep some aircraft flying, and therefore when a part was received for some hapless WRA already in AWP and it was placed back into testing, other parts may have been removed from it. This "displacement" of parts shortages resulted in growing numbers of WRAs being retained in AWP status, and fewer and fewer RFI units available for squadron needs.

The Lockheed study recommended that all parts in AWP should be declared as Beyond Capability of Maintenance (BCM), which would result in their being returned to manufacturers for repair. Presumably, this one-time surge of assistance from manufacturers would restore the AIMD repair system to equilibrium. However, this suggestion also implied that the only real problem with VAST WRA maintenance was a shortage of spare parts, an argument heard somewhat less forcefully in earlier studies.

Conclusions from Early Studies of VAST Shop Operations

While the apparent lack of WRA throughput was the motivation for these studies, none of the investigations considered variables outside the VAST shop as potential contributors. Indeed, there would seem to have been little reason to do so, since the AIMD model had worked so well for all other testers before VAST. Therefore, the implicit assumption of all these studies was that VAST was the culprit underlying low aircraft OR, but none of the earlier studies found a clear trail of evidence to support that assumption.

Overall, these studies were both inconclusive and frequently contradictory. They indicated that VAST seemed to be a common denominator in problems with low aircraft OR, but they did not clearly identify VAST as the cause of the problems. Several studies argued that training deficiencies were a contributor to VAST performance problems, but other studies suggested the deficiency pertained to ambiguity troubleshooting which was actually beyond the scope of the technician's job. The Q.E.D. study suggested that the relevant skill issue was that technicians had to deal with problems that were beyond the scope of normal operation, and therefore beyond what they had been trained for. (Some observers of the problem noted that a standard Navy reaction to any problem was to "train more," and so discounted the validity of the apparent training problem.) EMT was variable, but that was of no concern so long as WRAs were available from Supply when needed by the squadrons. EMT was found to be "inflated" somewhat by the VAST Build-Up/Tear-Down cycle and TPS troubleshooting, but the average length of maintenance time was a small fraction of the total time many WRAs spent Awaiting Parts. Some suggestion of VAST unreliability was made in a few reports, but the VAST stations themselves were exceeding designed availability specifications, and the use of automatic test procedures were not resulting in increased numbers of incorrectly removed failed parts relative to manual test methods. Finally, while operator confidence in VAST fault isolations was low, there did not appear to be a significant morale or motivation problem on the part of the sailors who worked in VAST shops. About the only finding not to be challenged was that under present conditions, VAST would not be able to repair both WRAs and SRAs.

The contradictions over training adequacy were interesting in one additional way. These results strongly suggested that the introduction of VAST into the maintenance workflow placed a different, and perhaps greater, burden on the operator. The difference was that with a more complex TPS, ambiguous fault isolations could now be attributed to the WRA itself, or the VAST station, which can malfunction, or the TPS. If the TPS were the culprit, this made resolution of ambiguities even more complicated, because the ambiguity could be rooted in only one part of the TPS, i.e., a flaw in the test program, a poor cable connection, or a poor ID connection. In a few cases, everything might be working correctly, but the WRA itself may have been incorrectly referenced in the master TPS index, and so a technician would be trying to repair a WRA with the wrong program. This could occur when specific configurations of WRAs were produced for particular mission applications, and while they appeared to be the same WRA and used the same nomenclature, they were not electronically interchangeable.

These problems illustrate a critical juncture in the operational design of automatic test equipment—how to get the best trade-off between production on one hand, and accuracy of fault-isolation on the other. When a fault is isolated, it might be traced to only a broad functional problem implicating several SRAs, to a more specific fault on one SRA, or more precisely to one small part on a single SRA. (The part or parts identified by the test program are called the *ambiguity group*.) If the objective of the VAST shop is to get WRAs tested and back to Supply quickly, then the design objective should be to make the ambiguity group as big as possible, to minimize the time spent searching for the problem within the WRA. On the other hand, if we want the job done only once, the ambiguity group should be as small as possible, recognizing that each WRA will take significantly longer to test completely. The trade-off problem with large ambiguity groups is that once a set of SRAs is removed, all of them must be tested and certified as working exactly as they should, i.e., they must be RFI; ambiguity groups of four generate twice the load of SRA testing as ambiguity groups of two. Thus, large ambiguity groups tend to enable faster WRA repairs, but at the cost of increased SRA-shop workloads, and vice-versa. In terms of a car repair, if we had a problem with the engine of the car, the question is whether we trace the trouble to a specific leaking injector and replace it, remove and replace the injector pump assembly, or remove and replace the entire engine. What mix of repair processes provides the optimum throughput for all components, and the highest OR?

During the time when these analyses were underway, the Navy was faced with a major problem in supporting its aircraft with VAST. Since it seemed clear that VAST could not support both WRAs and SRAs, and that in the case of the S-3A, the lack of RFI SRAs was creating interdependence stockouts of WRAs, NAVAIR decided to purchase automatic testers specifically for SRAs. The Hybrid Automatic Test System (HATS) was purchased from Lockheed to support S-3A SRAs, and the Common Automatic Tester, Version IIID (CAT-IIID) was purchased from Grumman Aerospace to support SRAs from the F-14A and the E-2C, both Grumman-manufactured aircraft. The DIMOTE system was acquired for A-7E SRAs; this purchase had already been planned for the Air Force, which also uses the A-7, and was expanded to provide testers for the Navy. These acquisitions, and a change in automatic tester philosophy, were announced in late 1976.[18]

The "change in tester philosophy" was a significant departure from the intended accession path for VAST, in that the Navy had decided to off-load most SRAs to other testers, which in turn resulted in a proliferation of automatic testers.   Since a large part of the original motivation for development of VAST was to eliminate tester proliferation, this was clearly a step in the wrong direction. But the Navy had no choice: 320 SRAs from the F-14A, in addition to the 35 tested on VAST, had to be supported; similarly, the S-3A had 419 non-VAST SRAs, and the E-2C had 107. In theory, VAST might have been expected to support 993 avionics SRAs and 480 of its own, but this was an obviously unattainable objective.[19]

A change in the support philosophy has implications for the entire logistics tail associated with VAST. To make more precise fault isolations for both WRAs and TPSs, VAST might need to be supported by a different logistics "tail" than first designed, with much more training, documentation, and associated support equipment, all provided to enable operators to deal with TPS problems which had not been envisioned in the original concept of the technology.   This is a significant change in the composition and distribution of the IP requirements in the repair cycle.

Chapter 3 referred to the VAST accession as an "experiment." The outcomes of the first VAST experiment (i.e., inserting VAST into the AIMD workflow) were unexpected, and were extremely undesirable. But whether the WRA production problems were really results of the introduction of VAST was ambiguous, and investigations of the VAST WRA workflow to this point produced no clear direction for resolution of the problems.

The VAST Shop Effectiveness and Efficiency Study

After review of the inconclusive results of these studies, NAVAIR contracted with the Systems Research Corporation (SRC) to do a comprehensive investigation of the VAST-shop workflow. The objective of this study was to try to reconcile the ambiguities from previous studies, and to recommend concrete changes in VAST shop procedures and logistics support. It was hoped that VAST performance would directly improve from implementation of study results.   In early 1977, Systems Research Corporation (SRC) assembled a team of researchers to study performance problems in the VAST shops. I was one of eight people contributing to the study, and in some ways my early participation was nearly incidental[20]—because a few findings from the earlier studies had suggested that shop management and priority-setting decisions influenced the performance of the shops, NAVAIR required the study team to include at least one member who specialized in matters of management and organization (we used two, in fact, and also included two human factors specialists to carefully examine the Navy's training program, one with primary responsibility for each coast). The majority of the team consisted of University of Southern California faculty, and since I was an assistant professor with USC at that time, I was asked if I might be able to contribute to the organizational analysis.

The method employed was straightforward—after familiarization with the earlier studies, development of an analysis strategy, and survey preparation, each of two teams was assigned to sites with the Atlantic Fleet (AIRLANT) and Pacific Fleet (AIRPAC). We decided to obtain our own data, since data from the early studies was very fragmented, and also to analyze selected empirical data on shop throughput from the Navy maintenance-data system. Our focus was on the VAST shops themselves, and the underlying assumption was that both the design of the Navy maintenance data collection system, and the data it collected were valid. We recognized a need to get more detailed data in some areas, as shown by the Q.E.D. study. The contract we were under required recommendations to improve the effectiveness and efficiency of the VAST shops; however, unlike earlier studies, our team was not constrained to consider only processes within the VAST shop. If we found contributing factors in relationships with units external to the VAST shop, or between variables outside the scope of the study, these were to be identified as possibilities for other action or more detailed investigation on their own.

In fact, the review of the study literature suggested that much of the variability in TAT, the throughput measure most directly related to aircraft OR, might be linked to other variables outside the VAST shop. Many of the existing studies had suggested examination of several of these variables, so these were given much more detailed attention in the SRC study.

The scope of the study is summarized in Table 4.2. There were two parts of the study requiring original survey preparation: (1) analysis of the decision and workflow control relationships within the VAST shop; and (2) analysis of the VAST paperflow and documentation.[21] For the first survey, we modified the linear responsibility charting method,[22] and called it the Hybrid Information-Decision (HID) matrix. We used the term "hybrid" because our purpose was to capture both objective information about decision-making in addition to perceptions of those processes by shop personnel. This was a simple matrix listing all workflow tasks and functions on the left side, and all shop and supervisory personnel across the top. At the intersection of each row and column, respondents entered a code indicating whether they performed an action independently, made a decision and subsequently notified superiors or others, made a decision in consultation with superiors, etc. Multiple responses were obtained from each survey site, and these were tabulated to determine whether shop personnel agreed on decision-making responsibility for important actions in the repair workflow. Of particular interest was whether the deployment of VAST had changed or distorted workflow decisions in unknown ways. The second survey was a standardized questionnaire used to record all aspects of workflow information in detail, both with respect to sources of information and to recording or disposition of that information.

Table 4.2   Scope of Systems Research Corporation study

Variable investigated	Method(s)
Turnaround Time analysis	Statistical analysis of Navy maintenance data
Maintenance/Supply interface	HID, paperflow, site interviews
Work Center management and decision relationships	HID
Workload prioritization alternatives	HID, site interviews
Personnel resources	Navy retention data; review of training curriculum; site interviews
NAVAIR structure	HID; site and NAVAIR headquarters interviews
Measures of effectiveness	Review of Navy maintenance data reporting system; site and headquarters interviews

Being located on the East Coast, I was assigned to perform site surveys at five locations. Two were shore sites, one for the E-2C at NAS Norfolk, Va., and one for the S-3A at NAS Cecil Field, Jacksonville, Fl. One carrier was included, the USS *John F. Kennedy*, based at Norfolk. The *Kennedy* air wing contained all three VAST-supported aircraft, and had four VAST stations. The other two sites I was assigned to were to conduct interviews with PRD Electronics, the VAST manufacturer, and NAVAIR headquarters personnel, in the second year of the project.

Other team personnel had assignments which depended on their area of expertise and their geographic location, as mine did. Team members surveyed other shore sites and carriers at both AIRLANT and AIRPAC sites; Naval Maintenance Training headquarters in Memphis, Tenn.; Aviation Supply Division headquarters in Philadelphia, Pa.; and Bureau of Personnel officers. The study began in January, 1978, and had a performance period of 20 months. The preliminary findings were reported in March, 1979, and final recommendations were submitted in October, 1979.

Since there had been several earlier suggestions that personnel issues, and particularly training, might have been significant contributors to poor VAST performance, we took a sample of 107 VAST operators, maintainers, and supervisors (from a total of about 400 in the entire Navy at that time), to ensure comprehensiveness and representativeness of our survey. We also interviewed VAST contractor representatives at each site, and representatives from several of the WRA and aircraft manufacturers. Finally, we included 33 personnel from other automatic test equipment shops (HATS and CAT-IIID), to permit some limited comparison of our findings to those from other shops using automatic testers.

The interviews we conducted sought two primary kinds of information. First, we were looking for information on logistics support and evidence of problems with VAST reliability or availability. Our primary interest in these questions was to guard against overlooking the obvious possibility that VAST was not working, although our emphasis was not an engineering analysis. Second, and of greatest importance, we had specific questions derived from the earlier studies as well as from the first-hand experience of several team members who were veterans and already quite familiar with the general military approach to maintenance; one team member was a Navy veteran who knew Navy avionics maintenance intimately. Thus, we were able to do our site research with sufficient background knowledge to comprehend and interpret our data with confidence.

We pretested our questionnaires and the HID matrix in a pilot study at NAS Cecil Field. This shore site is headquarters for the Atlantic Fleet S-3A wing, and provided an opportunity to test our data collection methodology at a base with a relatively complex aircraft and a heavy WRA workload. We spent a full week at this site, first gathering data and evaluating it, then making late-night changes to the instruments and trying them the next day, until we and the site personnel felt confident we were getting accurate data, on shop activities, documentation and paperflow, and a comprehensive overview of shop performance.

We were especially interested to learn how actual WRA repairs were accomplished. The intended (successful) shop workflow is shown in Figure 4.1. It portrays an endless loop of operation unless there are no WRAs Awaiting Maintenance (AWM). Some station time is allowed for both scheduled and unscheduled VAST maintenance, but the shop operates 24 hours a day. The workflow assumes First-In, First-Out (FIFO) WRA scheduling for repair. Once a WRA is released by the AIMD Production Control officer for repair, it is brought to the VAST shop, the Test Program Set (TPS) is collected, and TPS Build-Up is done. Testing goes on until the WRA passes its complete ("end-to-end") test, with or without replacement of SRAs. When the WRA passes, Tear-Down is done, the WRA is tagged as Ready for Issue (RFI), and the TPS is stored away. The sailor then goes to the holding area to fetch the next WRA, and the cycle is repeated.

Once testing begins, the technician has little to do until VAST identifies a potential fault, which the station monitor displays along with operator instructions. Much of the job is boring machine-tending work, and only one technician is actually needed at each station, so it has the potential to be both boring and lonely. Many sites found that having two technicians per station was actually more efficient under heavy workloads, since one could be doing Build-Up/Tear-Down of the TPS and fetching of parts, while the other monitored a WRA under test. The number of work cycles an operator completed on each shift was highly variable, depending on the outcomes of the testing. About 30 percent of tests resulted in no repair action being taken, since the WRA tested RFI. (This was an even higher percentage than the Q.E.D. study suggested.) The "no-fault" outcome can occur because the WRA was incorrectly identified on the aircraft as the cause of a problem; was pulled just to verify that it was OK; or had a fault that the VAST TPS could not find. Whatever the cause, an operator might have a "run" of these, and process many WRAs in a single shift. On the next shift, the station might get stuck on a WRA for which the program reports a fault, and which cannot be made to pass the test. In extreme cases, one WRA like this could tie up a station for several consecutive days.

At sea, personnel usually work 12-hour shifts; on shore, the typical shift is eight hours, and many sites use creative shift definition to give sailors free time. For example, sites in San Diego would often use three 12-hour shifts

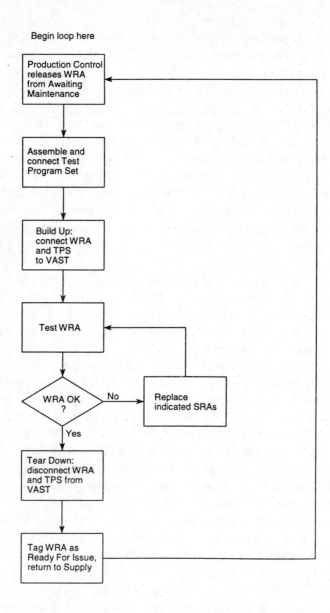

Figure 4.1 Simplified view of intended VAST shop test workflow

and one four-hour half-shift, enabling sailors to get to the beach for a long weekend, every weekend. Needless to say, such practices were popular.

Principal Findings of the SRC Effectiveness and Efficiency Study

Turnaround Time (TAT) analysis Unlike most previous work, the SRC study examined TAT more extensively than EMT. The TAT analysis for this study was performed by statistical analysis of data for a selected set of S-3A WRAs which were critical to several missions performed by that aircraft. This approach was taken for two reasons. First, the Navy had chosen not to analyze a data set for the entire group of VAST-supported WRAs, since the cost of extracting the raw data from the Navy recording system was high, and would have delayed completion of the project. (In the 1970s, data entry was done through manual recording of data on MAFs, then punch-card transformation for machine-readability, followed by use of custom Fortran programs to process data. Extraction of all raw data or specialized analysis was a major undertaking—having done exactly that for the data in Chapter 6, I can attest to this.) Data for these mission-critical WRAs was more readily available since they were already monitored closely and the raw data were extracted routinely. Second, these WRAs were considered to be representative of the range of technical complexity for the S-3A, and would provide adequate information for our purposes. Data were analyzed for 826 repair actions completed between 1 December 1977, and 30 November 1978.

Table 4.3 shows the results of this analysis. Each of the four components of TAT was evaluated individually: processing time, scheduling time, repair time (EMT), and Awaiting Parts (AWP) time. A "standard" time was determined for each of the TAT components, defined as the number of days required to perform that step for at least 85 percent of the WRAs going through the repair cycle. For example, at least 85 percent of WRAs were scheduled within three days of induction into the repair process; therefore, any scheduling action taking longer than three days was scored as having taken "excess" time. Note that in Table 4.3, "standard days" were counted as the actual number of days up to the standard, but less than the standard if fewer were actually taken. Thus, an EMT of 6 days would be recorded as 6 "standard" days; EMT of 11 days would be recorded as 8 "standard" days and 3 "excess" days. With exception to processing time, this procedure results in total "standard days" in the fourth column of the table which are not necessarily multiples of 826. For each of the 826 repair actions, actual times to complete each component were compared to these standard times, to identify those components of the repair cycle contributing to excessive TAT.

The results suggested that TAT could be improved considerably, from nearly 13 days on the average to something nearer the standard of 7.73; on the average, nearly a week more than the "standard time" was being taken by each WRA. As had been expected, the major cause of delays in the repair cycle was AWP time, which reinforced the perception that lack of spare parts was a bigger contributor to excessive TAT than VAST shop (EMT) performance. However, the analysis suggested that there was opportunity for improvement within the VAST shop, with an average of 0.77 excess days being taken for every WRA repaired. But insofar as TAT was concerned, and therefore the stock levels of WRAs, the problem of excessive time was real, not perceived.

Table 4.3   Results of Turnaround Time analysis for 826 S-3A WRA repairs

Action	Std. time (days)	Actual days (total)	Standard days (total)	Excess days (total)
Processing	1	1142	826	316
Scheduling	3	2925	1512	1413
Repair (EMT)	8	2319	1680	639
Awaiting Parts	20	4307	2371	1936
Average per WRA		12.95	7.73	5.22

The unexpected finding from this analysis was that the delays attributable to processing and scheduling were nearly three times as large as delays occurring within the VAST shop itself, and these two together were almost as great as the excess times accumulated by AWP. These processing and scheduling delays were largely matters of interunit relationships along the flow of work, not a function of parts availability or VAST station availability. The substantive work done at this part of the repair cycle is cleaning of the

WRA, sometimes involving only a surface cleaning, and sometimes requiring a solvent bath to remove exhaust deposits and other dirt. Cleaning is done both to expedite repair at later stages of the cycle, and as part of a Navy-wide preventive maintenance and corrosion-control program, so it is not an activity to dismiss. However, nothing in any previous studies had suggested that these shop-interface relationships might be material contributors to poor repair-cycle performance. Furthermore, even processing time held out potential for significant improvement. Site visits and crew debriefings indicated that the one-for-one exchange which was supposed to occur whenever a WRA was removed from an aircraft was being violated in many cases, particularly by squadrons at sea. The nature of the violations varied—aircrew would bring additional WRAs from their shore site and conceal them in crew quarters; one or more aircraft became "hangar queens" after their first breakdown (so termed because they never flew, and always "ruled the hangar"), and parts were stripped from them to effectively increase the pool of spares available to the squadron; during heavy flight periods, removed WRAs would be piled up in the Supply or screening areas to be processed "later," in order to serve squadron personnel quickly; and so on. Motivations for these violations also varied, but usually were based on some locally-optimal reason, such as being able to perform critical missions and keep squadron performance ratings up.

Maintenance and Supply interface   The findings on processing time supported our original decision to examine the maintenance-Supply interface closely. For our study of this relationship, we collected three types of data: site surveys and interviews, an analysis of paperflow and documentation within the shop and between units, and the Hybrid Information-Decision (HID) matrix. The HID analysis provided insights into the work center management and decision relationships and workload prioritization alternatives, which will be discussed in the next two sections. The present discussion will focus primarily on the results of the paperflow analysis and the site surveys and interviews.

What was discovered through these analyses, and was of greatest interest to us, was the degree of variability in the relationships between these units, with respect to the physical flow of WRAs and parts, the physical layout of facilities on ship and ashore, and the time required to complete transactions across workflow interfaces. In contrast to the designed one-for-one exchange, with all MAF and paperwork completed efficiently and on a timely basis, no site did things the same way.

There were many variables which affected the VAST-Supply interface relationship. Overall, we were able to categorize these into three principal types:

1. The location and size of the WRA, SRA, and bit-and-piece parts "pools," and in some cases the existence or non-existence of them. Bit-and-piece parts are technically known as "Pre-Expended Bins," or PEB, since the entire batch of small parts is considered "pre-expended" once they are released from Supply control to the work centers.

2. The willingness of Supply to lend SRAs and WRAs for use in troubleshooting on VAST, and to assist in batch processing in the VAST shops. Pools of components specifically designated for such troubleshooting assistance were termed Maintenance Assist Modules, or MAMs.

3. Control of stock levels and replenishment practices for SRA and bit-and-piece part (PEB) pools. Of particular interest was a special pool of parts which were difficult to repair, and therefore were sent back to their manufacturers, but tracked very closely to get them back to their sites quickly. This pool comprises the Closed-Loop Avionics Maintenance Program, or CLAMP.

Variations in this interface relationship as it affects the VAST shop are summarized in Table 4.4. This table shows findings from five shore sites and two carriers, and is representative of practices at Atlantic and Pacific fleet sites.

Much of the variation from location and size of pools was attributable to uncontrollable variables, the principal ones being physical space limitations (availability, layout, and proximity to tester work centers), and variability of workload. These factors interact with each other to create other types of variation as well. Particularly on carriers where both work centers and pools are located in different areas, a surge of repair activity might necessitate large numbers of individual "processing" trips by sailors to fetch RFI WRAs and take turn-ins to screening. The time required for many such trips could result in the build-up of large queues of WRAs waiting to be tested, and it is clear that a better strategy is to serve groups of WRAs, so that a cart of removals could be taken to screening and a load of RFI items brought from Supply on one trip. While more efficient, this practice inevitably violates the intended one-for-one immediate exchange and allows for mismatches of MAFs to WRAs and other kinds of paperwork errors. Our paperflow analysis

Table 4.4   Maintenance-Supply relationships at seven sites

Site	WRA pool access	SRA pool access, receipt time for SRAs not in pool but on site	Bit-and-piece (PEB) pool access
NAS Cecil Field, Jacksonville, Fl. (S-3A. AIRLANT)	None	SRA pool proposed but not established; receipt time 1 day	Central AIMD PEB pool; receipt time 30 minutes
NAS Norfolk, Norfolk, Va. (E-2C. AIRLANT)	None	CLAMP pool located in AIMD, receipt time 1 day; receipt time if not in pool, 1 day (pool also handles all SRA ordering and MAF paperwork)	Central AIMD PEB pool, accessible to technicians; contains about 250 items useful to VAST; no single person responsible to maintain stocks
NAS Oceana, Oceana, Va. (F-14A. AIRLANT)	None	CLAMP pool located adjacent to VAST shop, receipt time 1 day; receipt time if not in pool, 7 days	Free-access bin located in VAST shop; contains adequate depth and range of items; specialist technician controls inventory, completes MAF data
NAS North Island, San Diego, Ca. (S-3A. AIRPAC)	Located adjacent to VAST shop; easy to borrow RFI WRA if available; VAST shop holds 30 WRA MAMs	CLAMP pool located adjacent to VAST shop, but usually depleted; borrowing easy if SRA available	Free-access bin located in VAST shop
NAS Miramar, San Diego, Ca. (F-14A. AIRPAC)	Located adjacent to VAST shop; lent on as-needed basis	Pool of over 600 SRAs located adjacent to VAST shop, receipt time 10 minutes; receipt time for non-pool SRAs 1-2 days	Free-access bin located in VAST shop; of limited use to VAST shop
USS *John F. Kennedy*, Norfolk, VA. (AIRLANT)	Partial F-14 and S-3A SRA MAMs held in VAST shop; easy to borrow RFI WRA if available	CLAMP and regular-pool SRAs not available to VAST shop unless ordered; receipt time 1-2 days	Free-access bin located in Supply and VAST shop; of limited use to VAST shop
USS *Constellation*, San Diego, Ca. (AIRPAC)	None; SRA MAMs held in VAST shop	SRA pool accessible to VAST shop via phone call; pool receipt time 2-3 hours, nonpool receipt time one day	Free-access bin located in VAST shop; contains adequate depth and range of items; specialist technician controls inventory, completes MAF data

Source: *Productivity Enhancement of the Versatile Avionic Shop Test System: Site Evaluation and Final Report, Volume II Detailed Findings.* Leesburg, Va.: Systems Research Corp., 6 March 1979

indicated that a small number of errors (less than one percent) did result from such exchanges.

A more important source of variation came from local practices, several of which had developed over time as attempts to assist VAST and the SRA-repair work centers in doing their jobs. The Pacific Fleet (AIRPAC) sites and the *Kennedy* had MAMs pools for troubleshooting assistance, located in the areas shown in Table 4.4; AIRLANT shore sites did not. Sites using MAMs had significantly better success in repairing WRAs than others, because RFI parts could be put onto the VAST station to verify its status or the Test Program Set whenever there was an ambiguity that could not be readily isolated. These MAMs (or "loaners") were then returned to their holding area, either in Supply or a designated location in the VAST shop or AIMD. However, the practice of using RFI components as MAMs was officially not permitted, since a fault in a VAST station could create a failure in an RFI WRA when it was used to try to verify a VAST station; that WRA might be returned to the pool as RFI when it actually no longer was. Since there was no way to assure that every MAM would be retested (and most were not), this practice was discouraged at AIRLANT sites. Nevertheless, our study showed that the practice worked; for NAS Miramar it was especially effective, and will be discussed in more detail in Chapter 6.

SRA receipt time and pool access (i.e., time to acquire and fetch SRAs for a repair) was found to vary widely, from a minimum of 10 minutes for high-demand SRAs at NAS Miramar, to as long as two days for the same types of components at other sites. Non-pool components could take anywhere from one to seven days to acquire. These times may seem unreasonable, but given the physical and other variations already noted, and the theory of operation which assumed that adequate spare WRAs existed to support normal operations, such times were not unusual. There was similar variation in control of PEB parts, which in two cases were in the VAST shop but of little use to it, since many of the parts were consumed in other shops. At several sites, complete SRA pools had not yet been formed, so that central control of parts in these rotating pools had not yet been established. At sites where partial pools of rotating parts had been established for high-turnover components, other non-rotating parts were held in other locations on the site; and so on. Each of these variations created time delays in the local repair cycle for WRAs.

Control over PEB parts was very irregular. In essence, since these parts were "pre-expended," Supply had no further responsibility for them once they were issued to the shop or AIMD which held them. This meant that recording of PEB consumption, requisition of replenishment stocks, etc., effectively fell on the consuming unit. The PEB system had evolved as a stop-gap measure in earlier years, when the proliferation of these parts overwhelmed the Navy inventory system, and it had persisted. In fact, the PEB method worked rather well, but only because of local efforts to maintain the stocks and document component consumption in the repair system. This was done inconsistently, as Table 4.4 shows.

However, we found that PEB management was threatening to become a major problem in avionics repair. These parts were the ones used to repair the SRAs on which the VAST BBs and the WRAs depended. Since these parts were "acquired and forgotten" by Supply, demands for them were not being recorded accurately by the Supply system. A further complication was created by the Navy accounting system and the funding for local operational costs. Under Navy accounting methods contractor support was not counted as "local operational costs," and therefore PEB parts were often kept in stock by having manufacturers and other contractors bid to supply them. This procedure prevented local base operating money from being consumed for PEB parts, but it also meant that the Supply system had no real idea of the consumption rates for these parts and could not make intelligent decisions for either future physical parts requirements or for funding needs for them. Clearly, this was an area where immediate improvement in the documentation and data-acquisition system was needed.

Work Center management and decision relationships   The next part of the study was concerned with management of the workflow in the VAST shop itself, an area that had not been examined closely by any previous studies. In truth, many Navy personnel believed that the closed-system engineering concept of avionics maintenance which was designed into the AIMD workflow reduced management to a "common sense" function, which could be done by anybody who followed the rules. I faced several direct personal confrontations with people who regarded my activities on the project as a counterproductive nuisance factor, and made that clear in no uncertain terms. I humored them and got on with the job.

We used the HID matrix to collect information on two generic types of variables in shop management—who makes decisions and takes actions in the workflow, and what those decisions and actions were. However, we also asked who must concur with these decisions or be notified of them and any actions taken. The technique for doing this was relatively simple: a matrix was prepared specifically for the VAST shops, listing actions and decisions ("functions") on the left side of the page, and VAST shop, Supply, and AIMD personnel ("positions") along the top margin. Wherever a function intersected with a position, a code was entered to indicate whether the interviewee made the decision or took the action, had to concur with it, or had to be notified of it. Data were collected by members of the study team through interviews with site personnel. All managers and supervisors were interviewed, and a sample (at least 25 percent) of VAST operators and maintainers were interviewed. (VAST maintainers are operators who have had additional training to maintain the VAST stations themselves, and usually are personnel in at least their second four-year tour of duty.)

After data were collected they were analyzed for consistency (agreement) between positions. For example, if a shift supervisor claimed authority to decide to reconfigure a VAST station (to test a type of WRA the station had not been set up for), and also claimed only to have to notify his superior after the fact, we would check the superior's responses to see whether he agreed that only notification was required. These consistency analyses were made for the VAST shops, and for the interface relationships discussed in the section above.

I want to emphasize that response consistency *per se* did not necessarily mean that management or decisions were being exercised correctly, nor did lack of consistency mean they were not. The objective of the response consistency evaluations was to determine whether personnel in the repair system were aware of the interdependencies that affected AIMD performance, whether they were making necessary decisions, and were informing others on workflow decisions and actions that might affect those others. Given that VAST was a new technology and that previous studies had implied that workflow management could be a direct contributor to VAST performance, we did not want to assume that management practices developed for earlier technologies necessarily worked with VAST.

As an example, we found that Pacific Fleet sites were generally somewhat more productive than Atlantic Fleet sites. Analysis of the HID data showed that more AIRPAC people got involved in the general process of repair-cycle and VAST-shop decision-making, suggesting that information was more widely dispersed and made more available to personnel, enabling them to make the decisions necessary to keep production up. One example of this is the NAS Miramar decision to locate the most heavily-demanded SRAs close to the VAST shop and use a local "check-out" document to support trial-and-error repair work. Another was the tendency to involve personnel outside the VAST shop in many VAST decisions at Pacific sites, a practice we found to be uncommon at most Atlantic sites.

Many detailed findings emerged from this analysis, but they may be summarized into the following seven major conclusions:

1. Many VAST-specific authority relationships were unclear throughout the system. Most personnel were aware of general organization and authority relationships, since these are relatively standard throughout the Navy. However, we found considerable variability on who claimed authority to make decisions, who had to concur, and who had to be notified when decisions and actions peculiar to VAST were evaluated. For example, one of the common ways to deal with problems was to develop a local procedure or instruction; at the five shore sites, we found that the decision to do this was claimed by people as diverse as VAST operators, VAST maintainers, Supply personnel, Production Control personnel, shop supervisors, and contractor technical representatives. At all sites, at least one senior officer thought he should concur with these decisions; at three sites, however, no officers were ascribed that concurrence, and officers other than those expecting concurrence were identified as needing to concur at two sites.

2. Reporting requirements and expectations were unclear for many actions. This was illustrated by the point above, where many respondents indicated that no concurrence was necessary for local procedures to be implemented. A similar pattern of inconsistent expectations occurred with many VAST-related operational decisions.

3. Information needed to make workflow decisions was not acquired in a controlled fashion. An example of this problem was the decision to declare a WRA (and also SRAs, in some cases) Beyond Capability of Maintenance (BCM). BCM could occur for several reasons, and these reasons were coded on the MAF when the component was sent out of the shop: BCM-4 was the code for "lack of spare parts," and BCM-5 was the code for "shop backlog." One way of dealing with an overload in the VAST shop was to decide to BCM-5 some of the WRAs in the repair queue. BCM-4 could be used to the same effect, and was justified if parts took too long to arrive. By doing this, the WRAs would go to the manufacturer (or sometimes to a Navy depot) to be repaired, and then would be sent back to the site. While this would get the WRAs repaired, it diminished local stocks for as long the WRAs were gone. It would seem evident that this decision should be coordinated closely at least with AIMD Production Control and Supply, and sometimes with the squadrons as well. But at two sites, authority for these decisions was claimed by operators who did not identify others as needing to be notified that aircraft assets were

being sent off-site. At every site, there was at least one senior officer who claimed concurrence for this decision, but who was not identified as such by the decision claimant. In a case at Cecil Field, a training mission planned for the next day had to be delayed because a night-shift VAST technician had become frustrated with a particular WRA, "BCM'ed" a batch of four, and left the squadron without enough of that WRA to fly the four aircraft needed. The sailor simply was not aware that this was an issue.

4. Many decisions that needed to be made were not being made. The trade-off between the intended first-in, first-out (FIFO) processing and "batch" processing of WRAs has been discussed previously. We found that in some cases, this decision was not being made—if a particular officer had instructed that FIFO scheduling was to be used at a site, that procedure was followed until someone changed it even if a "natural" batch built up. In many cases, and especially at sea, the decision to go to one mode of operation versus the other needed to be considered on a shift-by-shift basis. But for many reasons, and sometimes simply from frustration, many VAST supervisors simply continued with what they had last been instructed to do.

5. Training and workforce skill utilization were not being coordinated. Training is a constant undertaking in the Navy, as noted, and was particularly important with a complex test technology like VAST. We found evidence that operator and site performance gradually improved with experience, and that doing on-the-job training and skill upgrading on a regular basis paid off. But as is the case in industry, on-the-job training was often delayed to keep production up.

6. Relationships with other interdependent work centers and AIMD units were not being monitored or coordinated. While our paperflow analysis showed that most of the information needed for interunit coordination was conveyed on the MAF and local documents, many of the variables which needed to be monitored to set workflow priorities and coordinate decisions with units outside the VAST shop were not. For example, the operator who BCM'ed the WRAs at Cecil Field had no idea of squadron needs, nor did anyone else outside the squadron. "Exception reporting" and use of the local "grapevine" were the common methods for exchanging coordinating information, and as is often the case, these methods do not include all affected parties.

7. Shop workflow was not being controlled. The major example of this problem was the setting of workflow priorities, which will be discussed in the next section. However, there were many other decisions and actions affecting VAST workflow which might have been taken and were often not. For example, if an operator got stuck on a WRA, should he continue to work on it until it was finally done, test for a limited time until it could be BCM'ed, or for only a specified number of hours before going to another WRA? In many strict FIFO situations, we observed a tendency to "cook the box" until it was either repaired or it was evident that nothing more could be tried that had not already been. Under these conditions, one or two WRAs could create bottlenecks and seriously degrade shop throughput.

Workload prioritization alternatives As indicated above, decisions to set priorities for WRA repairs and take other actions on the workflow to control and optimize shop throughput were often not being made. The need for such decisions is illustrated by Figures 4.2a and 4.2b, which show an expanded and more realistic portrayal of the shop workflow, although still highly simplified. These figures show three recurring decisions in the shop:

1. The decision to "batch process" accumulations of the same type of WRA, which increases efficiency by reducing the number of TPS fetches and Build-Up/Tear-Down (BU/TD) cycles, at the cost of violating the FIFO schedule (Figure 4.2a).
2. The need to decide how to repair a VAST station when a malfunction occurs, i.e., shut down completely or continue to use the station to test other WRAs for which it was still capable without the failed Building Block (Figure 4.2a). If repair work is to continue, which WRAs will be selected? This decision affects repair priorities, technician electrical safety, and raises a number of technical issues.
3. The need to remove WRAs for which no parts are available to Awaiting Parts (AWP) (Figure 4.2b). At most sites, AWP is a separate physical area of Supply or Production Control, reserved for storage of these WRAs until parts are received. AWP WRAs will go through multiple BU/TD cycles, reducing shop efficiency and delaying return of RFI WRAs to Supply. The alternative is to combine batch processing with cannibalization of similar WRAs, to repair as many WRAs as possible on each run of a batch, and minimize multiple passes of WRAs through the shop.

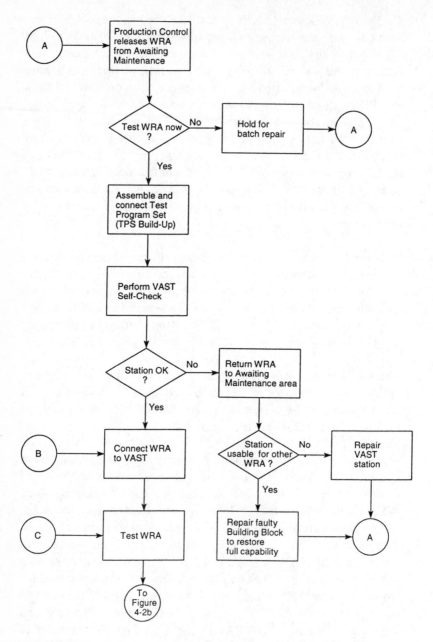

Figure 4.2a   Actual VAST shop WRA test workflow

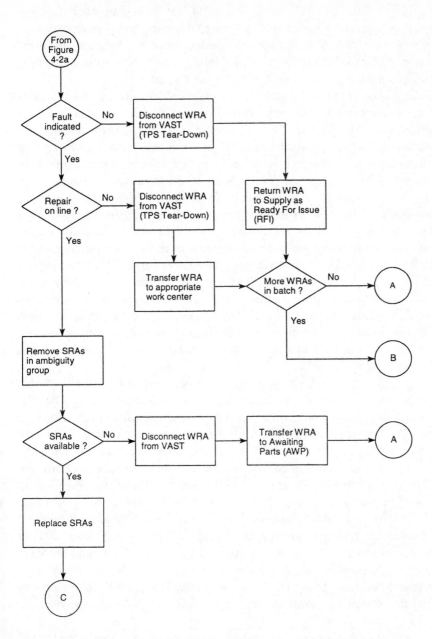

Figure 4.2b   Actual VAST shop WRA test workflow

Figures 4.2a and 4.2b reflect some of our more important findings regarding the actual flow of WRAs through the shop, and illustrate some of the processes that affect actual shop performance by departing from the intended FIFO workflow design. These figures constitute a general diagram, however, and summarize findings across diverse sites.

About the only thing that this flow diagram does not capture are cases where operators repeat tests when confidence in a fault-isolation is low. Test repetition is caused by many things, including simply a need to see that a test result is replicated at some point in the chain of tests. Another factor that contributes to test repetition is the problem of *configuration control*—over time, engineering changes in WRAs, in the VAST hardware, and in the TPSs were introduced, either to correct deficiencies or to generally improve performance. Because of these changes, some repair procedures did not work, some fault isolations were invalid, some TPSs did not properly isolate faults, and so on. Complete and coordinated information on the configuration of VAST stations, TPSs, and WRAs was needed to repair the WRAs, and this was not always available in timely fashion. The number of such changes was small, and configuration control was not a major contributor to repair problems when measured objectively; however, the possibility that an ambiguity could be a result of such configuration changes was a constant source of uncertainty, and a "noise" factor that contributed to repeated runs of a test or part of a test.

As would be expected, approaches to decision-making for workload priorities were as diverse as with other areas of decision-making. The HID data showed that the workflow unit which made repair-priority decisions could be Supply, Production Control, the avionics maintenance officer, the VAST shop supervisor, the VAST operator, or effectively no one at all, when a strict FIFO system was used without regard to any criteria except order of WRA arrival. Across all sites and both fleets, whenever the VAST shop became heavily backlogged with AWM WRAs, repair priority decision-making sometimes became chaotic—local decisions at individual sites might be made to maximize throughput, or minimize BCMs, or minimize EMT, or whatever seemed to be the most important criterion according to whoever made the decision. Even the decision-maker was a variable. At several sites, we found decisions being made by the Production Control officer on one shift, the system operator on the night shift, the VAST supervisor on weekends, and so on.

Such extremes as the latter case were observed only rarely, and never lasted very long (reduced levels of squadron operations eventually allow a catch-up breather for the shops). It was clear that most personnel in the repair system recognized that repair priorities had to be managed, but there was little agreement about how to do that. Many of these personnel would have disagreed that the throughput problem was management, in fact, which was a further complication. The scope of the problem was so large that the repair cycle was known to its members as the elephant is known to the blind men, and so while there was little disagreement that something had to be done to improve production, there was little agreement about what to do. A large number of Navy personnel and supporting contractors were convinced that the only real problem was lack of sufficient spare SRAs and bit-and-piece parts, and it was quite possible for them to construct plausible arguments in support of that position. Many others would identify VAST maintenance, or the ever-popular personnel training (which I address in the next section), and other variables. Overt conflict was rare, given that the Navy is a basic hierarchical system, but covert conflict was common. Unresolved disagreements across hierarchical levels were sometimes resolved by passive-aggressive behavior. I learned the expression "malicious compliance" from a shop supervisor who did exactly what his avionics officer directed after a repair-priority disagreement, knowing his actions would create a problem later. Much more often, the result of such covert conflict was frustration, and a resigned willingness to do whatever one was told to do, and hope for the best. If nothing else, workload backlogs frequently became so bad that the strongest motivation was for people to help each other out.

I do not want to create the impression that these factors interfered with shop production without recognition or action. The fact that people had time to argue over different approaches to shop decisions was partly a function of the fact that WRAs could be undergoing test while the arguments went on, and they did. But much more common were constructive, cooperative efforts to solve local problems as they were understood at the site. Some of those efforts succeeded remarkably well, and did so at the grass-roots level; in fact, one of these became a major impetus toward a long-term and permanent solution to the prioritization problem, and this will be discussed in the next chapter. There was widespread argument over priorities, but this was rooted in both the desire to solve problems and the lack of information to do it, and that was very frustrating. Even so, I was impressed by the high levels of motivation and concern for effective performance I found at every site I visited. That concern was one of the greatest sources of the frustration, which is no surprise.

Our study found three factors contributing to the workflow repair-priority problem, and despite many conflicting perspectives like those above, we came away with a strong impression that: (1) the overall objective of the

VAST shop was unclear; (2) that information needed to make more effective priority decisions was unavailable to those who needed it; and (3) that the amount of information needed to make effective decisions was often too much to handle without information-technology mediation. That mediation could take the form of data matrices, visual displays, or computerized systems (preferably the latter), but some form of mediation seemed necessary to cope with the information load the VAST shop generated.

These three factors pointed to the need for a scheduling algorithm operating against an agreed-upon and widely-recognized goal. Such an algorithm was needed to manage the quantity of repair-cycle information, and the goal was needed to transform information in ways that would enable the VAST shop, and other interacting AIMD units and Supply, to work toward system-optimal outcomes. Without the definition of a common goal, local optimality was the best the system could hope for.

Personnel resources The role that personnel capabilities played in VAST performance was studied as a function of three interacting factors: (1) the acquisition and retention of personnel, including staffing levels; (2) the acquisition and retention of skills; and (3) the use of non-military technical personnel.

First, we looked into acquisition and retention of personnel. Retention is a joint product of overall Navy recruiting to obtain replacements as normal attrition occurred, and morale and satisfaction issues which affected people's decisions to stay in the Navy or leave when their tour of duty was up. There was some concern about personnel levels from the perspective of demographics, since projections into the "baby bust" era of the U.S. population implied that inadequate numbers of new enlistees would join the Navy, and normal attrition would create a manpower shortage in a number of critical skills areas.

We found that there was a 30 percent turnover of VAST personnel each year. Fifty-five percent intended to leave after one tour of duty, and 79 percent indicated they would leave after two tours. Only 13 percent intended to remain in the Navy for a career. With the Navy's projected needs for VAST maintainers, which will be discussed momentarily, this did indeed support the view that a manpower shortage would be an issue within a few years.

However, major questions about this projection derived from the variability of estimates of the number of personnel required to operate a VAST site. Table 4.5 shows a number of estimates of personnel required, for shore sites and ships. Note that shore sites generally have more personnel than ships, since shore sites frequently have larger numbers of aircraft than the carriers, and do more training. Carriers use a minimum crew, and use maintainers to both operate and maintain VAST. At a training conference on 20 December 1977, the Chief of Naval Operations recommended that each ship should have 4 operators and 20 maintainers, or effectively one operator and 5 maintainers per station for a four-station ship. This, in some ways, might constitute a "minimum" crew, but as Table 4.5 shows, no ship had that

Table 4.5   VAST station personnel levels, 30 September 1978

Site	VAST stations	Personnel
NAS Norfolk	2	19
NAS Cecil Field	5	19
NAS North Island	5	43
NAS Oceana	5	14
NAS Miramar	6	28
USS *Forrestal*	3	11
USS *Saratoga*	3	6
USS *Independence*	3	9
USS *America*	4	12
USS *John F. Kennedy*	4	6
USS *Nimitz*	4	13
USS *Ranger*	3	7
USS *Kitty Hawk*	4	10
USS *Constellation*	4	12
USS *Enterprise*	4	7
USS *Dwight D. Eisenhower*	4	8

many personnel as of September, 1978; the *Saratoga* and *Kennedy* had only 6 people, and the *Ranger* and *Enterprise* only had 7. Only two shore sites had that many people, and these operated 5 and 6 VAST stations (North Island and Miramar, respectively). Thus, real "minimum" needs were probably closer to those reported by the ships. It is also worth noting that on the ships, from 50 to 100 percent of the personnel aboard were maintainers, with most ships having about two-thirds maintainers. This meant that the average shipboard skill level was higher than the shore sites.

VAST shop personnel, as noted in Chapter 2, consist of a mixed group of a few permanent technicians and supervisory personnel ("ship's company," aboard a ship), and a majority who are members of the squadron in the air wing to which they are attached, referred to as "air wing" or "operating detachment" personnel. These personnel travel with their squadron, and so rotate in and out of the VAST shop as their squadron deploys from, and returns to, its home base. The staff of a VAST shop over time is therefore a group of varying composition.

These variations made our job much more difficult, in that we could not fully evaluate the likelihood of a personnel shortage under all different conditions which might apply, and so we recommended a full study on that issue as a future task. For immediate purposes, staffing variability also confounded the relationship between skill levels and shop performance. For example, did it make sense to compare a ship with a few highly-skilled personnel to a shore site with a lower average skill level, but where more emphasis was placed on training so that mistakes were both expected and tolerated as a learning experience? We found evidence in our surveys to suggest the importance of skill levels to shop performance, but the variations across sites made generalization very difficult.

Next, we investigated the question of morale and its impact on retention and shop performance. We found that 70 percent of operators rated VAST jobs as in the top half of technical interest, and as professionally satisfying. However, only 41 percent rated VAST jobs in the top half with respect to impact on morale. Four primary negative factors affecting morale were: (1) that personnel were often detailed to non-technical jobs for a period of time following completion of the VAST curriculum, which was unavoidable but dissatisfying; (2) a perceived lack of career freedom, since 69 percent of technicians believed they could not transfer to other jobs because of a shortage of VAST personnel; (3) a difficult rating test that was almost universally perceived as unrelated to the skills actually required to operate VAST; and (4) loss of liberty in foreign ports because of the need to catch up on backlogs of WRAs on deployed carriers.

We found little to suggest a direct relationship between morale and either individual or shop performance, however. Since operation of VAST is mostly a machine-tending job once a test has begun, morale has little impact on what happens in the repair process. If a WRA turned out to be difficult to repair, or a fault-isolation was ambiguous, the relationship to morale was quite dependent on the individual sailor. One technician found such occurrences frustrating and demoralizing, while the next found this to be the most interesting part of the job. Overall, there seemed to be both effects within the overall group of VAST personnel, and they tended to have no identifiable net impact.

Where an impact was observable was in the motivation of some technicians to create careful records of test results and ambiguities and the resolution of the ambiguities. These records were often called "wheelbooks," after the notes of ships' pilots who would note how to make safe passages through harbors by relying on knowledge of landmarks, tides, and the like. A good wheelbook was worth its weight in gold, and those who maintained them took considerable pride in them; these people were recognized as a valuable resource to their units. The wheelbook served as a way of both responding to the frustration of difficult WRAs and as a creative outlet for a motivated individual. In this way, motivation did have a long-term impact on VAST performance. Further, we found that presence or absence of a good "wheelbook sailor" was often the primary determinant of the changes in shop performance that accompanied personnel rotations—that person was a training and troubleshooting information resource for the entire site.

For example, a comparison of VAST performance on two different carriers (both with the same aircraft deckload and four VAST stations) showed that the first carrier was getting about 50 percent VAST utilization while the other was reporting 95 percent. Much of the difference was attributed to one exceptional VAST maintainer on the latter ship. On closer examination of actual data on station availability from the PRD Electronics technical representatives aboard (the VAST manufacturer), we found that the difference was not as great as first reported (it was actually about 30 percent greater on the second carrier), but the technical representatives agreed that maintainer skill was one of several variables contributing to the performance differential. This was corroborated by observations of performance variation following ordinary rotation of personnel—improved performance followed the maintainer.

The second major factor investigated was skill acquisition, which is a product of formal training and on-the-job training. Since VAST was a new technology, we decided to examine the training program in detail to determine what impact training was having on shop performance. This was motivated partly by a general desire to validate the training program by the Navy, in part because of criticism from earlier studies, and to improve it where needed.

A typical career for a VAST operator would follow this sequence:

- Two months of boot camp
- Six months of basic electronics training ("A-school")
- Six to eight months for first sea tour
- Two to five months of basic VAST training
- Division assignment of approximately three months (frequently not on automatic test equipment)
- First assignment to the VAST Work Center

Thus, an operator might reach the VAST shop from 19 to 24 months after joining the Navy, and we found that most operators felt that they needed a year in the shop to really become proficient. Proficiency was therefore not being attained until about three years into the first tour of duty. For the typical sailor serving a four-year enlistment, the Navy had about a year of real return on its training investment, unless the sailor chose to re-enlist.

We made a number of interesting discoveries in our examination of the training program, many of which required initiatives beyond the scope of what we were contracted to do, and so could only become recommendations for future work. Among these findings were:

- Significant variations in training tracks and methods between the Atlantic and Pacific Fleets (for example, the length of training to obtain the basic Naval personnel rating for VAST operation could be from 8 to 17 weeks)
- Frequent cancellation of training courses due to lack of instructors and equipment
- No training for VAST supervisors, although some courses which might have been helpful were on the books, but had not been offered for years
- Perception of low effectiveness of the basic operator school—only 39 percent of new technicians felt they could really do their jobs after completion of basic VAST school, and 63 percent of experienced technicians believed they became proficient through on-the-job training and self-instruction

- Lack of training aids to support on-the-job training and reinforce classroom learning for new technicians.

The variations in course length and course sequence in training programs was particularly interesting. These occurred because the training sequences were designed by designated Fleet Replacement Aviation Maintenance Program (FRAMP) squadrons for each VAST-supported aircraft. These FRAMP squadrons had designed different programs, so that at the time of our study, there were no fewer than four different training tracks a VAST operator might follow. Furthermore, there were no FRAMP squadrons for the E-2C or S-3A in the Atlantic Fleet, so that all AIRLANT operators were trained on stations configured for the F-14A. This had very little impact on E-2C operators, but those assigned to the S-3A were often at a disadvantage, since the S-3A TPSs were built by Lockheed, unlike the other two aircraft, which were Grumman designs.

In addition, since more automatic testers were being acquired and planned by the Navy, most experienced technicians and officers felt that an automatic test equipment (ATE) skill rating was needed, rather than the general electronics test rating awarded at that time. Their perception was that there was a low level of skill interchangeability between VAST and other types of electronic testers, and because of the pressure to retain skilled personnel, it was very unlikely that a VAST technician could ever transfer into a non-ATE shop. Our recommendations therefore included creation of an ATE skill rating, in addition to thorough study and revision of the classroom curriculum and on-the-job training programs. We also recommended a thorough evaluation of the prospect of a personnel shortage, if future demographic developments actually diminished the number of recruits. Overall, we concluded that there were clear needs for change in the training program, but the problems we had found were also indicative of a program still in evolution and development, and far from mature.

Finally, beyond studying only the formal training program for enlisted personnel, we also looked into the use of civilian contractor personnel. These technical representatives, universally known as "tech reps," are employees of the WRA and tester manufacturers, and are under contract to Navy sites to provide technical support for their equipment.[23] They constitute a "shadow" work force of considerable importance to the Fleet, and virtually everyone who is familiar with the work they do agrees that the modern Navy could not function without them. They provide not only the depth of technical expertise needed to resolve operating problems with their company's equipment, but also provide a direct liaison to the company, serve as an indirect pipeline for supply of critical parts and materials for their equipment, and also assist military personnel in training and other tasks.

Tech reps are also considered to be a problem for some of these same reasons. Civilians are not supposed to go to sea, because they are not under control of ship's officers. In the event of a shooting war, no civilians are allowed to be placed in harm's way. Yet every ship, and most shore sites, are critically dependent on the tech reps, and they form a vital "corporate memory" for the Navy. In fact, most of the tech reps are former enlisted personnel, and not a few of them leave the Navy and go back to work on the same ship or on the same base they just left. The pay as a tech rep is considerably better than the Navy's, however.

The tech reps answer a large part of the question of how the VAST shops functioned in the process of evolving their training program, and how they functioned in terms of general productivity while other problems were being resolved. Unlike military personnel, the tech reps stay with their equipment and often stay at particular sites for a long time. They learn the idiosyncrasies of the machines, of the Test Program Sets, and of the personnel. Since most were former servicemen themselves, they know the Navy system and get along well with Navy personnel. The tech reps often conduct semi-formal on-the-job training programs, help indoctrinate new operators into the site, help build maintenance skills, and in extreme cases, even lend a hand when production backlogs build up. At the time of our study, they provided much of the personnel continuity that the Navy could not. They are a major information and IP resource which remained unseen for most official purposes.

The Navy maintained an official policy which was to "get the civilians off the ships." While there were good reasons for this, some of which were noted above, it never was achieved during this study, and never will be. But like the Navy, we found ourselves to be in a kind of love-hate affair with the tech reps. On the one hand, we understood the many contributions they made, and we might well have been willing to recommend a somewhat larger role for them, at least during the early years of deployment of any complex technology. On the other hand, since they were eventually supposed to "go away," we could not make such recommendations, especially since they could create false expectations for outside assistance (and increased cost).

Of course, the tech reps were a confound in our study. Their existence made it more difficult to identify and isolate sources of performance variation, and the wide roles they played made it difficult to factor their contribution out. At the same time, they were invaluable to us as sources of information. They would typically help us identify some of the best and some of the worst of personnel, both enlisted and officers. They helped us to be sure we had sampled thoroughly, and did not get either a "best foot forward" view of the shop, nor an unrepresentative "bitch session" perspective. They often answered technical questions to help us validate and interpret our own data when technical issues were important. We found that the large majority of them understood their roles very well. While they knew they were a hidden resource in training, they generally did not get involved in helping shop production. They understood the need to let the sailors make their own mistakes and learn from them, and it was much more typical of them to watch a sailor go through a full shift of frustration with a complicated TPS than to step in and fix a problem, even when they could. Across the Navy as a whole, we concluded that they were a constant factor with counterbalancing effects on shop performance: they helped overcome early deficiencies in the training program and supply pipeline, which helped shop production look better than it might have been, but generally did not intervene in the day-to-day processing of WRAs, even when "learning experiences" meant that performance suffered. We concluded that it was safe to regard them as a relatively constant and benevolent "background noise" in our study.

After observation of the net effect of all of these interdependent factors, our conclusions about the impact of personnel resources were considerably tempered relative to what the review of earlier studies had suggested. Our overall conclusions regarding personnel resources were that while the present supply of personnel was adequate, there could be a future shortage for reasons noted above. However, with respect to the direct impact of retention or training on shop productivity, there was a large and previously unreported impact from the tech reps. Retention actually was slightly above average for the VAST shops when compared to other electronic test ratings (45 percent planning to re-enlist, compared to 38 percent overall), and "hidden retention" was also provided by the tech reps, who augmented the classroom training with considerable expertise from their tours with VAST.

There did appear to be some validity to the observation that training for difficult TPS problem resolution might be deficient, but this could equally be categorized as a technical problem with the TPS, and one that needed resolution by the TPS contractor rather than a change in the training curriculum. For most of the severe TPS problems, this appeared to be the case. At the time we did our data collection, the Navy had proposed a formal course for TPS analysts to deal with these problems. Given these findings, about the worst thing one could say about the formal training program was that it was perhaps too conservative, in that it was kept very long to try to create proficiency, and that length may have been counterproductive.

Skill levels, independent of training considerations, were clearly an issue in shop performance. However, the perceptions of VAST personnel were not significantly different from those in other automatic test equipment shops as to where truly valuable skills were gained—41 percent of VAST operators said they learned most from on-the-job training or tech reps, and 31 percent of the HATS and CAT-IIID operators reported the same. The latter proportion is even more interesting in light of the fact that these testers only service SRAs and have a technically simpler and more uniform workload. Similar findings are often reported from other types of industrial and vocational training studies.

Our summary conclusion did not support the view that increased classroom training as such would have much benefit on VAST performance. We recommended that more emphasis be placed on structured on-the-job training, including job performance aids and other forms of self-instruction, and that this experience be provided earlier in the career of the VAST technician.

NAVAIR structure One of my responsibilities was to interview personnel at NAVAIR headquarters. The two objectives of these interviews were to determine whether adequate information on operations was being received through formal channels by NAVAIR personnel, and whether NAVAIR was able to respond to issues raised by operating sites. The issue was largely structural, in that the Navy matrix organization was complex, and it was possible for complex problems to "get lost in the maze." If that was happening, that could also be a contributing factor to less-than-satisfactory VAST workflow performance.

Using information from the HID matrices, which indicated when an organizational unit outside the VAST shop or AIMD was involved in a decision or action, my first step was to follow the logistics "tail" into the headquarters organization. Each logistics element (see Figure 2.1) was the responsibility of a specific unit. I reviewed my findings with each of the logistics managers, and found that individually they all were aware of fundamental issues before them, and usually had many of the items we were recommending on their "wish list" of changes. In fact, in most cases the SRC study team was viewed as an outside source of support for changes these managers wanted to have implemented. We found no evidence of information either being filtered or distorted beyond the normal kinds of "noise" one encounters in passing information through multiple nodes.

Perhaps the most important finding was that the confusion over what to do for VAST performance had worked its way up into NAVAIR, and there was as much disagreement over how to proceed at higher levels as at operating levels. Apparently, the elephant was just as hard to see from higher altitude as from the deck.

However, while we found the existing structure to be working well for those functions for which it was designed, there were several major problems residing outside those boundaries. Following the normal weapon-system development process, NAVAIR had created a project management office to oversee the contract while VAST was in development and test. Once VAST went into full-scale production, that office was disbanded, and responsibility for support of it was given to the logistics managers I had just interviewed.

In short, VAST had no program or project manager to serve as a single point of integration to resolve VAST-related operational problems. Each of the logistics functions was managed on a "management by exception" principle, which worked very well with most programs. VAST, on the other hand, had problems with apparent symptoms in multiple areas of logistics responsibility, but had no central point to coordinate them between the functions; this was true for budgetary matters as well as for functional problems. "Exceptions" for VAST frequently were not qualitatively the same as they were for other testers. To use a popular example, is an apparent skill problem in repair of a WRA a matter to be handled by the supply and training coordinator (AIR-411); the automatic test equipment manager (AIR-417); the Bureau of Personnel, Publications, or some other unit?

Our recommendations, in simple terms, were to establish a project management office for VAST, and to have all VAST operational and support problems be coordinated through that central office. We also recommended that central budget coordination should be provided, so that trade-off decisions with budgetary impact could be managed to truly obtain the most payoff and to attack the most pressing problems. The VAST manager was recommended to have concurrent authority with functional managers in areas of personnel assignments and training, coordination of WRA contractors and aircraft contractors in designation of future VAST workloads, avionics supply, and use of recurring operational funds.

I also found that numerous organizational compensatory mechanisms had been created to ameliorate the deficiencies of the formal structure. These served many of the same objectives as our recommendations, but did so more slowly and informally. Like the effect of tech reps, these mechanisms reduced the cost of operating the system as it was designed. These require some discussion on their own, and will be taken up in the next chapter.

Measures of effectiveness   As one of my tasks in the examination of the NAVAIR management structure, I evaluated the relationship between the performance measures used in the VAST shops and the AIMD to NAVAIR control and support. The objective of this task was to see whether the information being collected and reported by the Navy's data collection system gave management above the I-level the information needed for effective control and decision-making. The MAF collected a wide range of information about all aspects of the repair cycle, and the Navy's data processing system generated a large number of regular management reports and was able to create special reports, although several months were usually needed to fill such requests. We were interested in exploring the utility of this information for monitoring and control of the WRA repair cycle in more detail.

The most widely used measures, of course, were EMT and TAT, as discussed earlier. My conclusion was that while these measures were highly useful at the I-level, they unfortunately masked much of what NAVAIR management needed to know. EMT provides a useful average of combined time for the four activities needed to repair a WRA in a shop, and it can be calculated for individual WRAs to learn more about the variations within the full site workload of WRAs. However, EMT cannot be parsed into its components, and as we have already seen these individual parts of the repair process can be quite important, especially for difficult TPSs.

TAT measures overall performance for the AIMD, i.e., the full WRA repair cycle. It is the most relevant measure for the repair process, since it tells how long an average WRA requires to be returned to Supply in RFI condition, and this is the critical issue for readiness. Like EMT, however, TAT is a composite of many individual times, several of which are important in their own right, and each may provide useful control information. TAT as measured and reported was not differentiated into any of these component parts and, like EMT, masked control information.

Both of these measures share some common deficiencies for higher management. First, they only measure one element of performance, which is time for cycle completion (hours for EMT or days for TAT). Other factors, such as the importance of the WRA, the relationship of currently scheduled WRAs to mission requirements, or any factors more directly related to OR, are not reflected at all. Second, they are undifferentiated, and unable to provide performance information which reflects specific site missions. The primary issue here is the ability to improve performance on carriers as opposed to shore sites. Since the shore sites have a heavier training burden than the carriers, and conversely, the carriers have higher priorities for supply, personnel readiness and experience, among other factors, we argued that the measures should be able to provide management information on training and preparation for sea deployments. No measure of training or training effectiveness was available from the maintenance data system, however.

The other categorical problem was the high level of aggregation already noted. Neither Awaiting Parts (AWP) time nor Beyond Capability of Maintenance (BCM) frequencies were directly captured or reported to site managers. Thus, there was no way to monitor or control two important contributors to the length of the repair cycle, at either shop or AIMD levels.

The potential for local optimality and system suboptimization was constantly present, partly because of the properties of these measures. A "sensible" decision for a VAST officer faced with huge backlogs is to indirectly get some help from WRA manufacturers by BCM'ing all of the difficult WRAs in the backlog. Since BCM does not count against shop performance, the VAST shop would look good, WRAs eventually would get back onto the Supply shelves in RFI condition, and aircraft would be supported. However, during that BCM interval there would be major stockout problems, creating ripple-effect cannibalization of other aircraft and WRAs, and TAT would be driven through the roof.

Therefore, we recommended that specific methods and devices be created to collect data useful to local managers, particularly information which would allow disaggregation of EMT and TAT into their components when needed. At the same time, we created and recommended adoption of a weighted measure of aggregate performance which would be a more accurate assessment of site performance against mission requirements for NAVAIR. We recognized the realistic pressures on the VAST community to resolve more immediate problems, and did not expect that near-term adoption of these recommendations was likely; indeed, subsequent events bore this expectation out. At the same time, the need for some of these local measures was overcome by other events in the next few years, and I was able to contribute to that outcome, as will be discussed in the next chapter.

Technical issues   I have made little mention of technical issues up to this point, but I want to briefly summarize our findings in that regard. Our information on technical issues was collected from interviews with PRD Electronics, their tech reps at the sites, and operating personnel. We also obtained data from the NAVAIR program logistics office, AIR-417. An independent maintenance data collection and analysis system was being established at the Naval Air Engineering Center (NAEC) at Lakehurst, N.J., and preliminary data from NAEC supported information from AIR-417.

Our findings corroborated the outcome of the Q.E.D. Systems study— VAST itself was functioning very well. While there were a number of technical "bugs" in the VAST stations, VAST was meeting or exceeding design specifications for reliability and availability. Reliability is usually measured as Mean Time Between Failure (MTBF), and VAST MTBF was clearly better than required in the original specification; it was also improving. Numerous additional measures of station performance are routinely tracked by the Navy, and several of these were informative at the time as well. Mean Time Between Unscheduled Maintenance Actions (MTBUMA), which refers to breakdowns, was better than specified. Mean Time To Repair (MTTR), the number of hours to correct a breakdown, was being reported as within specifications. Overall, whether reliability was assessed as the number of breakdowns or preventive shutdowns, the frequency of these, or the length of time needed to get VAST back on line, the stations were working.

At the same time, there was considerable variance between sites and over time, and it was this variance which created the impression that VAST was not as reliable as the data showed. NAVAIR was aware of this variability, and was taking measures to improve the logistics support for VAST and resolve the technical problems which had arisen. This was a normal process of technology maturation, and VAST was progressing well, despite the concern of many in the Navy to have it move ahead even more quickly.

Conclusions

After evaluation of the masses of information we had generated through our study, what we found was rather contradictory to much of what was believed about VAST before we began work. We were able to identify many issues that required NAVAIR attention, and to make a number of recommendations to the Navy for immediate and longer-term corrective actions, as had been intended. But we were not able to find a technical or logistical "smoking gun" to explain apparent VAST production problems, and came away convinced that in terms of the usual logistic support and engineering criteria applied to test equipment, there was none.

The indication that the problems with VAST production were largely system-level and information-processing issues beyond control of the VAST shops began to emerge after several of our early site visits. Both for reasons of meeting the legal requirements of our contract, and for purposes of ensuring maximum data comparability across sites, we did not modify our data-collection or site-study methods after the initial changes from the pilot study at Cecil Field. However, we did expand the scope of our inquiry, as had been intended, and the information gained from that expanded scope helped us to delimit some of these broader systems problems.

Four major conclusions emerged from the information obtained from all the sources used in this study:

1. VAST worked. From a purely technical point of view, the first part of "Experiment 1," the accession of a new tester technology into an established and well-understood organizational workflow, was a success. The new test stations met or exceeded all of their design specifications for reliability, maintainability, and availability. The biggest "surprise" in the VAST technology was the TPS, which turned out to be a much greater source of exceptions and difficulties than the original concept of automatic test equipment had envisioned. But TPSs were not prepared by the VAST manufacturer, and technically were not part of the station—they were designed and produced by the aircraft WRA manufacturer, to the specification for VAST testability. Technical matters were being handled through the normal Navy processes of engineering investigations and technical changes, a routine pattern of technology maturation followed by all weapon systems.

2. VAST perturbed and overloaded the existing AIMD workflow management system, creating serious production bottlenecks and ultimately Supply stockouts. But analysis of throughput data, evaluation of interunit relationships, and investigation of either logistics support or the supporting organizational structure all indicated that the majority of variables affecting shop productivity resided outside the VAST shop—either they were problems traceable to relationships within the AIMD or they involved the complexity of the Test Program Sets and the WRAs which they tested. Failures in logistics support did not explain the WRA stockouts which were occurring along the VAST-shop workflow.

     Skill levels certainly affected VAST performance, but the skills most critical to resolution of production difficulties were those related to TPS problems, and a few areas of VAST maintenance. Training, suggested by some as deficient for the VAST program, was deficient primarily in the sense that it was not being provided for an unexpected area of difficulty, the TPSs. Indeed, in many respects our study suggested that looking at the VAST shops for explanations of WRA stockouts was to be looking in the wrong place, because most of the significant problems we found had nothing to do with VAST, beyond its position in the workflow. Thus, the insertion of a new tester technology as "Experiment 1" was far less successful in terms of its workflow consequences than the new technology itself.

3. The AIMD workflow disturbances resulting from introduction of VAST took the form of numerous changed requirements for information processing. This was evident from direct examination of the volume and variety of information about the WRAs, TPSs, and the stations that had to be acquired and processed, but mostly from the need to continuously monitor the progress of WRAs and their components through all phases of the repair cycle. As the information in this AIMD "database" changed, and squadron requirements changed, WRA-repair priorities had to change. In terms of the IP concepts introduced in Chapter 1, the VAST "experiment" changed the IP issue in the AIMD, and therefore the VAST shop, from a problem of uncertainty and exception resolution to a local problem of equivocality. Every time the composition of the repair queue changed or mission requirements changed, the issue of whether the VAST shop was working on the right problem had to be addressed.

A secondary IP effect could be seen through some of the technicians' responses to production problems. Technicians learned how to collect relevant information and use it analytically to resolve problems in the repair cycle, whether those problems dealt with the VAST stations, the TPSs, interaction with Supply, or use of alternative procedures to effect repairs. To the extent that operator motivation played a role in VAST shop performance, this was probably the most significant effect. Operators would accumulate "wheelbook" information to help them resolve workflow problems. Most of this, of course, was limited to resolution of uncertainties and exceptions at the shop level. Some of this information might easily have been incorporated into training courses, but much of what an effective technician had to know, and had to process, could only be learned through extensive experience with operational conditions. The differentiation between "training" and "skill levels" is most evident when considered from this point of view.

Even from the perspective of workflow within the VAST shop alone, the conclusion that seemed to be unavoidable to me was that VAST technicians and their supervisors were encountering IP capacity demands that were beyond their capability. Technicians, both operators and maintainers, were being confronted with requirements to acquire, store, and process information on TPS problems which were outside the VAST training curriculum. Ambiguities in many parts of some TPSs were occurring, including the test programs themselves, which were the most difficult and inaccessible part of the TPS. Not as immediately apparent, or as much a contributor to the throughput problem as the content of the TPS, was the fact that TPSs from different WRA and aircraft manufacturers were designed with differences in internal logic. This made a troubleshooting approach that was found to be effective with one TPS ambiguity ineffective on another TPS. At one point, as part of the standard Navy "fix," there were serious suggestions for the expansion of training courses to teach the specific operations of some WRAs, and to learn TPS programming. Both of these met considerable resistance, since they could have been recipes for disaster had they not been strictly controlled. As it turned out, neither was ever done.

Supervisors in the VAST shops were also facing IP problems they had never expected. The FIFO approach to WRA repair often simply did not work, because it required too many Build-Up/Tear-Down cycles when large numbers of AWM WRAs had accumulated. It was obviously faster to batch process groups of WRAs using a single TPS build-up, but that could only be done by violating the order of repairs sent from the Production Control Office. Various local methods were devised to try to overcome the problems inherent with batch processing, but without adequate IP capacity, none of these could ever hope to achieve more than serial forms of suboptimatization.

Whether viewed from a perspective of the VAST shop, the AIMD, the station, or the WRA, information processing was a key to site performance. In contrast to the technology of the VAST stations themselves, which worked well, the IP capacity of the AIMD workflow seemed obsolete and inadequate to cope with the IP consequences of VAST.

4.   The perceptability of these problems was made difficult by five key attributes of them. First, many of the relationships between events

and consequences were separated by *time lags*, making it difficult to perceive the connections, or interpret them when they were seen. Second, many system variables were *relational* rather than directly observable, and the relations were often subtle. For example, the outcome of "SRA shortages" at one site existed because of the policy at one site to use very tight control of Awaiting Parts (AWP) WRAs and not allow cannibalization of them; at another site, this problem did not exist because the local decision was to maximize cannibalization from AWP components, and deal with other consequences later. The "variable" causing "parts shortages" was the relation between a measure of performance (AWP control) and a flow of physical materials. Third, these relations were *contextual*, meaning that they varied from site to site for reasons ranging from physical site properties, site aircraft mix, or crew properties, to local relations between these. Fourth, because of the joint effects of relations and contexts, the problems were *polymorphic*—the same problem often took on different attributes, and appeared to be something else. Finally, all of these properties could exist in a state of *loose coupling* to the overall objective of the site, and to the whole Navy. Everyone agreed that OR was the common objective, but there was little agreement about how to achieve it. Local optimality and global suboptimality were therefore very common. VAST created tremendously higher levels of interdependence in the AIMD, and part of the problem was the common one of "everyone doing a good job" as an independent actor in a highly interdependent system.

That the changes VAST induced are difficult to identify can be seen by looking at Figure 3.8 once again. The avionics maintenance workflow after the accession of VAST looked exactly as it had with PGSE, except for the collapse of many repair flows into one. In exactly the same way, the support-of-support workflow remained unchanged after a BB was removed from a tester. As before VAST, some tester components had to go off-site for depot-level support, but this fact was not changed by VAST. Everything looked much as it had before, except there were fewer discrete testers to house and support after VAST than there had been before; if there was any noticeable change, it was that the AIMD workflow had fewer paths through it.

Because problems in the VAST repair cycle were polymorphic, problem attributes support different (and often inconsistent) interpretations. In the case of the VAST workflow, it was very easy to accept the air boss's perception that the job of the VAST shop was to fix the WRAs needed for the next mission to be launched. The VAST supervisor could easily agree, but with the caution that unless growing inventories of failed WRAs were reduced, there would soon come a point where the number operationally ready would be too small to support any mission. And the more that we disrupted the scheduled repair workflow, the bigger those piles would get. Thus, from this point of view, it made perfect sense to forgo one mission to gain others. Both the air boss and the VAST officer were trying their best to do a good job, but in the absence of the information buffers needed to make effective tradeoff decisions, neither was "right."

Linkages between the three major organizational units considered here show that the belief that one unit was not performing effectively was a motivation for others to create physical parts buffers to protect their units from degraded performance. To a considerable extent, these actions appear to be related to the inadequacy of information buffers, as just suggested. WRA buffers distort the AIMD repair cycle, and TAT and possibly EMT data thus reflect lowered performance as a direct consequence of the inadequacies of IP capacity in the repair cycle. That is, if squadrons behaved suboptimally to enhance their own unit performance because they did not have adequate information on the status of RFI WRAs, that same informational problem could be predicted to cause lowered performance within the repair cycle in the AIMD.

We categorized the problems we found as roughly 80 percent management and information processing issues, and 20 percent matters of engineering and technology and technical issues. For example, no one questioned the assumption that a WRA would be kept on VAST until it was repaired, but experience suggested the need to control the length of time a test would be allowed to continue without resolution. From one perspective, this is obviously a technical problem, and most likely with the TPS; but in the operating environment, it becomes a management problem, where continuous monitoring of the repair cycle is needed and proactive decision-making is required to maximize station availability, WRA production, and thus aircraft OR.

Consistent with other system dynamics studies (Hall, 1976, 1980, 1984; Kochan and Useem, 1992), the time lags between events and outcomes impaired correct interpretation of feedback and recognition of workflow problems. This, in turn, limited the ability of managers to correctly isolate and correct problems beyond the local level. As argued by Cyert and March (1993), managers used a localized "problemistic search" strategy, and the properties of the system usually allowed for a problem definition which seemed accurate when it was not; this was particularly true for problems with relational causes. These problems often caused positive feedback (or "hot feedback," to use the electrical term) within the system. Unlike negative feedback, the distinguishing feature of such hot feedback is its destabilizing effect on a system. Over the long time it took for these problems to become manifest, destabilization was clearly evident.

One example of the "hot feedback" problem was with management of bit-and-piece (PEB) parts—because the accounting system could be used to bypass Supply and protect local funds, Supply never really knew what PEB consumption was. Given data reporting very limited PEB consumption, Supply would order less PEB stock, aggravating the subsequent PEB "stockout problem" in the SRA repair shops. This created pressure to do something quickly, and the best way to respond was to use the accounting system to bypass Supply again, and to make that even worse by having tech reps bring parts directly from manufacturers as part of their "customer service." Similar hot feedback effects were observed from the relation between AWP management and WRA cannibalization on the regular WRA repair workflow.

From the simplified description of the AIMD repair cycle presented in Chapter 3, in addition to the studies and preliminary evaluations reported here, it would seem that the true sources of problems in the repair cycle should be easy to identify. This was far from the case, however. Appendix 4.1 summarizes many of the problems that were found in the AIMD workflow, based on surveys done in the late 1970s and early 1980s (including some of my own). Because of the time when the surveys were taken, these problems include findings from SRA work centers which tested SRAs off-loaded from VAST. Nevertheless, these problems were part of the overall AIMD information load that had to be processed if any production were to be gotten, and trying to sort out the "signal" about what was afflicting the workflow was quite difficult in the context of all the "noise."

Obviously, the avionics maintenance system had to function if the Naval Air Force was to be able to achieve its mission. Patchwork, local fixes, and the ingenuity of sailors and officers were necessary to keep aircraft in flying condition. What this section has reviewed is the nature of the most common error-reduction and correction methods used during the years when VAST was being studied and system changes were being considered. This discussion illustrates a range of adjustive responses to the problems occurring in the avionics workflow. It suggests that organizations can, indeed, achieve a much greater level of adaptability than either the population ecology model or the quantum view would suggest (Hannan and Freeman, 1977; Freeman and Hannan, 1983).[24] While not a smooth or linear accession, many of these adaptations foreshadowed larger system-level changes made in later years. As will be shown, nearly all of these methods involved intensive IP in this dynamic organization.

While there is much study of new technologies as they begin accession, there is little study of the information-processing impact of the new technology on the organization. In the case of VAST, organizational stability was assumed, even though many units of PGSE would be superseded by VAST. The unstated assumption was that VAST accession was a problem under uncertainty, and that exceptions would be managed using the IP system that had existed for an earlier generation of avionics-maintenance technology. Accordingly, there was no consideration of IP capacity as a concurrent requisite for the accession of VAST. VAST was "dropped into" an existing organization, with the MAFs, VIDS, periodic reporting processes, and other IP capacity determinants of that organization remaining unchanged. Most important, there was no increase in IP capacity to deal with larger information loads if they emerged, and they clearly did.

"Experiment 1," the accession of a new type of technology in the AIMD workflow, had produced some serious negative organizational consequences. But at the same time, local changes in IP capacity which were precursors to Experiment 2 emerged from this experiment—personnel at several sites had begun to recognize deficiencies in the IP system and take local corrective actions. The modified IP systems which resulted will be discussed in Chapter 5, and the full effects of these changes and the field quasi-experiment they became part of, in Chapter 6.

By the end of 1979, the final report of the Systems Research Corporation study had been turned in. The implication was that the IP variables shown in Table 4.2 offered more potential for resolution of the AIMD production problems than the standard set of elements in the logistics tail of aircraft and tester support. We felt we had gone a long way toward explaining some of the contradictory findings of earlier studies by examining that broader range of variables. The Navy had a great deal to ponder about correction of VAST operational difficulties, and many of the issues we had identified required an effort far beyond "fixing" a single technology. We were all tired, had other things to do, and so the group disbanded. But I learned an enormous amount with the SRC team, had the opportunity to work very hard with highly motivated, interesting people, and began some long-term relationships. The study we did, like many research and consulting projects, was both some of the hardest work I had ever done and some of the best fun I ever had.

Notes

1. *Bibliography for Automatic Test Equipment Work Center Effectiveness and Efficiency Study.* Falls Church, VA: Systems Research Corporation, 4 April 1978. Supported by contract no. N68335-78-C-1560.

2. *Productivity Enhancement of the Versatile Avionics Shop Test System Site Evaluation and Final Report.* Falls Church, VA: Systems Research Corporation, 6 March 1979. Supported by contract no. N68335-78-C-1593.

3. Kmetz, John L., An information-processing study of a complex workflow in aircraft electronics repair. *Administrative Science Quarterly,* Vol. 29 (2), June 1984: 255-280.

4. Four major simulations were performed over two years: Crockett, James J. and Paul Heimbach, *Tailored VAST (Versatile Avionics Shop Test) Computer Simulation Model* (Warminster, Pa.: Naval Air Development Center, June 1973); Kaufman, Philip F., *The VIEWS/ATE (VAST IMA Effectiveness by Workload Simulation/Automatic Test Equipment) Simulation Model* (Warminster, Pa.: Naval Air Development Center, November 1973); Kaufman, Philip F., *NAS Miramar/VIEWS—Simulation Model and Application* (Warminster, Pa.: Naval Air Development Center, June 1974); Kaufman, Philip F., *The Marine MMF (Mobile Maintenance Facility) VIEWS Simulation Model* (Warminster, Pa.: Naval Air Development Center, October 1974).

5. *VAST CVA Mock-Up Workflow Simulation Study* (Philadelphia, Pa: Naval Air Engineering Center, October 1973).

6. Makrakis, G. D., and Mackowiak, D., *Evaluation of Versatile Avionics Shop Test (VAST) AN/USM-247 (V), Sixth Interim Report* (Patuxent River, Md.: Naval Air Test Center, July 1973).

7. Makrakis, G. D., *Evaluation of Versatile Avionics Shop Test (VAST) AN/USM-247 (V), Seventh Interim Report* (Patuxent River, Md.: Naval Air Test Center, July 1973). This report found that VAST achieved Mean Time Between Failure (MTBF), the typical engineering measure of reliability, of 44.9 hours. In addition, VAST was found to be achieving increasing MTBF as the cruise went on. A similar conclusion was reached by an independent team responsible for VAST evaluation, as reported in *Assist in the Technical Evaluation of the Versatile Avionics Shop Test (VAST) System* (Norfolk, VA: Operational Test and Evaluation Force, August 1973).

8. Makrakis, G. D., *Evaluation of Versatile Avionics Shop Test (VAST) AN/USM-247 (V), Eighth and Final Report* (Patuxent River, Md.: Naval Air Test Center, November 1973).

9. Centralized Navy program restores readiness of F-14. *Aviation Week and Space Technology,* October 6, 1980: 67-72.

10. The $478 million program ended successfully in the summer of 1980.

11. Craddock, D. G., 5 February 1976. Letter from Commanding Officer, Naval Air Station Cecil Field to Commanding Officer, NAVAIR (Codes PMA-244, AIR-534, and AIR-417). Subject: *Avionics Versatile Automatic Testing and Repair, AN/USM-247 (V) VAST.*

12. *Opportunities for the Navy to Reduce its Requirements for Avionics Testing Stations.* (Washington, D.C.: U.S. General Accounting Office, June, 1976).

13. *Second and Last Partial Report on Project F/C 2, Follow-on Operational Test and Evaluation of VAST System (OPNAV Report Symbol 3960-12).* (Norfolk, VA: Operational Test and Evaluation Force, May, 1976).

14. *Summary of Maintenance Procedures and Problems at Fleet ATE Sites.* Virginia Beach, Va.: Q.E.D. Systems, Inc., 1977.

15. A "false removal" is an induction of a WRA that passes all its tests (i.e., no fault is detected) and is sent back to Supply as RFI. Although not a direct conclusion of the study, the large number of false removals probably distorted EMT downward, since a WRA with no fault will usually pass its test on the first run and require no further action.

16. Sauve, S. P., and Robinson, Donald D., *Analysis of failed parts on Naval avionics systems.* Preliminary Boeing Company Report for Naval Air Systems Command (AIR-340), undated. Date believed to be late 1976 or early 1977.

17. Kozlowski, H. J., *Study of S-3A components in Awaiting Parts status at NAS Cecil Field, Florida.* Burbank, Ca.: Lockheed California Company, April, 1977.

18. NAVAIR Letter on automatic test equipment (53424/MDM, 1 October 1976).

19. Data were obtained from Enclosure 2 to NAVAIR letter 53424/MDM, Ser 915. In reality, however, many of these SRAs would never have been placed on VAST, since they were from avionics devices such as radars and infra-red sensors which VAST was unable to support without extensive modification. The

principal departure from the plan for VAST support was the acquisition of the HATS and CAT-IIID testers, neither of which was intended when the Navy decided to develop Automatic Test Equipment.

20. The team consisted of James D. Bain (project manager), James Bick (statistics), Robert Canady (industrial management), Jo-Ellen Hayden (ATE management), James Martin (human factors), John Stanhagen (maintenance management), Gregory Smith (human factors), and me (organizational analysis). Everyone on the team had a primary specialty, but we all helped each other out in a lot of our work. This was a big undertaking, and it required that kind of cooperation. This was a great bunch of people to work with, and I think of them all fondly.

21. Most "paperwork" was making entries on the MAF, but some other forms and local logs were kept at most sites. For example, assistance given to another AIMD unit was recorded on a Support Action Form (SAF); each station had a logbook (the "passdown log") in which operators and maintainers would record information on the status and functioning of the station. This was of immediate value to the next shift, and also kept a running history of the station.

22. David I. Cleland and William R. King, *Systems Analysis and Project Management* (New York: McGraw-Hill, 1968: 196-224). The linear responsibility chart is best suited to a project management environment, where decisions must be coordinated across multiple line functions by project managers, an organizational relationship which tends to confuse people not experienced with it, and also tends to disperse decision-making in unplanned ways if not carefully managed. We decided to use this method because of the indications that interunit difficulties seemed to be a possible factor in VAST performance.

23. The Harris tech reps are formally known as Logistic Support Representatives, or LSRs.

24. I am not suggesting that the population ecology or quantum theories are necessarily incorrect. Rather, I believe that observation of many organizations suggests that while some cannot adapt to new situations, many others do. It is the latter we know least about, and the dynamics of these changes that need better explanation and understanding.

References

Assist in the Technical Evaluation of the Versatile Avionics Shop Test (VAST) System (1973), Norfolk, VA: Operational Test and Evaluation Force, August 1973.

Bibliography for Automatic Test Equipment Work Center Effectiveness and Efficiency Study (1978), Falls Church, VA: Systems Research Corporation, 4 April 1978. Supported by contract no. N68335-78-C-1560.

Centralized Navy program restores readiness of F-14 (1980), *Aviation Week and Space Technology,* October 6, 1980: 67-72.

Cleland, David I., and King, William R. (1968), *Systems Analysis and Project Management.* New York: McGraw-Hill.

Craddock, D. G. (5 February 1976), Letter from Commanding Officer, Naval Air Station Cecil Field to Commanding Officer, NAVAIR (Codes PMA-244, AIR-534, and AIR-417), Subject: *Avionics Versatile Automatic Testing and Repair, AN/USM-247 (V) VAST.*

Crockett, James J., and Heimbach, Paul (1973), *Tailored VAST (Versatile Avionics Shop Test) Computer Simulation Model.* Warminster, Pa.: Naval Air Development Center, June.

Cyert, Richard, and March, James G. (1993), *The Behavioral Theory of the Firm, second edition.* New York: Blackwell.

Freeman, John, and Hannan, Michael T. (1983), Niche width and the dynamics of organizational populations. *American Journal of Sociology,* 88 (6): 1116-1145.

Hall, Roger I. (1976), A system pathology of an organization: The rise and fall of the old *Saturday Evening Post. Administrative Science Quarterly,* 21: 185-211.

Hall, Roger, I. (1980), Decision making in a complex organization, in England, George W., Neghandi, Anant R., and Wilpert, Bernard (Eds), *The Functioning of Complex Organizations.* New York: Oelgeschlager, Gunn and Hain.

Hall, Roger I. (1984), The natural logic of management policy making: its implications for the survival of an organization. *Management Science,* 30: 905-927.

Hannan, Michael T., and Freeman, John (1977), The population ecology of organizations. *American Journal of Sociology,* 82 (5): 929-964.

Heimbach, Paul (1973), *Tailored VAST (Versatile Avionics Shop Test) Computer Simulation Model.* Warminster, Pa.: Naval Air Development Center, June 1973.

Kaufman, Philip F. (1973), *The VIEWS/ATE (VAST IMA Effectiveness by Workload Simulation/Automatic Test Equipment) Simulation Model.* Warminster, Pa.: Naval Air Development Center, November 1973.

Kaufman, Philip F. (1974a), *NAS Miramar/VIEWS—Simulation Model and Application.* Warminster, Pa.: Naval Air Development Center, June 1974.

Kaufman, Philip F. (1974b), *The Marine MMF (Mobile Maintenance Facility) VIEWS Simulation Model.* Warminster, Pa.: Naval Air Development Center, October,1974.

Kochan, Thomas A., and Useem, Michael (1992), *Transforming Organizations.* New York: Oxford University Press.

Kozlowski, H. J. (1977), *Study of S-3A components in Awaiting Parts status at NAS Cecil Field, Florida.* Burbank, Ca.: Lockheed California Company, April, 1977.

Kmetz, John L., (1984), An information-processing study of a complex workflow in aircraft electronics repair. *Administrative Science Quarterly,* Vol. 29 (2): 255-280.

Makrakis, G. D. (1973a), *Evaluation of Versatile Avionics Shop Test (VAST) AN/USM-247 (V), Seventh Interim Report.* Patuxent River, Md.: Naval Air Test Center, July 1973.

Makrakis, G. D. (1973b), *Evaluation of Versatile Avionics Shop Test (VAST) AN/USM-247 (V), Eighth and Final Report.* Patuxent River, Md.: Naval Air Test Center, November 1973.

Makrakis, G. D., and Mackowiak, D. (1973), *Evaluation of Versatile Avionics Shop Test (VAST) AN/USM-247 (V), Sixth Interim Report.*Patuxent River, Md.: Naval Air Test Center, July 1973.

NAVAIR Letter on automatic test equipment (53424/MDM, 1 October 1976).

Opportunities for the Navy to Reduce its Requirements for Avionics Testing Stations (1976), Washington, D.C.: U.S. General Accounting Office, June, 1976.

Overview of a Typical Aircraft Intermediate Maintenance Department (1983), Syosset, N.Y.: Harris Corporation, Government Support Systems Division, June, 1983. Harris Document Number 6002-83-017.

Productivity Enhancement of the Versatile Avionics Shop Test System Site Evaluation and Final Report (1979), Falls Church, VA: Systems Research Corporation, 6 March 1979. Supported by contract no. N68335-78-C-1593.

Sauve, S. P., and Robinson, Donald D. (undated), *"Analysis of failed parts on Naval avionics systems."* Preliminary Boeing Company Report for Naval Air Systems Command (AIR-340).

Second and Last Partial Report on Project F/C 2, Follow-on Operational Test and Evaluation of VAST System (OPNAV Report Symbol 3960-12) (1976), Norfolk, VA: Operational Test and Evaluation Force, May, 1976.

Summary of Maintenance Procedures and Problems at Fleet ATE Sites (1977), Virginia Beach, Va.: Q.E.D. Systems, Inc.

VAST CVA Mock-Up Workflow Simulation Study (1973), Philadelphia, Pa: Naval Air Engineering Center, October 1973.

Appendix 4.1

AIMD Workflow Problems

A number of significant workflow problems occurred in the actual repair cycle. Some were local problems due to the Automatic Test Equipment (ATE) shop and supply functions, and others were traceable to other sources.

Logistic and Supply Problems

The following logistic and supply problems were taken from site summary reports and firsthand information from Harris/GSSD Logistic Support Representatives (LSRS) aboard carriers and at land-based facilities:[1]

a. Supply support of bit and piece parts is weak. Many times Navy allowance items are not on board. Awaiting parts times are long; for example, 3 months is a common waiting time.

b. Shipboard supply has trouble locating onboard parts. The ship master-item stock-status listings appear to be incorrect in many cases.

c. Supply-to-AIMD interface is weak.

d. Supply is weeks behind in posting receipt documents.

e. Many of the Maintenance Assist Modules (MAMs) aboard are never used; other common failure items are not stocked as MAMs.

f. Support through LSRs thwarts the supply process at shore sites to a much greater extent than aboard a carrier.

g. Aircraft carriers are dependent on a supply pipeline, in that onboard aviation stores are not adequate to do the job.

h. Delivery times within the AIMD are too lengthy; deliveries often take 2 to 3 hours.

i. The Aviation Supply Office (ASO) does not properly establish or adhere to allowances. New allowances usually take up to a year to be filled.

j. Repair and replacement of Shop Replaceable Assemblies (SRAs) are often performed without the proper notification and documentation,

233

making it difficult to keep track of their status and location within the Work Centers.

k. Sole-source contractor-supplied items usually have very poor availability and delivery times. Such items can disable repair capacity for months.

l. Where substitute integrated-circuit "chips" are provided by Supply, they may or may not work when installed. There is no engineering support available to determine which chips will work at the AIMD. The result is wasted motion and time in the repair and test activity.

Technical Problems

a. ATE is highly susceptible to damage from voltage fluctuations.

b. Power surge conditions exist in the at-sea environment.

c. ATE is highly temperature-sensitive.

d. Hardware connections are not standardized.

e. ATE testing of Units Under Test (UUTs) requires a multitude of Interconnection Devices (IDs).

f. Test Program Sets are not properly maintained within the system, and the local personnel are not able to change them.

g. Use of Commercial Test Equipment (CTE) as part of ATE poses several problems. CTE is often less durable and reliable. Documentation is weak or totally lacking. CTE lacks preventive maintenance checks like other Navy equipment. CTE lacks self-test to fault isolate on station to one SRA.

h. WRA configuration changes require greater operator interaction. As WRAs are modernized, their component SRAs are changed. CTE will be a bigger problem.

i. Timing problems are very difficult to diagnose on ATE.

j. Overall environment at sea is plagued by vibration problems. The ship's motion, the catapults, and engineering plant create extensive vibration and shock.

k. Configuration of a Versatile Avionics Shop Test (VAST) system for a particular type of aircraft is lengthy. Reconfiguration is avoided whenever possible.

l. VAST operations frequently require longer times for Build-Up and Tear-Down of the station for certain UUT generic types than for test run times. BU/TD procedures frequently require 2 hours or more.

m. Hybrid Automatic Test System (HATS) is particularly unreliable for shipboard use. It was designed for vibration-free environment, with low humidity, and a cool and stable ambient temperature.

n. CAT-IIID has no maintenance plan at present; local personnel do not know which SRAs will be tested in future.

o. There are too many program languages, i.e., VAST Interface Test Application Language (VITAL) and Mini-VITAL for VAST, Abbreviated Test Language for All Systems (ATLAS) for HATS, and others like Waveforms Analysis Language (WAFL) for special procedures.

p. Contractors withhold certain technical data for proprietary reasons.

q. Cross-reference of interchangeable components is very limited.

r. Some technical updates and changes of avionics and electronics equipment leave the circuitry quite different, but looking the same. Identification of the actual configuration is confusing and slows the repair process.

s. The time that Supply needs to pick up WRAs from squadron may vary from 15 minutes to 2 hours.

t. There is clearly no decision support system directly controlling the repair priorities of failed equipment. Areas requiring control are items Awaiting Parts (AWP), the preferences of the individual operators, the ability to "batch process" a large number of WRAs and SRAS, etc.

u. A large part of the problem is AIMD and/or ATE system overload. The number of WRAs and SRAs backlogged and requiring repair work simply overwhelms the shop capabilities.

v. Cannibalization must be controlled or it may ultimately reduce the overall parts availability to [intermediate maintenance] shops. Cannibalization should be discouraged except in cases of extreme need. The difficulty, of course, is that cannibalization increases the cannibalized items turnaround time.

w. The decision to stop testing before a fault is found is now a widely considered option on the part of most VAST shop supervisors.

x. Many ATE maintenance decisions are initiated by ATE operators, and in some cases they bypass a bad ATE Building Block (BB) by changing to another type of WRA.

y. Manning levels should be reviewed throughout all ATE work centers. There is apparently no rhyme or reason in the manning of various ATE shops at the present time.

z.   There is a problem allowing some WRAs to continue in an iterative loop for the entire shift without any resolution; this means no WRAs are being repaired on that shift.

Repair Cycle Problems

a.   Workload fluctuates widely depending on flight operations, weather, and deployments.   The fluctuations are difficult to anticipate.   All PC scheduling is done manually and without detailed policy.   As a result, scheduling is difficult and often ineffective, and PC is often more involved in monitoring than controlling.   Work Center chiefs direct repair activities based on Expedite Repair (EXREP) lists.

b.   Communication between PC and Work Centers is often very weak. Work Centers lack knowledge of the materials that are Awaiting Maintenance (AWM) at PC.   AWM and in-work tasks are loosely managed.   Some AWM tasks are considered in-work by PC.

c.   Organization, layout, and operation of VAST Work Centers varies significantly from one location to another.   Individuals cannot transfer easily from one shop to the same shop at a different site without some relearning.

d.   The priority system is unreliable.   Priorities are established by Supply at the time of induction but are not updated.   As a result, the indicated priority does not reflect Supply needs.   Consequently, priorities are not worked exclusively.   Supervisors and operators use their own experience to determine what needs can be filled and they modify the schedule accordingly.

e.   The time available for repair work on ATE is significantly reduced whenever the station is needed for on-line maintenance efforts.

f.   In some cases, aircraft carriers begin deployment with ATE at reduced capability.

g.   While protective "bubble-wrap" is necessary, it creates identification and paperwork problems and requires unnecessary time expenditure.

h.   Backlogs of items Awaiting Parts (AWP) can be as high as several hundred items.   This volume requires special efforts to keep from losing assets at the supply-to-maintenance interface.   Special management attention is required for programs such as the Closed Loop Aeronautical Management Program (CLAMP), and for cannibalization actions. Additional civilian assistants, LSRs, or Material Control Coordinators (MCCs) are hired to expedite parts delivery.

i. Inexperienced operators send numerous UUTs to AWP for failure call-outs that later prove erroneous.
j. Cannibalization, if not carefully monitored, can lead to loss of assets.
k. Paperwork is complex and time consuming, which is detrimental to the primary goal of avionics/electronics repair.
l. The repair cycle can be entered by work request for either test and check only or by maintenance assist request. This dual method of entry provides a source of confusion that can lead to the loss of equipment.
m. Data analysis monthly summary reports are so long in formulation that they are not timely enough to be used as an onsite management tool.
n. Storage space is severely limited in many AIMD environments. Possibility for damage is greatly increased when Ready For Issue (RFI) or AWM gear is stowed on deck, even if only temporarily.
o. Microminiature repair capabilities do not exist in most Work Centers. Twelve hours or longer is typically required to send UUTs to a Microminiature Work Center in the module repair shop and back for retest.
p. After repair actions are completed, the AIMD loses track of delivery time to the operational maintenance activity. In many cases, 3 days elapse before the squadron gets its WRAs.
q. Collateral Duty Inspectors (CDI) do not verify that a WRA or an SRA has passed testing as a part of their quality control function.

Maintenance and Supply Interface

a. Local differences in operating procedures at each Intermediate Maintenance 3 (IM-3) site can mean that the time from when an operator requests an SRA until that requisition is filled may range from 10 minutes to a matter of hours or even days. Because of the degree of uncertainty and test ambiguity which exists within repair activities of the ATE system, this time differential has substantial impact on system production efficiency. The major reasons for this time differential can be attributed to:

    • Greater operator attention to the accuracy of part requisitions
    • Time lost and errors created through documentation
    • Time lost to material handling activities
    • Different requirements for test station reconfiguration.

b. Local arrangements for Supply support also differ at each site. It seems that these differences are the decisions of local management and reflect a combination of the organizational and service requests levied on the ASO by the various maintenance departments (O, I, D). Also involved are the ability and willingness of the supply department to meet these requests within the constraints of Supply personnel manning levels, and the flexibility of the ASO in creating local tracking systems for material to facilitate the maintenance workflow.

c. Several different Supply/maintenance working relationships exist. At the worst extreme, WRAs determined to be in need of parts were forwarded to the AWP storage area where several additional days or additional ATE-to-AWP storage iterations could transpire before the subject WRA was made RFI. Additional days were added to the Turnaround Time (TAT) cycle when supply personnel were "unable" to process the parts requisitions for several days after their arrival into AWP storage. When this occurred, it was not identified by the 3M system as a supply delay, but rather as a maintenance delay due to the way MAF entries are made. On the other hand, it could be shown that at the same site, operators had gone back for a specific part for a specific WRA as many as seven consecutive times. An examination of these data suggested carelessness and a lack of discipline in ascertaining that the parts requisition was properly filled out. These anecdotes serve to reflect one point: current system practices permit local environments to establish their own supply and maintenance interface, but often at the expense of the organizational goal.

d. There are several variables which are involved in the supply and maintenance interface as it relates to ATE, including:

- Existence, location, and size of WRA, SRA, and spare and repair part pools
- Willingness to lend SRAs and WRAs for use in troubleshooting/batch processing
- Stock levels and replenishment practices for SRA and spare and repair part pools

e. The most desirable situation for batch processing is one in which several WRAs are available for comparison of diagnostic program call-outs and for card swapping. This is augmented on the supply side by having an SRA pool closely situated to the ATE shop with SRAs available in minutes to the operator. The element of timing is very important because much time is lost if a WRA/ID/ATE configuration must be torn down while awaiting parts. If the build-up remains intact and the replacement SRA is inserted immediately into the WRA, testing can continue without an additional tear-down and build-up.

f.   The most desirable situation for SRA testing is to have a bit-and-piece part pool immediately available to the operator who is identifying the fault on the SRA. He then can select the parts required to RFI the board, and package them with the board for transfer to microminiature repair. The advantage of this system is a time savings. If the parts were not supplied with the board, the board would go into an AWP status.

g.   The supply of bit-and-piece parts for SRA repair has been an ever-increasing problem in recent years. Difficulties include the proliferation of microtechnology, questions of interchangeability, and the cost of complex components. Many bit-and-piece parts are stocked by the Defense Supply Agency (DSA); many others are stocked by the ASO. In either case, delays are often lengthy and the part received may not be interchangeable with the one removed. To circumvent these problems, NAVAIR has often bought initial stocks of spare parts to be sited at the AIMD for use in particular hardware programs. These stocks then are maintained by contractor inventory managers and replenished through the contractor's spare ordering chain.

h.   Although these were originally meant to be stopgap measures, the bit-and-piece part storage area (called pre-expended bin) has largely replaced the Navy supply system for certain portions of many intermediate maintenance units. Operation and replenishment of the pools is nonstandard, and varies from site to site. Most importantly, usage data from the pools often fails to enter the supply system. Thus, the system never registers a demand and parts are not procured.

Notes

1.   The data reported here are excerpted from the *Overview of a Typical Aircraft Intermediate Maintenance Department*. Syosset, N.Y.: Harris Corporation, Government Support Systems Division, June, 1983. Harris Document Number 6002-83-017.

5 Coping with Complexity in the Avionics Maintenance System

Introduction

As indicated in Chapter 4, the VAST accession induced unexpected IP demands in the avionics-repair workflow. The SRC study investigated more than logistics support alone, and this chapter reports the adjustments we found in the VAST shops and the AIMD to cope with the unanticipated IP demands that VAST brought with it. A number of formal and informal IP adjustments to workflow dysfunctions in the repair cycle were found, involving both "hard" and "soft" system variables. The chapter ends with descriptions of findings on early information technology (IT) interventions.

Background Developments

In the early 1980s, PRD Electronics Company, the VAST manufacturer, was purchased by Harris Corporation, and was renamed Harris/PRD. The relevance of this to my program of VAST research was that I had done part of the PRD surveys and much of the management and organizational analysis in the SRC study. Given that experience, I was asked by PRD to participate in a group the Navy uses to bring new weapon systems to maturity after they go into full-scale production and initial deployment. This group is known as an Integrated Logistics Support Management Team, or ILSMT. Since VAST is a tester categorized as "common" because it supports multiple aircraft, and is "automatic test equipment," the acronym CATE (i.e., Common Automatic Test Equipment) was also applied to the name of the organization; the full acronym is CATE/ILSMT.[1]

The ILSMT is an integrative structure which brings together all members of the community with mutual interest in a weapon system. In the case of VAST, this was NAVAIR, Harris/PRD, personnel from shore sites and carriers responsible for VAST and its operation, representatives of all of the support sites and logistics offices (training, Supply, etc.) and any others designated, requested, or in some cases, instructed to participate. The CATE/ILSMT met every six months in a conference format, alternating between the Atlantic and Pacific coasts, since the group was large and was responsible for VAST accession in both the Atlantic and Pacific fleets. The objective of the ILSMT meetings was to keep everyone involved in the accession of VAST and attendant systems aware of all technological, logistics, and operational problems, and track progress toward the resolution of those problems. It provided an opportunity for face-to-face meetings of all involved parties, and generated a list of action items from each meeting. At the next meeting, one of the first items of business was to follow up on the previous action items, to be sure problems were being resolved and information made available to all team members. Ideas for changes and modifications were also discussed, so that future system developments were also influenced by the ILSMTs. This pattern of activity has continued, and ILSMTs are still important integrative structures in the Navy.

My activity on the CATE/ILSMT was supported through Harris/PRD. Their interest in my involvement was that they knew that VAST worked, and that the production problems in the WRA repair cycle were not because of technical deficiencies in their tester. Since my area of expertise was in these organizational and management areas, they felt it was important to have that point of view represented at the meetings. Harris/PRD was actively developing newer versions of VAST for two other aircraft in pre-deployment testing, the F/A-18 Hornet, manufactured by McDonnell-Douglas, and a new antisubmarine-warfare helicopter; Harris wanted to make the transition of these testers to operational support of these aircraft as smooth as possible.

There was another area of manufacturer interest as well. The Navy had begun development of an automatic test equipment system for the growing Fleet-wide use of electronics. This tester was designated the Consolidated Support System (CSS), and it would eventually serve the electronic-test needs of the air, surface, and submarine fleets.[2] This was a major item of business, and the workflow limitations encountered with VAST in the AIMD might soon be facing all the other parts of the Navy, i.e., surface ships and submarines as well as the Naval Air Force. Being able to adapt the new technologies to their particular maintenance workflows, without being subjected to the early difficulties of the VAST accession, was important to everyone concerned.

As will be seen below, the CATE/ILSMT was important in its own right as an adjustive IP tool during maturation of the VAST technology. My ability to participate in it gave me access to much valuable research data.

Interim Information-Processing Adjustments to VAST Production Problems

As discussed in Chapter 4, there were numerous production problems found in the VAST avionics-maintenance workflow both on carriers and at shore sites. The broad problem categories investigated in the SRC study (see Table 4.2) had many similar components, ranging from problems specific to the VAST shop to those which were NAVAIR-wide. Again, most of these were found within the AIMD and the avionics repair cycle, and since SRC's charge was to investigate logistics support and any other factors affecting VAST performance, we collected data on both the problems we found and the coping mechanisms Navy personnel used to adjust for these problems during the early stages of VAST deployment. As reported in an earlier study,[3] most workflow problems fell into these nine categories:

1. Fluctuations in workload. Over the course of a deployment, the workload changes dramatically, particularly on carriers, and therefore demands for VAST shop activity vary.
2. VAST ambiguities. Fault isolations were often not clear or determinate.
3. Supply-VAST relationship. VAST had to keep Supply stocked, but many facets of the reciprocal relationship, whether providing full bit-and-piece spares or information on expected demands on Supply, were not consistent across sites.
4. VAST performance objectives. Related to item (3) in some ways, the definition of what VAST was to do, and who the shop worked for, was not consistent.
5. VAST maintenance and station availability. VAST required much maintenance to operate effectively, and when maintenance was not done well or delayed because of WRA workload demands, operator confidence in fault isolations decreased, and in some cases the stations simply broke down and were unavailable, either completely of for some WRAs.
6. WRA and VAST configuration control. Configuration control (or the perception of a lack of it) contributed to some test ambiguities and to operator repetition of tests for confidence in fault isolation.
7. VAST operator skills. VAST operator skills were sometimes not as well developed as perceived desirable; this was especially true (and probably most valid) in the area of TPS trouble-shooting skills.

8. Lack of central decision authority. AIMDs and NAVAIR in general did not have a central point for assessment and resolution of system-wide problems.
9. Inadequacies in the decision information system. A broad range of problems in this category were found within the VAST shops, the Supply system, within particular AIMDs, and peculiar to individual shore sites and carriers. In general, the VIDS/MAF system was not able to provide necessary workflow control information.

The Navy did not simply allow these problems and OR deficiencies to continue without reacting to them, as seen in Chapter 4. During the time when the SRC study and earlier research on the VAST workflow were underway, a number of adjustive responses were brought to bear on these problems. These adjustments consisted of IP mechanisms ranging from semi-formal organizational changes to informal on-site adjustments. Eight types of adjustment mechanisms were identified, all of which were helpful in correcting or ameliorating some of the operational difficulties described above, by enabling parts of the system to process the information necessary to keep VAST functioning. Among the most important of these adjustments were:

1. Formation of lateral relationships. Many local shop-to-shop arrangements were made for cooperative resolution of common workflow problems.
2. The CATE/ILSMT. In addition to technical, engineering, and logistic support as described earlier, the CATE/ILSMT helped resolve a number of coordination and other problems in the avionics workflow and NAVAIR organization.
3. Ad hoc goal and priority changes. While there was obviously no widely-accepted single goal for VAST to work toward, many local managers would change their working objectives in ways consistent with immediate mission or site requirements, in coordination with other local managers. While the local goals that were selected may have been suboptimal by other criteria, they were locally functional.
4. Outside contractors and "tech reps." As discussed in Chapter 4, these personnel were not "official" at the sites, and were provided to assist with operation of their employers' systems. In fact, they provided an important organizational linkage.
5. Ready-for-issue WRA comparison. A local adjustment to ambiguities in fault isolation was to create inventories of MAMs or

"golden" WRAs, which were RFI components taken from stock and used as comparison standards.

6. Ad hoc boundary adjustments.   Several kinds of boundary adjustments were made for local optimality of the repair system. These would be adjustments such as temporarily allowing an air boss to designate WRA repair priorities, to allowing Supply to make such decisions, or allowing the VAST shop to survey assets and make decisions; in some cases, WRAs were removed from Supply at the suggestion of VAST supervisors and "exercised" to be sure they really were RFI.

7. Cannibalization of WRAs. While generally not officially sanctioned, many sites would establish temporary or selective cannibalization policies to achieve production objectives. This not only effectively increased the pool of spare SRAs, but also minimized the number of WRAs and SRAs immobilized in the AWP locker.

8. Operator workarounds. VAST operators and maintainers were often ingenious troubleshooters and diagnosticians. When they would identify a known problem with anything in the repair cycle, they would often write up "workarounds" which would enable the WRA to be tested, a flaw in a TPS to be safely bypassed, etc. These were sometimes distributed widely by either the Navy or through tech reps, or in some cases were kept by individuals in the "wheelbooks" as described in Chapter 4.

Table 5.1 shows some examples of how these adjustment mechanisms were applied to the workflow problems.[4]   Several properties of these adjustments should be noted. First, adjustments were applied selectively and incrementally—not all adjustments could be used for all problems, nor would all problems respond to all adjustments. Some adjustments were more useful at sea than at shore sites, although most could be used at both. Second, problems were ameliorated through multiple adjustments, and many adjustments interacted with each other. For example, making a decision to change from FIFO to batch processing usually required that at least the site VAST officer, Supply officer, and Production Control officer would concur in the decision. Once elected, different resources and IP would be required to "work down" the batch of WRAs. Since this decision was often made under conditions where large queues of WRAs had built up, there was already pressure to maximize production, and the AWP locker might be temporarily opened, both to cannibalize parts (often officially unsanctioned, of course), and to simply reduce the number of WRAs in AWP storage. Given a diverse

Table 5.1 Information-processing effects of adjustments to VAST workflow problems at multiple sites

VAST workflow problem	Type of organizational adjustment							
	Lateral relationships	CATE/ILSMT	Ad hoc goal and priority changes	Outside contractors and tech reps	Ready-for-Issue WRA comparison	Ad hoc boundary adjustments	WRA cannibalization	Operator workarounds
Fluctuations in workload	Improve prediction and control of shop workload		Smooth production flow; change production schedule to minimize WRA backlog	Informal training; use of expertise to solve TPS problems during peak periods	Use RFI unit as redundant information to fault isolate during peak periods			Augment or bypass difficult or unreliable test programs
TPS fault-isolation ambiguities	Obtain information on kind of ambiguities and local mission impact	Identify major ambiguities and coordinate system-level investigation and response	Bypass ambiguities (decide to repair other WRAs)	External, redundant, unofficial information on ambiguity resolution	Verify VAST trouble-shooting information		Enable trial-and-error "swapping" of parts to resolve ambiguities, repair WRAs	Bypass, verify ambiguous test program sections
Supply-VAST relationship	Increase speed, accuracy in ordering WRA or VAST parts	Improve system-level information and parts flow and availability	Change objective from maximization of RFI WRAs to satisfying mission needs	External channels for information and parts flow		Position SRA pools close to VAST shop to speed Supply response, reduce unnecessary documentation	Increase spare parts stock; permit part comparisons in repair cycle	
VAST shop objective	Permit choice of batch or first-in, first-out production as needed for immediate mission		Adjust priorities to meet contingencies or capabilities			Acquire information on site RFI and parts stocks to evaluate present objective	Increase batch processing by increasing spares available and repairing WRAs AWP	

Table 5.1 continued

VAST maintenance and station availability		Improve system-level information and decision flow for VAST maintenance problems		Assist with difficult VAST fault isolation and maintenance tasks	Verify fault isolation on stations	Obtain information and "borrow" skills from other units if possible	Bypass, verify ambiguous test programs; substitute or assist procedures
WRA and VAST configuration control		Improve system-level information accuracy and configuration control for VAST BBs and WRAs	Permit changes in objectives to repair WRAs degraded station can test	Verify, update technical manuals and publications; secondary channel to manufacturers			Augment, bypass, experiment with test procedures when configuration uncertain
VAST operator skills		Define and improve training needs and procedures; better retention of personnel	Adjust priorities to match skills available	On-the-job training; assistance to operators; training feedback	Increase skills by verification of WRA fault diagnosis		"Wheelbooks" to record procedures for "bad actor" WRAs and TPSs
Lack of central decision authority	Integrate site workflow decisions; disseminate information among sites	Define system-level decision requirements; external relationships		Direct contractor decision support; internal AIMD contact		Decide local objectives on basis of immediate site or unit needs	
Inadequacies in decision information system	Increase formal channels; provide redundant channels	Define management information system needs; provide information and decisions		Increase formal channels; define formal system needs		Informally make functional structure more self-contained; modify information-processing methods	"Passdown" logs between shifts to inform later shifts of operational and maintenance status of station

set of IP adjustments, a site could deal with the exceptions that arose at least well enough to function; in addition, some information on uncertainties at the next higher imperfection horizon could be acquired and fed back into the system, where processing could begin to seek solutions to those problems.

In terms of the IPT framework in Chapter 1, these adjustments to the VAST workflow problems illustrate many of the major elements of IPT. All IP functions (acquisition, storage, transformation, and dissemination) can be found in Table 5.1, as well as all of the framework components (sensors, memory, processors, and accessors). Feedbacks, both at operating sites and in the larger logistics support system, are evident in many adjustments. Feedforward, especially in terms of site-specific planning and priority changes, is also common, and the dissemination of information about workflow problems through the ILSMT is coupled with feedforward to resolve the immediate problems and to achieve long-term correction of them. Finally, the management of risk is implicit in all the adjustment processes, with constant attention being given to the tradeoffs of one form of risk for another. The "physics" of IP, in my view, explains much of what Lindblom (1959) called "muddling through."

Beyond the VAST Shop: the AIMD Repair Workflow as a Complex System

The Systems Research Corporation System Analysis

As large quantities of data began to come in to the SRC study team from its site surveys, I began to work toward understanding the system in terms of how the participants in it responded to cues which were often contradictory and confusing. This desire was motivated by the fact that our results were consistent in showing that VAST worked, contrary to the impression many people had, and also because we kept finding that system variables other than those in the usual hardware and engineering logistics elements played important roles in determining repair system performance. Most of these variables were external to the VAST shop, and therefore outside the immediate logistics-element scope of the SRC study.

In short, I wanted to describe the system beyond its workflow and logistics properties alone, and instead try to understand it in terms of how two broader classes of variables were related to each other: "hard system" variables such as aircraft operational readiness, parts availability, etc., and "soft system" variables (Checkland, 1979, 1988) such as operator training and experience, interunit coordination, and similar variables not necessarily tangible or directly measurable. Further, I attempted to describe the system in terms of relationships between these variables, across all organizational units in the repair cycle, and to include the squadrons who were being supported by all this activity.

Figure 5.1 shows the model which resulted from this analysis. I created this model to organize all of the variables which had emerged from the SRC study of the VAST shops. The focal point of this analysis was identification of the most important variables affecting the successful repair of WRAs in the VAST shop and the nature of the relationships of these to other variables. "Effective repair of WRAs" means that TAT has been minimized, both for individual WRAs and in total for all WRAs processed. Since aircraft OR is the primary objective of all of the repair and Supply activities, the relationship of these variables to OR is considered. The variables shown in this figure are arranged by organizational unit. VAST shop variables are shown on the left, and begin with a "V-" prefix. Supply variables ("S-") are shown in the center area, and squadron or O-level variables ("O-") on the right side. Thirteen VAST-shop variables, four Supply variables, and 6 squadron variables were related to the ability of the VAST shop to return WRAs to RFI status. It is important to note that relationships between these variables are shown in terms of their effects on each other, not in terms of their repair-cycle flows or relationships. Some of these variables can themselves be decomposed into others, of course.

Within the AIMD, the most important variable was TAT (V-1). TAT itself was directly dependent on three other major variables. These are the ability to perform accurate fault isolations on the WRAs (V-2) and the availability of SRAs when demanded (V-6), a function of the production of supporting units. Both of these have a positive effect on TAT. The other direct variable was the amount of time required to document repair actions on the MAF (V-5), which could become significant for difficult WRAs; this obviously had a negative impact on TAT.

Fault isolation (V-2) had several interesting relationships to a group of variables. While TPS quality (V-9) had an obvious effect, other effects could be traced to the batching of WRA production runs (V-4), which reduced Build-Up/Tear-Down (BU/TD) time, reducing the probability of increased troubleshooting for difficult TPSs; the maintenance of pass-down logs to inform personnel across shifts of what the station was doing (V-13); and cannibalization of WRAs (V-3), to increase the pool of SRAs, to increase the size of batches processed, and to reduce BU/TD cycles. Two variables were also interrelated with several others—operator training (V-8) helped direct

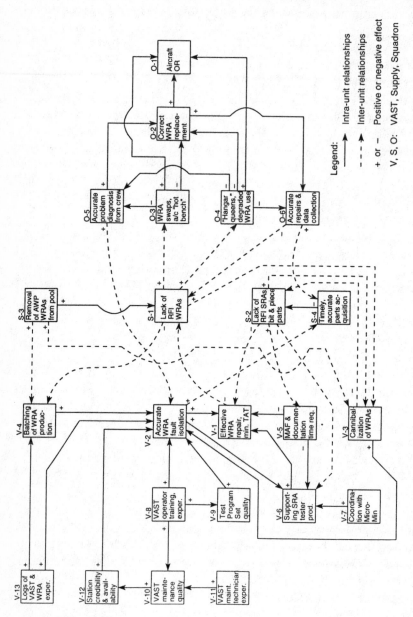

Figure 5.1 Analysis of hard-system and soft-system variables influencing performance of Naval avionics repair workflow

fault isolation, and benefitted TPS quality in a compensatory fashion, i.e., operators would acquire information about TPS problems and develop logs and workarounds (V-9); and station maintenance (V-10) was improved because operators would not misinterpret station problems as WRA problems, or were careful to check the station and request maintenance if the station were suspect. VAST station maintenance was enhanced by the experience and training of the VAST maintainers (V-11) and these relationships combined to produce a very important "soft system" variable which I term "station credibility" (V-12). A station which was both "up," and could be believed, reduced the amount of information processing technicians had to do when ambiguities came out of the test run, and as operator confidence improved, throughput improved.

An interesting "hot" feedback existed between VAST fault isolation (V-2) and supporting SRA testers (V-6). When the WRA fault isolations were accurate, the number of SRAs pulled from the WRAs was reduced, which reduced the workload on the SRA testers. That enabled the SRA shops to maintain high credibility for their testers because they had adequate time for maintenance, and good SRA tester performance helped keep up the stock of RFI SRAs. Both of these outcomes benefit VAST repair of WRAs. Similarly, the technicians' passdown logs (V-13) enabled supervisors to make better decisions regarding what a VAST station could do if it were not fully operational (i.e., a BB was malfunctioning), and could make better decisions about which WRAs to schedule while the station was restored to full capability. SRA tester production (V-6) was also enhanced by coordination with the Micro-Min shop (V-7), and in some cases it was decided to repair "non-repairable" SRAs to avoid a stockout of the "nonrepairable" item. Micro-Min was often able to repair parts which were originally thought to be too complex or difficult to repair in the field, and so were designated as disposable; these repairs were often done on a rolling ship, incidentally.

Variables V-1 to V-6, however, were related to variables in the Supply area, and these were not simple or isolated relationships. Further, Supply linked the repair shops to the squadrons, and so Supply variables were the intermediaries between what happened in the VAST shop and what happened on the flight line. The most significant variable in Supply was the availability of RFI WRAs for squadron demands (S-1). This is discussed in the negative, i.e., as the lack of RFI spares, because shortages had direct and immediate impacts on both the VAST shop and the squadrons. The only variable which directly affected RFI stock levels within Supply was the removal of WRAs from the Awaiting Parts WRA pool (S-3). All other relationships were between Supply and other units, and these relationships, in turn, were usually affected by multiple other variables. Decision-making to meet Supply needs was inherently an exercise in the management of tradeoffs, and conflict between unit objectives (both AIMD and squadrons) was inevitable.

Reduction of AWP levels was accomplished solely by testing the AWP units before returning them to the RFI pool, so reductions of AWP levels generated demands on VAST shop time. (Keep in mind that the WRA had become AWP only after at least one test, which fault-isolated to one or more SRAs which were not in stock.) Nevertheless, if the AWP pool was reduced, stocks of RFI WRAs were usually increased. Such reductions in AWP levels were best achieved by testing batches of WRAs and cannibalizing them, so batching of VAST runs (V-4) was directly affected by efforts to reduce AWP. But the need for RFI WRAs (S-1) had a countervailing effect on batching (V-4), because if specific WRA stocks were depleted, any of those in the repair queue had to be advanced to the highest priority, frustrating attempts to assemble batches. The cannibalization (V-3) needed to reduce the AWP levels was officially discouraged, of course. Nevertheless, the fact that all AWP WRAs needed unavailable parts created strong pressure to bend the rules and cannibalize as much as possible. This often resulted in one or two WRAs being stripped down to the frame, or very nearly, and some of those were never repaired.

The only other variable that had a direct relationship to another within Supply was that between the accurate acquisition of parts (S-4) and the level of RFI SRAs and bit-and-piece parts (S-2). The timeliness and accuracy of these acquisitions depended on two things—accurate WRA fault isolation in the VAST shop (V-2), so that the correct parts demands were generated, and accurate data collection on repairs in the squadron (O-6). When these were not accomplished the levels of RFI parts were diminished, and likewise the availability of RFI WRAs.

Shortages of spare parts created immediate effects elsewhere in the system. First, the lack of spares had two negative impacts: SRA testers could not keep up RFI SRA levels to satisfy VAST-generated demands (V-6); and the need to perform multiple tests (since many of the unfilled orders created AWP WRAs) increased TAT for the WRAs (V-1). Second, the lack of spare parts also created more time demands to document repair actions (V-5), adding a small percentage of time to each WRA needing multiple runs through the VAST shop. The lack of spares also increased pressure to cannibalize (V-3), but that pressure, in turn, distorted information on parts requirements (S-4), and reduced the accuracy of the information in the Supply "pipeline."

The squadrons, which often were viewed as a remote "customer" for all of these complex interactions, and therefore only indirectly involved in interactions in the repair system, were in fact actively engaged in several processes which strongly influenced the AIMD and Supply. Aircraft OR (O-1) depended on available WRAs, of course. When WRAs were not available (S-1), two compensatory practices were often put into effect by the squadrons. First, WRAs might be "swapped" between aircraft; this practice improved OR, but degraded aircraft configuration control and the replacement of the correct WRA (O-2). A related practice was "hot benching," in which a WRA was tried in one or more aircraft to determine if it could be used after another aircraft had indicated a fault with it. When certain WRAs acquired a reputation for being likely to be out of stock, "hot benching" was increased as a method of improving squadron OR levels.

The second compensatory practice was to designate some aircraft as "hangar queens" (O-4), and cannibalize parts from them to effectively increase the WRA pool; in some cases, WRAs known to be only partly functional were used to prevent downing an aircraft for a mission. These practices improved overall squadron OR, but distorted aircraft configuration control (O-2) and reduced the accuracy and timeliness of problem diagnoses from aircraft crew and squadron maintainers (O-5). The "hangar queens" also permitted O-level maintainers to literally hide some WRAs from Supply, so that critical items would be available under control of the squadron. Therefore, some incorrect diagnoses went on to the MAF, and then into the information system that the VAST shop depended on; accurate problem diagnoses from O-level personnel were very important to accurate fault isolation in the VAST shop (V-2) as well as to correct replacement of the WRA on the flight line (O-2).

The cumulative effects of these compensatory squadron practices was to degrade the timeliness and accuracy of information on repair requirements entering the repair system. Timely and accurate information on WRA failures was necessary not only for the VAST shop, but also to prevent distortions of the information required for Supply to perform effectively, and both of these were negatively affected by such squadron practices. The squadrons, of course, viewed the world from the perspective of immediate mission requirements, and considered what they did to be a necessary form of protection against other parts of the system that were not performing well.

Throughout this analysis, I expected technician motivation to be "soft system" variable of some importance, given anecdotal information to suggest such a relationship (see Chapter 4). However, motivation did not emerge as a directly important variable because of moderating relationships with information processing. Motivation was primarily related to IP, not performance—motivated sailors acquired more information, stored more in wheelbooks and other media, analyzed it more carefully and thoroughly, and disseminated it more widely. However, factors beyond the sailors' control had both positive and negative effects on the information they had to work with, and therefore the relationship of motivation to performance. For example, when a difficult WRA fault isolation was interrupted to put other WRAs in process, it frustrated efforts to resolve the TPS difficulties that were usually the cause of the problem. Motivation has been found to have an "inverted-U" relationship to performance, and in many cases the highly motivated sailors were frustrated by external circumstances and experienced "burnout." When things were running smoothly, on the other hand, the VAST station controlled the pace of work, and the sailor was primarily a machine-tender. This kind of work often became very boring. Ironically, the circumstances most highly motivating because of inherent problem-solving interest were often the ones most likely to lead to frustration. Different sailors had highly individual reactions to these situations, as well.

Motivation is an interesting variable in such technology applications, but it is not one which is simply or directly related to shop or system performance. Further, the moderating effects of information processing on motivation suggest that looking directly at motivation without understanding system IP will have little power to explain performance variation.

The Precursors to "Experiment 2"—Early Experiments with Information Technology in the AIMD Repair Cycle

While doing site surveys and data collection for the SRC study, some incidental and fortuitous findings suggested sophisticated understanding of some of the determinants of VAST performance on the part of Navy personnel. Some of these findings were particularly interesting because it showed that site personnel were recognizing the need for greater IP capacity in the AIMD workflow than provided by the Navy's VIDS/MAF system. In several cases this recognition led to development of unofficial or prototype information-technology systems to support avionics repair and supply management. There were four initiatives of this kind: a local Supply-VAST organizational arrangement at NAS Miramar; a semiformal computer application at NAS Oceana; a first effort at formally developing a decision support system; and a new management information system developed voluntarily by Harris/PRD. Each of these will be discussed briefly.

Supply-VAST Ad Hoc Organizational Changes at NAS Miramar

NAS Miramar is the primary Pacific Fleet F-14 shore site (and the home of the "Top Gun" fighter school popularized by the film some years ago). When the West Coast SRC team surveyed the site, they found that the Supply officer had decided to implement a practice he had observed on a previous carrier cruise, to create a "forward parts depot" for the benefit of the VAST shop. This "forward depot" consisted of moving the most commonly-demanded SRAs physically into the building where the VAST shop was located, putting Supply technicians there to control the stocks, and creating a local logbook to expedite trial-and-error use of a specific set of SRAs to troubleshoot WRAs. While not using computers or IT, the forward depot was beneficial to local IP capacity and organizational knowledge.

Three benefits derived from this forward depot. First, because the building housing Supply was located about 100 yards from the VAST shop, the forward depot reduced the amount of time required for the routine fetching of parts by shop personnel (often VAST technicians), with the EMT and TAT "clocks" running all the while. When the shop got busy, VAST technicians could not take the time to go fetch parts, and so mail runners were used; this often resulted in orders taking several days to fill. As was noted in Table 4.4, the forward depot cut average fetch time from between one and two days to 10 minutes. The lengthy fetching delays also contributed to more Build-Up/Tear-Down cycles, since the station often could not be kept idle until parts arrived.

Second, since many fault isolations were ambiguous, technicians sometimes had to try one part to see if it resolved a problem, and then another if that did not work, until they corrected the problem. This trial-and-error process could be quite time-consuming, and was made more so by the distance the sailors had to travel to get SRAs. Further, once tried and rejected, an SRA was supposed to be retested itself, to be certain that it was not damaged when it was inserted into the WRA, even though the actual incidence of such induced damage was low. This requirement, of course, generated many new work cycles for the SRA testers, and kept more SRAs off the Supply shelves for longer periods of time, increasing the probability of an SRA stockout and a consequent WRA becoming AWP.

The forward depot set aside a group of Maintenance Assist Modules (MAMs), an SRA pool consisting of between 600 to 700 SRAs, which was about 20 to 25 percent of total avionics stock on site. These SRAs were formally part of regular stock, and since they were not mixed with other

SRAs, they could be used as "loaners" to help troubleshoot WRAs. These often helped get past ambiguities much more quickly than other methods.

Finally, each trial of an SRA or group required MAF documentation, which had to be done every time SRAs were requisitioned from Supply. The paperwork requirement was considered onerous by the sailors, and indeed, it was hard to defend doing it fully for each trial, regardless of its success. To support the trial-and-error use of MAMs, Supply devised a local logbook which technicians used to sign out the SRAs they needed, until the sailor was sure the WRA had passed its tests. If a repair was effected, the full MAF was then completed; this procedure saved significant documentation time.

As part of the Miramar data collection, the SRC team collected data for ten mission-critical WRAs, i.e., WRAs that could ground an aircraft if they malfunctioned, and which had proven to be very difficult and time-consuming to repair. The analysis compared TAT and its components (as discussed in Chapter 4) at Miramar to Fleet performance overall and at other shore sites. Results of this analysis are summarized in Table 5.2. The data showed that there was a shorter cycle for every component of TAT for those ten WRAs (see Table, note 2). NAS Miramar completed the repair cycle in 77.3 percent of the time compared to the entire Fleet, and 70 percent of the time compared to other shore sites.

A more complete analysis of the performance data at NAS Miramar, with samples from the full set of WRAs repaired on the site, will be shown in Chapter 6. For the time, I want to conclude this section by noting that while the procedures used to create the forward depot at Miramar were technically violations of the Navy organization design, there was nothing lax or careless in the management of the depot. The forward SRA and MAMs pools were aggressively managed and controlled by Supply personnel there—one-for-one swaps of MAMs were absolutely required; no sailor was ever given a MAM or an RFI SRA without either signing the logbook or completing the MAF, and repeated attempts to cut corners (as were observed by one SRC team member) resulted in a meeting between the sailor, the VAST shop supervisor, and the Supply officer to "make it quite clear as to why that sort of thing wasn't done here." The system worked, but it was only as safe as its personnel made it. The new Supply officer, who came along one year later, decided that the forward depot was too unorthodox, and changed things back to the way they had been, i.e., the standard Navy structure. The effects of that reversal will be seen in the data analyzed in Chapter 6.

Table 5.2   Summary of TAT analysis for 10 mission-critical F-14 WRAs, NAS Miramar vs. other Fleet sites[1]

TAT component	Fleet-wide	Shore sites	NAS Miramar
Processing[2]	8.8	13.9	8.8
Scheduling	13.0	13.2	12.8
AWP	38.1	45.0	26.7
EMT	31.1	30.0	22.1
Total (TAT)	91.0	102.1	70.4

1   Source: *Productivity Enhancement of the Versatile Avionic Shop Test System: Site Evaluation and Final Report, Volume II Detailed Findings.* Leesburg, Va.: Systems Research Corp., 6 March 1979. Data are reported as the sum of average days required for each component of TAT for all 10 WRAs in the study group, and reflect repair actions taken at all sites from 1 December 1977 through 30 November 1978.

2   Processing time was distorted by one WRA which required much longer to process at Miramar. If that WRA were removed, the data for processing times would be 7.3, 11.6, and 4.8 days, respectively, showing an even greater improvement in performance at NAS Miramar.

Computer Support of Supply at NAS Oceana

A second local IP adjustment was the use of a rudimentary semiformal computer system at NAS Oceana. Oceana is the primary Atlantic Fleet F-14 shore site, and had experienced many of the same WRA stockout problems as Miramar, although not for the same reasons. Originally begun as a "bootleg" project, some "soft" money at Oceana was used to purchase a minicomputer for SRA control. This was later given formal support by the base administration, and the system was labeled the Specialized Program for Oceana Repairables Tracking (SPORT). In its initial form in 1978, SPORT did little more than automate some of the repair-transaction data entry for the exchange of SRAs. As time went by, the local personnel developed programs to print SRA "swap" forms, similar to those used at Miramar; to track the number of EXREP and POOL CRITICAL WRAs in the repair queue; and to report inventory status on a daily basis. The major benefit of the early

SPORT system, unlike the forward depot at Miramar, was to keep accurate records of WRA and SRA inventory.

The SPORT system was generally well-liked and perceived as helpful. When I interviewed site personnel about it, everyone from sailors to officers found it helpful, if only in small ways. Sailors liked the automated SRA swap forms; Supply officers and personnel found the daily listings of inventory status (both WRAs and SRAs) very useful, and inspection of the listings helped alert an experienced officer to impending shortages of SRAs before they materialized; Production Control also found the status reports useful to spot potential stockouts, and in conjunction with Supply and the VAST supervisors, had developed a practice of jointly reviewing the status reports to make production decisions. The scope of IP was broadened in multiple ways by this small application of information technology, and its early successes encouraged continued development over the next several years, with benefits to the overall WRA repair cycle.

The Fixed Allowance Module Management System (FAMMS)

In recognition of the operational difficulties with provisions of spare parts being experienced in the Naval Air Force, the Navy's Material Support Office in Mechanicsburg, Pa., began development and testing of a computerized system to monitor use of modules supplied to each site; this was the Fixed Allowance Module Management System (FAMMS). Without going into the technical details of "fixed allowances," such allowances were the standard way of provisioning any operating site. If an allowance is too low, stockouts will occur and mission capabilities will be degraded. Thus, any claims that stockouts are occurring will get the attention of the Material Support Office.

Since FAMMS was an inventory management system, its scope was limited to monitoring inventory status. Demands on the Supply system, status of all inventories from WRAs to bit-and-piece parts, Closed-Loop Avionics Maintenance Program (CLAMP) assets, and the like were monitored in FAMMS. Any stockouts resulting in non-operational aircraft were also reported by the system, and the resolution of those cases was tracked so that site managers could determine how quickly aircraft were being returned to operational condition.

FAMMS was initially developed at NAS Jacksonville. On my site survey at NAS Cecil Field, also located in Jacksonville, I spoke with two younger chiefs who had worked with FAMMS. In short, they were not particularly impressed with it, and had gone through all of the growing pains it had experienced up to that point. It had its share of software bugs, hardware incompatibilities, user unfriendliness, and similar problems that afflicted mainframe computer programs of that era. Having suffered through many similar problems with mainframe programs in academic systems, I found their complaints to be relatively predictable, and not of unusual difficulty, but they were nevertheless important limitations in an operating environment. The overall sentiment was that when FAMMS worked, it could provide useful information; however, it was crash-prone, and required much additional time compared to the VIDS/MAF system (to keypunch data and generate reports), so that in a busy environment, this delayed management feedback rather than giving timely information. I was told that the base commander was sufficiently unimpressed with FAMMS that he had the program transferred to NAS North Island when it went into its second phase of development. We will hear more of FAMMS at that location when we examine the data in Chapter 6.

The Harris/PRD Status Inventory, Data Management System (SIDMS)

The fourth initiative to improve avionics repair management IP was the voluntary development of SIDMS by Harris/PRD. SIDMS was a small system for processing single-site data on the major variables of importance to Production Control, and was more truly a management information system than SPORT was. SIDMS provided daily reports on production control status, i.e., a form of automated VIDS/MAF data in summary form, status reports on numerous things, including overall AIMD status data, individual work centers and status of testers, master equipment files for each work center, technical publications, AWP status, and the like. It provided a summary of personnel and skills on site, when different testers were scheduled for calibration, and, of course, Supply status data. Physically, it was a custom program operating on relatively generic minicomputer hardware. Data entry was through a video terminal, reports were generated through a standard line printer, and the minicomputer was a relatively small (for its time) machine which was linked by a local network to several terminals and printers.

SIDMS was installed as a demonstration project on the USS *John F. Kennedy* in late 1976, and it was there that I saw it in use the following summer. The system was well-liked by the large majority of people I interviewed. The reports it generated gave an overall snapshot of what was happening in the AIMD and the individual shops, showed the status of RFI inventories and components in the repair pipeline, and gave an overview of the availability of testers and shop capacity.

In several ways, SIDMS was well ahead of its time. It was the only system designed to collect and process data in such as way as to provide reports on the status of the AIMD. Rather than pilot the system at a shore site, as had been done with SPORT and FAMMS, SIDMS was demonstrated in an operational ship environment. Its scope was much more expansive than any other system, in that it tracked data on all important elements of the avionics logistics support system—technical publications, personnel, ancillary equipment, and so on. SIDMS might well have been the system to become a real decision support tool, had its development been continued.

Unfortunately, SIDMS had several limitations. Data had to be manually entered, so that when the *Kennedy* got busy at sea, not only was ordinary MAF paperwork required, but keying data into the system as well. The software had very limited error-checking capability, so that if bad data were entered, they often created confusion and required much time to correct. Reports were relatively ordinary transaction-accounting reports, so that time to scan them and assimilate data was required if decisions were to be truly supported. The machinery took space and power, always problems on carriers. Specialized training was needed to use the system, although it was much more user-friendly than most of its contemporaries. Finally, it was built by Harris, and for those for whom VAST had acquired a bad reputation, SIDMS was seen as a self-serving and somewhat inappropriate offering. One older Pacific Fleet chief once asserted that he would never have a SIDMS terminal in his office, because that was simply a way to pay Harris to clean up the mess it had created with VAST. We found that perception of both Harris and VAST to be unfounded and certainly not supported by the data on VAST or SIDMS, but it was as true then as now that "rationality" is a concept, not a working definition of how most decisions are made. As it was, SIDMS was so well-received by the crew of the *Kennedy* that by 1980 all Atlantic Fleet carriers were equipped with SIDMS. And, for reasons that one can ponder for many years, none of the Pacific Fleet carriers ever were.

Despite the lack of sophistication of these early systems, or the motives behind them, the common denominator in all of these efforts was recognition of the need to manage the large quantities of information being created by the avionics repair system. Most managers and personnel did not regard the issue as anything more than an information overload, but that alone was sufficient to motivate efforts to cope with it. Information technology seemed the most logical way to deal with the amount of data generated by the repair system. In many instances, personnel saw IT as simply a way to produce the reports higher management wanted and to get them off their backs so they could get some work done. Other motives included simple desire to use information to show that you were doing your job.

I titled this section of this chapter the "precursors to Experiment 2," which is the field quasi-experiment to be described in Chapter 6. What I mean by this reference to the beginnings of the experiment is that while these early systems, as individual programs, did not clearly demonstrate that information processing was of compelling practical importance in the avionics repair cycle, they set the stage for several tests of that idea. All four of these programs will be examined for their effects on AIMD performance in Chapter 6.

The Next Round: the Logistics Support Analysis Update Study

Background

At about the time SRC study was ending, NAVAIR contracted with Dynamic Science, Inc. to perform a Logistics Support Analysis (LSA) update study for VAST. An LSA is an evaluation all of the logistics elements described in Chapter 2 (Figure 2.1). Any new weapon system or technology is developed concurrently with an LSA, which specifies support requirements in all elements of the logistics "tail." As new weapon systems are deployed and become fully operational, the LSA is updated (essentially audited), to determine whether those elements are properly supported, and recommendations are made to NAVAIR for correction as needed. Outside contractors, rather than the system prime contractors, are usually retained for this purpose, although close liaison is maintained with both the prime contractor and NAVAIR. This is usually accomplished through direct contact and through the CATE/ILSMT. The original Dynamic Science contract was to perform the VAST LSA Update study, but because earlier studies suggested the value of a broader scope, the scope of work was expanded to do a complete examination of all variables in the AIMD workflow. Through my involvement at the CATE/ILSMT, I became a member of that team.[5]

Despite evidence from the early studies of VAST, the SRC study, or general awareness of the early IT applications just described, all of which strongly suggested that neither VAST performance nor its overall logistics support was the cause of repair-cycle problems, there had been no comprehensive formal study of the AIMD avionics-repair workflow. While many people inside and outside of NAVAIR had come to believe that VAST was not the cause of aircraft WRA stockouts, many others did. For that reason, hard data were necessary to support any conclusions about causes of poor performance, and more importantly, recommendations for change in the IP system. This support was necessary both for scientific rigor and because whatever conclusions were derived would be challenged, quite appropriately. The LSA Update provided the vehicle to do such a comprehensive study.

Work on this study began in early 1981. The first task, as required for the LSA, was to again survey the AIMDs and the VAST sites. The first order of business was to evaluate each of the logistics elements, so the surveys required reviews of publications libraries, personnel and skill allocations, Supply effectiveness, and so on. In addition to the normal logistics elements, the Dynamic Science team was also responsible for examining implementation of configuration changes that had been made in VAST. As noted earlier, when any new system matures, engineering changes are made to correct flaws and improve performance. Many of these changes are done by the issuance of engineering change "kits," and we were to audit the implementation of these engineering changes. Since prime contractors supply tech reps to help transition their systems into full deployment, we also were to evaluate the tech reps. Much of the "update" activity in the LSA update was concerned with these matters.

My primary responsibility in the LSA Update was to examine performance problems in the AIMD. That charge was both to look for evidence to evaluate the view that VAST was in fact not performing correctly, and to look for other factors in the AIMD that might explain performance problems, including simple poor management of the existing workflow.

Those who adhered to the view that VAST was not performing properly can be generally described holding the "engineering" view of the problem and the organization. Those who contended that the problem was not engineering held the "management" view. I was teamed with two others who held the "engineering" view, to represent both perspectives in our site survey reports. While we were only a very small cog in the whole machine of VAST development, enough controversy over the issues of VAST avionics support had been generated to necessitate as much balance and objectivity in our work as possible. The entire process of East Coast and West Coast site surveys was spread over 18 months, with interim reports, consultations, and guidance being provided through regular meetings with Harris/PRD and the CATE/ILSMT. During this time, I surveyed five shore sites and five carriers on both coasts.

LSA Update Findings

This section will briefly summarize the findings from the LSA Update study. In overview, there were no major surprises or unexpected results that emerged from the study. We performed the LSA Update and made a number of recommendations for logistical changes. Most of these were relatively ordinary changes and corrections, such as incorrect cross-references between two technical publications, a missing part number on a small Test Program Set cable, and the like. These were all reported routinely through NAVAIR offices and the ILSMT.

When the SRC study was done VAST was a new system, and personnel were willing to make allowances and adjustments for the process of going up the learning curve. By the time of the LSA Update, however, VAST was a much more mature system, and no longer the new technology at the beginning of its deployment. That had several consequences.

Engineering and logistics Relatively few changes or recommendations, in comparison to earlier generations of support equipment, resulted from the LSA Update findings. If anything, the amount of attention that had been devoted to VAST in its first years of deployment had resulted in faster responses to problems and engineering deficiencies than had occurred with many other testers, because the central importance of VAST to the carrier air wings had necessitated quick reactions to major problems. Over the course of many years, the Navy has learned how to respond to these technical needs quite well, and that capability was evident in what we found at all of the sites.

The nature of management information processing at this stage of VAST deployment was almost completely the processing of workflow exceptions. The majority of the adjustments we found to exceptions in the VAST shops and the AIMDs were highly constructive and creative, as shown in Table 5.1. Both sailors and officers had learned a great deal about the idiosyncrasies of the VAST system and individual stations. A number of engineering and technical documentation problems had emerged, as with any new system, and of course, the TPSs had experienced more operational difficulties than expected. However, the Navy has a number of established programs to deal with these types of exceptions, such as the program for correcting engineering problems: a Trouble Report (TR) can lead to a full Engineering Investigation (EI), an Engineering Change Proposal (ECP) if needed, and finally an Engineering Change (EC). If a change is needed, a "kit" of new or modified parts will be issued, and in most cases field personnel will install it and verify changes to the equipment. This process is used for any new equipment, whether a tester like VAST, a new WRA, or an aircraft. A similar process is followed for all types of software.

Management and workflow control In the area of AIMD management and workflow control, the findings were rather different. In general, we found a much higher degree of variability in AIMD management practices than might have been expected. From earlier surveys and studies, the experience of many team members (several of whom were veterans), and what we had learned from ILSMT and other meetings, we knew that the management of individual sites did not follow the Navy maintenance program in every detail, and was never intended to. Enough experience had been gained by all site personnel (as well as contractors and support personnel) to be able to cope with system dysfunctions to keep running, even under difficult conditions. However, we also found evidence of a number of dysfunctions having begun to emerge in the management and personnel of the AIMD workflow, and particularly in the VAST shops.

As was noted in Chapter 4, several new testers had been brought into the workflow to repair SRAs, and to relieve VAST of that workload. One tester, the CAT-IIID, worked extremely well in the F-14A and E-2C communities; on the other hand the HATS tester for S-3A SRAs was unreliable, both making inaccurate fault isolations and being prone to frequent station failures. Thus, the workflow had now become more complicated because the new testers created yet another interrelated path through the AIMD which had to be coordinated with others, and which increased the information processing burden on everyone, especially Production Control. The new testers helped improve aircraft OR in the F-14A and E-2C programs, but the S-3A program was still experiencing major problems.

Dysfunctional personnel adjustments Some dysfunctional adjustments to workflow problems had become evident. It was very common to find the relentlessness of the VAST WRA workflow to be wearing on personnel. Most shore sites ran 24 hours a day, with either half-shifts or one full shift devoted to VAST station maintenance; carriers ran two 12-hour shifts when at sea. The workload of Awaiting Maintenance WRAs never seemed to go away, and sailors often felt that whatever they did, there was no closure and no sense of accomplishment. Officers were constantly under pressure to make decisions for which they lacked information, to change priorities in the middle of on-going shifts, to train more thoroughly, to interact with tech reps (and site visitation teams), to coordinate with Production Control or the air wing, and the like. One haggard officer at a West Coast site told me that by his calculations, operating the VAST shop "by the regs" would require 18 stations. He had six, which was his full allocation, and felt he was constantly being beaten up by someone for not doing his part of the job. His solution was quite predictable—he was leaving the Navy.

The pressure to produce had begun to give rise to a small but measurable increase in attrition of VAST personnel, both technicians and officers. While not yet a crisis, the Navy was facing a period of mandated force reduction in the near future, and retention of skilled personnel was important. Even though VAST was perceived as a higher-skill job and a good assignment in many ways, its reputation for relentless work, canceled leaves at liberty ports (so the AWM backlog would be reduced when the ship resumed its cruise), and other characteristics, had begun to deter some skilled air wing sailors from accepting assignments to the VAST shop. Even when everything ran smoothly, there was the downside common to much machine-tending work—boredom. The experience of flying has been described by many pilots as "hours of sheer boredom punctuated by seconds of sheer terror;" many VAST technicians felt the same way about VAST, with the difference that the problems were what was interesting, while the boredom was simply boring.

Shop supervisors had begun to experience burnout, and it showed in several ways beyond the one case of someone leaving. NAS North Island responded to its production difficulties by keeping an earlier-generation tester that could be set up to do gross functional tests on several difficult S-3A WRAs. Sailors would often get stuck on these tests, and to avoid the frustration of very lengthy troubleshooting on VAST, they were allowed to take the WRA to the functional tester and run it there. In a matter of a few minutes (rather than about 1.5 hours), all of the major operations of the WRA were either verified or failed; if they were verified, an RFI tag was put on the WRA, and out it went. While not necessarily a problem, these kinds of tests did not actually test the WRA completely, and malfunctions could result. But this practice kept production up, AWM levels down, and good technicians less frustrated.

Supervisors had developed various defensive behaviors. Some would behave in a passive-aggressive manner, and simply abrogate control of the VAST shop to Production Control ("If they know so damn much, let them run this place."). Some simply waited until large batches of everything built up, and then ran in a nearly exclusive batch mode; if challenged over this decision, they would ask the dissatisfied party what they would suggest doing, or simply request orders to do otherwise. Some would simply go strictly by the TPS data and the technical-publication procedures, and anything that couldn't be repaired was "cooked" on the VAST station until the VAST officer ordered it to be taken off and another WRA tested. If parts were not available, others would simply consign every WRA to the AWP cage, where it was effectively lost to the system until parts arrived and it could be scheduled for retesting.[6]

These examples are the extremes, and in most cases and at most sites nothing like them ever occurred, or certainly never endured. But the incidence of them in an organization that often has to improvise and cooperate to get things done was troubling. "Adjustive wits," if I may use that term, mattered at all levels and in all positions of the VAST workflow, and if they were not used well the system soon broke down.

Constructive adaptations However, there was much being done that was proactive, creative, and effective as partial solutions to VAST and AIMD production problems, and these were much more common. First, we found numerous examples of the "wheelbooks" which had been found during the SRC study. Most squadron personnel assigned to the VAST shops had, by this time, acquired or developed one or more senior people on each shift. These individuals often operated as informal technical leaders, and kept careful notes on each of the WRAs, TPSs, and individual VAST stations they worked on, at both their master shore site and on the carriers. Numerous idiosyncratic characteristics of both hardware and software were noted, so that the ability to reduce ambiguities and improve fault isolations was enhanced. The "wheelbooks" were not "cheat sheets," as one critic of them once charged. In fact, these were information files created specifically to deal with uncertainties and exceptions in the repair process.

Two examples of these are illustrative: on the *Ranger*, we found one VAST station with a black "X" marked on the front of BB29. When we asked what that was for, the sailor opened a tool kit, took out a small rubber mallet, and said, "Nearly every time we run [a particular WRA] it tells us one card in it is bad. That's because the test causes a relay in BB29 to stick, so when we get that 'call-out,' we whack BB29 on the X with the hammer, and repeat the test. The WRA then usually passes, and the real problem is found somewhere else." In another case, sailors had noted that tests on a particular F-14 WRA were incorrectly identified as a set of failed resistors on one SRA; in fact, over 75 percent of these fault isolations were because the SRA had been jarred by hard landings. When the SRA was pulled out and reseated in its slot, the WRA usually passed and was RFI.

For as much as it costs, the F-14 was a leaky airplane, and water intrusion was a constant problem.[7] On rainy days, a group of F-14 WRAs would fail simply because they got wet. One ingenious sailor realized that by using a silicone sealant to cover certain screw heads on exposed WRAs, or to build "dams" around cooling air vents so that water would be deflected around the vents, large numbers of these failures could be prevented. This program was so effective that NAVAIR made it into an official maintenance procedure, and published posters with drawings showing the areas of the affected WRAs needing this treatment and specifying the correct sealant.

By far, the developments I found to be most interesting and exciting in this study were the early applications of information technology to workflow management. Two such applications are particularly noteworthy—one was the continued development of FAMMS, and the other was a completely spontaneous initiative on the *Forrestal*. These efforts succeeded almost entirely on the basis of the pluck and resolve of local personnel at the sites, and frequently in the face of considerable skepticism on the part of officers and others who were convinced that VAST itself was causing the workflow problem.

The FAMMS program, in the face of much of the skepticism surrounding VAST, had been moved to NAS North Island for continued development. North Island was an S-3A shore site, and had experienced major OR problems owing to avionics stockouts, as had Cecil Field. The Production Control (PC) office was particularly interested in improving AIMD performance, and had volunteered to accept the FAMMS software from NAS Jacksonville to try to use it there.[8] PC had tried to set up its own system in 1980, but found the task overwhelming. Even though FAMMS had been developed as a Supply tool, as noted earlier, North Island personnel had modified it to generate several reports more useful to PC and the AIMD, especially to identify those MAF documents which had resulted in an aircraft being either totally grounded or only partially mission capable (codes on the MAF made such identification possible). By using this information to schedule WRAs needed to get aircraft flying, OR had been improved. When no immediate critical repair needs existed, PC would allow the VAST shop to use batch processing to maximize the number of WRAs tested with a single TPS build-up. This action was coordinated with the VAST supervisor and officer, so that planned batch runs always considered the status of the VAST stations themselves along with aircraft OR requirements.

PC also worked with Supply to minimize the accumulation of AWM and AWP WRAs. This required continuous monitoring along with scheduling batch runs to process not only the AWM WRAs, but to bring those WRAs out of the "cage" and include them in the batch as well. Moreover, coordination with the SRA tester shops was necessary to ensure that adequate levels of critical SRAs would be available when needed to repair the WRAs. Even though FAMMS only did sorts by data field to find the basic data needed for these decisions, the ability to do those sorts quickly and accurately appeared to be improving production and OR, and was definitely reducing AWM and AWP levels. The combined number of SRAs and WRAs either in their repair queues or lacking parts had been nearly 2,700 items in 1980; when I surveyed the site in the summer of 1982, this number had been reduced to just over 1,300, or more than 50 percent. AIMD officers believed that within another two years, combined AWM and AWP would be reduced to not more than 1,000 items.

Ironically, the effectiveness of FAMMS depended heavily on having full and complete data on all AIMD repair-cycle transactions in the databases, and this was nearly the program's undoing. FAMMS did not have a dedicated computer—it was running on the base's mainframe, an overloaded machine that had to do everything from placing orders for cases of pork and beans to printing payroll checks. To keep it running, the base commander had directed that it be taken off line over weekends, when preventive maintenance and software debugging could be done. That improved the reliability of the computer system, but meant that no AIMD transactions done over the weekend could be entered until the next Monday. Aircraft flew continuously, however, and the repair cycle never stopped. The inevitable result was a backlog of data entry to be done on Mondays and Tuesdays, and some consequent delays in actual repairs. The combined effect of data-entry delays and undone maintenance had actually reduced the availability of RFI WRAs during 1981, and had hurt base performance. The base commander nevertheless supported the experiment, and by 1982, the payoff was becoming more visible. FAMMS was never a particularly effective MIS, but it was never intended to be one. A great deal of what was learned in attempting to improve its decision support utility benefitted the first actual MIS, which will be introduced in the concluding section of this chapter.

One of the most effective informal applications of information technology was made on the USS *Forrestal*, using "bootleg" Radio Shack TRS-80 computers. However, the *Forrestal* AIMD relied equally on "soft system" management processes to resolve operational problems in the repair workflow, as suggested by the SRC system analysis presented earlier in this chapter. The *Forrestal* flew the E-2C and the S-3A, but an older F-4 *Phantom* fighter wing; the ship therefore had only three VAST stations, but in some ways this was a more difficult management situation than the four-station carriers.

The *Forrestal* had a history of being an unlucky ship, and the VAST shop was no exception. Typically, a cruise began with three stations operating, and ended with one (and sometimes, none). WRAs would build up into huge AWM backlogs, and in fact most of them were not repaired at sea, but instead were brought back for repair at Cecil Field, the S-3A shore site for *Forrestal*. However, Harris/PRD received a report that she returned from a Mediterranean Sea deployment in November, 1981, with all three VAST stations up and running, and with no WRAs AWM or AWP. Further, the ship had been able to dedicate two of its three VAST stations entirely to S-3A WRAs, and that resulted in the Navy's all-time record for readiness for that aircraft. Since the LSA Update was underway, we quickly flew off to interview the ship's AIMD officers to learn how they had accomplished this feat.

The interviews began with my teammates asking questions about the standard logistics elements. For nearly every logistical issue they brought up, the AIMD commander's response was generally that there were no major problems or unusual difficulties, and those that were encountered were well within the scope of the Navy's standard correction procedures. "Clean" electrical power is always a problem aboard ship, and VAST was less tolerant of surges and low-voltage conditions than many other electronic systems. A new power generator had been installed aboard the carrier to provide clean power prior for this cruise, and the expectation was that a large number of performance improvements would be derived from that engineering change.

There was no doubt that clean power made many improvements—both VAST stations and the SRA testers broke down less frequently, allowing for less variability in production. That improvement benefitted Supply, in that irregularities in the flow of components were minimized, and they were less likely to have stockouts.

However, at this point of the discussion, it is useful to refer to Figure 5.1 again. In our survey, we found that a great deal of the improvement in performance resulted from a number of changes to the "soft system" which were installed at the same time the new generator went in, i.e., just before the Mediterranean cruise. All of these changes had direct consequences for the nature of the information processing done in the AIMD. One change was to physically modify the layout of the AIMD avionics maintenance office. By deliberately placing the Supply office and counterspace, the material screening unit, and the Production Control office and VIDS/MAF display boards in the same room, it was impossible for any of the officers or supervisors in these units not to overhear whatever was said, not to see the VIDS/MAF displays, or not to be aware of changes in the rate of inductions. Consequently, key decision-makers in charge of the Supply pool (all of the Supply variables, S-1 to S-4) and who determined the WRAs to process

(Production Control and the VAST shop supervisors, V-1 and V-5) were using consistent information to make decisions. Most of the priority-setting IP was done in this office.

This information was used in the form of a "consistent local algorithm" to determine which WRAs to schedule. The objective of the algorithm was to prevent any WRAs from becoming EXREP (meaning there was an aircraft grounded without the WRA). The screening unit inspected all incoming MAFs, and any which were already EXREP or POOL CRITICAL were scheduled for immediate repair. This was "consistent" in the sense that everyone in charge of the AIMD units, Supply, and the squadrons agreed on this objective, and took specific steps to be sure that information necessary to apply it was provided to all workflow units. As examples, a practice of putting notes on the MAF (beyond the standard EXREP, etc.) to inform Supply of the urgency of a requisition was used by Supply to decide which orders to expedite; the PC office grouped MAFs by the code number used to identify the WRA, and these could be visually scanned to identify accumulations of batches large enough to justify cannibalization; an identical layout for all VIDS/MAF boards was jointly designed by all units (they often differed between units to emphasize different information), so that everyone received consistent information by inspecting any of them. Maintenance personnel from the air wing were also consulted on their needs whenever EXREP WRAs were inducted. By including them in the decision loop, the priorities most important to the squadrons were met first (O-1, O-2, O-5, and O-6), which then diminished the pressure to "hot-bench" (O-3) and cannibalize "hangar queens" (O-4).

The information processing could be done manually, but the system was further modified through the lease of two Radio Shack TRS-80 computers. This decision was partly stimulated by SIDMS, in that the AIMD officer had heard of SIDMS, but *Forrestal* was not scheduled to receive SIDMS for nearly a year. The TRS-80 was among the earliest of the desktop microcomputers, with about 4K of memory and 8-inch floppy disk drives. These were not official Navy issue, and were leased using ship "soft money." One VAST-shop sailor was a computer hobbyist, and volunteered to write programs to automate the record-keeping for inducted WRAs and to track them through the repair cycle. These programs were databases which allowed unlimited fields to be defined for data entry, and could sort data by specifying up to five fields at a time. One computer was dedicated to keeping track of all transactions through Supply, which meant that all inductions, issues of RFI WRAs and SRAs, and spare parts for the testers were entered into the database. The database could then be searched for groups of high-demand WRA inductions or demands on RFI assets for which few spares were available. In overall terms, all inventory-status variables contributing to effective WRA repair (V-1) and minimizing the number and impact of stockouts (S-1) were stored and could be readily searched.

The second computer was used to maintain a database on the testers themselves, throughout the AIMD, and by selecting those SRAs and WRAs for repair for which the necessary testers were available, WRA EXREP was nearly eliminated. The same database software was used to monitor all testers throughout the AIMD, personnel status and assignments, calibration of testers, and Awaiting Parts components by work center, code number, MAF number, or stock number. A sort on any of these data fields gave a quick overview of the AIMD status to Production Control and AIMD officers. This expanded access to information on the status and performance of personnel and testers in other work centers interacting with VAST, Supply, and Production Control meant that decisions affected by these variables were much more tightly coordinated.

Other changes affected a broad range of soft system variables. VAST operators often found themselves confounded when ambiguous fault isolations occurred because there was no way to determine whether the source of the ambiguity was the WRA or the VAST station. To resolve this problem, VAST maintainers were teamed with the operators whenever ambiguities occurred, and together they could usually resolve the ambiguity, and do it with less time in parallel than sequentially. In a number of cases, it was helpful to have storekeepers in the Supply area who were knowledgeable of VAST and the WRAs it tested to ensure that correct parts were obtained. The tester shops and PC trained these storekeepers and then reassigned them to Supply when openings occurred. Not only did this practice help the storekeeper understand the specific needs of the VAST shop, but it also meant that personal relationships between units were formed, and these could help when problems came up. These changes linked variables V-8 through V-12 much more closely and positively.

A final illustration of these soft-system variables was in the motivation of shop personnel. As noted earlier, the flow of WRAs through the shop often became relentless, and sailors began to suffer "burnout" because of the unceasing flow of WRAs. A large part of that problem was the lack of closure on the queue, and sailors often felt frustrated by the seeming lack of progress they made at working down the queue. Whenever an EXREP WRA was inducted, its code and description were typed on a strip of stiff paper about one-quarter inch by six inches, and this strip was placed on a special clipboard used to monitor EXREPs. Whenever an EXREP item was taken from the queue, its strip was removed from the clipboard. A simple solution to the burnout problem was to tape an empty foam coffee cup to an in-out tray on the Production Control Officer's desk. When an EXREP WRA was repaired, the strip for the WRA was placed in the cup, and the operators could easily see how many EXREPs had been processed on their shift. This simple feedback device was credited with having a significant benefit on morale, and often operators would become competitive to see which shift could repair the most EXREPs. A second cup for general repairs was soon added.

The results of this simple algorithm and the supporting IP changes in the soft system were quite significant, and very much a departure from previous *Forrestal* cruises. As the cruise went on, the VAST shop would occasionally run out of AWM WRAs, so that a shift literally had nothing to do. In these situations, shop managers and supervisors would run a full VAST self-test, a process requiring 8 or more hours, which required the use of several complex TPSs specific to VAST self-test. These were complicated procedures, but when done, they often identified problems in the stations or in components of the TPSs themselves, since they could also be tested. The result of these tests was to keep the VAST stations and its TPSs "clean," which further reduced the probability of ambiguous fault isolations and lost time from that source in the repair cycle. This was an excellent example of a negative feedback loop reducing variance in the system, and contributing to system performance.

Finally, it should be noted in passing that many of the VAST shop supervisors and officers had begun to generally recognize that management of the shop workflow required processing of much more information than that provided by the VIDS/MAF board or the EXREP or POOL CRITICAL designations on the MAFs themselves. As one illustration of this, a shop supervisor at NAS Oceana had developed a personal algorithm he used to select WRAs for repair. He considered five variables: the levels of RFI components in Supply; operator skills; the time required to repair a particular WRA; the status and configuration of the VAST stations; and the compatibility of the station with the WRA (some stations experienced fewer problems with BB57 on some tests, for example). He also maintained a good working relationship with Supply, so that he could casually go into the storage area and "eyeball" the levels of RFI WRAs. Even though one type of WRA might have been next in the queue, this supervisor might delay it because there were two in stock, and the WRA was not likely to be demanded soon. Finally, he cannibalized WRAs routinely, by first repairing as many WRAs in a batch as possible without cannibalization, and then cannibalizing to get as many repairs from the one TPS build-up as possible, so long as no

EXREPS came into the shop. Observation and analysis of his own experience had enabled this young supervisor to create a very effective IP and decision process, and he felt that he was usually on top of things on his shift (a perception corroborated by his superior officer).

The "engineering" interpretation of AIMD workflow problems persisted, however, even in the face of growing evidence that factors other than logistics and hardware seemed to play a major role in site repair performance. My DSI teammates, therefore, found the *Forrestal* visit to be largely a disappointment. We knew that the *Forrestal* had just had its most successful cruise ever, in terms of its ability to keep its VAST stations operating and repair WRAs, and they expected that the primary reason for this success was the installation of the new generator for the VAST shop. While the benefits of this new generator were acknowledged and fully appreciated, it was the bootstrap management system that was considered by everyone we interviewed on the ship to be the major contributor to the performance improvement. The engineering perspective of the problem had difficulties accommodating that information.

The Aircraft Intermediate Maintenance Support Office

One other development occurred in parallel with the LSA Update, and bears on the research to be reviewed in the next chapter. This development was the creation of the Aircraft Intermediate Maintenance Support Office (AIMSO) at NAS Patuxent River, Maryland. "Pax River," as this base is known, is the Navy's primary test and development center for aircraft programs, and in this capacity it also is the technical evaluation site for testers, including VAST. AIMSO was formally established on 1 October 1979 to provide management assistance to intermediate-level aviation maintenance. The Chief of Naval Operations (CNO) decided that problems with Naval aircraft maintenance and readiness demanded direct attention at high levels. AIMSO was created to provide that level of attention by reporting directly to CNO, and to examine requirements for improved readiness that went beyond the usual engineering and logistics approaches.

The LSA Update study was initiated in late 1980, at about the same time that AIMSO was fully staffed and operational. Our LSA Update team was soon independently coordinating its efforts with AIMSO as a result of contact through the CATE/ILSMT, and by 1982 we had developed a continuous working relationship. AIMSO personnel had independently come to the same conclusions we had, i.e., that the resolution of problems in the AIMD workflow would be achieved through improved management, and particularly IP changes, not improved engineering. Thus, one office had begun to work on a true management information system to support avionics repair, and its first specific objective was to try to improve the management of the VAST workflow. In that connection, work had begun on development of the VAST Automated Management Program (VAMP, of course). When operational, VAMP would acquire and process information on the entire flow of work from WRA induction at Supply, through scheduling in Production Control, and through all parts of the repair cycle (including Awaiting Maintenance time and Awaiting Parts, if any) until the WRA was restored to RFI status and sent back to Supply.[9]

VAMP was the first comprehensive effort to apply information technology to management of the AIMD workflow, and a full description of its effects on IP will be given in the next chapter. A great deal of the learning necessary to create VAMP had come from the FAMMS experience at North Island. In late 1982, North Island's AIMD Production Control office got a new minicomputer, and this was used as a test site for much of the final development of VAMP software. VAMP was almost fully debugged and operational by early 1983, and the results, as we will see in Chapter 6, were dramatic.

Notes

1. The challenge is always to be able to say the name and the acronym in one breath. Like the "QWERTY" keyboard, invented to slow typists so that they could not type too fast for the mechanical linkages in early typewriters, the Navy's use of acronyms dates back to the use of semaphore flags on wooden ships, where a flag code like DXG meant something very specific, and has never gone away.

2. This tester was later given the designation Consolidated Automated Support System, or CASS. The World Wide Web URL for CASS given in the Foreword refers to this system.

3. John L. Kmetz (1984), An information-processing study of a complex workflow in aircraft electronics repair, *Administrative Science Quarterly*, 29 (2): 255-280. Not all of the relationships discussed here were covered in the *ASQ* article, principally in the interests of simplifying the article and reducing its length.

4. All data reported in this section were reviewed and approved for security clearance by officials of the Naval Air Systems Command.

5. This work was supported by NAVAIR contract N00019-79-C-0543.

6. The most extreme AWP situation I encountered was in a case where the Supply officer in control of AWP simply started moving a partition wall outward every time the "AWP cage" filled up. He refused to release any AWP unless it was strictly "by the book." The only way total AWP was reduced was to start working down the levels when this officer was not on duty, and then physically move the cage partition inward. To guarantee no increase in volume, shelves were built against the outside of the cage wall and moved with it.

7. The F-14A is a "swing-wing," or technically a "variable geometry" aircraft, and so it is very difficult to seal all of the areas inside the fuselage from water. In a salt-water environment, that can cause major problems with many electrical and electronic components, but the larger problem was actually rain. Sealing the leaks would have cost an estimated $1,000,000 per aircraft, and so the Navy elected not to do it.

8. I particularly want to thank Lt. Robert Bachmann and ASDC Marcus Oakley. Both of them were very helpful in demonstrating how they were using FAMMS, and their enthusiasm was contagious throughout the site.

9. I especially want to recognize the efforts of Mr. John Gray. John was a key member of the AIMSO team, and more than anyone else kept the development of VAMP moving forward. He was a delight to work with, and I learned an enormous amount from him.

References

Checkland, Peter (1979), Techniques in 'soft' systems practice, Pt. I: Some diagrams—some tentative guidelines. *Journal of Applied Systems Analysis*, 6: 33-40.

Checkland, Peter (1988), Soft systems methodology: An overview. *Journal of Applied Systems Analysis*, 15: 27-40.

Lindblom, Charles E. (1959), The science of "muddling through." *Public Administration Review*, 19: 79-99.

NAVAIR contract N00019-79-C-0543. Phoenix, Arizona: Dynamic Science, Inc.

Productivity Enhancement of the Versatile Avionics Shop Test System Site Evaluation and Final Report (1979), Falls Church, VA: Systems Research Corporation, 6 March 1979. Supported by contract no. N68335-78-C-1593.

6 "Experiment 2"—IP Capacity, Organization Performance, and Organization Slack

Introduction

This chapter reports the results of "Experiment 2."[1] This experiment examines the effects of changes to the information processing capacity of the avionics repair workflow on the performance of that workflow over time. These effects are measured at both the level of the VAST shop and the AIMD, i.e., at both the site and system levels. The general model of IPT predicts that positive changes to IP capacity should benefit performance, and that negative changes should reduce performance.

Embedded within this experiment is an investigation of organization "slack," which while theoretically and practically significant is extremely difficult to isolate and measure. The circumstances of the VAST technology accession created an opportunity to estimate the effects of slack as defined in Chapter 1, as both positive and negative performance payoffs over time.

Fundamental to the IPT model is that the IP structure must support the processing of information needed for goal attainment. Both positive and negative changes in IP capacity over time should be followed by corresponding positive and negative changes in performance. Obviously, trying to measure these effects is very difficult, especially for reduced performance. Not only is the researcher attempting to measure things that "didn't happen" (i.e., lowered or lost performance in the case of reduced IP capacity), but most organizations simply change too quickly to permit measurement of such effects.

The workflow in the avionics repair cycle, however, is stable enough over a long period of time to enable such a study. When it became apparent that the deployment of the VAST Automated Management Program (VAMP) would allow a thorough study of changes in the IP system, and that "hard" data on both shop and AIMD performance could be obtained, I designed this

277

experiment to see whether changes in IP would actually result in the predicted changes in performance. The LSA Update Study provided the justification to collect raw data from the Navy's VIDS/MAF system and perform an independent analysis of the effects of the IP changes described in Chapter 5.

Obviously, one of the confounds in any field research of this kind is the possibility that variables not measured or otherwise taken into account might be the explanation for observed "effects." Fortunately, so much importance was attached to VAST performance that by late 1983, all of the studies reviewed in Chapters 3, 4, and 5 had been done; from that body of work, we fully understood the context of the research, and were confident that unknown variables were not likely to exist, let alone have significant effects on performance. In short, what was done in the avionics repair workflow was known exactly, and it had been determined that none of the variables in the logistics "tail" could explain poor avionics production through the VAST shops.

The earlier studies had also established a baseline for interpretation of performance changes. Not only were the characteristics of the overall workflow known, but the details of operations at all of the major shore sites and for quite a number of carriers as well. By 1983, VAST had achieved a high degree of technological maturity, with most of the technical problems associated with deployment of a new system having been resolved. The one exception to this statement pertained to the TPSs; but while they were still a source of problems, even those had been isolated well enough to know that they were not problems with VAST but were specific to the TPSs themselves. Further, many of the most troublesome TPSs had already begun to receive corrective attention, whether in the form of formal Engineering Investigations (EI) or through informal "workarounds."

Description of the Study

General Study Design

"Experiment 2" is a multiple-wave, quasi-experimental field study (Cook and Campbell, 1979). The experiment examines the relationship between changes in the information processing capacity at different shore sites and objective Navy performance measures (both EMT and TAT) at those sites. The changes in IP capacity examined are all relative to the Navy-designed flows of materials and information as shown in Figure 3.8 and discussed in

Chapter 3; the VIDS/MAF system for management information processing support is therefore the baseline IP system for all sites. A two-wave study of F-14A sites was conducted, using data from 1978 and 1981; a three-wave study was done for S-3A sites, using data from 1978, 1981, and 1983. Data from Cecil Field (an S-3A site) provides a control group, since this site never adopted any of the information processing changes enacted at any other bases. Supplemental carrier data from 1981 are also examined. All data are based on large samples taken from Navy-supplied tapes of raw maintenance data. Finally, descriptive follow-up data from 1985 to 1989 are also examined briefly.

This study is considered a quasi-experiment because it was not possible to fully control the timing and exposure of the repair-cycle units to the "experimental treatment" (Cook and Campbell, 1979). Also, the specific "IP treatments" were not the same in all cases, and it was only possible to have a control group for the S-3A sites. However, the sites were matched on two key variables known to be sources of performance variation: the type of site (ship *vs.* shore), and the type of aircraft supported at the site. It was also possible to construct comparison baselines for all research sites in 1978 from interview data provided by site personnel in the first wave of data collection. Since there were two pairs of sites, within- and between-time changes in IP capacity and performance could be measured and compared for each aircraft type.

Measures of Performance

I obtained tapes of raw MAF data from the Navy for the full year of operations at each site for each of the three study years, and extracted random samples of EMT and TAT data for each study site from them, using a description of the coding system the Navy also provided.

Table 6.1 summarizes the nature of the four shore sites included in the study. The sites for the experiment were the master shore bases for both Atlantic and Pacific Fleets for two of the three major aircraft supported by VAST, the F-14A and the S-3A. This allows comparison of data from two different geographic sites, each of which supports the same aircraft, and each of which has the same number of VAST stations. The only exception is that Miramar supports two aircraft (the F-14A and the E-2C), but the majority of that workload is from the F-14A; further, both aircraft and their VAST TPSs were manufactured to similar engineering specifications by Grumman

Aerospace Corp. The effect of the two-aircraft mix on performance is likely to be very small if the TPSs are similar, as earlier studies suggest.

Data for the cross-sectional comparison of carrier performance in 1981 reflect a full deckload of all airborne and non-airborne WRAs. These WRAs are shown in Table 3.1, and the performance comparison is for all carriers in the respective Atlantic and Pacific Fleets.

Table 6.1   Four NAVAIR shore sites studied in "Experiment 2"

Naval Air Station	Fleet	Aircraft supported	Number of VAST stations
Cecil Field (Jacksonville, Fl.)	Atlantic	S-3A, A-7E[1]	6
North Island (San Diego, Ca.)	Pacific	S-3A	6
Oceana (Virginia Beach, Va.)	Atlantic	F-14A	6
Miramar (San Diego, Ca.)	Pacific	F-14A, E-2C	6

1   The A-7E made very limited demands on VAST resources. The large majority of the workload at this site was from the S-3A.

Samples and Sample Size

An analysis of Ready For Issue (RFI) rates performed by Q.E.D. Systems assisted in determination of sample sizes.[2] This study was an analysis of Navy production data which examined changes in aggregate RFI levels between the same two time periods as my first waves of data collection, i.e., 1978 and 1981, and was done independently of my study. Table 6.2 shows the range of monthly WRA workloads processed through the VAST shops at three of the four shore sites in my study, and from 11 carriers. For reasons that are not explained in the Q.E.D. memorandum, data for NAS North Island were not examined. I have shown the ranges only to indicate that the sample sizes selected for my study are always the equivalent of at least a month of production, although my data are sampled from the entire year to minimize the effect of variables which may be cyclical or otherwise distort data from a single month alone. Given variability in carrier deckloads and air wings,

I used much larger samples for the cross-sectional comparison of carrier data from 1981.

Table 6.2   Minimum and maximum monthly WRA production at selected research sites for 1978 and 1981[1]

Site	Minimum production	Maximum production
Cecil Field (S-3A)	163 (May, 1981)	350 (July, 1981)
Oceana (F-14A)	219 (October, 1981)	521 (July, 1981)
Miramar (F-14A)	156 (June, 1981)	534 (December, 1981)
Carriers	105 (USS *Independence*, February, 1981)	589 (USS *America*, May, 1981

1   Minimum and maximum values both occurred during 1981. The maxima were most likely to be found exclusively during 1981 since the deployment of VAST stations was nearly complete by this time.

IP Capacity Changes

No attempt was made to "measure" IP capacity in terms of a fixed set of variables; instead, workflow diagrams of the IP system operating at each of the sites during each wave of the study are used to illustrate changes in IP capacity in descriptive terms. The reason for this choice of descriptive rather than empirical assessment of IP capacity is very simple: as will be seen, none of the sites used exactly the same elements of the IP system over time except for NAS Cecil Field, the "control" site for the S-3A study. This prevents meaningful common measures from being taken, even if IP capacity scales had been developed.

The similarity in formal organization design used at all sites enabled me to construct a baseline description of "databases" used or generated in each shop and material and information flows, which is shown in Figure 3.8. Changes to those databases and flows could thus be examined for effects on performance, where other variables were effectively held constant or their effects were known from other research.

Each of the tables of results is preceded by a specific description of the workflow at each of the research sites. Modifications of Figure 3.8 graphically illustrate these descriptions by showing how the IP capacity in the workflow was changed at each study site. These diagrams show changes in terms of the databases and information flows affected, as described in Chapter 4. In each of the AIMD shops or units shown in Figure 3.8, there is an acronym to designate at least one database which is specific to that shop or unit. IP capacity is increased by either expanding the number or type of databases used to control the workflow, or by augmenting the flow of information by increasing the number of linkages, or with information technology. In IPT terms, if the IP structure is expanded or more dynamic linkages are included in workflow decision-making and control processes, then IP capacity is enhanced. Reducing or eliminating any IP structure elements, i.e., databases or linkages, reduces capacity.

Relative to the baseline VIDS/MAF system, IP capacity changes could be interpreted as changes to the scope of decisions as suggested by Galbraith (1977: 98). He describes "decision scope" as a relationship between the comprehensiveness of the database (either "local" or "global"), and the frequency of decisions (either "periodic" or "continuous"). If the decision process within any unit is expanded to include additional information, whether by increasing the number of databases or increasing the flows of information between them (especially if such changes increase the frequency of decisions), the scope of the decision has been increased.

Effects of these IP modifications are evaluated in terms of percentage changes in VAST-shop EMT and AIMD TAT, i.e., effect sizes, between sites and between times. Also, *t*-tests are used to evaluate the probability of sampling error (as discussed in Appendix 1.2). EMT is a "local" measure of performance, since it reflects only the time to process a WRA within the VAST shop. TAT is a "global" or system-level measure, since it reflects all actions necessary to complete a repair through the AIMD. Depending on the site, IP changes may or may not include the use of information technology.

It may seem somewhat unusual to use *t*-tests for large samples such as these, but there were two reasons for choosing this approach that I found to be compelling. First, we know that many of the distributions of EMT and TAT for individual WRAs are skewed toward longer times, as suggested by the review of the S-3A TAT data in Table 4.3. In examining the distributions of many WRAs from all three aircraft, I found this to be a common pattern. We know that the *t*-test is robust in cases of non-normal population distributions, and as the samples get larger, distorting effects of nonnormality on the t statistic diminish (and the distribution of t approaches normality, of course).

Second, I wanted to do specific comparisons of means between different sites or between different times at the same site. The exhaustive preliminary studies we had done on logistics support and other variables in the workflow had effectively eliminated these logistics elements, along with staffing levels and skill mixes, as contending explanations for performance variability. Yet performance variability clearly existed, and these same studies had suggested that changes in the way that the workflow was managed, and particularly changes in the way information about the work was managed, might be a better explanation for that variability.

A summary of the IP system in use at each site for each wave of data collection is shown in Table 6.3. For the 1978 and 1981 performance comparisons, IP capacity changes had been made at least 12 months earlier. The 1983 performance changes at the S-3A sites were measured within the year during which the VAST Automated Management Program (VAMP) was being fully implemented for the first time.

"Experiment 2" Results

Performance Effects of Information Processing Changes at F-14A Sites (NAS Miramar, NAS Oceana)

Figure 6.1 (based on Figure 3.8) shows the IP system in effect at NAS Miramar in 1978, when the forward SRA pool and the pool of Maintenance Assist Modules (MAMs) were located near the VAST shop. The databases and material and information flows affected by these changes to the baseline have been emphasized relative to Figure 3.8, and other databases not affected have been deleted from the diagram. As the figure shows, only two databases and two flows were affected by these IP changes; a supplemental information flow was also created with the use of MAMs, shown by flow 11a, which does not exist in the baseline workflow diagram.

IP changes at NAS Oceana are shown in Figure 6.2. At the time of the first round of Oceana data collection in 1978, the SPORT computer system was being used to provide supplemental local documentation for the "swapping" of SRAs in WRA repair (see Chapter 5). By 1981, nearly all inventory in the Oceana VAST workflow was in the SPORT system databases, making timely data available to Production Control and the VAST

Table 6.3 **Management information processing system in effect at sites studied in "Experiment 2"**

Site and aircraft supported	Fleet	Wave of data collection		
		1978	1981	1983
Oceana (F-14A)	Atlantic	VIDS/MAF system only	VIDS/MAF system plus SPORT	Not included
Miramar (F-14A)	Pacific	VIDS/MAF system plus forward parts detachment	VIDS/MAF system only	Not included
Cecil Field (S-3A)	Atlantic	VIDS/MAF system only	VIDS/MAF system only	VIDS/MAF system only
North Island (S-3A)	Pacific	VIDS/MAF system plus FAMMS running on base administrative computer	VIDS/MAF system plus FAMMS running on dedicated computer	VAST Automated Management Program (VAMP) plus automated MAF data entry
Carriers (all VAST-supported aircraft)	Atlantic	Not included	VIDS/MAF system plus SIDMS	Not included
Carriers (all VAST-supported aircraft)	Pacific	Not included	VIDS/MAF system only	Not included

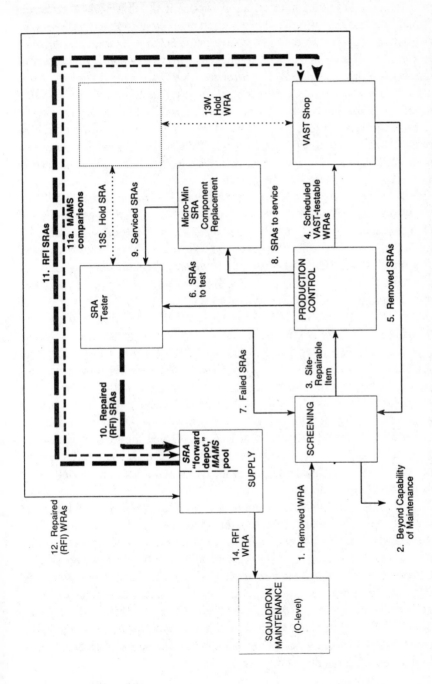

Figure 6.1   NAS Miramar information processing modifications to the AIMD workflow, 1978

shop officers. SPORT included all component databases, and the local inventory accounting system had been augmented by automated SPORT data entry on inventory movement. (The Navy provided reports to operating sites from data entered on MAF documents, but these always lagged months behind current operations, so that prior to SPORT current inventory status was seldom known with accuracy.) In a strict technical sense, SPORT provided no new information relative to the VIDS/MAF system; however, it did eliminate delays in feedback, and contributed greatly to ensuring that site inventory data were current and accurate. From this perspective, SPORT transformations provided new information to site managers. Again, these IP capacity changes are shown in Figure 6.2.

EMT effects from these IP capacity changes are shown in Table 6.4. As the 1978 row in Table 6.4 shows, the Miramar VAST shop was processing a WRA in less than half of the EMT taken at Oceana. The effects of SPORT on EMT can readily be seen in the Oceana column of Table 6.4, where EMT had been reduced by over 35 percent. However, when the second round of data were collected in 1981, the SRA forward pool at Miramar had been eliminated and the repair cycle had reverted to the original design of Figure 3.8. 1981 EMT increased nearly 56 percent at Miramar relative to 1978.

Effects on TAT shown in Table 6.5 were even more dramatic. Average TAT was nearly five days less at Miramar in 1978, meaning that Miramar completed the average repair over 27 percent faster than Oceana. Both sites showed improvement in TAT between waves of data collection, as would be expected for maturing technologies like VAST and the F-14. However, the improvement of almost 17 percent at Miramar was far exceeded by an improvement of almost 81 percent at Oceana. Given the large variances in TAT, the change over time at Miramar might have been a chance fluctuation at the .05 level of significance, but improvements at Oceana clearly were unlikely to be from chance.

All of these performance effects are as IPT predicts, and are most dramatic in terms of their effects at the system level, i.e., on TAT. The addition of IP capacity and the change in scope of the decision system to a more nearly continuous basis, as was done at Oceana between waves of data collection, clearly improved performance. At the same time, when IP capacity was reduced at Miramar between waves, slack in the form of lower performance adjusted for the diminished IP capacity. The effect of removing the forward SRA pool at Miramar was more localized, i.e., principally affected EMT within the VAST shops, given the local scope of changes to the workflow and IP between waves.

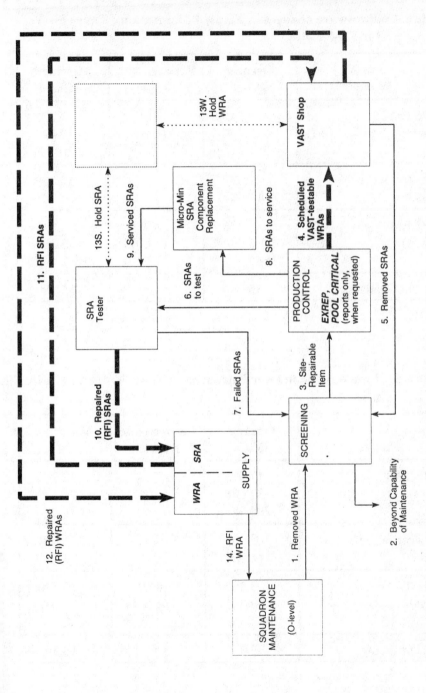

Figure 6.2   NAS Oceana SPORT system database and SRA exchange tracking, 1978

Table 6.4 Two-wave changes in Elapsed Maintenance Time (EMT) for F-14A sites

Wave		Oceana (Va.)	Between-site t value	Miramar (Ca.)
1978 EMT	M	6.545	7.60	3.226
(hours)	SD	7.306	(<.001)	2.497
	n	294		678
Between-wave t value		9.09 (<.001)		10.069 (<.001)
1981 EMT	M	4.236	8.70	5.032
(hours)	SD	5.992	(<.001)	5.289
	n	843		1212
Percent Change		-35.28		+55.98

Table 6.5 Two-wave changes in Turnaround Time (TAT) for F-14A sites

Wave		Oceana (Va.)	Between-site t value	Miramar (Ca.)
1978 TAT	M	17.575	2.24	12.736
(days)	SD	32.688	(<.03)	26.330
	n	294		678
Between-wave t value		9.09 (<.001)		1.664 (n.s.)
1981 TAT	M	3.267	8.70	10.510
(days)	SD	9.392	(<.001)	26.682
	n	843		1212
Percent Change		-80.84		-16.59

Performance Effects of Information Processing Changes at S-3A Sites (NAS Cecil Field, NAS North Island)

Three waves of data were collected at the S-3A sites. The first two were taken at the same time as the F-14A data collections, but a third wave was collected in 1983 at the conclusion of the LSA Update, and because of the introduction of the full VAST Automated Management Program (VAMP) during 1983, that wave was split into the first and second halves of the year. Large samples were taken for each six-month period, and performance effects of VAMP were assessed for each half of the year.

Changes in the IP system over three waves   As Table 6.3 shows, there were major differences in the nature of the IP systems used to manage AIMD workflow between the two S-3A master bases, NAS Cecil Field and NAS North Island. The most important aspect of this difference is that Cecil Field essentially served as a "control" for Experiment 2, since no significant changes to the VIDS/MAF system were put into effect between 1978 and the end of 1983; the VIDS/MAF IP system there was unchanged during the entire experiment. North Island, in contrast, went through an evolutionary period of experimentation with the Fixed Allowance Module Management System (FAMMS) in 1978 and 1981, and then installed and began fully operating the VAMP during the course of 1983. 1983 was a year of progressive learning and improvement with the use of VAMP, which was the first true decision support system to be used in an AIMD.

Figure 6.3 shows the IP changes that occurred at North Island during 1978 and 1981. During these two waves of data collection, FAMMS was operating and continuously being expanded and improved. When VAMP was installed in 1983, the entire set of databases and information and material flows in the AIMD were included; that is, VAMP was comprehensive of the entire AIMD avionics repair process as shown in Figure 3.8. While differences in aircraft and TPS design make comparisons between S-3A and F-14A sites less straightforward than they might be, the workflow described in Figure 3.8 was used at all sites, and the functioning of the VAST shops, the AIMD, and Supply was the same.

The scope of the VAST Automated Management Program   VAMP was developed and deployed through the efforts of the Aircraft Intermediate Maintenance Support Office (AIMSO), as noted at the end of Chapter 5. The primary mission for AIMSO was to improve intermediate-level aircraft maintenance management, since studies which motivated AIMSO's creation

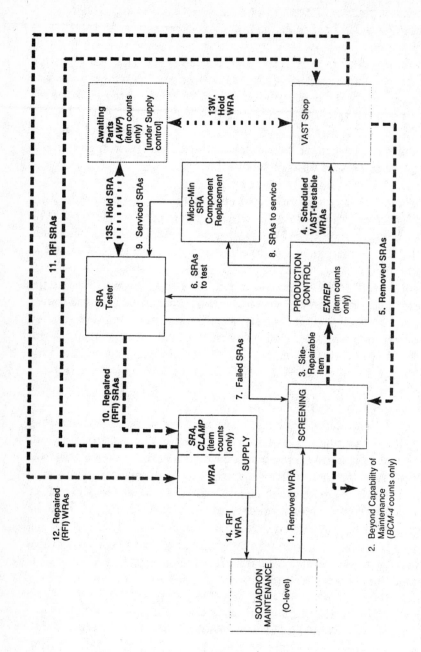

Figure 6.3 NAS North Island workflow with FAMMS induction and inventory data systems, 1978 and 1981

showed that little attention had been paid to AIMD management issues. AIMSO took several initiatives, including the writing of a comprehensive guide to the management of the AIMD using the VIDS/MAF system. This guide was known as the Readiness Maintenance Management System, and it established the majority of the data tables needed for VAMP. These tables included the "soft" system components of personnel and training records, so that skill levels became an explicit part of the information used to make operational decisions in the AIMD.

AIMSO personnel used the lessons learned from experimental or local IP systems such as the SPORT and FAMMS programs, most of which were facilitated by the CATE/ILSMT. By late 1980, AIMSO proposed full development of VAMP, and targeted its first deployment for late 1982, a two-year effort. I became involved in this process in 1982, principally to contribute what I had learned from my VAST and AIMD investigations to AIMSO, and to provide an outsider's point of view in the latter stages of VAMP development.

VAMP was developed in modules during 1981 and 1982., i.e., between the last two waves of data collection. As noted in Chapters 4 and 5, the S-3A had been experiencing significant operational difficulties owing to unavailability of RFI WRAs. Hence, S-3A shore sites were selected as the first bases for testing and development of the program, in the hope that VAMP would improve operational readiness for the S-3A. Since I was already involved in independent data collection and evaluation for two waves of data for 1978 and 1981, my scope of data collection was increased to include data from the S-3A sites for 1983.

Unlike other programs which provided very limited information transformation activity (largely accounting or sorting functions), VAMP was structured around a decision algorithm which selected WRAs for repair on the basis of their contribution to aircraft operational readiness. The Navy maintained information, some of which is classified, on the mission-essential characteristics of individual WRAs, and this constituted part of the algorithm's selection criteria. The entire site repair queue was evaluated each time a new WRA was inducted into the repair cycle from a squadron. Those WRAs which had the greatest impact on readiness, had the highest Supply priority (EXREP or POOL CRITICAL), and had the highest historical demand rate, were moved to the head of the repair queue. VAMP, in short, maximized performance on the highest-level criterion of the system. While other criteria, such as throughput rates, RFI rates, or local EMT or TAT were significant, they were not used as the most important performance criteria by VAMP; but as will be seen, these measures were directly affected by the

VAMP algorithm. This permits comparison of 1983 EMT and TAT measures with the two earlier waves of data.

As developmental experience with the VAMP modules was gained, additional decision-support information was incorporated into the VAMP algorithm, and many of the additional variables from both the "hard" and "soft" systems, as shown in Figure 5.1, were also added. For example, data on VAST station status were added, so that the algorithm could evaluate whether a station which could repair the next WRA in the repair queue; if a VAST station were completely down or operating in degraded status, a station for that particular WRA might not be available at the moment. In such a case, the algorithm would select the next-highest-priority WRA, and evaluate the queue as soon as maintenance data indicating that the degraded VAST station was back up to full capability were entered. Data on operator and maintainer skills and ratings were added, so that the algorithm could assign some weight to the difficulty of the repair. "Difficulty of repair" was defined as two experience variables with the WRA, which were EMT data on the WRA, and the percentage of that WRA which had been sent off-site as Beyond Capability of Maintenance (BCM). The effect of expanding both the scope and number of databases, and hence the variables in the algorithm, was to make the VAMP increasingly sensitive to all factors which affected repair-cycle performance.

One design feature of VAMP was quite noteworthy. VAMP enabled direct terminal entry of all MAF data, and a printing routine was designed to allow VAMP to work in parallel with the VIDS/MAF system during its early deployment. This allowed VAMP to produce MAFs which could be posted on the VIDS/MAF display boards. However, all of the data from the Navy's repair policy and procedures had been entered into a reference database, and when a technician made an entry through the keyboard, the program would prompt the worker if an erroneous or incomplete entry was made. To complete a MAF, both VAST operators and maintainers had to be sure they knew the repair procedures and data requirements; data entered through the VAMP interface were therefore "clean" and correct, and data used for the decision algorithm from site databases were therefore increasingly accurate. Since the data were entered as part of the "real-time" repair process, all decision data were current, unlike FAMMS, which was never able to acquire or provide data less than 24 hours old. These features also enabled the North Island personnel who were working with AIMSO to create databases containing information from technical publications used in the repair process, and to cross-reference these to data entered by the sailors. Numerous discrepancies and errors in the technical publications were eventually discovered through this subroutine of VAMP. The feedback effect was to greatly increase operator confidence in the actions they were taking during the repair cycle in the near term; the long-run effect was further improvement in technical-data logistic support throughout the VAST repair cycle.

A final point to be aware of is that VAMP, unlike FAMMS, was developed on its own minicomputer, which was purchased as part of the VAMP program. The computer was installed in the Production Control office at North Island, and site personnel were selected and trained to operate it. These people were kept at North Island throughout the development and debugging of the VAMP program.

Before examining the effect of VAMP on EMT and TAT at the S-3A sites, it may be useful to summarize the impact of VAMP on avionics-maintenance IP capacity relative to the VIDS/MAF system. This impact may be described in terms of the IP structure defined in Chapter 1:

Function effects. The primary VAMP effects on IP functions were on acquisition, storage, and transformation, with some important feedback effects through information dissemination:

> Acquisition—a standard MAF-format entry was used, with an error-checking subroutine to require technicians to enter all data as specified by Naval Aviation Maintenance Program guidelines.
>
> Storage—local on-line, interactive databases were established for all data needed for control of the AIMD workflow.
>
> Transformation—an OR-driven decision algorithm was used for all WRA repair-priority decisions. Relative to the VIDS/MAF system, more variables were likely to be used in the algorithm (tester status, crew training, etc., although some PC officers already were considering these, as we have seen). VAMP continuously monitored the repair queue and assessed priorities whenever any variable which affected OR changed. VAMP also generated diagnostic outputs.
>
> Dissemination—VAMP continuously reported priorities to Production Control and Work Center supervisors; provided troubleshooting outputs, e.g., false removal reports; and cleaned up technical data discrepancies. General feedback was dramatically improved.

Framework effects. All parts of the IP framework were affected by VAMP, primarily through information technology mediation; there was limited effect on accessors, although users could request standard outputs:

Sensors—data entry was performed through local terminals rather than the MAF.

Memory—use of databases was expanded; a broader range of variables was available to the decision algorithm; however, no new data collection was required for VAMP. Memory was also linked to accessors so that information quality was monitored and improved over time, and errors were prevented.

Processors—VAMP was provided with a dedicated Wang minicomputer.

Accessors—continuously-updated WRA repair priorities were available on user request; VAMP was capable of printing standard Navy-format reports when hard-copy documentation was requested; printed MAFs were provided to support the VIDS/MAF system during transition; and feedback was given to technicians on MAF data entry.

"Experiment 2" Results at S-3A Sites (NAS Cecil Field, NAS North Island)

Table 6.6 shows changes in EMT for the S-3A VAST shops. Again, Cecil Field used the VIDS/MAF system at all times, while data from North Island reflect effects of the FAMMS local experiment in 1978 and 1981, and the effect of VAMP in 1983. As the table shows, EMT in 1978 was over 40 percent greater at North Island as compared to Cecil Field, in large part because of the enforced delays needed to enter MAF data into the FAMMS program when the base administrative computer was not available over weekends. By 1981, both sites had degraded to over five hours EMT per average WRA repair. This was a cause of considerable concern within the NAVAIR community. However, the proportionate degradation at North Island was less than at Cecil Field, and although the two sites were roughly comparable (i.e., equally bad), North Island EMT had actually declined very little. By mid-year 1983, when the VAMP had been in use for about six months, EMT at North Island had improved back to about its 1978 level, while continuing to degrade at Cecil Field. By the end of 1983, with VAMP fully operational at North Island, S-3A EMT had dropped to its lowest levels ever; Cecil Field, on the other hand, continued to worsen, achieving record-high EMT levels for the S-3A.

Table 6.6   Three-wave changes in Elapsed Maintenance Time (EMT) for S-3A sites

Wave		North Island (Ca.)	Between-site t value	Cecil Field (Fla.)
1978 EMT	M	4.679	9.93	3.048
(hours)	SD	4.868	(<.001)	2.404
	n	1296		663
Between-wave t value		2.46 (<.02)		14.070 (<.001)
1981 EMT	M	5.145	1.045	5.421
(hours)	SD	5.188	(n.s.)	5.343
	n	1493		1583
Between-wave t value		3.206 (<.01)		2.079 (<.05)
January-June,	M	4.686	3.285	6.70
1983 EMT	SD	1.745	(<.01)	17.849
(hours)	n	1218		885
Between-wave t value		25.090 (<.001)		0.27 (n.s.)
July-December,	M	3.031	6.418	6.93
1983 EMT	SD	1.666	(<.001)	17.939
(hours)	n	1502		894

Table 6.7 contrasts the North Island TAT effects with FAMMS and VAMP to those with the Cecil Field VIDS/MAF system over the three waves of data collection. The results parallel those for EMT. In 1978, both sites were taking nearly a month to repair the average WRA, with Cecil Field again doing slightly better than North Island under the restrictions of the FAMMS program. Over the next three years, TAT improvement was both statistically and practically significant at both sites, but this was largely because of the Navy's investment in large numbers of additional SRAs (an experimental disturbance which will be discussed shortly), and a program of

operating minimum numbers of S-3As at shore sites so that they could be stripped for WRAs to send to sea with deploying squadrons. The two sites achieved approximate parity in the first half of 1983, but as VAMP became fully effective at North Island in the second half of 1983, TAT fell to about five and one-half days. At Cecil Field, TAT continued to increase beyond its 1981 and mid-1978 levels.

Table 6.7   Three-wave changes in Turnaround Time (TAT) for S-3A sites

Wave		North Island (Ca.)	Between-site *t* value	Cecil Field (Fla.)
1978 TAT	M	29.253	1.189	26.712
(days)	SD	52.346	(n.s.)	40.347
	n	1296		663
Between-wave *t* value		7.308 (<.001)		8.881 (<.001)
1981 TAT	M	16.115	1.045	11.423
(days)	SD	40.823	(<.001)	28.374
	n	1493		1583
Between-wave *t* value		3.538 (<.001)		0.810 (n.s.)
January-June,	M	12.207	0.384	12.830
1983 TAT	SD	11.203	(n.s.)	47.301
(days)	n	1218		885
Between-wave *t* value		15.449 (<.001)		0.401 (n.s.)
July-December,	M	5.503	5.099	13.750
1983 TAT	SD	11.317	(<.001)	47.541
(days)	n	1502		894

Experimental disturbances common to all research sites At the beginning of this chapter, it was noted that this study was a quasi-experiment rather than a fully controlled true experiment. Although mentioned many times, it should be noted that the continuing maturation of the VAST technology over the research period was an experimental disturbance common to all sites and supported aircraft and avionics components. This is a background "noise" factor which cannot be eliminated, but is important because the expectation for any weapon or support system is that it will become increasingly reliable and maintainable over time. The Navy provides extra support and contractor services for any new system, but these are withdrawn as the technology matures. Between data collections there were three specific changes which affected all aspects of the repair cycle at all sites, and these must be regarded as disturbances to the experiment:

1. TPS modifications. Both NAVAIR and the weapon system contractors continuously correct deficiencies in the VAST test program sets. These changes affect both TPS hardware and software, and would be expected to slightly reduce mean EMT and TAT across data collections. This is an ordinary aspect of technology maturation for any complex system.

2. VAST and WRA hardware modifications. The WRA and VAST manufacturers also correct equipment deficiencies as necessary, although the proportion of circuitry affected is small. These modifications gradually reduce failure rates and make VAST test results more accurate, which principally reduces mean EMT. To the extent that engineering problems causing false failure identifications are corrected, there should also be some benefit to TAT. This is also an ordinary aspect of system maturation.

3. Personnel retention. A service-wide problem in the late 1970s was the poor retention of skilled personnel, and thus retention of organizational learning. The VAST community had experienced proportionately greater retention problems than the rest of the Navy. As retention had begun to improve slightly by the 1981 data collections, it would be expected that both mean EMT and mean TAT would benefit from the overall increase in personnel experience levels.

Experimental disturbances specific to S-3A sites Three disturbances specific to S-3A sites occurred over the data collections, and these should also be noted:

1. Loss of training on S-3A WRAs. VAST training detachments at the two S-3A sites (North Island and Cecil Field) were eliminated in 1979-1980, and all VAST training was assigned to detachments at F-14 bases. There are some significant technical differences between S-3A and F-14 test programs, and this change could slightly impair S-3A WRA repair performance.
2. Unreliable SRA tester. As discussed in Chapter 4, early experience with VAST showed that VAST could not effectively repair both WRAs and SRAs. NAVAIR procured the Hybrid Automatic Test Set (HATS) to repair SRAs for the S-3A. Unfortunately, because HATS and its TPSs proved to be unreliable, many SRAs had to be sent to depots or manufacturers for repair, and shortages of SRAs at these sites were aggravated by this problem.
3. Additional parts procurement. NAVAIR procured approximately $46,000,000 in spare SRAs for the S-3A between the 1978 and 1981 data collections. As noted in the Systems Research Corporation study, past evidence indicated that additional spares would reduce TAT, but would have very little effect on EMT.

The effects of these three disturbances tend to counteract each other. The loss of training and unreliable HATS tester could be expected to increase both mean EMT and TAT, while the spares procurement would reduce TAT; the net effect is not estimable for either performance measure.

On the other hand, earlier studies of VAST and experience with previous generations of testers (and with avionics maintenance in general) would not suggest that changes in EMT and TAT of the magnitude and direction seen for either aircraft type could be explained by these disturbing variables. Since some of the disturbances had been studied independently in the SRC study (effects of training and skill levels, for example), and found to have limited impact on performance, this further decreases the likelihood that changes in EMT and TAT at any of these sites could be attributed to these disturbing variables. Finally, staffing levels, which were seen to vary widely in Chapter 4, also have little impact on EMT or TAT.

Figures 6.4 and 6.5 summarize the changes in EMT and TAT, respectively, over all waves of "Experiment 2." Several things can be seen in the figures even more strikingly than from the data. Figure 6.4 plots the EMT data from Tables 6.4 and 6.6. For both types of aircraft, it is clear that lack of IP capacity degrades EMT, as IPT predicts. The Navy's concern over the EMT trend for the S-3A was obviously justified, in the sense that as VAST matured and was withdrawn from contractor support, EMT was getting worse, not better (this and related issues are discussed below). It was not until VAMP became fully operational at North Island that EMT was restored to its original level. The degradation of EMT at Miramar when the forward SRA pool and local swap forms were removed, coupled with the continuous degradation at Cecil Field (the VIDS/MAF "control" site), did much to make the Navy willing to try VAMP.

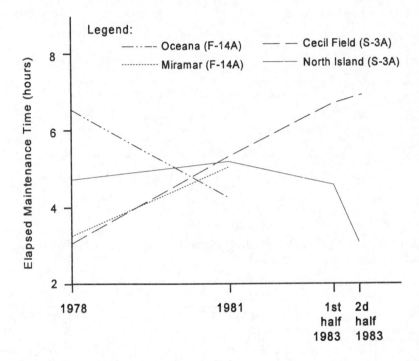

Figure 6.4 Plots of three-wave changes in Elapsed Maintenance Time (EMT) at all sites

The benefits of both maturation and improved IP capacity for TAT can be seen in Figure 6.5 (based on TAT data in Tables 6.5 and 6.7). The combined effect of both processes can be seen at both Ocean and North Island; the effect of maturation alone can be estimated from the trends at Miramar and Cecil Field. Again, the trend at Cecil Field under the VIDS/MAF system alone begins to degrade after 1981, and at slightly increasing speed through 1983.

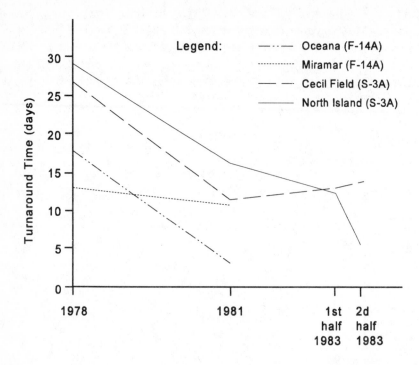

Figure 6.5 Plots of three-wave changes in Turnaround Time (TAT) at all sites

Performance Effects of Information Processing Changes on Carriers in 1981

A final cross-sectional comparison was made in conjunction with the second wave of data collection in 1981. As noted in Chapter 5, Harris Corporation had designed the Status Inventory and Data Management System (SIDMS) to function as a minimal decision support system for avionics maintenance. SIDMS had been placed on the USS *John F. Kennedy* in 1978, and was in use on all Atlantic Fleet carriers by 1981. This permitted me to collect data on the performance of the two fleets on a cross-sectional basis in 1981, and the results are shown in Table 6.8. Clearly, the average TAT was nearly 45 percent less for the Atlantic Fleet using SIDMS than for the Pacific Fleet. EMT was not materially affected between the Fleets, and given the variability between AIMD layouts among the carriers this was not surprising or unexpected; however, TAT performance at the AIMD level was obviously better by far with SIDMS support.

Table 6.8 1981 cross-sectional comparison of EMT and TAT for Atlantic Fleet and Pacific Fleet carriers

Fleet		Elapsed Maintenance Time (EMT) in hours	Turnaround Time (TAT) in days
Atlantic (using SIDMS)	M	5.692	8.536
	SD	7.009	28.140
	n	2777	2777
Between-site *t* value		0.26 (n.s.)	11.20 (<.001)
Pacific (not using SIDMS)	M	5.761	19.032
	SD	7.317	37.630
	n	1067	1067

Further Performance Improvements at North Island Subsequent to Experiment 2

Given its status as a formal AIMSO project, VAMP developments at North Island were monitored on a number of criteria besides effects on EMT and TAT. Much of this data collection was done in parallel with my work. Concurrent with the reduction in EMT and TAT (which AIMSO data independently verified), numerous other improvements in AIMD management occurred. Some of the most significant of these were:

- Technical publication discrepancies were discovered and corrected. A total of over 300 such discrepancies were found by mid-1984 by comparing data entered into VAMP directly to the data entered from the MAF documentation at Cecil Field.
- Component pool management and readiness improved markedly at North Island over the next year. EXREP was decreased by 67 percent; components Awaiting Maintenance (AWM) decreased at least 65 percent compared to pre-VAMP levels; and Awaiting Parts (AWP) similarly decreased nearly 50 percent.
- VAST availability at North Island doubled during 1983, and enough station time was gained to initiate a rigorous preventive maintenance

program on VAST (this was supposed to have been done from the outset, but workload demands seldom permitted time for preventive maintenance, especially full self-test). With VAST running "clean" because of the preventive maintenance program, a number of ambiguous fault isolations were correlated with TPSs, rather than the VAST station, the WRA, operator error, or other potential sources. With this information, the Navy had enough reason to launch seven formal Test Program Set Engineering Investigations to modify the TPSs. The combined effects of these two programs greatly increased station performance, for both technical reasons and because of increased operator confidence in fault isolations. By the end of 1983, VAST availability had improved so much that two stations at North Island had been shut down for two months owing to lack of work, and all six stations had been idle for lack of work on three separate occasions.

These improvements continued over the next several years. By the end of 1985, VAMP had been put into use at all master jet bases, and further program development had extended VAMP to be applied to non-avionics components, including engines, hydraulic systems, and some ordnance items. During the Reagan Administration, four new carriers were put into construction, all of them requiring VAST stations that were no longer being produced. The VAMP program succeeded in freeing 15 stations from shore bases, enough to outfit the new carriers without having to restart the VAST production line. This alone may well have saved between $300 million to $500 million.

At North Island, a number of other benefits were derived from VAMP. The SRAs which had originally been intended to be supported by VAST, but had required other testers because VAST could not manage the workload (see Chapter 4) had been returned to being tested on VAST. This workload increase was accomplished while simultaneously releasing three stations from the site for new carriers, and using one of the remaining three as a dedicated maintenance station. In effect, two VAST stations were now successfully doing much more work (both WRA and SRA testing) than six had been doing before VAMP. It is difficult to measure exactly how much of an increase this constituted relative to the original 156 WRAs supported by VAST, but it was a very significant per-station increase in workload. By the end of 1985, WRA TAT at North Island was typically down to one day or less, and often being achieved within one shift of 8 or 12 hours, depending on the shift.

These performance improvements benefitted the maintenance system in other ways. With the creation of large databases of valid data, investigations of repair-cycle and engineering problems could be much more easily resolved. A number of WRAs were notoriously difficult to maintain, either because of their own complexity or their incorporation of troublesome SRAs; these WRAs were known as "bad actors," and one of the programs undertaken was to identify the bad actors and isolate the reasons for their frequent failure. By 1986, this program had determined that roughly 10 percent of SRAs in the inventory were generating nearly 25 percent of maintenance demands, for both WRAs and SRAs. These were targeted for engineering investigations and special corrective procedures. The release of VAST stations for maintenance work meant that additional stations were available for investigation of problems with Test Program Sets. TPS failures could occur from things as elementary as bent or broken pins in the cables to failures of circuitry in the Interconnecting Device, or as complex as test program problems requiring lengthy software engineering investigations in combination with the component being tested. These were often the most difficult to resolve, and one of the factors limiting these investigations was station time. More of that time was now available, and VAST and AIMD performance both benefitted from it.

I had intended to gather a final post-VAMP wave of data during the late 1980s, but did not. A minor reason was that funding reductions had required the Navy to restrict access only to current contractors, and I was no longer one of them. However, the major reason is that the environment and configuration of the VAST workload had changed so dramatically from the effectiveness of VAMP that comparisons with earlier waves of data could no longer really be drawn. The number of stations per site had changed, workload composition had changed, operational conditions had changed, and the context of the experiment was lost. VAMP had become a "hot" feedback on the whole AIMD system, and now not only processed information more effectively, but had altered the composition of the VAST workload before VAMP, all with highly positive effects. From a taxpayer's perspective, this was a rather pleasant problem.

Conclusions

This chapter began with a major question, which was whether VAST performance depended on IP capacity or whether performance was a function of technical and logistical variables. What the data strongly indicate is that the latter have limited impact on VAST and AIMD throughput, and more specifically, that the deficiencies affecting what was labeled "VAST performance" were in fact deficiencies in the IP capacity of the AIMD.

Particularly from the last wave of the study, when VAMP was fully operational at North Island, we can see that IT-mediated changes in IP capacity had major impact on the productivity of the AIMD. Both the VAST-shop EMT and AIMD TAT improved. Of the two, EMT improved by as much as 50 percent, with both F-14A and S-3A shore sites having average EMT of just over three hours by the end of 1983. Average TAT was greatly improved, with a reduction to only about 18 percent of pre-VAMP duration at North Island; this is a highly conservative estimate of the actual extent of improvement, since it was being achieved with a larger and more diverse workload and fewer VAST stations. Both EMT and TAT continued to improve for the remainder of the decade, while workloads were increased.

The findings also indicate that within the VAST shops, the average EMT level is rather sensitive to even minor improvements in information processing capacity. Whether local changes consisted of things like simplifying MAF documentation, reducing fetch times for parts, or more complete development of within-shop IP capacity, EMT would drop measurably. TAT, on the other hand, was much less affected by such local changes, and practically significant improvement in TAT required more ability to capture information on variables in the larger AIMD system.

The second question in this chapter was concerned with organization slack. Again, a major question is one of whether inadequate or reduced IP capacity is adjusted for by a reduction in the level of performance. Results from the F-14A sites, where both positive and negative changes to IP capacity were made over the first two waves of the study, indicate that even at the level of the individual shop, performance declined in the case where IP capacity was decreased, and improved where it was increased. The data from the S-3A shops suggests the same conclusion, particularly at North Island in 1983 where IP capacity was increased.

The nearest approximation to a decrease in IP capacity at S-3A sites was seen in the second wave of data collection at North Island (1981), where the decision to force all data into the FAMMS system meant delay in data entry when the site computer was not available; compared to Cecil Field, North Island performed rather more poorly than it had before FAMMS was imposed, which is consistent with IPT predictions. However, the contrast in TAT between 1981 and the end of 1983 at S-3A sites strongly suggests that negative performance payoffs will result from inadequate IP capacity. The plots in Figure 6.5 illustrate the obvious continuing degradation of TAT at Cecil Field while VAMP was dramatically reducing TAT at North Island.

The "experimental control" of the constant VIDS/MAF system at Cecil Field gives us reason to suggest that other variables, particularly the normal progress of maturation typical of nearly all technologies, is not the explanation for changes in either VAST-shop or AIMD performance. Taking all experimental disturbances into account, especially the acquisition of large quantities of additional spare parts, along with the effects of technology maturation, the changes in EMT and TAT at Cecil Field are far smaller than those at North Island. Results at the F-14A sites where no experimental control was available suggest the same effects, and also indicate the importance of IP capacity on TAT. The greatest percentage change in TAT at the F-14A sites occurred at Oceana, where the SPORT system was in place by the second (1981) wave of data collection. Finally, the cross-sectional evaluation of carrier data in 1981 suggest the same effect from the experience with SIDMS in the Atlantic fleet.

The empirical data from these studies is also supported by the qualitative data from earlier site visits. Practices discussed in Chapter 5, particularly "hot benching" as a means of avoiding induction of WRAs into the system, and the removal of so many parts from some aircraft that they became "hangar queens" are two examples of the kind of lowered performance in the system that can derive from inadequate IP capacity. In contrast, the experience of the *Forrestal* with its primitive microcomputer decision support systems, and its deliberate soft-system changes to enhance the availability and sharing of information, suggest the benefits of increasing IP capacity. In comparing the cases of the *Forrestal* and FAMMS at North Island, the suggestion again is that even the simplest improvements in IP capacity (in forms such as the storage of information and acquisition of that information) improve performance when they are done in a timely way, and that performance decreases when IP capacity is diminished.

The engineering studies of the VAST technology prior to its deployment reported in Chapter 4, did not detect the sensitivity of the IP system in the AIMD to the effects of a change in tester technology. The early evaluations of VAST after its deployment also did not identify the WRA production problem as one of information processing capacity or system management. It was not until the SRC studies that some of these possibilities were first demonstrated, and not until years later that confirmatory data were available. That "insiders" to the industry have difficulty seeing such limitations is not an uncommon or original finding. Senge and Sterman (1992) summarized studies from numerous different industries, including airlines, consumer products, government organizations, and others, all of which had experiences parallel to VAST, i.e., that major dysfunctions occurred because of failure to understand important properties of the system. In particular, they point out that when decisions have indirect, delayed, nonlinear, or multiple feedback effects, optimal decision-making is very difficult; but this is exactly the environment in which many managers work. Hall's (1976, 1984) studies of the old *Saturday Evening Post* showed how management of that publication made counterproductive decisions and, moreover, acted on their incomplete information in ways that eventually destroyed the magazine. One has to wonder about the total cost of such lack of system understanding, and the negative slack which adjusts for that lack of IP capacity, to American industry. Technology-based industries are especially subject to many of the IP-system risks this research has identified.

An implied question in this connection is whether investment in information technology to augment IP capacity increases performance; this also appears to be strongly supported. While there has been much debate over the payoff of information technology in the past decade, as noted in Chapter 1, the results of Experiment 2 certainly support the argument that information technology can have major impact on the performance of an organization. The Navy is keenly aware of the large amounts of money tied up in maintenance and spare parts, and constantly monitors the effect of different logistics systems in minimizing that cost. Operational readiness is a problem in military effectiveness, while cost containment is a problem in logistical efficiency; the Navy, like the other services, is always struggling to find an acceptable balance between inherently irreconcilable outcomes, and the findings of this experiment suggest that investment in IT and IP capacity may be helpful in finding that balance.

No previous research has shown such clear IT effects on performance. For all the investment in IT over the past three decades, particularly in the U.S., the payoff of this technology is still largely a matter of trust, and quite difficult to measure. Strassmann (1985, 1997) argues that in many cases, computers are used to automate obsolete and inappropriate work methods, and are often poorly appraised before becoming part of a major investment program. Others have argued that computers really make up little of the total capital stock in the U.S. (Sichel, 1997), and that for that reason and also because of the time lags required for new technologies to have a significant payoff, the impact of IT has not yet fully appeared.

Compounding both of these problems is the difficulty in measuring the payoff of IT. This problem is illustrated by the work in this chapter. Had a set of standard measures of IP capacity been devised, they could not have been applied across all different sites studied without missing a major component of the variance in EMT and TAT, simply because of the variety of methods used to modify IP capacity. In industrial situations, one should expect that investment in other forms of IT beyond computers alone (such as modified telephone and data services, now very common), also diffuses IP capacity effects across many different types of performance variables. In the AIMD it was possible to examine physical-production payoffs in what is essentially a service workflow. This is not possible in the large majority of organizations, and in pure-service environments measurement of payoffs themselves is extremely difficult.

Having said all that, I want to be clear that I do not mean the results of this chapter to imply that any organization having performance problems should immediately invest heavily in information technology, in the belief that such tools will solve performance problems. In this particular case, an enormous amount of effort had been devoted to learning about workflow parameters and relationships, and to doing limited, localized experiments with IT before major IT investments were made in the AIMD.

From a pragmatic perspective, this work does not constitute "proof" that IT will always mediate performance problems. On the contrary, an organization that has not made its goals specific, nor inventoried its stock of information, nor examined whether it has the IP structure to process that information, nor examined the dynamic relationships between these parameters, is unlikely to know what to do with IT. At the end of the day, we still have to do enough homework to know how to use IT tools to good effect.

At the same time, this does not mean that the only effective way to invest in IT is to conduct such exhaustive, expensive experimentation. What I am suggesting is that the question of whether IT can "pay off" has been supported. From an academic perspective, the fundamental scientific question of whether significant performance variability can be attributed to changes in IP capacity and IT mediation seems to be one that can be answered in the affirmative; all possible avenues to find countervailing explanations have also been explored, and appear not to be explanations of that performance variability. This research does not constitute "proof" that IP capacity is the best explanation to the question of performance variability, but for the time it appears that IT can have strong effects.

This chapter largely concludes the discussion of the major technology accession in the Naval avionics world, the accession of VAST over earlier generations of manual testers. However, it is not the end of the story or the last we will hear of VAST. As I have indicated earlier, there was already a program underway to design the next generation of automatic test equipment even as these studies were being done. The next accession had already begun, and while VAST was becoming mature, the new generation of test technology was being born in much the same manner as VAST. In the next chapter, we will turn our attention to some of what was learned from the VAST experiment and incorporated into that design process for the new generation of testers; we will also look at several continuing issues in automatic tester technology accession.

Notes

1. All data reported in this chapter were reviewed and approved for publication by officials of the U. S. Naval Air Systems Command.

2. Comparison of 1977/78 and 1980/81 "I" level data. Q.E.D. Systems memorandum, February, 1982.

References

Cook, Thomas D., and Campbell, Donald T. (1979), *Quasi-Experimentation: Design and Analysis Issues for Field Settings.* Chicago: Rand McNally College Publishing.

Comparison of 1977/78 and 1980/81 "I" level data (1982), Q.E.D. Systems memorandum, February, 1982.

Galbraith, Jay (1977), *Organization Design.* Reading, Mass.: Addison-Wesley.

Hall, Roger I. (1976), A system pathology of an organization: The rise and fall of the old *Saturday Evening Post. Administrative Science Quarterly,* 21 (2): 185-211.

Hall, Roger I. (1984), The natural logic of management policy making: its implications for the survival of an organization. *Management Science,* 30 (4): 905-927.

Senge, Peter M., and Sterman, John D. (1992), Systems thinking and organizational learning: acting locally and thinking globally in the organization of the future. In Kochan, Thomas A. and Useem, Michael (1992), *Transforming Organizations.* New York: Oxford University Press.

Sichel, Daniel E. (1997), *The Computer Revolution.* Washington, D.C: Brookings Institution Press.

Strassmann, Paul A. (1985), *Information Payoff: The Transformation of Work in the Electronic Age.* New York: Free Press.

Strassmann, Paul A. (1997), *The Squandered Computer.* New Canaan. Ct.: Information Economics Press.

7 New Technologies and "Experiment 3"

Introduction

This chapter describes developments in the years since the end of Experiment 2. There are four cases with implications for IPT and technology management and accession. These are not discussed in exact chronological sequence, but that is of little importance, since these events occurred in stages over the period from about 1983 to the present. Each of these is a case which could be described in as much detail as the development and deployment of VAST. I have chosen to describe these in summary terms, and to include only that information most relevant to the IPT and technology accession issues already raised by the case of VAST. These cases are derived from the VAST experience and discuss the continuing development of ATE in the avionics repair cycle. After a short discussion of each case, I will briefly summarize those implications as they relate to the research discussed in previous chapters. Integration of these conclusions into IPT will be done in Chapter 8.

The first of these is the experience of the Canadian Forces with a modernized version of VAST. I review this briefly since one variable in the avionics maintenance system can be compared between the Navy's AIMDs and the Canadian Forces land-based maintenance operation, and that is whether the difficulties with U.S. AIMD workflows could be attributed to the requirement of working at sea. The Canadian Forces do not operate in a carrier environment, even though their primary fighter is a U.S. Navy design. The analysis I performed for the Canadian Forces, however, shared the same IPT perspective as my work for the U.S. Navy, and drew considerably on that experience.

The second case is the continued development of the VAST Automated Management Program, which is now a fully-fledged module of a much larger Navy repair-process and logistics management program, the Naval Logistics Command Management Information System (NALCOMIS).

The third and fourth cases are closely related. The next generation of ATE technology, the Consolidated Automated Support System (CASS) was in early development while the VAST studies were underway. CASS is now being deployed, although that deployment has been delayed and slowed owing to technology-accession problems, including technical problems in the development of TPSs, in the selection of aircraft to support, and in the transition of VAST TPSs to CASS. The E-2C has now been transitioned from VAST to CASS, but the F-14 (A and B models) and S-3 (B model) are still heavily dependent on VAST. There is also the issue of integrating CASS with NALCOMIS, which is more complicated than first envisioned in the CASS design. The final case is the transition of VAST support to CASS and other testers while the accession and continuing development of CASS is still underway, and this constitutes a still-incomplete "Experiment 3."

The Canadian Forces ATE Experience

One variable that was repeatedly suggested as a cause for many of the problems that VAST and other ATE encountered was the environment that equipment worked in, which was the carrier. Much of this perception was unspecific and was given little credibility. On the other hand, there was a grain of truth in the argument that the design requirements for VAST were all limited by the characteristics needed to work on a ship, and that meant that many mechanical, electrical, and physical space parameters were severely constrained. In a land environment, so this argument went, many of the production problems of the AIMD were not likely to occur, or at least not as severely as the Navy had experienced. I was able to examine that hypothesis first-hand through my work with the Canadian Forces.

The Canadian Forces contracted to buy the McDonnell-Douglas F/A-18 in 1980 to replace their older fighter inventory. When delivered, the aircraft was configured as the CF-18, and the advanced and updated digital version of VAST, known as the Automated Test Set Version 1 (ATS V1), was procured with it for avionics support. ATS V1 was known in the industry as "mini-VAST," since it was manufactured by Harris Corporation (like VAST), used several Building Blocks from the original VAST, and was designed to operate in the same environment as VAST (the U.S. version is deployed on carriers). SRAs and some smaller modules were tested using a second new product, the Hybrid Test Set (HTS). The main workload from the CF-18 was supported by the ATS V1, similar to the relationship of VAST to the aircraft it supports.

The CF-18 procurement was a much more gradual, phased transition from older aircraft and logistics support than had been the case when the U.S. Navy acquired VAST; VAST and the avionics from three aircraft to support arrived nearly at once. (The CF-18 deal, incidentally, has become a somewhat famous illustration of offset trade in international business, showing the relationships between foreign policy, trade policy, and defense alignments.) The total order was for $2.9 billion with deliveries to be made over eight years. As it turns out, the basic F/A-18 design was excellent—the aircraft has proven to be a highly effective multi-role "strike fighter," and very reliable. The significance of this is that whatever readiness problems the Canadian Forces experienced with CF-18 avionics were not rooted in fundamental design shortcomings.

There were also significant differences between VAST and the ATS V1, nearly all of them positive. The ATS V1 was a great technical improvement over VAST, being much faster, smaller, more reliable, and able to test a wider range of avionics; it had benefitted enormously from experience with U.S. Navy and Marine Corps air units using it to support the U.S. F/A-18, so that there were very few "bugs" for the Canadians to work out of it; and further, the Canadians used it in a ground-based hangar mode, more like the U.S. Air Force and free of the space restrictions and other problems associated with carrier deployments. Unlike other aircraft VAST supported, the F/A-18 used much more digital avionics, and was one of the first in the U.S. inventory to use "fly by wire" technology, where computers and electronic devices intervened between the pilot and the control surfaces of the aircraft. This digital design also included many of the weapons the aircraft carried. Finally, the ATS V1 workload was lighter than for either VAST or U.S. versions of ATS, since the Canadians had fewer aircraft and trained differently (although no less intensely) than U.S. forces.

Nevertheless, by 1988 the Canadians were experiencing exactly the same WRA and SRA stockouts the U.S. Navy had experienced when VAST was in early deployment. The Canadian Forces asked Harris to help them design a course to give to shop managers, in the belief that management skills were the cause of their supply problems. I was contracted by Harris to go to Canada, study their repair-cycle operations, and write a management manual for their shops. The Canadian Forces have two domestic bases for their air force: one in Bagotville, Quebec, and the other in Cold Lake, Alberta, and both of them operate the same way. I surveyed the Bagotville site to collect data on their repair workflow and management system in the fall of 1989. Based on that information, and working with Canadian Forces personnel, I then wrote a management course and took it to Cold Lake to present and turn over for internal use in the summer of 1990.[1]

What was interesting to observe was that periodic WRA stockouts would occur, and these were typically attributed to either ATE shortcomings or to inadequate stock levels for spare parts as with VAST. While the ATE with the heaviest CF-18 workload was the ATS V1, several other ATE devices were also used for radars, analog electronic WRAs, electro-optical WRAs, and electronic warfare and electronic countermeasure WRAs. Being the most heavily used, ATS was frequently blamed for stockouts when they happened, and much the same rationale for increased sparing levels and more test stations were heard there as had been the case with VAST at the U.S. bases. I first heard this at Bagotville in 1989, and again at Cold Lake in 1990.

I toured the maintenance organization at Bagotville and met with site managers and the Harris tech rep there to learn how the site intermediate maintenance workflow operated, how repair data were documented, how the units were organized and run, and the like. Of major importance to me were the data on ATS operational availability and maintenance, and the data were clear—ATS had met and exceeded its design specifications by a considerable margin. It worked, its TPSs were reliable, and when it needed repair or calibration it was well supported. This information was confirmed in separate meetings and discussions with operators and shop supervisors. While they could not directly document their beliefs or support them with hard data, the personnel who had any significant experience with ATS V1 did not believe that WRA stockouts could be attributed to the tester.

To make matters more difficult, the Canadian Forces did not have an automated scheduling algorithm like VAMP, or even its simpler predecessors. The workload at both bases was small enough to be managed manually, so that investment in information technology beyond that needed for routine data recording and office automation was not considered justifiable at that time. Lack of IT for workflow management prevented timely feedback from reaching shop supervisors and managers, and made it difficult to see how repair priorities had to be continually updated after each induction of a WRA into the repair cycle. Further, the absence of a scheduling algorithm, along with the perception that the accession of ATE over earlier generations of testers was a straightforward substitution of machines, made it difficult for the Canadians to recognize the need for different levels of information processing capacity in the intermediate repair workflow.

One of the tasks before me at the turnover and training presentation in 1990 was to articulate a new way of perceiving the relationship between repair-cycle processes and stock levels. I devised the description of the "relevant pool" of WRAs as comprising all WRAs in all aircraft, in the repair cycle, and on stock shelves, and this seemed to be effective. Repair priority decisions needed to be made on the basis of the most critical WRA in the entire pool, including those already installed on aircraft in addition to those in inventory and in the repair cycle itself. The absence of information technology to demonstrate this made the job more difficult, but experience with the U.S. Navy was extremely helpful. We spent a considerable amount of time at the Cold Lake presentation discussing and clarifying what this change in definition of the "relevant pool" meant, and why it was needed. However, I am quite sure there were about 10 percent of the participants in that group who remained unpersuaded to the end—they still contended that fixing the "engineering problems" and increasing sparing levels was the answer to their problems.

The principal question of importance to me was whether the carrier environment seemed to be of much importance in causing stockouts, i.e., whether a land-based environment would not experience production problems similar to those of the U.S. Navy. Clearly, this was not the case. The pace of new aircraft introduction was relatively gradual, and the aircraft itself was an excellent design throughout, including excellent maintainability. In addition, the CF-18 experience suggested that the size of the avionics workload was of less importance than was often perceived. It was fairly easy to attribute many of the U.S. Navy's stockout problems to overloads in the repair cycle, especially when at sea and running full flight operations. But as the experience with VAMP at North Island strongly suggested, VAST was probably being underutilized in most cases, and with the correct workflow IP capacity, it could process many more components than first believed. In Canada, some stockouts occurred with even much lower levels of flight operations; the volume of work never approached that of U.S. units, but the "stockout problem" occurred anyway. Therefore, it seems reasonable to conclude that the stockout problem is a function of IP capacity and the accession process itself, not the tester or the environment in which the tester functioned.

The Continued Development of the VAST Automated Management Program

Following its initial successes at North Island, the VAST Automated Management Program (VAMP) was extended for application to several other deployed systems. VAMP was expanded to be used for the other VAST-supported aircraft (having been initially developed for the S-3A), and demonstrated at NAS Miramar. Following these extensions, the basic program structure and workflow-management algorithm of VAMP was rapidly modified for use in other repair processes, including other electronic testers, power plants, and aviation life support items. As with VAMP, these were tested and debugged on site, and not deployed until they had been demonstrated to work effectively. Given the complexities of the avionics repair process, which is probably the most complex of all AIMD workflows, the transition of VAMP into these other areas was much simpler and faster than its original development.

By 1986, VAMP was absorbed into a much larger overall Navy program, the Naval Logistics Command Management Information System (NALCOMIS). When rewritten and integrated into NALCOMIS, the name of the program was changed to the Automated Production Management Module (APMM), and it is still functioning under that name today.

NALCOMIS is a very ambitious undertaking in its own right, and was intended to both modernize and standardize the numerous MISs which had developed throughout the Navy and Marine Corps. NALCOMIS was originally chartered in June, 1975, and was scheduled to be implemented in at least 98 shore sites by the end of fiscal year 1990.[2] Its scope of IP support was intended to cover only the intermediate maintenance and Supply units at those sites, but has been expanded to cover O-level operations as well. With the inclusion of the APMM, it is now an important management tool for the AIMD and may eventually become the decision-support MIS for the CASS testers, which will be discussed in the next section.

However, NALCOMIS is far behind schedule, in large part because of the expanding scope of the project and simultaneous changes in information technology. It is now proceeding through a phased development process, and is presently in Phase II. In its present stage of development, NALCOMIS contractors provide hardware, system software, training, spares and integrated logistics services for use at the organizational maintenance level (i.e., squadrons) for U.S. Navy and Marine Corps aviation units. As of 1995, 58 NALCOMIS Phase II sites were operational. Phase II replaces Phase I by providing real-time management information, automating and validating source data collection at the intermediate maintenance level, and giving reporting capability to those sites for higher levels of command. NALCOMIS is merging with two other major Navy information technology projects which were begun independently, the Shipboard Non-Tactical Automated Data Processing (SNAP) program and the Maintenance Resources Management System (MRMS) program. The merged units operate under one program office, the Navy Tactical Command Support System (NTCSS), which meant transfer of NALCOMIS from NAVAIR to the Space and Naval

Warfare Systems Command (SPAWAR) during three fiscal years from 1995 to 1997.[3]

Under SPAWAR command, the designer of the overall logistics information system (including NALCOMIS) is now the Navy Management Systems Support Office (NAVMASSO). NAVMASSO was established in 1978 to support three existing fleet information technology systems operating at 81 sites. In 1981, NAVMASSO underwent a major change in mission when it was given responsibility to automate the entire fleet with logistic support applications. With over 900 sites around the globe, NAVMASSO is now working to re-automate the fleet with logistic applications that are compatible with both existing tactical systems and commercially available off-the-shelf hardware and software applications.[4]

Thus, VAMP and NALCOMIS have clearly become absorbed into a merged technology accession of massive proportions itself, and in my view one which will probably be an indefinite and continuous process. As we will see, it is not the case that all of VAMP or the decision support it provided have transitioned along with these larger systems. However, a conclusion which seems warranted from this development process is that the IP changes which were the core of VAMP are applicable to other workflows and technologies, not just avionics repair alone.

The Next Generation of ATE

The next generation of ATE was begun even as VAST was still being brought up to full productivity in the AIMD, and proceeded through roughly three phases. First, the combination of stockouts, difficulties with some testers or Test Program Sets (TPSs), and the continued evolution of more complex avionics, had resulted in many competing proposals to deal with the Navy's test and repair requirements. In part, this led to construction and purchase of testers the Navy had never intended to own (see Chapter 4), and many in the logistics community feared a proliferation of ATE systems, similar to what had been the case with WRA-specific testers (i.e., PGSE) in the earlier generation. Accordingly, I refer to this as the *proliferation of ATE* phase in the history of this accession. Given the need to cope with repair-cycle production pressures and the rapidly developing technologies in both avionics and automatic test, the Navy semi-formally adopted a *family of testers* concept for its ATE from roughly the middle 1970s until the 1980s, and this was the second phase. In response to these and other pressures, NAVAIR announced the concept of the Consolidated Support System (CSS) in 1980.

CSS was to become the universal tester to meet all electronic-test needs, and would eventually serve other parts of the Navy beyond the Naval Air Force. This has evolved into the Navy's current phase, the development of the Consolidated Automated Support System (CASS).

Difficulties associated with the introduction of VAST into the AIMD were very much in the mind of NAVAIR when the pre-CASS CSS program was begun. NAVAIR thus imposed a requirement on all contractors who intended to bid for CSS: they would have to demonstrate understanding of the AIMD environment and the management of the avionics workflow as a preliminary condition to bid. To demonstrate this knowledge, all bidders were required to develop a computer simulation of the AIMD, known as the System Synthesis Model (SSM) and to pass a NAVAIR test of that model. This would be accomplished by thorough documentation of the SSM, showing understanding of how repairable components and information moved through the repair cycle, and then by demonstrating the model using problem sets provided by the Navy in a controlled competition.[5] The competitive problems were a set of workload data and operating parameters written by a NAVAIR evaluation committee. When the SSM competition was held in 1983, all bidders had to run their simulation to show how their design concept for CSS would meet the operational demands contained in the problem sets. AIMSO personnel played a key role in both the development of the problem sets and the evaluation of the results, so that thorough understanding of the AIMD environment was present on the NAVAIR side of the evaluation team as well as on the contractor side.

I supported Harris Corp. through the 1983 SSM competitions, providing information on AIMD workflow processes and information needs. Harris did well on the simulation, but unfortunately did not win the CSS hardware concept design round of competition that followed in 1984.[6] That eliminated Harris from the bidder's pool, and eventually a team led by General Electric won the contract to develop CSS. By this time, the name of this new generation of testers was changed to the Consolidated Automated Support System (CASS), the name under which it is still operating.

Following the reduction of the final bidders to two teams, I was engaged to support the General Electric team in preparation of its final bid in 1986 and 1987. GE won the contract, and I had the opportunity to work with them in the last rounds of prototype evaluation before full production of CASS.[7] One of the responsibilities I undertook was to assist in demonstration of the Operational Management System (OMS) which was to be built into CASS. The OMS was required to be a local system which could provide many of the same functions as VAMP did for the VAST workflow in the AIMD.

Specifically, it was to provide a scheduling algorithm, to track performance data, to automate the completion of MAF entries for repair-cycle documentation, and monitor the status of the test station itself. In addition, GE designed CASS to fully automate the display of all technical publications needed for the CASS station and any WRAs it supported. This became the Automated Technical Information (ATI) system, in which a document is displayed in the hard-copy format required by the Navy on the station monitor, and could be printed in an exact What-You-See-Is-What-You-Get (WYSIWYG) format on the station printer.

CASS represented a major technical advance over VAST. In the two decades between initial VAST and CASS designs, electronic technology had advanced enormously, especially in the areas of miniaturization, digital electronics, and component integration. This was also true for many of the electronic systems now deployed on other weapon systems, including ships and submarines as well as aircraft, so that need for new test capabilities was being created in parallel. Design and manufacturing technologies had also advanced. CASS therefore was designed to permit "technology insertion," so that as parts of CASS technology became outdated or unnecessary, they could easily be upgraded or replaced. CASS is much more modular than VAST or earlier testers, but like VAST it is built of groups of "racks" which share a common core of computers, an operator console, and associated equipment needed by any tester configuration. If an entirely new type of avionics were developed, requiring test capabilities not envisioned when CASS was designed, new racks of equipment could theoretically be built and attached to CASS in the future. From a technical perspective, then, CASS solves a major problem underlying much technology accession by being designed to be continuously upgraded throughout its service life.

The first-generation tester technology for CASS is now complete. There are both stationary and mobile versions of CASS, so that it can serve as an intermediate-level tester in a wide variety of settings. The rate at which CASS will be applied to new test roles depends on two factors. The first is the rate of TPS development, which is a lengthy and expensive process. The second factor is the cost-effectiveness of different modes of test and repair, including the alternative of simply disposing of failed components rather than repairing them. Both of these issues will be discussed in more detail below.

The CASS design is modular, to permit a central "core" station which contains the computer and operator console to be mated with a number of other racks.[8] Each set of mated components creates a different type of test station, and CASS presently has five station configurations: Navigation and Communication, Radar, Electro-Optical, Electronic Warfare, and Electronic

Countermeasures. CASS is now being introduced into the Fleet, and is being used at all three levels of repair (organizational, intermediate, and depot), as well as by contractors for TPS development. However, owing to a variety of technical changes, problems, and external factors,[9] CASS has fallen far behind its original schedule for deployment.

The development of CASS, by now, is being paralleled in the other services. The U.S. Department of Defense has organized an Automatic Test Systems (ATS) program, which will coordinate ATE development for all the services and serve as an information clearinghouse.[10]

VAST and CASS in The Fleet: "Experiment 3"

The third and final "experiment" to be discussed in this book is one that is now underway, and for which the results will not be known for years. This experiment is the accession of CASS into the Fleet, with the objective of making CASS the universal electronic-component tester for all Naval applications.

CASS is presently in a program of continuing test and evaluation in operational conditions. As of September, 1995, the Operational Test and Evaluation Force in Norfolk, Virginia, had concluded over 25,000 hours of follow-on test and evaluation to confirm CASS performance while using weapon system operational (i.e., not factory or developmental) TPSs (Martin, 1995). The formal evaluation used nine production CASS stations at six different shipboard and shore sites. Shipboard evaluations were done on the USS *Constellation,* USS *Nimitz,* and USS *Carl Vinson.* U.S. Marine Corps air units participated with CASS in a mobile facility. Shore sites participating were the NAS Miramar AIMD, and the NAS Patuxent River CASS test facility. Weapon system TPSs selected for the test included 13 WRA TPSs from both the F-14D and non-airborne systems.

In NAVAIR's view, the test reconfirmed satisfactory CASS results from previous tests, in 14 operational categories ranging from diagnostic capability to reliability and supportability. The CASS stations experienced a 96 percent operational availability rate and over 1,936 hours mean time between operational mission failures. This compares favorably to much more mature systems.

I refer to the CASS deployment as an "experiment" because in my view it has similarities to the original deployment of VAST decades ago. VAST was intended to fulfill the roles of many different kinds of earlier manual test equipment, and ultimately did. Nevertheless, one aspect of the original experiment, the "universality" of the tester, still remains to be fully appreciated in terms of its impact on information processing demands and the consequences of technology changes on maintenance management. Rather than being the sole tester for all the WRAs and SRAs VAST was supposed to support, additional testers were needed and as these came on line there began a proliferation of ATE devices, quite the opposite of what was intended. One important similarity of this design for universality is that the units outside the range of those supported by compatible decision-support systems, particularly those developed to work with CASS in aviation units, are similar to those outside the scope of the VAST shop when VAST was first deployed. VAST collapsed many component repair flows into one, and therefore had major effects on AIMD information flows. CASS may have similar effects in some of its new operating environments, and those environments may not be prepared to meet the demands of CASS on workflow management IP capacities.

A second parallel, and one which is unavoidable in a military environment, is the operation and management of the old technology along with the new. In fact, I consider this to be the major factor in the overall problem of technology accession in any environment—the full process of accession requires simultaneous operation of the old technology with the new, until the older one is completely supplanted. In many aspects of technology management, we tend to be dazzled by the new technology, and the assumption is that when it comes on line, all of our problems with the old technology will be solved by accession. That is only possible if the IP requirements of existing parts of the system are completely compatible with the new technology, and in the rapidly-changing worlds of electronics there is every reason to anticipate that such compatibility will not be the case. This challenge is now confronting CASS in several areas. I will briefly discuss two of these, one primarily technical, and the other primarily managerial.

The continuing technical problem: the Test Program Set As I have noted briefly, VAST Test Program Sets are now being transitioned (or "rehosted") to other testers as VAST approaches the end of its service life. The TPS has become very much a focal challenge for automatic test equipment. The TPS is embedded in the support logistics "tail," and thus imposes major support-of-support requirements in its own right. Whenever a TPS is designed, it requires a computer program, a set of technical manuals and instructions, connector cables which will correctly mate with the hardware interfaces on both the component being tested and the test station, and a training curriculum that shows the operators how to do all of this for the specific tester. If any element of the TPS is changed, everything else must be changed correspondingly. This means that the TPSs for each WRA now supported by VAST must be modified to operate on CASS—CASS-compatible test programs must be written, tested, and documented; cables and adapters must be made to permit physical coupling of the WRAs to CASS ports and connectors; and so on. In short, the entire logistics "tail" shown in Figure 2.1 must be reconstructed or reconfigured as necessary, and validated. This has been a slow process, and one which has taken much longer than first envisioned.

The technical problems in making a component testable on ATE are a major part of the TPS challenge. To be sure that a part can meet a specified range of capabilities, the part must be designed to perform at the extremes of its range without damage, and the tester must be designed to apply stimuli that stay within the appropriate range. For example, a chip may contain transistors that operate between +5 and +7 volts, and which amplify that power 100-fold; applying +7.5 volts to be sure it can withstand +7 may "fry" everything downstream of the chip. These kinds of technical problems exist with every new tester and TPS. TPS "bugs" of this kind were a major problem for VAST in its early years—most of them were temporarily resolved by developing the "workarounds" discussed in previous chapters. Full correction of these problems, however, took years of effort, and in fact have only been resolved in the late 1980s. The VAST TPSs were finally "clean" at about the time they were originally scheduled to be replaced by CASS. This is a long and costly process.

Validation and verification of a TPS is also a technical challenge. The issue is straightforward: how can one be sure that a TPS will actually correctly identify faults in a component? The usual approach is to verify that a TPS will find a known percentage of faults in a test, since not every one can be detected in a real-world environment. Long-established procedures for acceptance testing of TPSs have been established by the military,[11] although for many years they were not well understood or applied (Baroni, 1986). Poon *et al.* (1990) categorize approaches to diagnosing faults into three types: (1) modeling them using software; (2) simulating them from empirical knowledge of failure modes; or (3) using knowledge-based systems based on diagnostician expertise. The acceptance-testing method generally used is to create simulated faults in a component and then see whether the test program finds them. This can be done by a variety of methods, such as attaching jumper wires to simulate short circuits, deliberately applying out-of-range power to a component, inserting a wrong part to simulate a failed part, and so on. One can never find all faults, and this becomes a problem because undetected or incorrectly diagnosed faults appear after the deployment of a TPS—these become the problem of getting the TPSs "clean," as described above.

An interdependent issue is the problem of general technological obsolescence. The computer that originally operated VAST had less computing power than the programmable calculators of a decade later, and are hopelessly obsolete in today's terms. Miniaturization has had a major impact—many of the electronic test functions needed by VAST required a large drawer full of electronic components in the 1970s; equal or greater functionality is now provided by a single chip. Thus, there is almost no possibility to migrate the computer code from one tester to another, and the entire program has to be rewritten for the large majority of TPSs. When VAST was designed, it was necessary to design computing and related equipment as custom components for the tester. Since that time, especially with the rapid adoption of ATE in commercial and civilian markets, much of modern ATE can use a "rack-and-stack" design built around commercially available hardware and software. The cost savings are considerable, both for initial acquisition and later logistic support, but achieving such integration of commercial equipment is not a trivial matter.

Thus, the cost of avionics testing remains extremely high. Typical testing costs are as high as 50 percent of cost of a component (Weiss, 1994). These high costs are a result of two continuing problems. One is a constant need to "reverse engineer" at each stage in the component's life cycle to obtain essential information necessary for testing; the second is the relative inability to reuse information gained at one time in similar situations later in the life cycle of the component. The root cause of this limited capability to reuse information is the dependence of TPSs on particular software languages, instrument(s), or technologies. In turn, this inability to reuse the components of the TPS causes each TPS developed to be an "expense" in testing, rather than an "investment" which might be reused with newer generations of ATE. But high cost is a recurring issue in the development of TPSs (Pullo and Salvarezza, 1986), and is itself driven by multiple interdependent variables, such as the ability to control vendor costs in development (Burkhart, 1986); different test requirements in factory development versus deployment (Lanterman, 1986); and problems with software and system migration (Bergeron, 1990). If a component is too expensive to test or repair relative to its acquisition cost, the better alternative may simply be to throw failed components away, and stock enough of them to meet demand with new items. Computer models for analysis of the appropriate level of repair and stocking levels are used regularly to assist the military and the contractors with these repair-or-discard decisions.[12]

However, cost issues are not the only criteria a military organization must consider. Commercial computers may serve perfectly well in ordinary conditions, but a carrier is often a hostile environment for electronics, with "dirty" power, humidity, and other environmental problems. In the event of a nuclear detonation, the electromagnetic pulse generated will destroy all commercial electrical and electronic devices; military electronics are "hardened" to withstand such a pulse, and are thus not really interchangeable with commercial equipment even if the latter performs the same function. Finally, with the rapid rate of obsolescence of electronic and digital devices, there is a question as to whether the manufacturer will be willing and able to support an item as long as the military will need it. VAST is a case in point—the plants where it was manufactured are closed, the workforce retired or employed elsewhere, and the division of Harris Corporation that manufactured it no longer exists in the form that manufactured VAST. The full responsibility for keeping VAST functioning for the remainder of its service life now falls on the Navy. Fortunately, as VAST stations are removed from service, they can be cannibalized and used for spare parts; in addition, the Navy has depots with the manufacturing capability to make any new parts needed, albeit at very high cost. But it is questionable whether any commercial equipment would ever be supported for so long.

In the case of the accession of greatest immediate interest, the transition of VAST TPSs to CASS, there are still other complications. One is that an orderly progression of test capabilities from one tester to the other must be planned out, so that we do not find ourselves needing more, rather than fewer, testers in each AIMD. That is, if the idea is to replace VAST with CASS over the remainder of this century, we want to do it in a manner that permits VAST stations to be removed from sites (particularly carriers) as their WRA workload is taken over by CASS; otherwise, we need both testers on site, with their full logistics "tails." Which TPSs to transition is a decision driven by a far wider range of variables than just the order of change—cost-effectiveness is a key consideration, as noted, and is more difficult in a transition because some of the supported weapon systems are also changing significantly, or becoming obsolete. For example, the F-14 now operates in three versions, the A, B, and D models (and is due to be replaced by the F/A-18E). VAST supports some WRAs from all of them, but as aircraft were upgraded to newer models, more digital and advanced WRAs were installed on them, and these are better suited to support by CASS. As many of the older installed components reach the end of their service lives, their failure rates go up (see the "bathtub curve" in Figure 2.4), creating more demands on testers already deployed. Given the issues already summarized above, this becomes a significant cost tradeoff decision to be managed along with the others (Wood, 1989), including operational readiness.

Configuration management (CM) becomes a key challenge when many test stations are being widely deployed to support many different components, although historically CM has often not been done well with TPSs (Merlenbach, 1992). The system software for CASS contains approximately three thousand modules and nearly two million lines of source code (Darling, 1994). This software is currently being used on several different configurations of CASS stations at multiple sites to develop and run numerous TPSs. Because of the complexity of the software, the vast quantities of code, and the large number of users, proper configuration management of the CASS system software is crucial to the overall success of the CASS program. In addition to the usual CM issues in TPS development (primarily hardware, software, and documentation), configuration control also involves management of re-usable test objects, data management, tester resource management, and user interface management (Rathburn, 1994). ATE "universality" clearly brings with it a greatly increased scope of work to manage all the information necessary for the test equipment to fulfill its requirements.

This transition cannot be made without consideration of the other ATE already deployed in the field. There is always the possibility of a "lateral" transition, where VAST TPSs can be modified for a tester other than CASS. This is what was done for support of the E-2C. Since CASS deployment had fallen behind schedule, and many of the avionics, radars, and communications WRAs on the E-2C had been modernized multiple times, the decision was made to transition all E-2C TPSs to the CAT-IIID. (The CAT-IIID was discussed briefly in Chapter 4; it was designed primarily as an SRA tester for the F-14A, but has shown itself to be quite versatile and highly reliable.) Thus, transition of TPSs from VAST to CASS now needs to be concerned with only two of the aircraft originally supported by VAST, and this is a somewhat simpler problem for the near term. But inevitably the accession from VAST to CASS will have to be accomplished for all supported avionics.[13]

In closing this section, I want to be sure that I do not leave the impression that any of these problems are unknown to professionals in the field. On the contrary, much attention is paid to these issues at numerous meetings and conferences each year, and in the industry generally. Standards for making TPS data independent of testers, and test methods independent of test resources have been under consideration for years (Hanna and Horth, 1991). Such standards can do much to improve the consistency, reliability, and transportability of TPSs. They can help to automate the TPS development process, and thereby reduce the costs associated with TPS development and from rehosting existing TPSs to new testers. In addition, applications of new approaches to resolve many of the problems inherent to TPS design are regularly considered in the profession. These include the use of computer-aided software engineering for TPSs (Scully, 1987); artificial intelligence applications to both develop the TPS and use it in deployed test environments (Dill, 1990; Levy and Pizzariella, 1990); and investigation of the prospects for rehost of TPSs from dedicated station computers to commercial PCs (Scherer *et al.*, 1994), among many others. Nevertheless, these interdependent variables make the process of orderly accession resistant to simple resolution. The benefits of many of these thrusts remain for the future, and from the perspective of technology accession from existing systems, they remain problematic. The implication that many of the fundamental equivocalities and uncertainties that surrounded the development of VAST TPSs persist in the development of the next generations of TPSs, and the transition of older ones, is indeed strong.

The continuing managerial challenge: integrating CASS and NALCOMIS
When the VAMP was first deployed, it resolved several problems with the integration of a critical tester "upward" into the larger AIMD system. In this sense, VAMP was oriented toward solution of specific operational problems centered around the VAST shop itself. A challenge facing the designers of NALCOMIS was that they were attempting to integrate "downward," using an information system designed from the top down to meet many organizational- and intermediate-maintenance and supply information needs, and incorporate the operational particularities of each shop into the overall information system. This is a very challenging process, even in a workflow environment as outwardly standardized as avionics maintenance.

Two examples suggest some of the difficulties. First, consider security. Some TPSs contain hardware or software which is accessible only to personnel with appropriate security clearances. Additionally, an element of the VAMP (and therefore now the APMM) is a subroutine which places the highest priority on WRAs which are most critical to aircraft performance of specific missions. These decisions are based on an internal Navy list that shows the relationship between what a WRA does and its importance to those missions, and it is called the Mission Essential Subsystem Matrix (MESM). Weights from the MESM are used as part of the VAMP repair-priority algorithm, and many of these data are classified. In order to fully integrate all shop maintenance operations and data into an MIS, some method for resolving security issues must be implemented, and there are many to choose from. All of them, however, require time and costs that are not an issue in shops doing only unclassified work.

Second, consider the question of safety in different types of maintenance shops. High-pressure tires are a completely different kind of safety problem than high explosives, and both must be handled in different shops. Paints, solvents, adhesives, and numerous other materials are found in some shops and not others, and most of these require specific safety measures and documentation not found in other shops. Electronic testing is concerned with electrical safety, of course, but also with handling precautions for many chips and integrated circuits which can be damaged by static electricity and other hazards.

The point is that to design a top-down information system like NALCOMIS to meet the demands of all of these shops is a much greater challenge than the design of specific local-purpose systems like VAMP. Technology accessions which fail to consider such issues are almost certain to be at greater risk of being informationally isolated, in the sense that information needed for the supported technology either cannot be obtained from the larger system, or that the operating technology center cannot provide adequate feedback and feedforward into the larger system. Being aware of that risk is only a first step—there is a huge volume of work to be done to make and implement decisions about the resolution of it. This is the situation that has been facing NALCOMIS since its inception.

When CASS was developed, an Operational Management System (OMS) was developed for it. The OMS provided necessary shop-level decision support before NALCOMIS and APMM were available at all CASS sites. The OMS provides most of the same decision support that VAMP did for VAST, in other words; it has been used only in the CASS work centers, however, since the Navy has had NALCOMIS under active development for many years and intends to use it at all work centers. Unfortunately, this has also decoupled CASS from integrated development with NALCOMIS, so that integrating them is now a more difficult issue than it might have been.

NALCOMIS was developed independently of VAMP or CASS, but in parallel with them. Much of the stimulus for development of NALCOMIS came from the needs of the aviation maintenance community, and in large part from avionics. But since CASS and NALCOMIS were not really developed jointly, there has been a significant degree of divergence between them in some areas. To complicate matters, not only does the relationship between CASS and NALCOMIS not completely overlap, but neither does CASS overlap all test applications, nor NALCOMIS all data-management and decision-support applications. CASS therefore will need its OMS for those applications not covered by NALCOMIS for a considerable time into the future (Holland, 1995), and new developments in the OMS will need to consider requirements of Shipboard Nontactical Automated data Processing (SNAP) and Maintenance Resources Management System (MRMS) IT systems until they are all merged into a single information system (Batchelor, 1995).

Either joint development or parallel development has its merits, but long involvement in this process has brought me to the conclusion that one of the most effective ways to prevent true system integration is for each agent in the development process to do the best individual job possible. For the best of all reasons, some of the worst of all outcomes is assured—in this case, the desire to show how well the prime contractor could design and develop the OMS meant that it would certainly be different from the APMM, and the "Not Invented Here" syndrome would be alive and well.[14]

At present, an active discussion is under way regarding the integration of OMS into NALCOMIS, and therefore eventually into the much larger logistics support MIS the Navy is developing for the future. The CASS OMS can automate acquisition of data required by NALCOMIS and support automation of decision processes within NALCOMIS. This includes both data on the processing of components, as well as the "health" of the individual CASS stations. Much of what is provided by the OMS for production management in the CASS shop should be available to NALCOMIS, especially data on the "health" of the individual station (Holland, 1995), a variable found to be quite important in the original VAMP. Because of the development of APMM to serve the needs of many shops which did not use ATE, this level of detail was not preserved in NALCOMIS, although the functional similarity of the two systems is quite high. Current CASS project management recommendations are to provide this functionality through the OMS interface, so that NALCOMIS is transparent to the user, and to make necessary changes to the OMS so that it can be fully merged with NALCOMIS (Holland, 1995).

The parallels between the issues facing integration of OMS and NALCOMIS, and the earlier integration of the VIDS/MAF system with VAMP, are difficult not to draw. They imply that any technology accession will require a corresponding IP and workflow process accession as well.

Conclusion

This chapter has summarized the developments of approximately the decade since the major workflow problems with VAST were resolved and VAST finally achieved its full productive potential. VAST is still in the Fleet, and "humming right along," according to personal communications I have had with several VAST operating personnel. Each of the separate programs mentioned in this chapter has its detailed story to tell, but the major accession has been the one from manual to fully automated test equipment, and the principal bridge between those eras is VAST. New ATE has benefitted in many ways from what has been learned from VAST, but at the same time some lessons for the future may need to be reinforced or made more central to the accession process than they presently are. Some recommendations in this regard, along with a return to some of the theoretical and integrative issues raised in Chapter 1, will be taken up in the next and final chapter.

The prime contractors for all of the testers discussed in this chapter, as well as the Navy offices responsible for them, are committing major efforts toward making their development processes accessible to each other, and to prevent and correct errors early in the deployment of CASS. It is difficult to fully integrate all of the IP implications of the CASS accession while there are also large numbers of technical issues to resolve, as was the case with VAST. A very encouraging note is that all of the major contributors to the CASS system have created World Wide Web sites, and the use of them is growing. However, as with earlier generations of technology, the engineering and technical issues predominate the discussion of the Technical Working Group and the prime contractors alike. For example, as of 1 August 1996, the "Lessons Learned" directory for CASS had not been updated since 1 May 1995; and of the large number of references in the directory, only one pertained to the OMS, and NALCOMIS was not mentioned at all.

VAST, at long last, is entering the retirement phase of its life cycle. At the end of 1996, about 50 percent of the transition was complete. By the end of fiscal year 1997, the last nuclear carrier cruise with VAST is scheduled, and the first full CASS deployment shortly thereafter in 1998.

The unanswered question, and one which will not be resolved for years, is the extent to which NAVAIR and others in the ATE development community have been able to capture the lessons of the VAST experience and incorporate them into the development of the next generations of testers. Whether they have been able to engage in the kinds of descriptive and prescriptive analyses needed to integrate the evolving new ATE technologies into the organizations which will use them is unclear. However, for all the technology development effort devoted to ATE over the past three decades, no sustained attention to the organizational IP problem has been given. The CASS SSM competition was the closest approximation to such a development. My present concern is that the properties that made the impact of VAST on AIMD performance difficult to understand are also found in the context of CASS and NALCOMIS. The personnel are different, the contractors are different, the electronics and information technology have advanced tremendously, and the military mission is no longer that of the Cold War. For these reasons and more, it is possible that many of the outcomes of the VAST experiment will be repeated when CASS and new testers are deployed into organizations not yet prepared to cope with the IP demands those new technologies create.

In short, the past decade has finally seen the resolution of the VAST-related problems with WRA throughput in the AIMD. Nearly the entire period of original VAST deployment, until 1985, was needed to achieve the potential of the technology, but this sometimes excruciating process had little to do with the technology itself (and was not sufficient for the TPSs). Instead, the larger AIMD system surrounding VAST, and the nature of the IP capacity within that system, was responsible for the problems attributed to the VAST technology. Five rather cautionary conclusions seem justified in view of this experiment with the avionics repair cycle:

1. Technology history seems to repeat itself. It is difficult not to associate the experiences we see here with the old adage that each generation must learn anew.

2. The "technical imperative" that still appears to dominate the development and accession of new technologies, while making a major contribution to the technology itself, has potentially significant dysfunctional organizational and management consequences.

3. Technology and accession management place a premium on the ability to visualize performance in terms that reflect the interdependence of the technology-intensive units with others in the organization.

4. Related to conclusion (3), technology and accession management clearly require consideration of information processing implications which lie beyond considerations of the technical issues alone.

5. Finally, technology accessions focus the organization on different levels of information imperfections (see Chapter 1) than those specific to the technology-intensive units. The results of this study strongly suggest that as new technologies create greater

interdependence in complex systems, the relevant information imperfections will be found at the next higher level. Although only an inference from this study, some technologies might reverse that direction of change. In either case, one should not assume that the organization designed for the previous generation of technology will accept the new generation without having to reevaluate its information processing capacity or the level of imperfection most relevant to performance after the accession.

In Chapter 2, I suggested that the accession process is likely to be messy, nonlinear, and discontinuous. This certainly was true with VAST, and seems to be the case with many of the newer technologies. This has been a major reason for adopting the term "accession" rather than "succession" as a label for the process of technology change in this book. The study of many technologies, automatic test equipment included, suggests that "succession" is a poor term to describe how technologies progress and evolve over time.

Notes

1. I want to once again thank my Canadian hosts for their hospitality at both sites, and for both a challenge and a lot of fun with the Cold Lake group. That unit is the 10th Field Technical Training Unit, or 10 FTTU, which of course has to be "ten-foot-two."

2. Lavely, L. W., *Naval Aviation Logistics Command Management Information System briefing.* Naval Air Systems Command, Project Office PMA-270 (officially undated; believed issued September 1983.)

3. Steven W. Batchelor, *FY 1996/1997 Biennial Budget Estimates: Narrative Statement for Major Automated Information Systems, Naval Aviation Logistics Command Management Information System (NALCOMIS-V60).* Department of Defense, Department of the Navy, October 2, 1995.

4. *NAVMASSO Description,* Navy Management Systems Support Office, Fleet Logistic Information Systems.

5. Guidelines for model evaluation were being published by the General Accounting Office at the time. An abridged version of those guidelines was provided by Saul I. Gass and Bruce W. Thompson, *Guidelines for model evaluation: An abridged version of the U.S. General Accounting Office Exposure Draft.* Operations Research, 28 (2), March-April, 1980: 431-439.

6. One of the difficulties Harris had to overcome was that the perception that VAST had not worked well was persistent, even though performance and engineering data from several sources (including mine) showed otherwise. To some extent, this created a rationale to seek a new prime contractor, and may have disadvantaged Harris in the minds of some judges. In complex, long-term competitions such as this one, factors like these always play some role, but we can never know how much. Global competition in commercial aircraft between Boeing and Airbus Industrie probably reflects some of these same pressures, and the acceptance of new airliner offerings waxes and wanes accordingly.

7. CASS has since changed hands. GE sold the CASS division to Martin Marietta in 1992, and in 1995 Martin Marietta merged with Lockheed to become Lockheed Martin, which is now the prime contractor.

8. Since all the components fit into a cabinet with different slide-out racks, and the components are positioned one above the other in the cabinet, this design is referred to in the industry as "rack and stack."

9. For example, the first aircraft to be fully supported by CASS was intended to be the V-22 Osprey tilt-rotor aircraft. For a long time, however, the entire V-22 program was in doubt, and thus the development of CASS assets to support it. The V-22 was only put into full production in mid-1997. Uncertainties of this kind ripple throughout other programs as well, and have major schedule impacts.

10. For those interested in automatic test issues, the World Wide Web address is http://www.navair.navy.mil/ats/ats.htm.

11. The applicable standard during the VAST era and the early development of CASS was *MIL-STD-2077(AS), General Requirements for Test Program Sets*. Department of the Navy, Naval Air Systems Command, 9 March 1978.

12. The type of model used is a Level of Repair Analysis (LORA) model, and is done as part of the overall logistic support planning process. The specific model used during the early days of CASS development was the 1977 Naval Weapons Engineering Support Activity MOD III Level of Repair model. This has since been updated and changed considerably, and now operates on desktop computers.

13. This is fully appreciated by the CASS Technical Working Group. Not only is the transition of VAST TPSs a responsibility, but TPSs are in development for the F-14D, the V-22, The F-18 E and F models, and numerous other systems.

14. I want to be very clear that I mean no disparagement of anyone working at GE, then or now. In fact, I was very impressed by the quality and conscientiousness of the GE people I had the pleasure to work with, and I would recommend them to anyone. The larger problem is that if we reward performance on the basis of individual activities when continuity of team performance is needed, there is a strong disincentive to coordinate present efforts with what has gone before; this problem is common to all organizations. The question before GE at the time the CASS OMS was developed was whether there was a need to develop something new, or to closely coordinate OMS development with what had already been achieved with the VAMP. My argument was for the latter, so that "system integration" between the technical and informational components of the system would be inherent. Obviously, I did not prevail.

References

Baroni, R. Anthony (1986), Understanding and applying sequential analysis to TPS acceptance test procedures. *IEEE AUTOTESTCON Proceedings.* IEEE, Piscataway, N.J. (86CH2299-6): 79-84.

Batchelor, Steven W. (1995), *FY 1996/1997 Biennial Budget Estimates: Narrative Statement for Major Automated Information Systems, Naval Aviation Logistics Command Management Information System (NALCOMIS-V60),* Department of Defense, Department of the Navy, October 2, 1995.

Bergeron, Jay C. (1990), Migrating TPSs to next generation ATE. *IEEE AUTOTESTCON Proceedings.* IEEE, Piscataway, N.J. (90CH2793-8): 281-286.

Burkhart, Richard M. (1986), Putting the fun back into TPS development. *IEEE AUTOTESTCON Proceedings.* IEEE, Piscataway, N.J. (86CH2299-6): 217-224.

Darling, W. P. (1994), CASS system software configuration management. *IEEE Systems Readiness Technology Conference AUTOTESTCON Proceedings.* IEEE, Piscataway, N.J. (94CH3436-3): 7-14.

Dill, Harry H. (1990), Test program sets—A new approach. *IEEE AUTOTESTCON Proceedings.* IEEE, Piscataway, N.J. (90CH2793-8): 63-69.

Gass, Saul I., and Thompson, Bruce W. (1980), Guidelines for model evaluation: An abridged version of the U.S. General Accounting Office Exposure Draft. *Operations Research,* 28: 431-439.

Hanna, James P., and Horth, Willis J. (1991), A new methodology for test program set generation and re-hosting. *IEEE Systems Readiness Technology Conference AUTOTESTCON Proceedings.* IEEE, Piscataway, N.J. (91CH2941-3): 279-285.

Holland, Tim, LCDR (1995), *NALCOMIS—CASS Integration via OMS and IMA: Proposal Recommendations, PMA 260 Briefing.* http://cass1.nawcad.navy.mil/cass/twgmin/twg7/oms-3b.html. U.S. Naval Air Systems Command, PMA-260D21.

Lanterman, Doug (1986), Vertical compatibility—issues and answers. *IEEE AUTOTESTCON Proceedings.* IEEE, Piscataway, N.J. (86CH2299-6): 255-261.

Lavely, L. W. (undated), Naval Aviation Logistics Command Management Information System briefing. Naval Air Systems Command, Project Office PMA-270 (believed to be issued September, 1983).

Levy, Arthur, and Pizzariella, John (1990), Dynamic sequencing of test programs. *IEEE AUTOTESTCON Proceedings.* IEEE, Piscataway, N.J. (90CH2793-8): 93-97.

Martin, Marianne (1995), *High Reliability and Availability Proven in Latest follow-on test and evaluation (FOT&E)*, Washington, D.C.: Department of the Navy, U.S. Naval Air Systems Command.

Merlenbach, Chris (1992), Importance of configuration management: An overview with Test Program Sets. *Annual Forum Proceedings—American Helicopter Society, vol. 1.* Alexandria, Va: American Helicopter Soc.: 315-323.

MIL-STD-2077(AS), General Requirements for Test Program Sets. Department of the Navy, Naval Air Systems Command, 9 March 1978.

Naval Weapons Engineering Support Activity, *NAVWESA MOD III Level of Repair model, release 2,* 1 June 1977.

Poon, Andrew, Bertch, William, J., and Wood, Jay B. (1990), Next generation TPS architecture. *IEEE AUTOTESTCON Proceedings.* IEEE, Piscataway, N.J. (90CH2793-8): 51-61.

Preliminary APMM Functional Description (1986), Lexington Park, Md.: Mantech Services Corporation.

Pullo, Frank A. and Salvarezza, Michael (1986), ATTS: ATLAS template translation system. *IEEE AUTOTESTCON Proceedings.* IEEE, Piscataway, N.J. (86CH2299-6): 211-216.

Rathburn, Kevin (1994), Managing automatic test systems in the 90's. *IEEE Proceedings of the National Aerospace and Electronics Conference, vol. 2.* IEEE, Piscataway, N.J. (94CH3431-4): 1233-1240.

Scherer, Carol S., Osman, Richard J., and Vasquez, Sandy L. (1994), Test station controller replacement using commercial products. *IEEE Systems Readiness Technology Conference AUTOTESTCON Proceedings.* IEEE, Piscataway, N.J. (94CH3436-3): 455-463.

Scully, John K. (1987), Case techniques in integrated TPS development. *IEEE AUTOTESTCON Proceedings.* IEEE, Piscataway, N.J. (87CH2510-6): 277-283.

Weiss, Daniel H. (1994), Achieving tester independence. *IEEE Systems Readiness Technology Conference AUTOTESTCON Proceedings.* IEEE, Piscataway, N.J. (94CH3436-3): 321-327.

Wood, N. O. (1989), ATE for older systems—An engineer's perspective. *IEEE Proceedings of the National Aerospace and Electronics Conference, vol. 3 (of 4)*, IEEE, Piscataway, N.J.: 1414-1418.

8 Extending IPT, ATE Lessons, and a Technology Accession Model

Introduction

This chapter summarizes and synthesizes material from earlier chapters, from both theoretical and applied perspectives. I have organized the chapter into four sections. The first deals with the overall issue of technology management and the implications of this research for the IPT theoretical framework. The second section is a theoretical-to-pragmatic transitional discussion of some of the decision-making implications raised by the VAST and ATE research. A brief third section touches on some pragmatic "lessons learned" and some implications for ATE accession. The final section is a pragmatic model of technology accession. I am a firm believer in the adage that nothing is as useful as a good theory, and given that perspective, the "theoretical" and "practical" are interwoven throughout this chapter.

A very brief summary of IPT and the research relevant to it that was done in this book is useful before further discussion of the model. Chapter 1 provided the basic IPT model, of course, and Chapter 2 an overview of the background of the U.S. Navy test technology environment (i.e., VAST), which was both a stimulant for development of IPT and provided data to test it. Chapter 3 described the Navy's avionics-repair organization and workflow, which embodies the three major variables (I, S, and C) of the IPT model.

Chapter 4 reviewed the major studies of the accession of VAST; more importantly, this chapter reviewed all data on the impact of logistics support on VAST performance. Each element of the VAST logistics support tail was potentially a variable with some power to explain WRA stockouts on the VAST workflow. Obviously, if logistics support was found to be a plausible explanation for poor performance, the IPT argument is not supported. Chapter 5 examined the logistics-support question again, and expanded the inquiry into a wider set of variables than logistics alone. This had been suggested by some of the earlier work reported in Chapter 4, including early efforts to mediate AIMD IP with information technology. None of these studies provided strong evidence that logistics support explained poor WRA repair performance.

Chapter 6 directly examined the role of IP capacity on AIMD performance, using objective performance data to test the model. The results strongly support the IPT model, and show that performance varies directly with IP capacity in the AIMD. IT mediation of IP capacity was shown to exert a powerful effect on performance.

Chapter 7 briefly examined a potential environmental variable as the explanation for WRA production deficiencies in the land-based environment of the Canadian Forces, and found that the change in environment did not prevent the type of problems experienced with VAST in the U.S. Navy. Chapter 7 also considered some of the IPT implications for the new generation of testers now in development and deployment, as well as for the overarching IP design the U.S. is developing for the Navy and its other forces as well.

Theoretical Implications of the ATE Study

System Complexity, Information Load, and Information Value

From the beginning of this book, I have argued that technology management and accession is fundamentally an issue of *information processing*, as conceptualized in terms of the IPT model. The "system" under study in most of this book is a very complex system, partly because of its structure, partly because of its size, and partly because of the sheer number and diversity of tasks necessary to support a technically advanced, geographically dispersed military organization.

Streufert and Swezey (1986) conceptualize "complexity" in a way which centrally incorporates IP—they characterize organizational complexity as an interaction of the organization's physical structure, the IP characteristics of its personnel (individually and as groups), the information acquisition techniques personnel use, the flows of information through the organization, and the relevance of its outputs (and they specifically note decisions as a key output, an issue which will be discussed later). They emphasize that most of all, we need to determine whether "integrated" IP is used across levels and processes within the organization.

They argue that if we characterize the total amount of information entering the system as the information *load*, then the way that load is processed and distributed enables the organization to understand its task environment:

> To the degree to which relevant, undistorted, and sufficiently complete information is distributed within an organization, the potential for flexible integration of that information exists (1986: 99).

They derive two arguments from this premise: first, adequate IP requires that uncertainty be decreased when possible, but that "residual uncertainty" must be accepted and used for contingent planning. Second, they argue that impermeability of the organization's boundaries, and distortions of information, can feed "mechanical" views of the organization and contribute to organizational inertia.

These conceptual arguments certainly seem applicable to the accession of VAST into the AIMD. To the extent that organizations become more complex over time, and to the extent that they insulate themselves from information which challenges their view of functional IP requirements, they make themselves inflexible and at a disadvantage when circumstances change. The list of AIMD workflow problems seen in Appendix 4.1 certainly suggests the extent of the information load. What is perhaps more important is that this list suggests the problems facing anyone who wants to sort out the "signal" from the "noise." It is probably not an exaggeration to say that during the VAST accession, there was overload of both signal and noise. Organizational inertia, under these conditions, should not come as a surprise.

The results of the soft-system and hard-system analyses done in this study suggest that slack, in the undesirable form of lowered performance, will be the adjustive mechanism if such "inertia" exists. The demanding technical issues confronting ATE and other complex technologies are the "large current" problems of performance (Edwards, 1964); the IP issues are the "small current" problems of control. What the studies here suggest, however, is that small *currents* can have large *effects*.

Thus, in complex organizations technology accession is an IPT issue, with the emphasis on *processing*. Even if people are given the information they need to understand the system, but not the ability to synthesize it and take globally effective actions, dysfunction is inevitable. This is an issue of *equivocality*, as discussed in Chapter 1, not of uncertainty—more information alone will not fix it. The VAMP program, from this perspective, was an equivocality-resolving technology, not an uncertainty-reducing one. Although VAMP did not require any inputs beyond those already recorded on the MAF as a part of the regular data acquisition in the avionics repair cycle, VAMP created new accessors by removing delays in feedback.

The VAMP algorithm included data on the VAST station status as a variable affecting the ability of the AIMD to meet its production objectives; this information already existed in the AIMD and was not new. The new information from the VAMP transformation was evaluation of the repair queue status at the time each new WRA was inducted, and designation of repair priorities according to the new population of the queue.

VAMP resolved equivocality by creating new access to information, i.e., knowledge, at the operating level, and for the first time allowed continuous decision-making on the basis of the true status of the repair queue and the test technology. Knowing the status of the repair queue through feedback enabled continuous feedforward to the shops. By focusing on the unified system goal of taking those actions that maximized the repair of the weapon-system assets with greatest "value," global objectives were achieved. But this was only possible with IP capacity sufficient to process all information about that system and its goals.

Consideration of the impact of workflow changes was necessitated by a new generation of tester technology, not because the new technology did radically different things than its predecessors, but because it changed the flow of work through the system, which in turn required a parallel change in system IP capacity.

From an IPT perspective, the findings on ATE evolution and operation in this book suggests an interesting conundrum about the perception of the *value* of information in technology management and accessions. Within the context of ATE development, and particularly in our early studies of VAST and the AIMD workflow, I pointed out that we frequently encountered resistance to the "intrusions of management types" into what was seen as purely a technical problem. The technical perspective was also dominant in the early TECHEVAL and OPEVAL assessments of VAST, and in the later analyses of the problems surrounding operational WRA throughput. In many respects, the value of additional information outside the technical realm was regarded as not only lacking in value, but as an unwanted addition to an already heavy information load, i.e., information with *negative* value. Indeed, Drèze (1987:111) argues that information may actually have negative value under some circumstances (an impossibility in much of classical decision theory, incidentally):

> To sum up, the significance of additional information in a decision
> is generally twofold. First, information adds flexibility to the course

of action, since the decision may vary with the message received. The benefit arising from this flexibility is usually called [the] "value of information." Second, information may modify the set of feasible courses of action; in particular, information that an event is true precludes betting on that event; more generally, it precludes "trading" (or negotiating) under ignorance about that event. This modification of the set of feasible courses of actions can be advantageous or disadvantageous, depending upon circumstances. It entails a sort of "opportunity cost," which is logically distinct from the value of information.

Drèze's arguments may be valid in circumstances where classical risk (e.g., wagers or negotiations regarding future outcomes) is facing the decision maker, and belief in the "engineering perspective" implies that reducing the amount of information available to personnel in a complex system might benefit performance by removing distractions. Given the vector properties of information I describe in Chapter 1, however, I would argue that this logic does not apply in most organizational decisions; yet it is common for people to behave as if it does, and particularly in technology-intensive organizations where attention to technical matters must come first. This is particularly likely when we treat "past perfect" information as if it were an absolute, or categorize "non-technical" information as irrelevant. The seductive logic of attending solely to the "obvious" technical problems results in an unintended and dysfunctional "success-through-ignorance" approach to problem solving.

There are many reasons why reducing information is an impossibility, not the least of which is that human beings are *active* information processors. Attention is directed toward those things we do not comprehend, or perceive as dysfunctional. The absence of information feeds the dysfunctions. Even if human beings were not such active processors (and not all of us are, of course), the dynamics of a complex organization are a stimulant to many kinds of IP. A very general assumption of IPT, then, is *that organizations should never be expected to be informationally passive.* The paradox is that if we do not provide information, the system personnel will create it, ascribe value to it, and act accordingly.

This paradox was clearly evident in the "soft-system" analysis in Chapter 5, and seen through the ingenuity and adaptability of system personnel in the other analyses in that chapter. If nothing else, one has to be amazed at the ingenuity of sailors and officers in the system to find ways to get the job done when needed (as well as to find ways to "beat the system" when they felt it was appropriate). In most cases, however, the lack of IP capacity to deal with control and management issues led system personnel to seek solutions in the technical realm they thought was "valuable," and they still could not solve their problems.

The value of information about the system state is supported by findings from other sources and larger-scale technical systems, particularly in the arena of factory and production-facility design. In analyzing many findings from a variety of sources on Japanese technology-management practices, Liker *et al.* (1995: 380) concluded that

> ...All these themes can be viewed as an outgrowth of a more basic observation, that Japanese managers tend to think in terms of *systems*. That is, whereas U.S. managers usually focus on individual skills, techniques, departments, disciplines, and organizational structures, Japanese professionals and managers tend to concentrate on the *connections* [emphasis added] among these elements. When the tasks cannot be managed in their entirety by particular people or groups, the problems can always be broken down into smaller units, but the connections among these units still are not lost in the disaggregation.

The increasing level of factory automation, particularly advanced manufacturing technology (AMT) and flexible manufacturing systems (FMS) during the past decade has required attention to problems and issues similar to many of those found in the VAST accession. Bessant (1993) reviewed a number of AMT studies and experiences from the decade of the 1980s, and concluded that the errors of that period reflected a lack of strategy for technology management in AMT. Beatty (1993) reviewed AMT experiences in 10 Canadian firms over a three-year span, and concluded that a "two-tiered" organization structure, with one tier focused on more intensive planning for technology integration, resulted in more successful implementation of AMT. Thomas *et al.* (1994) summarized data from six continuing case studies of "technology assimilation," and concluded that managerial attitudes and beliefs both affect and are affected by the assimilation process. They argue that the interaction of elements of the technology and the managerial belief system create a technology which is specific to every firm. Much the same conclusion is drawn by Lindberg's (1994) case studies of factory management system implementation by three firms, in which "latent uncertainty" makes for an almost inevitable misalignment between types of technology, the management system, and strategic controls.

By and large, there are still many unanswered questions about the relationship between organization and technology (Sun, 1994). However, these field studies suggest that whether successes or failures are used as examples, the effective implementation of these new manufacturing technologies requires simultaneous attention to the properties of the technology and to the management of its accession process; this is fundamentally an IP issue.

Einstein has reputedly defined "genius" as "the ability to see the obvious." (This, of course, was after most of a lifetime of hard work to see what was "obvious.") After huge amounts of analysis, it seems obvious that successful technology accessions of any kind require full understanding of the organization as a complex system, no matter how we approach the question of accession, and no matter what kind of technology is at issue. The technology creates a high degree of initial equivocality and uncertainty, followed by exceptions as it matures. It is seductively simple to argue that until issues surrounding the nature of the technology itself are resolved, there is little point in wondering how an organization will be able to use it. Many organizations, therefore, concentrate most of their accession efforts on the technology, and assume that the organization will come along if we can make the right predictions about the nature of the technology.

But as Neils Bohr has said, "Prediction is very hard, especially when it's about the future." Because technology accession is a system-level problem, it is much more complex than simple technology forecasting. I had to go up a huge learning curve to master all the acronyms and jargon that come along with the military automatic-test arena (language is a major IP problem, in that regard). But no single individual can learn all that needs to be known to really understand and diagnose a complex-technology system, and the accession process has to be undertaken by fully-participating members of all subsystems and disciplines. When we add people from different disciplines (and different cognitive IP orientations) to the process, it is often very frustrating to those with other perspectives. The accession process, in short, is necessarily a product of a group of people who, from the perspective of each other's professional background, "don't know anything." It is very easy under such conditions to conclude that communication problems are the underlying issue, when the communication difficulties are symptoms of more complex IP problems. Most organizations have a hard time dealing with that kind of challenge, and that is part of what makes fully understanding a system difficult, too. The difficulties these accessions pose, in cases like that of ATE, are frequently underestimated even by close observers of the scene.[1]

Technology accession, then, is much more than simply a transition from one generation of hardware and software to another. It is the *interaction* of the technology transition with the organizational transition that must accompany it. If both are not fully appreciated and managed as interacting processes, technology accessions can be very difficult and take a long time, indeed. I use the term "appreciated" because the paradox of accession is that it is unlikely both can be fully understood before committing to new technologies.

Information Processing and Requisite Variety

A frequently-cited concept in the literature of complex systems is W. Ross Ashby's (1964) "Law of Requisite Variety." As an abstract way to express the idea that a system can vary in many ways, and that managers who would control a system must have as many ways to vary their control processes as the system can vary, it is an excellent insight. It suggests that if managers or system observers can characterize the "variety" in a system in meaningful ways, better understanding of the system should enable better control and better performance, by reducing error in ways comparable to those suggested by Monge (1993). One inescapable conclusion of the VAST experiment was that VAST created a kind and degree of variety that was completely unexpected and unintended, and which was difficult to recognize because it lay outside the boundaries of the Navy's normal technical or organizational problem-solving methods.

The concept is limited, however, in that it does not specify what "system variation" is, or how one recognizes it when it is there. The VAST experiment is again a case in point—if one substitutes one tester for many, and adds only one new work center to the organization while eliminating need for many others, did that increase or decrease the "variety" in the system? Add to that the question of how one can measure change in variety, when the lengthy development and evaluation process the military uses is designed to eliminate as many unintended technical variations as possible. Further, if the new technology has been designed and developed to fit into the same organizational workflow as all other test technologies, why should there be any reason to suspect that the behavior of the system should change in ways that cannot easily be detected within the existing sensor framework?

These are all questions that the Law of Requisite Variety can suggest explanations for after the fact, but which it cannot predict except in general terms. The underlying problem is rather obvious—how does one establish a baseline for "variety" which permits us to assess changes in the future? Organizations, people, technologies, physical locations, and many other things in organizations change all the time, and there is no unambiguous way to detect when one of these changes might be important to the functioning of the organization. If one thinks about the number of ways that any of these variables can change over time, the scope of possible variation is literally overwhelming.

Theoretically, a change in "variety" may be conceptualized as a change in the level and nature of the information imperfections the organization induces. That is, we may conceive a change problem as an "exception" when it is now an uncertainty; similarly, uncertainty-level issues could be transformed into problems of equivocality. I believe this is exactly what occurred with the accession of VAST—workflow problems which had been uncertainties and exceptions at the shop level with PGSE tester technology became equivocality problems at the AIMD level after the accession of VAST. None of the performance cues or stimuli in the system after VAST was introduced made this apparent, however.

I would like to suggest that there is a way to make the Law of Requisite Variety more concrete, and to apply several tests of its implications. This is to conceptualize "variety" in terms of IPT, in the form of changes in IP structure and cybernetic system properties, as discussed in Chapter 1. All throughput and control processes in organizations are fundamentally information processes, and therefore both "variety" and changes in variety can be envisioned in terms of effects on IP structure and information content, i.e., "flows" and "stocks" of information.

This raises a very good question—how do we find such effects when they happen? Here are two examples of potential approaches, both of which are very pragmatic. First, one can use a matrix technique, a general method which has been used for applications ranging from the venerable Kepner-Tregoe (1965) decision matrix, to linear responsibility charting, to more recent applications such as Taguchi's (1986) Quality Function Deployment. IPT suggests use of IP structures as the matrix. Each of the four functions and four framework components of IP structure can be evaluated in terms of the "W's" used in the Kepner and Tregoe method (and in the fundamentals of journalism): what, who, when, where, why, and how. The result is a ninety-six-element matrix— ((4 functions x 4 frameworks) x 6 questions) = 96 elements. Since many of the questions may have associated responses, there may be fewer than 96 unique responses. It is also possible that multiple categories of responses could increase the total number of responses. At first glance, such a matrix may seem daunting, but compared to the huge number of other variables one might consider in a complex system, this matrix is likely to produce a smaller set of variety elements to evaluate. Many of these are likely to be correlated, as seen in the descriptive analysis in Table 5.1, and some may be completely redundant. Table 5.1, incidentally, consists of 72 cells.

Second, one can use the familiar systems-model concept of input–process–output relationships (see Figures 1.6 and 1.7) to evaluate organizational IP. Both the throughput and control processes of the organization can be described in terms of these general system variables. Thus, variety can be described as databases, flows, feedbacks, and feedforwards. This is the approach that was used to describe the repair workflow in the AIMD and the functionality of the VAMP in this book. Description of what an organization does at one time, and comparison with differences at a later time, can provide considerable insight into the variety of processes in an organization, as seen in Chapters 5 and 6. Delays and lagged relationships, in particular, are more likely to be detected using such methods.

For the analyses discussed in Chapters 5 and 6, I chose to use matrix approaches. An example of a matrix analysis was the analysis of the workflow adjustments shown in Table 5.1. An example of an empirical assessment based on a systems-model approach was given in Chapter 6; this, in turn, was based on the model of the repair-cycle flow shown in Figure 3.8, which allows us to examine the effects of IP changes on each of the flows and databases in the repair cycle under different conditions. As we have seen, different IP capacity existed at different sites and times over a span of approximately ten years, and with knowledge of changes in IP capacity over time, this analysis allows both "variety" and performance (and the relationships between them) to be evaluated.

IPT thus provides a robust and flexible framework to describe how systems behave. Relatively simple matrix approaches can be employed to describe a system in static terms, and if observations are made across time, some properties of system dynamics can be ascertained. Static descriptions can often be accomplished through a formal workflow analysis, which is discussed later.

Modeling may be used for system analysis. Modeling is more demanding of resources, but brings the benefit of potentially enormous improvements in system comprehension and system performance. The most complete modeling methods are those based on full simulation of the workflow, which requires thorough understanding and description of the system as a prerequisite. Such descriptions are costly to develop, but as the results of

VAMP have shown, they may pay tremendous benefits. Modeling was used early in the development of CASS and its OMS. Suggestions for prescriptive methods will be given in the concluding section of this chapter.

It is probably impossible to describe all the ways that a system can vary, but then, it is probably unnecessary to do so. If the members of organizations are able to describe what they do and how they do it, much can be achieved to improve performance and reduce the amount and severity of "error" (Monge, 1993) to a manageable level. Experience from several divergent undertakings, including historical cost reductions achieved through experience curves, or with product improvement through quality management programs, suggests that the capability of organizations to understand their processes and improve their functionality is widespread, and sometimes quite dramatic, as shown in this study by the success of the *Forrestal* on her Mediterranean cruise. Exhaustive description of all possible forms of "variety," then, is not a precondition for its control.

Variety, Risk, and Organization Slack

In Chapter 1 I reviewed the three categories of risk which are given specific consideration in the development of military-technology systems—technical, schedule, and cost risks. One of the implications of the study of organization performance and slack in Chapter 6 is that our conceptualization of risk is too narrow to deal with the complexities of the technological world. My recommendation is that we need to add an additional category to the three discussed in Chapter 1, which I call *process risk*.

Process risk refers to the possibility that in any new or changed organizational context, the dynamics of the organization may be affected in ways which expose the organization to new losses or dysfunctions. Process risk thus becomes a variable in the net payoff of imperfect information, or organization slack, in a definitional sense. However, process risk also creates a new category of risk which can be explicitly assessed, and the data from VAST and ATE experience provides ample reason to investigate this category. It also suggests a broader reconceptualization of risk, as shown in Table 8.1 below.

Table 8.1   System resources and system risks

System resources	System risks	
Information	Technical	Process
General	Schedule	Cost

Table 8.1 suggests two changes to our concept of risk. First, it restates risks in terms of relationships to two key *system resources, information* and *general* (i.e., non-information) resources. General resources refer to all financial, physical, personnel, and other tangible or legal resources which the organization uses. The principal risks to which these resources are exposed are those concerned with time or schedule commitments, and with cost. Information resources, on the other hand, face risks from technical issues and from unknown "process" risks. *Process risk* refers to *the impact of a new or changed technology on the workflow processes the organization must carry out to achieve its goals.*

Two types of risks are primarily associated with each of the system resources: technical and process risks are primarily a matter of our knowledge of what we do—the knowledge being managed in the organization, and the organization design to mobilize and exploit that knowledge. The second category of risks is related to general resources, such as money, people, and time. These are risks to schedule and to cost. Appropriately, we can argue that the diagonals in Table 8.1 represent large-current and small-current risk issues: the technical-cost diagonal is the large-current question of whether we can solve a technical problem before we go broke; the schedule-process diagonal is the small-current problem of knowing what we are doing in time to control it. The technical-cost diagonal is largely static, and the schedule-process diagonal is largely dynamic.

My argument is that process risk is fundamental to any kind of technology management and technology accession, and to organization change in general. In the specific experiment of VAST accession, process risk was obviously unrecognized and unappreciated, but for good reasons. A review of Figure 3.8 would not suggest that replacing PGSE with VAST would affect the workflow, since the only change in the AIMD process would be the removal of many nodes in the system and the replacement of them with one; however, that change resulted in the queueing-priority problem shown in Figure 3.11. Even if these two figures are considered together, they would not suggest a problem with system throughput; indeed, all technical evaluations indicated that VAST was able to do its job.

Because it is dynamic, process risk can be subtle and difficult to detect. The many Navy and civilian evaluators of VAST were bright, knowledgeable, and experienced people, and the overwhelming majority of them are highly motivated to help the Navy succeed. But none of these factors alone are enough to make visible the impact of technology changes on the "invisible" flow of task information through an organization. I want to be very clear that I intend no disparagement or disrespect for the many Navy and civilian personnel who worked with me on this experiment—on the contrary, I would be glad to have them on a team with me at any time. Process risk is simply difficult to detect, and when we have a methodology such as exhaustive engineering investigations at hand, we tend to use it and believe it, with good reason; but the "law of the instrument" still applies.[2]

The research reported in this book strongly suggests that process risk is conjoint with technology accession. I mean this to imply that at any level of an organization, a change in technology brings with it a corresponding process risk. Further, I would argue that as the scope of change affects larger numbers of subsystems and subsystem elements, both the range and degree of process risk increases correspondingly. If so, this analysis suggests that the VAST process "experiment" may be repeated at higher levels of the individual services and the Department of Defense with some of its current programs.

To make that point clear: unlike the history with VAST, there is now a major effort underway to bring all ATE-derived information into a larger-scope information system, and to coordinate that with other logistics elements as well. This is the effort surrounding the accession of NALCOMIS. As we saw briefly in Chapter 7, NALCOMIS has taken a long time to develop and to integrate with other information systems and workflows. To design a top-down information system to meet the demands of all of these workflows is daunting, to say the least. But technology accessions which fail to consider IP issues such as process risk are almost certain to face performance problems, because the organizational knowledge needed for that accession either cannot be obtained from the larger system, or because the operating unit lacks the IP capacity to provide adequate feedback and feedforward for the larger system. Being aware of process risk is only a first step toward its resolution—there is a huge volume of work to be done to make and implement decisions about the resolution of it. This is the challenge that has faced NALCOMIS since its inception.

In terms of the present ATE initiative, we can see some of this problem through the VAST experiment and the experience of the Canadian Forces at a more microcosmic level. Bringing VAST on line, or the ATS V1 for the Canadian Forces, required a change in the definition of the relevant "asset pool" from the "rotatable pool" to "total assets," including those deployed on aircraft. In the PGSE world preceding VAST, the "rotatable pool" of WRAs and SRAs was the only concern of the AIMD, because each separate repair workflow only needed to be concerned with the stock levels of the assets the AIMD testers serviced. When the asset flows were combined to go through a common tester, that concept of the "pool" was no longer valid—the "pool" had to consider the total number of assets in the queue, to begin with, and since the queue could affect the stock levels, it then also had to consider the assets deployed in aircraft which might become elements of the queue. Similar changes, many of them subtle, might well be expected to accompany accessions to newer technologies now under way.

This observation suggests an important additional property of organization slack, one not observed in previous literature. From an IPT perspective, slack provides the linkage between high-level equivocality and operating-level exceptions. No managers can ever be certain they have taken all variables or perspectives into account when planning the goals and processes of an organization, and so some degree of mismatch between projected and actual system performance will always exist. Of course, these differences are never visible until after the fact. Slack provides closure between these levels of IP, and makes it possible to adjust for high-level decisions at the operating level and to feed the results of these adjustments back into the system; this can be done far faster than can ever be done by deliberation and decision at high levels alone. In many ways one can argue that highly fragmented systems like market economies work this way; the limitations of high-level planning are clearly visible in Central and Eastern Europe, for example.

IPT, System Dynamics, and System Coupling

The AIMD workflow is clearly highly interdependent. The VAST accession increased an already high level of interdependence: IP prior to VAST required less depth and scope of information in both the individual work centers and for Production Control. After VAST, more "databases" and flows had to be monitored and processed, and this processing had to be done continuously, not periodically. Several implications may be drawn from this change and data on its effects on the workflow.

First, the extensive technical evaluation of VAST described in Chapter 4 suggests the need for complementary evaluations of the organization as part of any technology accession. The Navy, which formally refers to the kind of technical evaluation VAST went through as TECHEVAL (see Chapters 4 and 7), thoroughly evaluated VAST on all of its engineering parameters. Its reliability and maintainability were investigated, along with myriad technical parameters such as power consumption, cooling airflow, and of course, logistical requirements. What these analyses did not provide was insight into the workflow processes in the system VAST was entering. How VAST was related to the flows of avionics in the repair cycle was understood only from the perspective of how the tester fulfilled technical requirements in a specific subsystem (i.e., one shop).

In my view a corresponding "ORGEVAL" is a requirement for any significant technology accession, but this was never done for VAST. In all of my field studies and literature reviews, I never found any reference to the possibility that this new technology could have a significant impact on the organization and IP requirements of work in the AIMD, or consequently, an impact on aircraft operational readiness. That, however, is the norm—I seldom find explicit consideration of such factors in any organization, and then usually only in the context of having to rearrange the office furniture; in the case of VAST, organizational "stability" was assumed, even though many units of PGSE would be superseded. Accordingly, there was no consideration of IP structures or procedures as a concurrent requisite for the accession of VAST. VAST was "dropped into" an existing organization, but with the same MAFs, VIDS, periodic reporting processes as used with earlier tester technology, and without change in IP capacity. No consideration of the effects of VAST on interdependence within the AIMD workflow, or of linkages within the workflow, was given until the SRC study.

Second, the unstated assumption was that the information imperfections relevant to the VAST accession were uncertainties and exceptions; the nature of the question to be answered by VAST was believed to be fully understood. The equivocalities inherent in the accession of this new technology were unrecognized by the formal reporting system for years, partly as a result of being masked by the huge volume of data on the technical issues related to VAST, and from lagged reports of operational data from the Navy system.

The "engineering" concept of the organization was pervasive. Within the VAST shop itself, most supervisors and officers could respond to our survey questions only with information regarding station reliabilities, operational peculiarities, and the like. Few seemed able to conceptualize the VAST-related WRA production shortcomings in terms beyond the technical and engineering characteristics of the testers and the repair system. Very few ever suggested that the problems had informational implications, and when that assertion was made, it was always in the form of justification for more technical documentation (i.e., the logistics "tail"). Indeed, NAS Cecil Field had obtained copies of the actual electronic schematic diagrams for VAST, and kept them available in the VAST shop for technician reference. A regular topic of heated discussion at several CATE/ILSMT meetings was the question of expanding the VAST training curriculum to include information on the electronic operation of the WRAs VAST supported. Another controversial topic was the potential for technicians to be trained to modify TPS programs. At any level, however, the issue of VAST performance in the workflow was almost invariably perceived as a matter of adjustment for exceptions and reduction of uncertainty. The equivocality issue of whether we were working on the right question was never heard from within until AIMSO began to focus on the issue. Even then, many saw VAMP development as a useless, wasteful endeavor. I heard many remarks as disparaging of the potential contribution of VAMP as I heard regarding my own investigation of workflow management and IP.

In IPT terms, these observations suggest the dynamic linkages in a system are related to information imperfections and the "parameters" each type of imperfection imposes on OIP. Table 8.2 summarizes these relationships. If the information imperfection facing the organization is an exception to a plan or intended outcome, the information parameter is "error," and the dynamic response is to create buffers of information to deal with these errors (Kmetz, 1984). However, if the imperfection is uncertainty, then the parameter is the quantity of information (more information is required than is available), and the primary linkage needed is feedback. Finally, if the imperfection is one of equivocality, the parameter is the frame being used for the problem, and the system linkage needed is feedforward. The distinctions between these in an operational environment are often quite subtle. The difference between using system sensors (framework components) to simply stockpile more information, versus directing them toward asking a question anew is only a matter of selecting the issues to which we attend. All IP functions use the same framework elements to "frame" problems, but not in the same way, and the creation of buffers is certainly not the same as planning; buffering, in fact, often hides the need for better planning.

Table 8.2   Information imperfections, parameters, and system linkages

Information imperfection	Information parameter	System linkage
Exception	Error	Buffer
Uncertainty	Quantity	Feedback
Equivocality	Frame	Feedforward

The subtlety of these relationships can also be seen in terms of the effects on system variety, as discussed above. The divergent workflow paths of the PGSE era preceding VAST required very limited decision-making in the workflow; indeed, the only "decision" required was the selection of the appropriate shop to which to send a WRA after it was inducted (see Figure 3.10). After the accession of VAST into the workflow, variability was increased dramatically by the dynamic relationship between individual WRA repair priorities for all WRAs in the queue and the interaction with station status. The information load this dynamic relationship created was far beyond the IP capacity of the VIDS/MAF system, and adjustive slack in the form of lowered performance resulted. Where information buffers such as documents or tech reps could resolve the errors of the PGSE system, VAST changed the shop parameter to at least the level of uncertainty, where more feedback loops were needed to evaluate a queue of WRAs that had not existed before. Similarly, the AIMD faced new parameters in the form of changes to IP framework elements, which were necessitated by the constant feedforward that VAST required if it were to avoid induced interdependence stockouts, as discussed in Chapter 3.

What was unrealized was that the VAST accession greatly increased *interdependence* between units within the AIMD because of the WRA queues that built up when workloads were high or when TPS anomalies interfered with the rate of shop throughput. A decrease in hardware and work center variety, relative to the earlier PGSE model, increased the variability of throughput, and the adjustment choices were to expand the IP capacity of the system or lose production.

Interdependence is the determination of outcomes through interacting processes. The fact that different functions are interdependent does not mean that they are well integrated—in fact, the opposite may be true. For organizations, the effects of interdependence on performance may be moderated by using a combination of system linkages, i.e., buffering, feedback, and feedforward. The analyses in Chapter 6 suggest that if this is not done, then performance will adjust downward until the IP capacity of the system is able to cope with the information load generated by current levels of variety and interdependence. Thus, it is clear that highly interdependent processes have the potential to adversely affect performance if they are not matched with adequate IP capacity.

It also follows that *coupling* is a subset of interdependence. A *tightly-coupled* organization has a highly interdependent relationship between various processes. Tight coupling implies that buffering is used relatively less than feedback or feedforward, and also implies that delays between interdependent activities are reduced relative to looser coupling. Tight coupling, therefore, requires greater IP capacity than loose coupling, irrespective of the degree of interdependence. IPT thus provides a conceptual framework to integrate interdependence, system IP capacity, and system performance. As Table 8.2 suggests, more "variety" in system linkages is a requisite of increased interdependence. Interdependence is an informational phenomenon, as the study of the VAST and ATS V1 accessions already show, and the experience with an expanding NALCOMIS suggests.

We may conceive of interdependence as a requirement for *information consistency* across functionally interacting units, where information consistency is defined as *agreement on the content and the locus of information needed by both units*. In short, if both the "what" and the "who or where" of information required for effective workflow interaction is the same, the units can coordinate what they do to contribute to system performance. From the perspective of a focal unit, then, consistency *lag* is the *time to achieve information consistency*, which can be expressed as

$$consistency\ lag = \frac{time\ to\ consistency\ at\ focal\ unit\ (nominally\ 1)}{time\ to\ consistency\ at\ interacting\ unit}$$

and a *lag coefficient* (LC) can be computed as

LC = (1 - lag),
where $0 \le LC \le 1$.

The "locus" of information in this relationship is considered to be dependent on the type of storage and processors used in the IP structure. Information need not be physically located with the operating unit if appropriate IT mediation has been provided.

Thus, an organization with high interdependence and low consistency lag would be predicted to perform well, where greater lag at the same level of interdependence (i.e., longer time to consistency) would predict poorer performance. Therefore, *interdependence can be expressed as the extent of imperfect information between units.* As with any other imperfection, coping with imperfections between units requires resources; thus, the cost of interdependence can be expressed as part of the net payoff of imperfect information, i.e., organization slack. Similarly, buffering of information or physical assets can be expressed as a cost, as can lowered performance.

Figure 8.1 illustrates the concept of consistency lag. From some nominal time 0, the cost of information inconsistency is the area under the curve, until the curve becomes asymptotic to some minimum cost level, which is a function of the organization design itself. I have labeled that minimum level the "systematic" level, corresponding to the concept of the level of irreducible risk in financial models. There is, of course, an irreducible level of risk in using any type of organization design, so that choice of parallel models is quite deliberate. Time 0 can correspond to the beginning of an event such as a reorganization, a major change in markets or clientele, or any other event that requires the organization to adjust and respond to it.

As the figure shows, two organizations with different structural designs will incur very different costs of operation over time. There is evidence to suggest such relationships in the literature—the different market-response capabilities of Unilever and Procter and Gamble in consumer products, for example, is one very clear case.

To the extent that either the Navy or hardware contractors understood organization slack, it was appreciated only as the "front-end" cost of technology transition; coordination and the costs of coordination were not recognized or factored into the technology accession process. Thus, the avionics-repair system had to evolve new methods of coupling over time to cope with the inherent stresses between conflicting performance demands, incomplete diagnoses of interdependent problems in the workflow and the VAST shop, and lack of an IP structure designed to cope with the information load these interacting factors generated. The slack that resulted was both the loss of performance relative to what might have been achieved (a quantity we can estimate fairly well after the fact), and the additional costs of coordination through mechanisms such as those shown in Table 5.1. Table

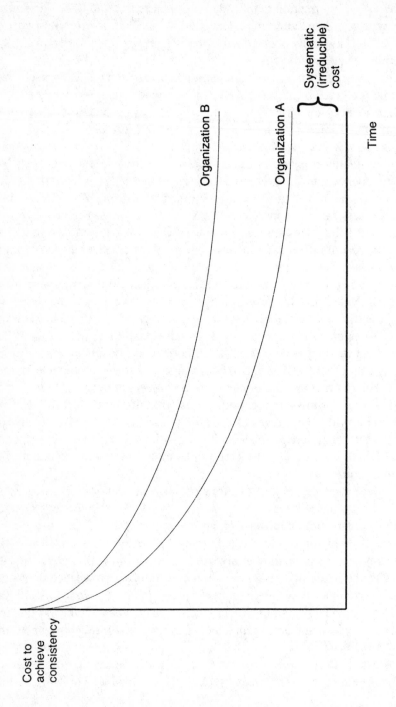

Figure 8.1   Consistency lag and structural consistency cost

5.1, it bears repeating, is not an exhaustive list of all factors affecting performance or IP deficiencies, or the compensations for them.

Decision Making in Technology Accession

One of the issues that the VAST experiment raises is the nature of the decision processes used in technology accession and management, a process I have alluded to several times. With hindsight, the IP implications of this study seem completely unambiguous—how did many of the decisions about the VAST accession and its impact on the AIMD workflow apparently miss numbers of obvious facts?

I want to emphasize that decision theory is not a central area of my personal research expertise. I am much more a "consumer" of decision-theory research than a contributor to it. Nevertheless, my experiences in the general electronic-test arena stimulated many questions about the decision-making process. Of particular interest was the question of how decisions made in a technical and scientific field could appear to be so biased as to exclude possible explanations of system performance from consideration. That is, if the normative model of decision-making parallels the process of scientific investigation, why were some plausible alternative explanations for VAST or AIMD performance deficiencies not considered very early in the VAST deployment?

Nutt (1984) did an empirical study of the types of actual decision processes used in organizations (i.e., rather than normative processes) and the nature of the stimuli which evoked them. The activities he observed were grouped into five separate stages of the decision process, and all decisions in his study were evaluated against the five stages to determine which were activated by each type of process and which were not. The five decision stages are: (1) formulation; (2) concept development; (3) detailing; (4) evaluation; and (5) implementation.

He found that actual decisions among his research-subject companies could be placed into five categories of models. These models, in turn, could be evaluated to determine which of the five stages of activity they evoked and the frequency of their application. The models were:

1. *Historical* models, which basically adopted the practices of others in a decision. These were used 41 percent of the time, and activated stages 1, 3, and 5.

2. *Off-the-shelf* models, which feature aggressive and overt search for information. These were used 30 percent of the time, and omit only stage 2.
3. *Appraisal* models, which feature themes of seeking a rationale for a decision. These were used only 7 percent of the time, and omit stages 2 and 3.
4. *Search* models, primarily used for passive and defensive search, were also used only 7 percent of the time, and activate only stages 1 and 5.
5. *Nova* models, which actively sought new ideas. These were used in 15 percent of the cases, and activated all five stages of the decision process.

Two observations from Nutt's analysis seem relevant here. First, the pattern of studies performed both to initially evaluate the feasibility of VAST and newer ATE support his observation that nothing like the normative decision process so widely taught in management courses was found in his data. Most of the studies of VAST operation in the TECHEVAL, OPEVAL, and later performance investigations fall into the "historical model" category, where the "engineering" perspective dominated. In many respects this has been true in the development and accession of most ATE technologies. However, a qualification of Nutt's findings must also be made—while the overall process never fully conformed to a classical rational-decision model, many of the individual studies of VAST performance did, in the sense of being rational models constrained by the prior belief that engineering and logistic variables were at issue. These studies were limited to collect data on the problem they had been charged with, but within that limited purview, they were somewhat closer to the classical model than others.

This leads to the second observation, and in my view the most important. The underlying difficulty facing managers in Nutt's study and in the ATE studies reported here was very similar—definition of the problem. How to correctly identify the problem one wishes to solve is one of the most critical aspects of any decision process, and also the one which is an inherent paradox. It is arguably the most important decision issue in many aspects of technology management.

In IPT terms, the "problem-finding" issue was one of equivocality, rather than uncertainty. By defining the problem, the scope of search and attention are both delimited, and thus the scope of the solution. A fundamental premise of systems theory is that all systems are both subsystems and supersystems, depending on one's point of view. While an IPT perspective cannot guarantee selection of the "right" problem, it can broaden and increase the generation of options, a criterion for quality in decision-making from both a theoretical perspective and from empirical research (Janis and Mann, 1977). Technology accession, as illustrated in the ATE studies in this book, clearly needs to consider the effect of newer generations of technology on different levels of information imperfection.

One of the issues that must be faced in the process of technology management and accession is that of how to cope with inadequacies of human (cognitive) IP and decision-making within the process. For example, if a matrix of IP issues as suggested earlier had been used, would it have been assured that the IP effects of the VAST accession would be recognized? Would an alternative model, perhaps one which focuses much more directly on IP, such as Janis and Mann's (1977: 70) model of "vigilant information processing," detect the workflow impact of a technology accession? The answer might still be "no," since we had no way to evaluate the full effects of VAST deployment on the AIMD.

For this reason, it seems worthwhile to consider use of more normative, structured approaches to acquire information, so that the decision maker is forced to consider a wide range of technology and organizational issues. Two methods seem well suited to that purpose. One is to use simulation tools, which are now much more accessible to managers through the power of information technologies like the desktop microcomputer. The second is to follow a somewhat more structured accession procedure, and the model being proposed in the next section is such a tool.

An outgrowth of this study of ATE accession for me is to critically re-examine much of our basic thinking about decision-making. My proposal is that none of our literature of decision-making adequately takes into account the issue of the conditions that lead to information acquisition in the first place. One must literally get the attention of a decision maker about an issue before any decision model or process will be applied, and the principal issue is one of "problem finding," as suggested above. If that attention is not given, none of the IP activities proposed in any models of decision-making will be activated. I propose that much decision-making is subject to an individual's personal level of arousal, or "comfort," within the context of the immediate environment and one's personal level of skills to cope with a decision within that environment; this basic concept is well-grounded in cognitive psychology. Every individual behaves as if there were a threshold level on a personal "index," so that if an observer were to measure the position of someone on that person's index, anyone over the threshold would behave as if there was no issue to resolve (i.e., all information is "past perfect"), where those not at their threshold would perceive a problem or an issue to resolve. I refer to this hypothetical scale as a personal *Comfort/Capability Index,* or CCI.

An individual's CCI redirects attention toward those immediate stimuli which are subjectively most important at any time. A person at or above the "comfort" threshold of the CCI is dealing with the subjective functional equivalent of perfect information. An illustration of the CCI in operation can be made by careful observation of driver behavior. Since the University of Delaware is located near one of the most heavily-traveled sections of highway I-95 in the U.S., I have an ideal vantage point to observe how people behave in a hazardous environment. During the rush hour, men will be shaving, women will be putting on makeup, many drivers are on their cellular phones, and many will be going through purses and briefcases to be sure they have all the things they need for that day; people will also be seen reading magazines and newspapers in moving traffic. I have taken non-scientific quizzes with many of my classes and consulting groups, and asked whether the informal rule of driving is "keep right except to pass." Although not a uniform legal requirement in the U.S., most people are aware of that rule and recognize the safety advantage of passing on one side of traffic. Yet many drivers pay no attention to traffic behind them at all, and settle into a comfortable pace in the left lane, blocking passing traffic. The effect is to create what I call "relativistic parking lots," where large numbers of vehicles are moving together in the same direction, but unable to move around each other at different speeds. Such behavior illustrates the level of "rationality" many apply to an environment which poses the greatest threat to their lives they will ever face.

The growing body of decision-making research shows the tendency of most individuals to attend selectively and sometimes inappropriately to stimuli, and to draw incorrect conclusions from that information (Bazerman, 1994). The effect of being at or above one's CCI threshold is to reduce one's attention to new information, and also to reduce the weight attached to new information. Unless the threshold can be raised or the focal person's index lowered, most of decision theory is unable to help improve decisions in technology accession and management. After all, if one is above the threshold, why is there a problem?

Lessons Learned about Technology and ATE Management

One conclusion to draw from the review of post-VAST ATE development in Chapter 7 is the difficulty of applying system learning to larger segments of an organization, or even to development of related technologies. The fact is that there is nothing fundamentally new facing the relationship between CASS and NALCOMIS that was not an issue between VAST and the VAMP (now APMM). Of particular importance is the need to have an effective production algorithm which meets the needs of all users, for avionics and other electronics repair as well. The CASS OMS provides this for the CASS avionics work centers, but the desire to effectively integrate CASS with NALCOMIS adds a new demand for information processing capacity; this is analogous to that first experienced with VAST when it created the need for decision support beyond that available from the VIDS/MAF system.

Like the earlier situation facing VAST in the AIMD, the relevant node in the system was considered to be the shop (i.e., the Work Center). AIMD production control was a process managed beyond the shop level, and so there was no immediate recognition of the impact of VAST on higher levels of system IP and performance. This is very similar to what is now being experienced with CASS—the Navy is committed to the use of a single electronic module tester, and intends for CASS to fill that role for all the Navy services—air, surface ships, and submarines. However, each of those "other Navies" has developed its own operating processes which are not like those of NAVAIR or the Naval Air Force, and the impact of CASS on these units is to create demands for information processes (data and information acquisition, formats, storage, etc.) not consistent with these other units. The development of NALCOMIS and the desire to integrate NALCOMIS with CASS requires resolution of the uncertainty and equivocality inherent to these system differences before either CASS or NALCOMIS can perform to its full potential.

NALCOMIS has been delayed for many years, in part because it has been intended to eliminate the demon of duplication, in addition to being effective for all users. Yet, the services within the overall Navy are so differentiated that every time NALCOMIS is expanded, a new layer of complexity for the information technology is created because of changes in the IP structure. Rather than be concerned with whether the CASS OMS duplicates part of the functions of NALCOMIS, then, it might be preferable to determine what information linkages and interfaces are needed to correctly incorporate and reflect the interdependencies of the system relative to readiness goals. The crucial issue is not to design whatever system is selected to incorporate every *data* element for every possible purpose, but instead to be sure that the interfaces give access in both directions to the *information* needed for the whole system to operate effectively and be intelligible to managers. If a combination of OMSs in different shops can feed critical information into NALCOMIS so that the overall logistics mission is successful, and vice versa, that may be highly effective despite the near certainty of some cost for duplications. The technical issues are usually discussed as familiar "interface" matters in the IT design. But we might well ask what the cost of lowered performance is, while waiting for the more comprehensive system to be worked out.[3]

Figure 8.2 conceptualizes this relationship as one between performance (large-current) outcomes and the cost of IP capacity (small-current) costs. If combined costs are too low, performance is reduced because the organization lacks the IP capacity to cope with its information load. The organization's capability to cope with any form of information imperfection is diminished, and it therefore misses opportunities and suffers lowered performance relative to desired or projected levels. Conversely, excess investment in IP capacity may reduce overall performance because resources are wasted and costs are excessive (performance may actually be good, but the excessive costs of imperfect information and process risks reduce it). More commonly, organizations design inappropriate structures, and these may become so elaborate relative to their information load that they induce large costs through delay and the loss of opportunity. At either extreme, performance suffers as a result of the incorrect matching of IP capacity to information load. Examples of the "excess" case are numerous; examples of the "insufficiency" case are largely anecdotal. The results of Experiment 2 in Chapter 6, however, provide direct empirical evidence of the effect of inadequate IP capacity on performance.

This relationship implies that for IT mediation of many workflow processes, the construction of decision-system and other modules which will be discarded after a period of transition may be the most effective strategy to follow. While this is often approximated in technology transitions it is also frequently decried because it is perceived as a stopgap measure. Rather than attempting to get a perfect fit between disparate systems and their respective data elements on the first try, it may be better to implement local systems which support local units, and only integrate these informationally at higher levels of system functioning. This issue has been confronting the development of NALCOMIS for much of its existence. VAMP evolved into the APMM, which is now part of NALCOMIS (see Chapter 7); this was a "bottom-up" software migration. As it merges with other systems under

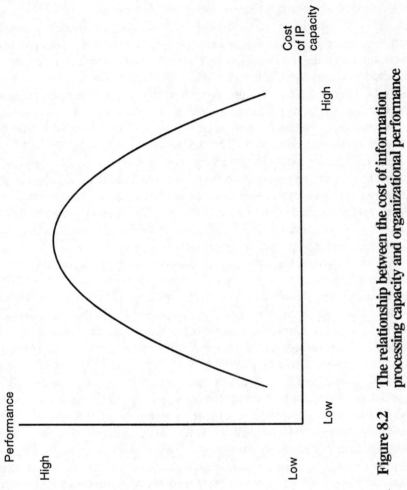

Figure 8.2   The relationship between the cost of information processing capacity and organizational performance

control of NAVMASSO, NALCOMIS has become a very different system to that which was first envisioned, and the IT integration is now a "top-down" challenge to merge several large programs and decision systems into one.

One of the persistent implications of the engineering concept of technological systems is that they somehow get "finished." This is interpreted to mean a stable design, a known set of parameters which define the system and its relationships to the rest of the world. Once these characteristics are known, the "final" design is implemented, and everything works as intended. One of the lessons to be learned from technology accession, and for those who must interact with socially-constructed realities like organizations, is that the design is never "done," and there will never be a final system which incorporates all the best elements. Whether we like it or not, equivocality will always accompany technology development and accession, and we are forever in need of revisiting the issue of whether we are asking the right questions.[4] For the near term, it may be preferable to construct interfaces between systems like NALCOMIS and others which will ultimately be discarded as newer ones are implemented. Imperfect information comes at a cost, no matter how it is paid.

It is very difficult for any complex organization to incorporate learning into the system in ways that benefit subsequent rounds of technology accession. One of the implications of this research is that the way that we manage technology accessions may make it more unlikely that we will learn from experience, not less. Several examples illustrate the potential for this problem. The resolution of some VAST engineering issues created uncertainties and positive (destabilizing) feedbacks in the AIMD workflow, and the relationship of these to production may never be fully understood or appreciated. An example of these effects can be seen in the experience with VAST self-test. As discussed in Chapter 4, a full VAST self-test is a time-consuming process, and when self-test was most needed was when there were heavy production demands on the shops. That was the least likely time for a supervisor or operator to run self-test, because of the loss of station time. However, experience at several operating sites (the *Forrestal* being one) where local managers had insisted on using self-test, had demonstrated the value of running "clean" stations. The result for stations not running clean was that ambiguities were much harder to isolate and resolve, and production suffered; but so long as the station was "working," the perception was that production was not being lost. Controlled experiments with self-test were never done to fully evaluate this trade-off.

A second problem has been with the cables used to connect components to testers. At one of the first CATE/ILSMT meetings I attended , I learned that these cables had been a source of problems and ambiguities since the earliest days of peculiar support equipment (PGSE), a fact I had observed first-hand in the VAST shops. These "cables" are bundles of wires ranging from a dozen or so up to one monster which had 256 separate wires in it. If a wire broke, a pin was pushed back into its holder, or bent, the result was always an incorrect fault identification. Despite this, a cable tester had never been purchased by the Navy, and much time was often taken by a technician to manually test each wire in the cable when it was suspect. Only with CASS has cable self-test finally become an integral part of the TPS.

Third, TPS design and verification are continuing engineering challenges. The CASS Technical Working Group (which can be found on the World Wide Web) has done an admirable job of making the design process as visible and open to commentary as it can, but exceptions and uncertainties are the norm in TPS development and operation. In the VAST experiment, the technical complexity of TPSs posed several problems. TPSs were designed from different engineering perspectives, so that dissimilar technical processes had to be used to resolve test ambiguities and to correct problems. With exception to a limited number of Lockheed TPSs, there was no self-test capability for the TPS itself and, like cables, these could be the source of several types of ambiguities. Training curricula for TPS operation inserted only a few faults into the WRA for the TPS to find, and in deployed conditions the variability of failure modes greatly exceeded those used in training. Operators thus needed much more time to become proficient than originally projected. Numerous TPS problems were discovered after deployment, and these created a backlog of Engineering Investigations that took decades to complete. Transition of VAST TPSs to CASS has been the primary problem with transition of CASS into the Fleet in the 1990s.

The TPS created an interorganizational OIP interface between the partners in a large scale "alliance" of WRA contractors (allowing for the reality that the original alliance was forced by NAVAIR). The TPS alliance represents the general problem of OIP perfectly—all elements and aspects of the need to process information effectively and to manage cybernetic and dynamic relationships are present, both within and between the organizations in the alliance. There are potentially valuable lessons to be learned from this experience as we move into a more tightly integrated global economy, with much higher levels of opportunity and competition.

Through purely technical advances, newer technologies have enormously improved self-test and TPS reliabilities. But if there are possible throughput implications of self-test, cable-test, or other operational capabilities and these are not explicitly evaluated, similar production problems may afflict the new generations of testers; the greater problem may be from unanticipated technical difficulties. One way to assess some of the potential for technical "surprises" is to use the CASS developers' workflow simulation model (or a similar model), and insert technical bottlenecks into the workflow. In fact, I would argue that development of the workflow simulation model and CASS should be done in parallel, but I am not aware of any such development or application at the present time. In my view, one of the principal "lessons learned" from the VAST experience should be the consequences of not considering the organizational impact of new or changed technologies, but I see little evidence that this has been learned. The present approach seems to be almost totally dominated by the engineering perspective.

A Model for Technology Accessions

Figure 8.3 shows a general model for the technology accession process. Like the many other diagrams in this book, it shows a dynamic relationship between the stages of an accession and the information processed in each stage. While general, this model can be adapted to many organizational circumstances. It is an iterative model, and for simplicity the diagram shows a linear sequence of activities. Each "stage" represents a phase in the process where multiple IP activities will be performed as shown in Figures 1.2 and 1.3. It is unlikely that such simple linearity as shown in the diagram will be found in real situations; rather, a cycle of evaluations and assessments will occur between initial system description and final implementation, and this sequence can stimulate change and reassessment.

The first phase in this model is to describe the existing system baseline. This description must consider not only the nature of the workflow, but explicitly consider and articulate the goals and objectives that workflow is intended to accomplish as well. The IPT tools and diagramming methods I have illustrated in earlier chapters are the basic methods for system description. The baseline must be described in terms of both the static IP structure presently in use and the dynamic properties of the workflow. This description should be provided for each of the units on the affected workflow, i.e., those parts of the organization subject to the accession of technologies. The static description should detail the IP structure, identifying the function and framework elements of that structure. An ancillary part of this analysis which may be supported by it is to develop a "wish list" of IP improvements and changes.

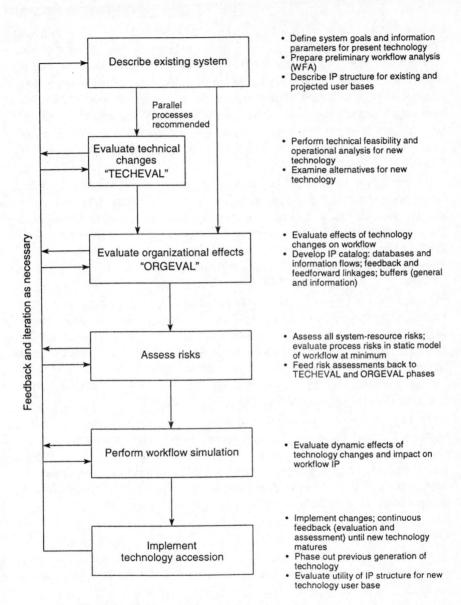

Figure 8.3 A model of technology accession

The dynamic properties of the system are developed through diagramming of the workflow in ways similar to those illustrated in this book. Nodes and information bases in the system must be identified, along with the flows of materials and information between them. The syntax or structure of the IPT "language" used for description of system dynamics is Workflow Analysis (WFA). Much of this process is now referred to as "workflow mapping." Detailed analysis of workflows is what has occupied the largest part of this book in Chapters 3, 4, and 5; a structured investigation of performance outcomes based on that workflow analysis was shown in Chapter 6.

Workflow analysis and mapping is not an idea that is unique to this book, or to any particular field. In many ways, it is a thinking process whose origins are so diffuse as to be lost. Part of its roots are the general model of reductionist scientific inquiry, and my first exposure to the idea of structured analysis can be traced to high-school experiences in a chemistry laboratory. Very similar ideas surfaced later, when I learned to do computer flowcharting to write programs in FORTRAN and COBOL. Application of this idea to organizations is also not new—in fact, the use of diagrammatic tools and structured analysis was formalized in early writing on systems management (e.g., Cleland and King, 1968; 1972). The earliest application of the conceptual use of workflows as a basis for organizing that I have found is that of Chapple and Sayles (1961).

Systems theorists have long recognized the value of WFA as a way to conceptualize dynamic systems, and an entire 1975 issue of a now-extinct academic journal, *Organization and Administrative Sciences*, was devoted to systems analysis including the application of WFA techniques to systems (although the term "workflow analysis" itself was never used). I believe that the underlying intuitive appeal of WFA has been the same throughout— workflow analysis is a way to describe the relationship between elements of organization structures in terms of mutual interactions and interdependencies, and in terms of jointly determined outcomes. In that connection, workflow analyses of the kind used in Chapters 3 and 4 were the basis for the "hard system" and "soft system" analysis in Chapter 5, and for the evaluation of performance and organization slack in Chapter 6. WFA is a very robust methodology.

It is also worth noting that the idea embodied in WFA and IPT is closely related to much of what is now termed "business process reengineering" (BPR), or simply "reengineering."[5] The concept of designing organizations around their logical workflows, from process initiation to ultimate customer satisfaction, is one that WFA and the application of systems analysis supports very well. The other major development of recent years has been the need to document workflows for ISO 9000 and other quality-system certifications. Organizations must "document what they do, and do what they document" to be awarded an ISO 9000 certificate, and that has propelled WFA into the spotlight in ways we never dreamed of when we were doing it in connection with Navy repair workflow analyses. Appendix 8.1 summarizes an approach to WFA that I teach to many users, many of whom are planning to apply it to an ISO 9000 or related quality program and increasingly to support project management.

The analysis of the workflow requires understanding of what is done in order to explain it and to document it correctly. At the minimum, an IP "catalog" will be developed which identifies all relevant databases and information flows in the focal organization. Whether the resulting description is correct is an empirical matter, and can be determined by audit, a step which is highly recommended for complex systems. When the WFA and IP catalog are complete and correct, they enable investigation of the workflow in static terms. This can be used for changes in design, whether for technical or informational purposes. This step is fundamental to quality certifications, incidentally.

The second phase in the process is to perform the necessary evaluation of technical changes from a technical perspective. The Navy process of TECHEVAL is an excellent model for this part of the process, although more exhaustive than many commercial organizations might find cost-effective for some accessions. This will be a continuing activity within the accession, in much the same way as we have seen with all generations of ATE. This method is undoubtedly the best-developed of all in the accession process. TECHEVAL is necessary for any accession; but it is never necessary and sufficient. This phase can be run in parallel with the third phase, and in my view should be whenever possible.

The third phase in the accession process is to perform "ORGEVALs" in parallel with TECHEVAL. It is possible to gain considerable insight into the workflow by evaluating the process changes that accompany different technologies in static terms.[6] For example, it is interesting to consider what might have been the effect of evaluating even a simple diagram of changes such as shown in Figures 3.10 and 3.11. Realization that VAST would collapse multiple discrete workflows into a single stream might have alerted NAVAIR to be vigilant for TAT delays from queueing.

While the second phase of the model is concerned with technical evaluation and the possible acceptability and utility of technical alternatives, the third is concerned with the potential impact of any of these alternatives on organizational IP and performance. A principal reason for the recommendation that these two phases should take place in parallel is that the interaction of the new technology with the workflow may have unpredictable performance consequences. The earlier in the process such outcomes are recognized, the more likely that the final solution will be satisfactory, and the shorter the maturation period for the technology when deployed.

The fourth phase in the accession process is to evaluate the risks that accompany the change in technology. The four risk categories associated with system resources in Table 8.1 must be evaluated. Process risk is the most difficult of these to assess, and to some extent can only be fully evaluated through system simulation. For simpler organizations or technology accessions of limited scope, however, static analysis of schedule, cost, and technical risks may be adequate. Whatever assessment is done, however, should be fed back to phases (2) and (3).

The next phase is to simulate the workflow, using dynamic simulation models if possible. Simulation is strongly recommended for all complex systems. A first step in such simulation is to evaluate a baseline model, which is the focal workflow in its present form. Experience with quality certification programs has shown that even static workflow evaluation is likely to reveal many anomalies and inefficiencies, and it is likely that some system modifications will result from that step alone in parallel with the process. However, it is recommended to model the system in its present form, so that the model can be validated against existing performance data. If one can simulate system inputs and processes, then simulated output measures should be similar to actual ones, and this is the nature of the validation. Changes in processes or system properties which result from the accession of new technologies can then be evaluated dynamically, with relatively high confidence.

The final phase in the process is implementation of the technology change. In complex systems, even careful analyses will not capture all possible forms of system variability, and so continuous monitoring of the changes will be needed until the technology matures. The issue of system variability is especially significant with the "soft" system variables, and how the new technology will finally integrate with the human elements of the system can only finally be known through the actual "experiment." The accession is complete only with phase-out of the earlier generation.

In this model, the structure of IP can be evaluated at any relevant point in the workflow, so that functions such as the location of decision-making authority, for example, can be placed at the best point in the workflow consistent with performance and control requirements. Similarly, modifications to the framework for IP can be evaluated. Through WFA or simulation, if we observe that we cannot determine where necessary control or operational information is located, transformed, or disseminated in a system, or what part of the system acquires control information, then we are probably observing a system we cannot control. These characteristics of workflow IP become apparent as the workflow is diagrammed and analyzed.

It is worth noting that while the WFA symbols and the text figures shown in Appendix 8.1 are simple, the process is not. Significant investments of time and energy went into the development of all of the workflow diagrams shown in this book.[7] In doing highly detailed analyses for NAVAIR, we soon learned that the most valuable tools in preparing a paper WFA chart were erasers, scissors, tape, large sheets of paper, and pencils (*never* pens), in that order. Many hours were spent preparing a diagram in great detail, only to find that when we validated it with a user, the answer was "That's almost right, except for this part here..." That was when the erasers, scissors, and other change tools came out, and we went back to our respective offices to try to get the diagram right on the next pass. There is a lot of hard thinking that goes into this process.

Fortunately, in the intervening years since we did that work, software has made the job much simpler. Many programs now exist which can do the drudgery of WFA preparation and modification quickly and easily. Further, it is simple to "nest" diagrams together, so that "drilling down" from a high-level diagram into the details of a workflow is also simple, and changes at any level are immediately recorded throughout, at the user's control. Information technology has made WFA almost fun. The hard thinking remains, however, and there is no software to do that part.

There are other additions to the analytical tool kit. In 1986, Elihyu Goldratt published *The Goal,* a book which has had considerable impact in the manufacturing world. This volume was the first example of what Goldratt has since developed into the "theory of constraints." While not something I have personally applied, my reading into the theory of constraints suggests that it may also be a helpful tool for dealing with practical problems in complex workflows. The graphical technique developed by Monge (1990, 1993), discussed in connection to the dynamics of organizations in Chapter 1, enables the manager and organization designer to select properties and variables and monitor them over time. Experience with the accession of VAST suggests that had such techniques been applied to several of the key variables in the AIMD workflow, avionics repair effectiveness might have been brought up to needed levels of readiness much more quickly and cheaply than was the case. As with the theory of constraints, I have not had personal experience with the application of Monge's methods, but the logic behind them and the wide application potential are both appealing.

The important breakthrough in new tools, in many respects, is the development of simulation software and visual programming tools that allow someone with knowledge of a system to create a computer model of it relatively easily. In the years when I learned the value of these tools, entire staffs had to be dedicated to the creation and validation of these models, and they were often a nightmare to run. It is now much easier for an organization to be able to use such simulations to see how a dynamic system will be affected by changes, whether technology accessions or other types. I do not want to give the impression that these are "walk-in-the-park" programs to use—on the contrary, some significant investments of time and energy are needed to operate them well. But with that cautionary note, it is likely that someone who knows a system well will be able to construct a much more accurate image of that system than someone who is an expert in simulation alone. That potential for the system designer to directly be the system simulator is a major change from the past. In addition, the literature of such simulation applications is growing, and models and examples of simulation are becoming increasingly available to aid the user (Richardson, 1997).

The model of technology accession presented here requires parallel development in understanding how the system operates as an information processor as well as being a medium for achievement of technical objectives. There is a great need to compensate for inability of human decision makers to comprehend the nature of dynamic systems (Senge and Sterman, 1992), and this model provides an IP framework that assists the human analyst to understand all operational aspects of the technology itself and the organization in which it is embedded.

Conclusion

This book has been a long journey through a territory that is probably quite strange to most of us. While the content may be different from that ordinarily found in academic research, I think there are several important conclusions we can derive from this study.

First, I believe that the information processing theory of organizations is a useful combination of concepts and tools, for both the comprehension and implementation of technology accession, and for technology management more broadly. Moreover, I have always believed that the information processing perspective of organization is robust and applicable to a wide variety of organizations; some static-analysis research into the relationship between different models of structure and performance supports that contention (Kmetz, 1981). I am prepared to argue for its universal utility; readers may not want to go that far yet, and that is perfectly fine with me. I will take it as a mission to try to provide more evidence in support of that argument in the future. For the present, I think IPT has shown itself to be capable of describing the way that complex technologies manifest themselves in organizations. The conceptual and practical strength of IPT is its ability to portray the symbiosis between organization and technology, through modeling the organization as an entity and the technology which the organization mobilizes. Both are necessary to attain the payoffs of technological advances.

Technology management is a distinct and important sub-discipline of management, but development of theory in this area has been limited by a lack of both a conceptual basis for it or tools to apply to it. IPT contributes toward these needs. Much of the literature of technology management seems to me to be struggling for an identity, and for a means to express relationships between technologies and organizations which would appear to be almost intuitively obvious, yet remain elusive. In many ways the problem is parallel to the broadening effect of travel—anyone who has traveled is aware of the changes in perspective that come from it, but articulating those effects is extremely hard to do.

In my view, much of what we categorize as the issue of "innovation management" is really the problem of accession management. There is a lot of evidence to suggest that inventing new ideas is often less a problem than getting them to market, and once in the market, getting them to become the "standard" so that integration of the technology into a broader system of activities and applications occurs. One estimate suggests that at least 80 percent of all basic research and development done in the private sector yields essentially nothing—neither a marketable product nor a product that is an economic success (Mansfield, 1981).

Even success at innovation is no assurance of success in the marketplace. Famous examples of technologies developed by companies but never commercially exploited by them are all too common: the videotape, invented by Ampex, and never developed for home use; the invention of the graphical user interface, the mouse, and networking by Xerox, and never developed by them beyond being internal tools; the laser diode, discovered by an American university researcher, supported and developed by Hitachi, and the heart of the compact disk player in which American firms have no position; and the examples of "IBM" personal computers and Apple computers, both of which are stories of great success and great failures at once, depending on the perspective taken, but neither having taken either of those companies quite where they wanted to go. The firms noted for having done better at this process in recent years have done so by building closer relationships between R&D units and marketing (Clark and Wheelwright, 1993), an IP maneuver if ever there was one!

The focal technology in this study has been automatic test equipment. ATE is not something the large majority of us know of, or need to know of. It does what it does with high reliability, but remains invisible to the large majority of us. By now, the application of ATE has become commonplace, with most automotive repairs and diagnostics having been automated, and increasingly becoming embedded in many consumer products as built-in test. This book has focused on only one part of this progression, having stayed close to home by looking at the issues confronting complex military organizations with highly specialized missions. In that sense, I have been more concerned with events at the "edge of the envelope" rather than the more widespread adaptations of the technology to consumers.

The study of IPT in a complex organization leads me to conclude that there are two fundamental asymmetries in information processing, which are somewhat counterintuitive and therefore hard to recognize and manage. First, the relationship between IP and the three levels of imperfection is asymmetrical. Suppose one sets out to "beat cancer." Does that mean development of a vaccine (prevention), development of a cure (therapy), or development of a control (management)? Once the fundamental equivocality of this question is resolved, the uncertainty related to the research process, and the exceptions that arise as the research is carried out, can be adjusted for and integrated into the program. However, resolving exceptions under any of these three strategies tells us nothing about whether the strategy is a better question to be working on than another. In simple terms, therefore, "doing things right" is no guarantee that we are "doing the right things." The "technical imperative" falls into this trap; and in my opinion, so does most of business process reengineering.

Second, a comparable asymmetry exists between organization slack and IP capacity. Decreasing IP capacity will cause performance to decline, but dropping performance (or throwing resources at a problem) does not necessarily increase IP capacity. This is a major reason for my recommendation that slack be defined as the net payoff of imperfect information. If we decide to put more resources into an organization, or allow ourselves more "wiggle room" in our budgets, there is no assurance that such additional costs will be applied to IP capacity. Even if they are, the ability to adjust depends on whether higher-level information imperfections have been resolved first. We constantly have to make tradeoffs between proaction and reaction, or between anticipation and adjustment; both of these require resources, and both require the processing of information.

Increasingly, and perhaps somewhat belatedly, economists and business people are recognizing that technology is the key to economic growth. Technology (especially information technology) is a major tool for international business, which is the direction of the future global economy. Technology accession is an important variable in the development of international businesses, which are increasingly dependent on new technologies to process business information, and as components of other products and services. For these and other reasons, I regard the development of a coherent theory of technology management to be a timely undertaking. As the impact of new and changing technologies becomes globally distributed, much value can be derived from a better understanding of how companies, organizations, and individuals can effectively integrate these changes into their lives.

Such accessions are also significant variables in the transition of the former planned economies of Central and Eastern Europe and the former Soviet Union. In many respects, these economies and their managers have a problem very similar to that faced by the U.S. Navy with VAST—how to learn the lessons of a new technology of management while changing and modernizing their organizations. Their problem is made more difficult in many respects, since it is assumed that the old physical technology is obsolete and in need of replacement; learning to reconceptualize the world is a bigger challenge. But Navy managers had to learn to reconceptualize the world with ATE. My article in the *Proceedings of the U.S. Naval Institute* (Kmetz, 1986) was a rejoinder to a retiring admiral who argued that the amount of maintenance data collection being done in the modern Navy was a worthless "paper chase," and that we would be better off having a maintenance card stored in a hatch under the aircraft tailplane, as we did in the days of wooden decks and propeller-driven *Hellcats*. The new challenge is the technology accession of Western and capitalist management into the former centrally planned economies. The economic problems inherent in the "crony capitalism" that resulted in economic devastation of several former Asian "tigers" is yet another example of this. These economies are still dealing with the most fundamental form of information processor, ourselves.

The very last thought I want to leave is that none of this book is intended to criticize or diminish the many people, military and civilian alike, who have been involved in the development, debugging, and operation of all generations of military ATE. More than anything else, whenever I went to a ship or a shore site to work on these studies, I came away deeply impressed with the dedication, motivation, intelligence, and persistence of the people who needed to make these new technologies work. By its very nature, new technology will always be the substance of "experiments" like the ones we have seen here, and whatever information we have will always be imperfect; because of that, we will always be at the edge of the envelope in technology accessions. There will never be a direct, linear, or predictable path to the future. What has made these new technologies work has always been the resourcefulness of the men and women out there with them.

Notes

1. McCullough (1989) referred to the "demise" of VAST by the mid-1970s, following its technical obsolescence. While it is true that the state of the technology has moved quite far, VAST itself was not scheduled to be fully retired until the end of Federal fiscal year 1997.

2. The "law of the instrument" is a tongue-in-cheek way to express the tendency for a technique to be applied exclusively to all circumstances where it seems appropriate, even when it may not be. My favorite expression of this law is, "give a small child a hammer, and everything in the world needs pounding."

3. There is a striking degree of parallelism to me between the attempts to work out a complete technical solution to these problems before they are implemented, with my observations of the land-restitution process in Bulgaria. In the early 1990s, the "reformed" Bulgarian government decided to return land and properties to those who owned them before they were seized by the State in 1946 and 1947. This is a hugely complicated process, but the first 80 percent of the job could be done pretty quickly, and might well have been. Instead, little restitution was done because the Parliament wanted to restore everything perfectly in one fell swoop. The result has been a classic parliamentary logjam, with far too little accomplished, and by 1996 the economy had fully collapsed. The need for resolution of potentially life-threatening technical issues makes the technical evaluation process extremely important, but the focus on technical issues alone creates a "past perfect" form of information that masks the reality that there have always been unwanted surprises in the accession of any new technology. I suspect that is true in most technology-intensive organizations, not just the Navy.

4. This belief is not even borne out in the physical world. Any military aircraft undergoes a program of constant change and updating throughout its life cycle, and many of these are significant changes. As one example, the original design of the F-14A required that a small triangular winglet known as a "glove vane" had to pop out of the stationary wing surface above the air intakes when the aircraft transitioned to supersonic flight. (These can be seen in the diagram of the F-14A in Appendix 2.1.) The glove vane was needed because the center of lift shifted toward the rear of the aircraft at supersonic speeds, and the aircraft would pitch down. Later design modifications were investigated to correct this problem, and on some the glove vane was eliminated. Along with it went several servomechanisms, a firmware program on the main air data computer, and a component of the logistics "tail." Even an aircraft responding to basic laws of physics is never "done."

5. Although I want to be clear that I disassociate myself from reengineering. In my view, as reengineering has been widely used, it has been a damaging and costly misapplication of a poorly-articulated business fad. The mistaken belief that OIP could be mediated so thoroughly by information technology that the CIP contributed by individuals was unnecessary and often subject to off-handed "obliteration" is a fantasy, and even the originator of reengineering has had to acknowledge that fact (White, 1996). As practiced, most reengineering is fundamentally deficient in its understanding of organizations or OIP. It is often little more sophisticated than the "engineering model" we found in NAVAIR and many defense contractors.

6. In going through the workflow analysis necessary to obtain its ISO 9002 certification in 1992, the Dupont UK polyester-resin plant reduced its tests from 3,000 to 1,100, and increased first-run process yields from 72 percent to 92 percent. This was in a purely technical chemical process, which the company had thought it completely understood and had completely under control.

7. I certainly cannot take credit for having invented or developed much of what I am now terming WFA. I do take considerable responsibility, for better or worse, for usually being the first one in a new analysis team to begin drawing diagrams of relationships between functions and processes in organizations, and encouraging others to use the method to understand the system. My experience and observations were that while flow or system diagrams were widely used in programming and engineering, they were seldom found in organization analysis, and the only examples I knew of were from the texts and sources I have cited in this chapter.

References

Ashby, W. Ross (1964), *Introduction to Cybernetics.* New York: Wiley.

Bazerman, Max H. (1994), *Judgment in Managerial Decision Making, third edition.* New York: Wiley.

Beatty, Carol (1993), Critical implementation decisions for advanced manufacturing technologies. *International Journal of Technology Management,* 8: 189-196.

Bessant, John (1993), The lessons of failure: Learning to manage new manufacturing technology. *International Journal of Technology Management,* 8: 197-215.

CASS Technical Working Group (1996), http://spectra.crane.navy.mil/cass/

Chapple, Eliot D., and Sayles, Leonard (1961), Chapter 11: Workflow as the basis for organization design. In Chapple, Eliot D. (1961), *The Measure of Management: Designing Organizations for Human Effectiveness.* New York: Macmillan.

Clark, K. B., and Wheelwright, Steven C. (1993), *Managing New Product and Process Development.* New York: Free Press, 1993.

Cleland David I., and King, William R. (1968), *Systems analysis and project management.* New York: McGraw-Hill

Cleland David I., and King, William R. (1972), *Management: A systems approach.* New York: McGraw-Hill.

Drèze, Jacques H. (1987), *Essays on economic decisions under uncertainty.* Cambridge: Cambridge University Press.

Edwards, Elwyn (1964), *Information Transmission.* London: Chapman and Hall.

Goldratt, Elihyu M., and Cox, Jeff (1986), *The Goal: A Process of Ongoing Improvement, revised edition.* Croton-on-Hudson, N.Y.: North River Press.

Janis, Irving L., and Mann, Leon (1977), *Decision Making: A Psychological Analysis of Conflict, Choice, and Commitment.* New York: Free Press.

Kepner, Charles H., and Tregoe, Benjamin B. (1965), *The Rational Manager.* New York: McGraw-Hill.

Kmetz, John L. (1981), Comparative prediction of organizational structure and effectiveness from four models of structure. *Proceedings of the 41st Annual Academy of Management,* San Diego, Ca.

Kmetz, John L. (1984), An information-processing study of a complex workflow in aircraft electronics repair. *Administrative Science Quarterly,* 29 (2): 255-280.

Kmetz, John L. (1986), Paper worth chasing. *Proceedings of the U.S. Naval Institute,* 112 (7): 103-107.

Liker, Jeffrey K., Ettlie, John E., and Campbell, John C., eds. (1995), *Engineered in Japan.* New York: Oxford.

Lindberg, Per (1994), Management of uncertainty in AMT implementation. *Logistics Information Management,* 7: 10-21.

Mansfield, Edwin (1981), How economists see R&D. *Harvard Business Review* 59 (6): 98-106.

McCullough, Bob (1989), Military test: Downsizing and standardization. *Electronics Test* (9): 26-29.

Monge, Peter R. (1990), Theoretical and analytical issues in longitudinal research. *Organization Science,* 1: 406-431.

Monge, Peter R. (1993), (Re)Designing dynamic organizations. In Huber, George P. And Glick, William H. (Eds), *Organizational Change and Redesign.* New York: Oxford University Press.

Nutt, Paul C. (1984), Types of organizational decision processes. *Administrative Science Quarterly,* 29: 414-450.

Richardson, George P. (Editor) (1997), *Modeling for Management: Simulation in Support of Systems Thinking* (two volumes), Brookfield, Vt.: Dartmouth.

Senge, Peter M., and Sterman, John D. (1992), Systems thinking and organizational learning: acting locally and thinking globally in the organization of the future. In Kochan, Thomas A. and Useem, Michael (1992), *Transforming Organizations.* New York: Oxford University Press.

Streufert, Siegfried, and Swezey, Robert W. (1986), *Complexity, Managers, and Organizations.* New York: Academic Press.

Sun, Hongyi (1994), Patterns of organizational changes and technological innovations. *International Journal of Technology Management,* 9: 213-226.

Taguchi, Genichi (1986), *Introduction to Quality Engineering: Designing Quality into Products and Processes.* Tokyo: Asian Productivity Organization.

Thomas, Richard, Saren, Michael, and Ford, David (1994), Technology assimilation in the firm: Managerial perceptions and behavior. *International Journal of Technology Management,* 9: 227-240.

White, Joseph B. (1996), 'Next big thing': reengineering gurus take steps to remodel their stalling vehicles. *The Wall Street Journal,* November 26: A1.

Appendix 8.1

Workflow Analysis

By now, readers are familiar with workflow analysis (WFA), whether they realize it or not, from having looked at the numerous workflow diagrams throughout this book. All of these diagrams have a number of common characteristics, and I want to be sure they are observed. First, they all consist of the same five symbols. Second, these symbols are always used in the same way within any particular workflow diagram. Third, the same symbols are used at different levels of the organization, so that high-level, aggregate processes can be shown in one diagram, and the same symbols can be used to show details within one part of the high-level diagram. The symbol set used for all of these diagrams is shown in Figure A8.1.1.

The choice of symbols for my version of WFA is not accidental. In much of my analytical work in the VAST studies, I found it helpful to diagram exactly what I meant when I talked to people about abstractions like "workflows" and "systems." At first, drawing largely on my training in flowcharting for computer programming, I constructed complex diagrams using as much of the full suite of typical flowcharting symbols as possible. Thus, I differentiated between manual processes, computer processes, and automated non-computer processes; between types of inputs; between types of storage; and so on. What I soon found was that I had to spend as much time explaining the symbols as I did the logic of the workflow, and that was simply not effective.

To resolve this problem, I eventually extracted a simple set of distinctive, widely-applicable symbols which can be applied to almost any kind of problem and are easily learned and understood. These are the symbols in Figure A8.1.1. There are only five of them, and of these, only three are used for the majority of WFA diagramming: the process box, the decision diamond, and the flow-direction arrow. I decided to retain the "document" symbol because of the fact that many processes require the input or output of specific, documented information. Like it or not, the "paper trail" is a reality. The connector symbol can be used to simplify diagrams and eliminate crossing flow lines, to serve as "start" and "stop" terminators (my purist friends from the programming world delight in informing me that this is

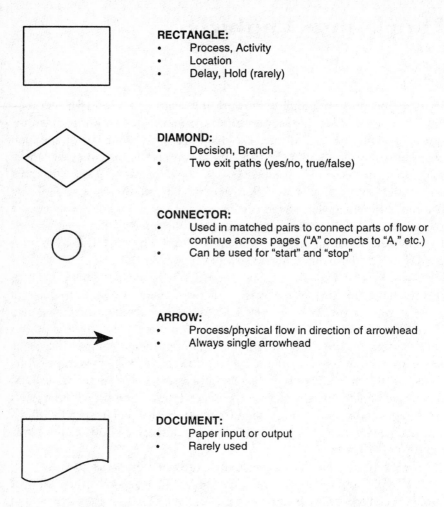

RECTANGLE:
- Process, Activity
- Location
- Delay, Hold (rarely)

DIAMOND:
- Decision, Branch
- Two exit paths (yes/no, true/false)

CONNECTOR:
- Used in matched pairs to connect parts of flow or continue across pages ("A" connects to "A," etc.)
- Can be used for "start" and "stop"

ARROW:
- Process/physical flow in direction of arrowhead
- Always single arrowhead

DOCUMENT:
- Paper input or output
- Rarely used

Figure A8.1.1 Basic flowcharting symbols for workflow analysis

incorrect, and that terminators should always be ovals), and to connect across pages, of course. Five symbols is a number that stays at the lower limit of the "magic number 7, plus or minus two" (Miller, 1956). I assume that no matter how capable my audience may be, they must contend with many competing stimuli, and fewer symbols is better than more. Further, all of the symbols are visually and operationally distinct—there is no way to confuse a decision or branching point with a process.

I teach a course on WFA to students who are largely drawn from the business community and are applied practitioners of WFA. I also teach it in a senior undergraduate course on systems management, and require a field application project from those students. As noted in Chapter 8, the application most of them want to use WFA for is quality programs, and within that group most are striving to obtain ISO 9000 certification. Having taught my approach to WFA to many users, I have found that this system works well, and I encourage others to use it as widely as they can. Fortunately, software has taken almost all the drudgery out of the diagramming process, and this is certainly one area where IT has paid off enormously.

Reference

Miller, G. A. (1956), The magical number seven plus or minus two: Some limits on our capacity for information processing. *Psychological Review,* 63 (1): 81-97.

Index

References from Notes indicated by an 'n' after page reference.